Internal Audit Quality

Internal Audit Quality

Developing a Quality Assurance and Improvement Program

SALLY-ANNE PITT

WILEY

Library of Congress Cataloging-in-Publication Data:
Pitt, Sally-Anne.
  Internal audit quality : developing a quality assurance and improvement program / Sally-Anne Pitt.
      pages cm
  Includes index.
  ISBN 978-1-118-71551-2 (hardback); ISBN 978-1-118-71550-5 (ePDF);
  ISBN 978-1-118-71549-9 (ePub); ISBN 978-1-118-77721-3 (oBook)
  1.   Auditing, Internal. 2.   Quality control. I. Title.
  HF5668.25.P58 2014
  657'.458—dc23

                                                                                       2014018631

Printed in the United States of America

10 9 8 7 6 5 4 3 2 1

This book is dedicated to my amazing family—Michael, Steph, and Ethan—because without them, why bother?

Contents

Preface

This book will assist chief audit executives and internal auditors to develop a quality assurance and improvement program and embed processes that enhance the quality of their internal audit function. The book looks at what constitutes quality, and how a greater understanding of quality drivers can lead to more valuable internal audit practices.

Most internal auditors understand quality and performance. Good internal audit practice benchmarks organizational areas and activities against commonly accepted criteria. This book provides similar criteria for internal audit functions to benchmark themselves against.

Chapter Elements

Each chapter includes a number of elements:

- **Figures** illustrate specific models or practices and support the narrative associated with these examples.
- **Extracts** from the Institute of Internal Auditors' *International Standards for the Professional Practice of Internal Auditing* are included where relevant to a specific element of internal auditing.
- **CAE Quotes** provide practical advice, tips, and warnings from senior and experienced internal audit professionals from 11 different countries.
- **Examples** of better practices allow internal auditors to benchmark themselves against other internal audit functions.
- **Common Quality Issues** allow internal auditors to learn from the errors of others and to ensure they are not repeating these same mistakes.
- **QAIP Hints** provide examples of key process areas that could be used in a maturity model, and key performance indicators that could be used in a balanced scorecard or other performance measurement tool. These will assist chief audit executives and internal auditors to build a quality assurance and improvement program and embed quality in daily activities.
- **Quality Questions** provide hints for chief audit executives and internal auditors undertaking internal assessments or quality reviewers undertaking external quality assessments.

Chapter 1: The Various Faces of Internal Audit

Chapter 1 focuses on the history of internal audit and the development of the profession. It places modern internal auditing into its historical context and considers how internal audit has evolved to cater to the specific assurance requirements between jurisdictions, sectors, and organizations.

This chapter highlights the centrality of the Institute of Internal Auditors (IIA) to the professionalization of internal auditing. It discusses the importance of professional standards to ensuring the integrity of internal audit and overviews the development of the *International Standards for the Professional Practice of Internal Auditing.*

Chapter 2: Quality, Performance, and Value

Chapter 2 discusses the interrelationship between quality, performance, and value. It provides an oversight of the emergence of quality models and quality management systems since the 1950s.

This chapter also examines processes for measuring performance, focusing particularly on logic models, maturity models, and balanced scorecards.

Chapter 3: Developing a Quality Framework

Chapter 3 argues the need for chief audit executives to embed a structured approach to internal audit quality. Typically this is in the form of a quality assurance and improvement program, incorporating both internal and external assessments.

Chief audit executives should have a good understanding of the inputs required to deliver a quality audit outcome. This allows the internal audit function to focus on the key drivers of quality and develop performance processes and metrics that target critical areas. The chapter discusses logic models, which can assist chief audit executives in identifying the key drivers of quality. It looks at the way in which performance measures can also be used to embed quality and provides guidance for developing appropriate measures that could be incorporated into a balanced scorecard or other performance framework.

The chapter overviews responsibilities for internal audit quality and acknowledges that primary responsibility resides with the chief audit executive.

Chapter 4: Internally Assessing Quality

Chapter 4 discusses processes for internally assessing audit quality. These assessments are critical to delivering, and continuously improving, value to the organization. The chapter provides guidance to chief audit executives and internal auditors undertaking ongoing or periodic assessments. It presents ways of linking internal assessments to maturity and logic models, which can then form a key part of quality assurance and improvement programs.

The chapter provides guidance on the key elements of periodic internal assessments, sometimes referred to as health checks. It also looks at processes for measuring and responding to levels of client satisfaction, and the use of benchmarking to determine how the internal audit function compares to those in other organizations.

Chapter 5: Externally Assessing Quality

Chapter 5 discusses processes for externally assessing audit quality. These assessments provide assurance that the internal audit function is delivering value to the organization and operating in a professional manner.

The chapter recognizes external assessments as a key element of the quality assurance and improvement program and introduces the three common types of assessments: full external assessments, self-assessments with independent validation, and peer reviews. It presents arguments for undertaking external assessments and the value to be gained from these.

The chapter also provides specific advice on selecting a quality reviewer and considerations when choosing the self-assessment approach.

Chapter 6: Internal Audit Strategy and Planning

Chapter 6 argues the importance of developing an audit strategy that addresses the needs and expectations of internal stakeholders. It identifies the key inputs to the strategy as the internal audit vision and value proposition, risk management and resource planning, articulation of key responsibilities and types of work to be undertaken, and the internal audit charter.

The chapter provides advice to chief audit executives and internal auditors about understanding the needs and expectations of different stakeholders, and linking these to internal audit's value proposition. This understanding is important to ensuring the quality assurance and improvement program is targeted toward areas that are most critical to achieving the value proposition.

The chapter includes specific guidance for ensuring internal audit's value to the audit committee and undertaking adequate planning to maximize the potential for internal audit's success.

Chapter 7: Areas of Responsibility and Nature of Work

Chapter 7 discusses the different areas within an organization for which internal audit is responsible for providing assurance and the types of engagements that may be undertaken by internal audit. It looks at the differences between assurance and consulting activities and provides advice to internal auditors on balancing the benefits to be obtained from each.

The chapter looks at engagements that may add significant value to an organization and provides suggestions for increasing the value and quality of individual engagements. It provides a number of specific examples for different types of engagements, including governance audits, performance/operational audits, and risk management audits.

Chapter 8: Internal Audit Charter

Chapter 8 discusses the need for a charter to define the mandate and purpose of internal audit functions. It provides advice regarding the key elements that should be included in a charter and suggestions for ensuring that the internal audit function has appropriate authority to undertake work that will deliver value.

Chapter 9: Internal Audit Staffing

Chapter 9 highlights the importance of staffing to internal audit quality. It provides guidance for chief audit executives considering different staffing models for their internal audit function and looks at the benefits associated with in-house teams, outsourcing, and co-sourcing.

The chapter includes specific advice to chief audit executives outsourcing internal audit engagements; outlining a potential process for undertaking procurement activities and identifying the risks that should be considered in each stage of the process.

The quality of an internal audit function is directly affected by the staffing resources available to it. The chapter discusses the competencies and capabilities needed to build effective audit teams and assists chief audit executives looking to undertake capability planning. It recommends ways to design jobs that support quality outcomes including the use of flexible work practices.

The chapter also includes strategies for recruiting, inducting, and retaining the right staff to optimize the mix of skills, experience, and personalities within an internal audit function.

Chapter 10: Managing and Measuring Staff Performance

Chapter 10 provides advice to chief audit executives and internal auditors about managing and measuring staff performance to maximize internal audit quality. It discusses performance management, provides examples of processes that can be used with internal auditors, and includes a framework for managing underperformance.

The chapter provides guidance for chief audit executives to implement effective team development processes, and discusses the value of mentoring and team meetings. It also argues the importance of individual professional development, and the need for internal auditors to cultivate both technical and interpersonal skills.

Chapter 11: Internal Audit Professional Practice

Chapter 11 provides guidance for chief audit executives and internal auditors on embedding quality into professional practices. Doing so maximizes the potential for the internal audit function to deliver a quality product and add value to an organization. It looks at ways to build a quality practice from scratch, or to reinvent an existing internal audit team.

The chapter discusses the role of policies and procedures in guiding internal auditors to operate consistently and professionally. It recommends the types of policies and procedures that may be required for an effective internal audit function and provides an outline of a typical internal audit manual.

Chapter 12: Annual Audit Planning

Chapter 12 discusses the need for chief audit executives to undertake audit planning to ensure that the internal audit function maximizes its value to the organization. It provides advice for planning in a way that addresses organizational objectives and the risks that relate to these objectives, and includes different models for identifying and rating these risks.

The chapter provides guidance for developing an audit universe as a precursor to the annual plan. It also discusses the value of assurance mapping during annual audit planning and recognizes that the budget allocated to internal audit will significantly influence its ability to undertake comprehensive, quality work. The chapter includes models for an audit universe, assurance map, internal audit budget, and annual plan.

Chapter 13: Planning the Engagement

Chapter 13 emphasizes the importance of an engagement plan to a quality audit outcome. The chapter provides guidance to internal auditors on the key elements of an engagement plan and includes specific recommendations and examples for increasing the quality of each of these elements.

The chapter incorporates an extended discussion of analytical procedures and data analysis, recognizing that some internal auditors may be less familiar with these approaches, which when incorporated into an engagement plan, have the potential to significantly enhance the quality of audit evidence.

The chapter identifies the risks related to performing engagements and recommends these be considered during the planning phase.

Chapter 14: Performing the Engagement

Chapter 14 discusses the fieldwork, or conduct, stage of an internal audit engagement and associated processes the chief audit executive can implement to ensure audit quality.

During fieldwork, internal auditors should collect sufficient and appropriate evidence to support the engagement findings. The chapter describes the nature of relevant and reliable evidence and includes examples of appropriate evidence.

The chapter incorporates an extended discussion around interviewing techniques, recognizing that interpersonal skills are critical to an effective audit engagement. It argues the need for internal auditors to understand the true significance of audit findings to determine the causal factors in adverse events, and includes a model for identifying root causes. It also discusses what constitutes a quality engagement finding and ways for sharing these findings with engagement clients.

Chapter 15: Communication and Influence

Chapter 15 identifies effective communication as a critical element of modern internal auditing. It recognizes the importance of written, verbal, and nonverbal communication and discusses their respective roles in influencing positive outcomes within an organization.

The chapter examines ways for chief audit executives and internal auditors to identify their key stakeholders and to understand stakeholder needs. It recognizes that the nature of internal auditing means that conflict is always a possibility, and includes specific tools to manage conflict.

The chapter includes a structure for an engagement report, highlighting the key elements that should be included in each section, as well as a range of better practices.

It discusses the value of report ratings and includes a number of different models for these.

Internal auditors regularly use influence to achieve their goals, meet the requirements of their engagements, and implement their plans and strategies. Effective chief audit executives can influence the audit committee, senior management, audit clients, other assurance providers, and internal audit staff. The chapter provides tools and techniques for using influence.

Chapter 16: Knowledge Management and Marketing

Chapter 16 advises chief audit executives and internal auditors about how to leverage knowledge management and marketing processes to enhance internal audit quality. It provides a range of knowledge management tools that could be incorporated into internal audit policies and procedures, as well as examples of marketing activities.

Chapter 17: Quality and the Small Audit Shop

Chapter 17 identifies the specific quality challenges associated with small audit shops and recommends a range of options for addressing these challenges.

Appendix A: International Standards for the Professional Practice of Internal Auditing

Appendix A includes an extract of the *International Standards for the Professional Practice of Internal Auditing* produced by the Institute of Internal Auditors.

Appendix B: List of Quality Questions

Appendix B summarizes the quality questions that are included at the end of many of the chapters. These questions can be used by chief audit executives and internal auditors to develop a quality assurance and improvement program as they highlight areas within an internal audit function that influence, or are impacted by, internal audit quality. They also provide a useful reference for reviewers undertaking external quality assessments of internal audit activities.

Appendix C: List of Key Performance Indicators

Appendix C summarizes the key performance indicators that are included in the chapters. This summary allows chief audit executives and internal auditors to select those most relevant to their own circumstances.

Glossary

The Glossary defines a number of commonly used internal audit and quality terms.

Acknowledgments

Very special thanks to my Pitt Group colleagues, and in particular Michael Pitt, John Campbell, and Brooke Pitt. Without them, I would not have had the time or inspiration to complete this book.

Thanks also to Chris McRostie for first indulging me in my quality endeavors, and to *the people of quality*—Judy, Max, Tak, and Archie.

The following people generously shared their time and expertise in either interviews or through the sharing of better practices for this book. Their commitment to internal auditing is reflective of the many thousands of internal auditors working tirelessly to improve organizations: Carmen Abela, Brad Ames, Gibby Armstrong, Dr. Sarah Blackburn, Jørgen Bock, Goh Boon Hwa, Jackie Cain, Karen Chia, Angie Chin, Dr. Len Gainsford, Allan Gaukroger, Judy Grobler, Max Häge, Allison Hill, Greg Hollyman, Ana Figueiredo, Rune Johannessen, Vanessa Johnson, J. Graham Joscelyne, Mike Lynn, Cesar L. Martinez, Bob McDonald, Bill Middleton, Takuya Morita, Constance Ng-Yip Chew Ngoh, Chin Ooi, Tan Peck Leng, Takeshi Shimizu, Trygve Sørlie, Teis Stokka, Shannon Sumner, Eileen Tay, Goh Thong, Archie R. Thomas, Matt Tolley, and Bruce Turner.

PART I

Internal Audit and Quality

CHAPTER 1

The Various Faces of Internal Audit

Internal auditing is an independent, objective assurance and consulting activity designed to add value and improve an organization's operations. It helps an organization accomplish its objectives by bringing a systematic, disciplined approach to evaluate and improve the effectiveness of risk management, control, and governance processes.
— Institute of Internal Auditors, Definition of *Internal Auditing* (2013)

Internal auditing is an internationally recognized profession guided by a common commitment to enhancing governance, risk management, and control processes. Although the nature of internal auditing may vary between countries, jurisdictions, and organizations, central to its purpose is a desire to support management to improve operational, and ultimately organizational, outcomes.

There is no single correct approach to internal auditing. Internal auditing should look and feel different for each organization. The best internal audit functions will reflect the priorities and values of each organization. Senior managers and audit committees across organizations will each have their own expectations of the internal audit function. The challenge for chief audit executives is to understand and, wherever possible, reflect these expectations in their operations.

History

Internal auditing can be traced back to the Persian Empire. Murray (1976) attributes the start of internal auditing to Darius the Great, "who ruled his people from 521 to 425 B.C." Darius exercised his rule at different times of the year from four scattered capitals in different parts of the country—Persepolis, Ecbatana, Susa, and Ctesiphon. His empire was divided into 20 provinces, each administered by a *satrap* who paid taxes to the empire according to the wealth of the province. In order that the honesty of the rule of the satrap could be established, Darius sent representatives out to all parts of his empire. They became known as "the eyes and ears of the king"—possibly the first internal auditors.

Despite the early beginnings of internal auditing, the profession did not experience considerable growth until the nineteenth century, when the Industrial Revolution resulted in the large-scale systemization of processes, and an enhanced focus on quality and consistency of outputs. Its growth continued into the twentieth century with the development of management theory and practice and the emergence of the "manager" as a distinct role in corporate operations.

The Institute of Internal Auditors

The first major book on internal auditing was authored by Victor Brink in 1941. Around the same time, a small group of professionals were looking to establish a professional association for internal auditors.

The Institute of Internal Auditors (IIA) was established in the United States in 1941 with 24 members. The IIA developed a *Statement of Responsibilities of Internal Auditing* in 1947. According to Flesher (1996), the statement intended "that internal auditing dealt primarily with accounting and financial matters, but may also properly deal with matters of an operating nature. In other words, the emphasis was on accounting and financial matters, but other activities were also fair game for the internal auditor."

The role of the internal auditor was to evolve quickly, however, and as early as 1948, Byrne recognized the potential for internal audit to add value to organizations. He stated, "Management has broadened the internal auditor's horizons and it is the auditor's responsibility to take advantage of the opportunities presented in order to realize the true value to be obtained from a dynamic internal audit program" (Byrne 1948).

Flesher (1996) found the emphasis on accounting and finance matters in the IIA's 1947 statement had significantly changed by the release of a revised statement in 1957, which allowed the internal auditor to provide services to management, including:

- Reviewing and appraising the soundness, adequacy, and application of accounting, financial, and operating controls.
- Ascertaining the extent of compliance with established policies, plans, and procedures.
- Ascertaining the extent to which company assets are accounted for, and safeguarded from, losses of all kinds.
- Ascertaining the reliability of accounting and other data developed within the organization.
- Appraising the quality of performance in carrying out assigned responsibilities.

In 1978, the IIA released the *Standards for the Professional Practice of Internal Auditing*. The IIA established its first international chapters in 1948, and by 2012, membership had grown to over 180,000 across 190 countries.

According to its website, the mission of the IIA is to provide dynamic leadership for the global profession of internal auditing. The IIA has identified activities that support this mission:

- Advocating and promoting the value that internal audit professionals add to their organizations.
- Providing comprehensive professional educational and development opportunities, standards and other professional practice guidance, and certification programs.

- Researching, disseminating, and promoting knowledge concerning internal auditing and its appropriate role in control, risk management, and governance to practitioners and stakeholders.
- Educating practitioners and other relevant audiences on best practices in internal auditing.
- Bringing together internal auditors from all countries to share information and experiences.

The IIA is governed by a board of directors elected at an annual meeting of the membership. Under the board of directors sit a number of committees comprised primarily of volunteer members. Operationally, the IIA is supported through an office in the United States, which has a dual role of providing services directly to North American chapter members, as well as supporting a network of global institutes. Internationally, individual country institutes are often supported by their own office.

Types of Internal Audit Functions

Internationally, internal auditing is recognized as a profession with a number of common elements—most importantly, a set of recognized professional standards. However, the nature of internal auditing varies considerably between organizations.

Although most internal audit functions share a number of features, the nature of internal auditing will differ between public-sector organizations focused on the efficient and effective expenditure of public money and corporate entities focused on delivering profit to shareholders.

Internal auditing may also vary between countries and even states and regions within countries. Differences can be created or exacerbated by legislation, governance structures, cultures, language, and education systems.

Internal auditing takes on a different style and approach, depending on the nature of the audit work undertaken. In less-mature organizations, where there may be limited ability to rely on management to operate in accordance with agreed processes, the internal audit function may be focused on providing financial and control assurance. However, as organizations mature, and greater reliance can be placed on management, the internal audit function might operate more as a source of strategic advice and less as a compliance enforcer. These different types of roles and areas of responsibility are discussed further in Chapter 7.

Internal Auditing in Different Sectors and Organizations

Although internal auditing is an international profession, different countries, and jurisdictions within countries, have their own regulatory environments and cultures that affect the nature and operation of internal audit.

Likewise, the composition of the public sector, also referred to as public service or civil service, varies between, and even within, countries. Understandably then, the models for public-sector governance also vary. This has a direct impact on internal audit, and the configuration, roles, and responsibilities of internal audit functions. Some jurisdictions include mandatory requirements for internal audit and audit committees, while others operate on a voluntary basis.

Examples 1.1 to 1.6 illustrate differing jurisdictional approaches to internal audit.

Example 1.1 The Impact of the Sarbanes–Oxley Act on Internal Auditing in the United States

The *Sarbanes–Oxley Act* (SOX) (2002) has had a major influence on the role and nature of internal auditing in listed companies in the United States.

Section 404 of the act requires management's development and monitoring of procedures and controls for making its required assertion about the adequacy of internal controls over financial reporting, as well as confirmation by an external auditor. Section 302 requires management's quarterly certification of not only financial reporting controls but also disclosure controls and procedures.

Internal audit's roles in SOX-compliant organizations can range from advice regarding initial project design to project oversight, ongoing monitoring, and documentation and testing of key controls.

Example 1.2 Internal Auditing and the Japanese Kansayaku

Japanese corporate law prescribes the role of the *kansayaku*, or statutory auditor, for listed companies (*kabushiku gaisha*). Statutory auditors are appointed by the chief executive officer and board and endorsed by shareholders. Their role is to audit the directors' execution of their overall duties, including those related to accounting.

Some Japanese corporations will have both *kansayaku* and internal audit functions, although these are in the minority. However, in these cases, it is the responsibility of the *kansayaku*, rather than the internal auditors, to assess the performance of the board and chief executive officer.

Example 1.3 Internal Auditing in Portuguese-Listed Companies

Portugal operates similarly to the United States–based SOX regime. Its requirements for listed companies include the development of an internal control and risk management framework and an annual assessment of its effectiveness. In addition, companies are required to establish an audit committee or supervisory body and an internal audit function. However, unlike the United States, there are no criminal penalties for breaches of these requirements.

Similar to a number of other jurisdictions, regulations are stricter for the financial services industry. In this case, there is a requirement for separated internal audit and risk management activities.

Example 1.4 Public Sector Internal Auditing in the United Kingdom of Great Britain and Northern Ireland

The United Kingdom operates primarily (although not exclusively) as a three-tier government model, with a central government and often two tiers of local government. Some aspects of government are assigned to the Scottish and Welsh governments and Northern Ireland executives.

The UK government comprises ministerial and nonministerial departments and a large number of agencies and other public bodies. Departments are directed through Treasury guidance to establish an audit and risk assurance committee and an internal audit function operating to UK *Public Sector Internal Audit Standards*. The requirements for audit committees within agencies and other public bodies vary.

Local authorities—county, district, and borough councils—constitute the second and third tiers of government. There is no requirement in England for local authorities to have an audit committee, although guidance from the Chartered Institute of Public Finance and Accountancy (CIPFA) strongly recommends audit committees. Other parts of the United Kingdom have differing expectations regarding audit committees.

The *Public Sector Internal Audit Standards* came into effect in the United Kingdom on April 1, 2013, covering the whole of the public sector. The standards are based on the Institute of Internal Auditors' *International Standards, Definition of Internal Auditing*, and Code of Ethics.

Example 1.5 Internal Auditing in the Australian Government

There are three tiers of government within Australia: the federal/Commonwealth/Australian government, state/territory government (for each of the six states and two territories), and local government (for multiple municipalities or councils within each state or territory).

Commonwealth departments at the federal level operate under the *Financial Management and Accountability Act* (1997) and associated regulations, which require the following:

- Chief executives must establish and maintain an audit committee.
- Audit committees must have, wherever practicable, at least one external member.
- Audit committees must advise the chief executive about the internal audit plans of the entity.
- Audit committees must advise the chief executive about the standards used by internal audit.

State and local governments have different requirements for internal audits, depending on state legislation.

Example 1.6 Internal Auditing in the Canadian Government

Similar to other Commonwealth countries such as Australia and the United Kingdom, Canada operates three tiers of government at the federal, provincial, and regional levels.

The *Federal Accountability Act* (2006) designated deputy ministers (chief executives) as accounting officers, accountable before the appropriate committee of Parliament, and required agencies to establish appropriate internal audit capacity and audit committees.

In addition to the Federal Accountability Act, the Treasury Board of Canada has developed a Policy on Internal Audit and Internal Auditing Standards for the Government of Canada based on the IIA's *Standards*.

The *Policy on Internal Audit* requires departments and agencies to:

- Establish an internal audit function that is appropriately resourced and that operates in accordance with the policy and professional internal auditing standards.
- Establish an independent departmental audit committee that includes a majority of external members who are not currently in the federal public service.
- Approve a departmental internal audit plan that addresses all areas of higher risk and significance and that is designed to support an annual opinion from the chief audit executive on departmental risk management, control, and governance processes.
- Ensure that management action plans are prepared that adequately address the recommendations and findings arising from internal audits, and that the action plans have been effectively implemented.
- Ensure that completed audit reports are issued in a timely manner and made accessible to the public with minimal formality.

Internal Audit Standards

The *International Standards for the Professional Practice of Internal Auditing* (*Standards*) produced by the IIA are the only set of internationally recognized standards for internal audit. Although a number of countries have developed their own internal audit standards, these are based in large part on the IIA's *Standards*.

International Professional Practices Framework

The *International Professional Practices Framework* (IPPF) is the IIA's authoritative guidance to the professional practice of internal auditing. It incorporates both mandatory and strongly recommended guidance.

The mandatory guidance consists of the definition of internal auditing, the *Standards*, and the Code of Ethics. The strongly recommended guidance comprises position papers, practice advisories, and practice guides.

INTERNATIONAL STANDARDS FOR THE PROFESSIONAL PRACTICE OF INTERNAL AUDITING

According to the IPPF (2013), the *Standards* are principle-focused and provide a framework for performing and promoting internal auditing. The *Standards* are mandatory requirements consisting of the following:

- Statements of basic requirements for the professional practice of internal auditing and for evaluating the effectiveness of performance. The requirements are internationally applicable at the organizational and individual levels.
- Interpretations, which clarify terms or concepts within the statements.

The *Standards* are divided between Attribute and Performance standards. The *Attribute Standards* encompass the attributes of organizations and individuals undertaking internal auditing, whereas the *Performance Standards* describe the nature of internal auditing and quality criteria against which performance can be measured. Table 1.1 identifies the different series within the *Standards*.

Further detail regarding the *Standards* is provided in Appendix A.

TABLE 1.1 IIA Standards

Standard Series	Standard Number
Attribute Standards	
Purpose, Authority, and Responsibility	1000
Independence and Objectivity	1100
Proficiency and Due Professional Care	1200
Quality Assurance and Improvement Program	1300
Performance Standards	
Managing the Internal Audit Activity	2000
Nature of Work	2100
Engagement Planning	2200
Performing the Engagement	2300
Communicating Results	2400
Monitoring Progress	2500
Communicating the Acceptance of Risks	2600

Source: IIA (2013).

CODE OF ETHICS   The IIA (2013) identifies the purpose of its Code of Ethics as being to *promote an ethical culture in the profession of internal* auditing. The Code of Ethics incorporates the principles that internal auditors are expected to apply and uphold and the rules of conduct for internal auditing.

The principles and rules of conduct are subdivided into four categories: integrity, objectivity, confidentiality, and competency.

Integrity

Internal auditors:

- Shall perform their work with honesty, diligence, and responsibility.
- Shall observe the law and make disclosures expected by the law and the profession.
- Shall not knowingly be a party to any illegal activity or engage in acts that are discreditable to the profession of internal auditing or to the organization.
- Shall respect and contribute to the legitimate and ethical objectives of the organization.

Objectivity

Internal auditors:

- Shall not participate in any activity or relationship that may impair or be presumed to impair their unbiased assessment. This participation includes those activities or relationships that may be in conflict with the interests of the organization.
- Shall not accept anything that may impair or be presumed to impair their professional judgment.
- Shall disclose all material facts known to them that, if not disclosed, may distort the reporting of activities under review.

Confidentiality

Internal auditors:

- Shall be prudent in the use and protection of information acquired in the course of their duties.
- Shall not use information for any personal gain or in any manner that would be contrary to the law or detrimental to the legitimate and ethical objectives of the organization.

Competency

Internal auditors:

- Shall engage only in those services for which they have the necessary knowledge, skills, and experience.
- Shall perform internal audit services in accordance with the *International Standards for the Professional Practice of Internal Auditing*.
- Shall continuously improve their proficiency and the effectiveness and quality of their services.

The Need for Standards

Standards establish a professional framework for undertaking internal audit engagements. They provide assurance that internal auditors operate in a responsible, ethical manner using commonly accepted practices. Applying standards assures management, as well as other key stakeholders like the audit committee, that the internal audit function is operating in a professional manner.

Using standards automatically builds excellence into internal audit engagements and results in quality practices being embedded within daily activities. Perhaps even more important, conforming with recognized standards sets an example for the organization that internal audit is operating in accordance with professional norms and sets a benchmark for the rest of the organization.

Some internal auditors are mandated to use standards. Usually, this is due to (1) professional membership requirements, (2) legal or regulatory requirements, or (3) procurement and contractual requirements. As an IIA member, individuals are required to conform with those standards identified as being applicable to individuals. However, chief audit executives who are members of the IIA are obligated to conform with all of the IIA *Standards*.

Why Use the IIA's *Standards*?

The IIA's *Standards* are the only set of internationally recognized standards specific to internal auditing. The IIA *Standards* are principles based and designed to guide the way internal auditors operate. Being principles based, the *Standards* are neither prescriptive nor inappropriately restrictive. They do not prevent internal auditors from being creative or innovative but provide criteria for internal auditors to operate against. They establish a framework that allows internal auditors to benchmark themselves against other professionals and can guide internal auditors in the way they perform their work.

Conclusion

The establishment of the Institute of Internal Auditors has been a major contributor to the professionalization of internal auditing. Through the application of a set of internationally recognized standards, internal auditors can demonstrate their professionalism and provide assurance to management and the audit committee that they are operating in an ethical, transparent, and impartial manner.

References

Byrne, J. T. S. (1948, August). Current trends in internal audit programs. *New York Certified Public Accountant, 597.*

Canadian *Federal Accountability Act.* (2006). http://laws-lois.justice.gc.ca/eng/acts/F-5.5/page-1.html.

Commonwealth of Australia. (2007). *Financial Management and Accountability Act.*

Flesher, D. L. (1996). Internal Auditing Standards and Practices: A One-Semester Course. Altamonte Springs, FL: The Institute of Internal Auditors.

HM Treasury. (2013). *Public Sector Internal Audit Standards: Applying the IIA International Standards to the UK Public Sector.* http://www.gov.uk/government/uploads/system/uploads/attachment_data/file/213372/Public-Sector-Internal-Audit-Standards-December-2012-plus-DH-Info.pdf.

The Institute of Internal Auditors. (2013). *International Professional Practices Framework.* Altamonte Springs, FL: The Institute of Internal Auditors.

The Institute of Internal Auditors. (2004). *Internal Auditing's Role in Section 302 and 404 of the U.S. Sarbanes-Oxley Act of 2002.* Altamonte Springs, FL: The Institute of Internal Auditors.

Murray, A. (1976, January). History of internal audit. *Journal of Accountancy*, 98.

Treasury Board of Canada Secretariat. (2012). *Internal Auditing Standards for the Government of Canada.*

Treasury Board of Canada Secretariat. (2012). *Policy on Internal Audit.* http://tbs-sct.gc.ca/pol/doc-eng.aspx?id=16484&section=text.

United States of America. *Sarbanes–Oxley Act,* 2002. Pub. L. 107–204, 116 Stat. 745, enacted July 30, 2002.

CHAPTER 2

Quality, Performance, and Value

Quality means doing it right when no one is looking.

—Henry Ford

Successful organizations have a clear understanding of what value looks like to their customers and stakeholders. They strive to meet quality expectations by measuring performance, and they look for opportunities to continuously improve processes and products.

The quality management movement of the mid-twentieth century was pivotal in today's understanding of the interdependence of quality, organizational success, and customer satisfaction. What is now considered standard management practice was first described by revolutionary practitioners like J. Edward Deming, Joseph Juran, and Kauru Ishikawa.

Internal auditors are perfectly positioned to embrace quality processes to improve their own internal audit function. They should have a clear understanding of the organization's strategic priorities, providing them with insight into the areas where they could add maximum value to the organization as a whole. Internal auditors should strive to meet stakeholder expectations by embedding performance measurement processes focused on the most efficient and effective use of limited resources.

Understanding Quality, Performance, and Value

Quality, performance, and value are interrelated concepts. Quality processes can enhance performance and increase value, and performance improvements can drive quality. All three elements are important for ensuring operational success.

Quality

Quality is both relative and unique. As a relative concept, the existence of quality can only be determined by comparing two products or assessing a product against an accepted set of standards. However, there is also a level of subjectivity associated with quality—what constitutes quality for one individual might not be shared by another. Perceptions of quality are intrinsically linked to perceptions of value.

Aghapour and colleagues (2011) describe a *triangulation relation* between organizational success, customer satisfaction, and quality. This is illustrated in Figure 2.1.

FIGURE 2.1 Quality Triangle

Delivering quality products, or outcomes, can enhance customer satisfaction, and ultimately support organizational success. Internal auditors should consider quality from two perspectives. First, internal auditors should look to enhance the quality of their own products and services. This will increase satisfaction of their own customers—management and the audit committee—and ensure demand for their services. Second, internal auditors should focus on areas that will improve overall quality for the organization. This requires consideration of key organizational strategies and objectives.

Performance

Performance is both the manner in which organizations achieve results (i.e., the way they behave and operate to effect actions) as well as the outputs and outcomes of these actions (i.e., the results they achieve). Performance measurement should consider both the ongoing activities of the organization as well as the ultimate results.

Examining operational performance is a key activity for internal auditors. Likewise, internal auditors should routinely measure their own performance to ensure that they are delivering quality products and services and satisfying their own customers.

Value

Warren Buffett (2014) quoted investment guru Ben Graham when he wrote, "Price is what you pay—value is what you get." Like quality, value is an abstract and subjective concept. It will vary from individual to individual and organization to organization. However, an understanding of value will be central to every organization's success. It will also be pivotal to internal audit success.

Quality Management Systems: Deming, Juran, and TQM

A number of models have emerged since the 1950s focusing on the management and assurance of quality. Many of these quality management systems and processes concentrate on continuous improvement and the involvement of staff across an organization in delivering quality.

J. Edward Deming

Deming was a pioneer of the quality management movement, focusing on the need for continuous improvement of organizational processes. His theory of quality was premised on the belief that all processes are vulnerable to loss of quality through variation—if the levels of variation are managed, they can be decreased, and the overall quality rises.

His quality philosophy incorporates the following 14 elements (Deming 1986):

1. Create constancy of purpose toward improved products and services.
2. Adopt the "new philosophy"—appreciate the new economic age.
3. Cease dependence on mass inspection.
4. End "lowest tender" contracts.
5. Constantly improve systems.
6. Institute on-the-job training.
7. Institute leadership.
8. Drive out fear—encourage effective two-way communication.
9. Break down barriers between departments.
10. Eliminate slogans and targets calling for zero defects and implement leadership.
11. Permit pride of workmanship by workers.
12. Permit pride of workmanship by management.
13. Encourage education and self-improvement.
14. Put everyone in the company to work to accomplish transformation.

The Deming approach was summarized in the continuous improvement (or Deming) cycle (see Figure 2.2).

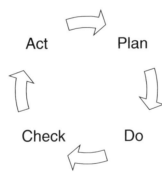

FIGURE 2.2 Deming Cycle

Deming stressed that organizations should move away from quality control–focused inspection and rigid managerial control to embrace continuous improvement and participative processes. His work with Japanese organizations following World War II led to the development of the Japanese philosophy known as *kaizen*.

Kaizen

The Japanese quality approach of *kaizen* (literally, change for good or improvement) focuses on the improvement of quality, cost, and delivery (QCD) and the philosophy that solutions often exist at the *ground level*, on the factory floor and among workers.

The *kaizen* concept stresses the need for a supportive and leadership role for management to encourage people to improve everything they do in their work environment. For it to work effectively, *kaizen* must be emphasized from the top of the organization, and it must be supported by total employee participation through an attitude of openness and controlled change.

Joseph Juran

Like Deming, Juran worked in Japan from the 1950s to the 1980s. In 1951, his *Quality Control Handbook* was released; by the fifth edition, it was known as *Juran's Quality Handbook*. It introduced the *quality trilogy* incorporating quality planning, quality control, and quality improvement.

Quality planning focused on the identification of customers and their needs. Quality control was the process of meeting quality goals during operations with minimal inspection. Quality improvement was the creation of beneficial change to achieve "unprecedented levels of performance." There are 10 steps in quality improvement (Edmund and Juran 2008):

1. Build awareness of the need and opportunity for improvement.
2. Set goals for improvement.
3. Organize to reach the goals.
4. Provide training throughout the organization.
5. Carry out projects to solve problems.
6. Report progress.
7. Give recognition.
8. Communicate results.
9. Keep score.
10. Maintain momentum by making annual improvement part of the regular systems and processes of the company.

QUALITY CONTROL TO QUALITY ASSURANCE   Unlike Deming, who discouraged excessive quality control–based inspection activities, Juran believed that quality control formed part of the quality trilogy. However, similarly to Deming, he saw that significant improvement in quality would not be achieved through inspections-based practices, but through dramatic quality improvements. To a large extent, these improvements were the forerunner to quality assurance activities.

Quality assurance focuses on determining whether a product or service meets the customer's expectations. Quality assurance generally involves a suite of preventative activities that help achieve a particular outcome (i.e., a quality product or service). In contrast, quality control is generally more limited in focus and determines whether a product or service is of substandard quality.

Quality assurance activities should be structured and systematic. Although quality assurance originated in the manufacturing sector, its principles can be readily applied to other fields, including internal audit. In general, quality assurance activities are preventative rather than retrospective.

Total Quality Management (TQM)

Total quality management (TQM) emerged as a concept in the 1940s and 1950s, spearheaded by both Deming and Juran. TQM is essentially a collection of organizational strategies focused on the improvement of quality. It relies on all members of an organization working together to meet the changing needs and expectations of both internal and external customers by getting it right the first time. It is based on these principles:

- Focus on customers and stakeholders.
- Engage everyone in the organization in participation and teamwork.
- Support a process focus with continuous improvement and learning.

Although approaches to TQM can vary, its implementation principally involves the following steps:

1. Training
2. Improving
3. Measuring achievement
4. Implementing project management
5. Creating organizational structures

Stace (1994) refers to TQM as "a process of continually improving one's ability to satisfy customers through a systematic company-wide effort." TQM gained prominence in the United States and Europe in the 1970s and 1980s, although to some extent it now competes with other quality approaches such as reengineering and Six Sigma.

QUALITY CIRCLES   Dr. Kauru Ishikawa, famous for the Ishikawa (fishbone cause-and-effect) diagram, was a key driver of the Japanese quality control movement of the 1950s and 1960s, along with Deming and Juran. He created the notion of quality circles, with these goals:

- Contribute to the improvement or development of the function or enterprise.
- Promote human relations, contentment, and job satisfaction within the workshop.
- Maximize the utilization and development of the available human capabilities.

A typical quality circle has between 5 and 10 volunteers from an organizational area, who aim to introduce and implement their own quality improvements. Quality circles are often integrated with TQM and other quality programs and form an important link between staff and management.

Six Sigma

In the 1980s, Motorola developed Six Sigma as a quality and process improvement tool. The name reflects a statistical standard requiring that errors be extremely rare. It was subsequently adopted by a range of companies, including General Electric, Siemens, Nokia, American Express, Boeing, and Sony.

The Six Sigma approach is essentially a business problem-solving methodology that supports process improvements through an understanding of customer needs, identification of causes of quality variations, and disciplined use of data and statistical analysis. These are referred to as the *define, measure, analyze, improve,* and *control* (DMAIC) approach.

Effective implementation of Six Sigma, like many quality models, relies on a number of critical success factors:

- Management commitment
- Project selection and leadership
- Project metrics and a measurement assurance system
- Application of the right tool mix (which can include histograms, Pareto charts, simulations, etc.)
- Linkage to customers and suppliers
- Training of staff and use of cross-functional teams
- Cultural change including promotion of problem solving

ISO 9000

The International Organization for Standardization (ISO) first published its ISO 9000 series of quality standards in 1987 as a model for quality assurance standards in design, development, production, installation, and service. The system provides a universal framework for quality assurance and quality management.

ISO 9000 requires that organizations do the following:

- Document operations and activities according to ISO 9000 standards.
- Work according to these documents.
- Keep records to show the quality system is working.

The ISO Standards were significantly updated in 2000 by incorporating a greater focus on process management, as well as TQM principles and procedures.

The ISO 9000 family incorporates auditing requirements that, in some organizations, are aligned with internal audit. Although there is no formal requirement for these activities to be aligned, at a minimum, internal audit should be aware of any ISO 9000 activities and ensure that these are incorporated in the organization's assurance map.

Models for Measuring Performance

There are many models for measuring both quality and performance. Some of these are embedded within broader quality management systems (such as TQM and ISO 9000) while others complement or support broader systemic approaches. The following three models all complement, rather than replace, quality management systems.

Balanced Scorecard

Robert Kaplan and David Norton first proposed their balanced scorecard approach in 1992. The scorecard focused on translating strategy into actions, and promoted a move away from traditional financial measures. Instead, organizations were encouraged to develop a broad range of financial and nonfinancial lead and lag measures that provided insight into overall operating performance.

The balanced scorecard measures were categorized into four perspectives: financial, customer, internal processes, and learning and growth. The structure of a typical scorecard is described in Figure 2.3 (Kaplan and Norton 2007).

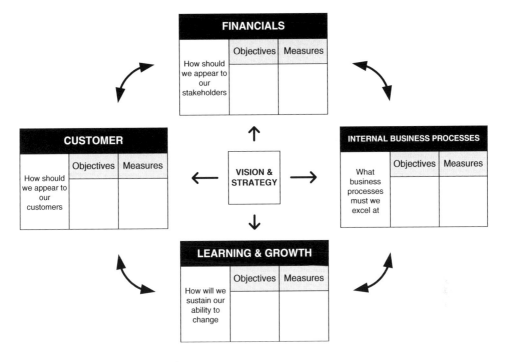

FIGURE 2.3 Balanced Scorecard

Venkatraman and Gering (2000) identify four essential elements to the successful implementation of a balanced scorecard:

1. *Make the strategy explicit.* The organization's strategy must be made explicit and made to form the basis for the scorecard.
2. *Choose the measures.* The performance measures must be aligned with the strategy and the relationships between the measures must be clearly understood.
3. *Define and refine.* Performance measures must be put into place so that the scorecard becomes the language of the company.
4. *Deal with people.* Above all, people and change management must be properly managed.

Logic Models

Logic models can be used to determine the effectiveness of programs or activities and are based around a graphical representation of the program or activity. While more correctly a program evaluation model, rather than performance measurement model, they describe the interrelationship between resources available, activities proposed, and results intended.

Although logic models were initially conceived to measure performance by government and not-for-profit organizations, they lend themselves toward measurement of internal audit performance. Their value lies in the focus on outcomes and outputs, rather than the achievement of profit, and the approach acknowledges that measuring outcomes is not always easy. Figure 2.4 outlines a typical logic model.

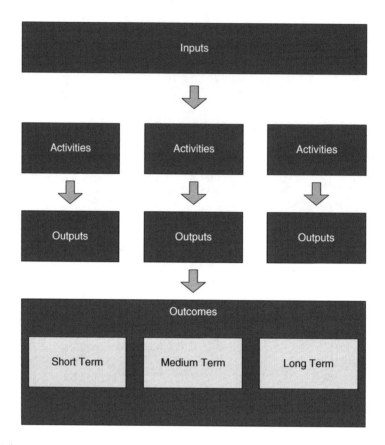

FIGURE 2.4 Logic Model

Maturity Models

The first maturity model, known as the Capability Maturity Model, was released by the Carnegie Mellon Software Engineering Institute in 1991. It was originally designed to improve the process of software development, but its broader applicability was recognized, and the model was expanded in 2000 to apply to enterprise-wide process improvement.

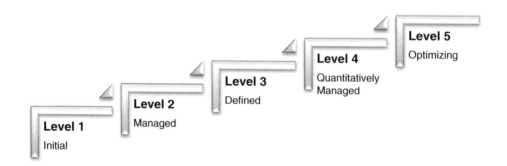

FIGURE 2.5 Maturity Model

The maturity model promotes continual process improvement through evolutionary steps rather than revolutionary innovations and generally utilizes five levels of maturity (or capability) as shown in Figure 2.5.

Although the descriptions for each level can vary, commonly they range from unpredictable, poorly controlled, and reactive processes in level 1, to defined and predictable processes in level 3, through to a focus on good practice and process improvement in level 5. Each level incorporates a range of key process areas (KPAs) that outline key processes required to achieve that level of maturity.

Conclusion

Internal auditors needn't be experts in quality management to benefit from the work of practitioners like Deming and Juran. Internal audit functions can incorporate continuous improvement into quality assurance processes. Doing so ensures that internal auditors maximize their value to stakeholders.

Balanced scorecards are commonly used by organizations to provide a multifaceted approach to performance measurement that transcends traditional financial reporting. They incorporate both lead and lag measures to provide insight into past performance in addition to positioning the organization for future success. Internal auditors can utilize a balanced scorecard approach to great effect. Similarly, internal auditors can use logic models to determine the effectiveness of their service delivery outcomes and maturity models to identify their actual and ideal levels of capability and maturity.

References

Aghapour, A. H., M. Manafi, R. Gheshmi, R. Hojabri, and M. Salehi. (2011). An exploratory journey into TQM practices and its association network. *Interdisciplinary Journal of Contemporary Research in Business* 3(6): 800–806.

Atkinson, A., and M. Epstein. (2000). Measure for measure: Realizing the power of the balanced scorecard. *CMA Management* 74(7): 22–28.

Balanced Scorecard Institute. (2014). "What Is a Balanced Scorecard?" http://balancedscorecard.org/BSCResources/AbouttheBalancedScorecard/tabid/55/Default.aspx.

Birkett, W. P., M. R. Barbera, B. S. Leithead, M. Lower, and P. J. Roebuck. (1999). *Assessing Competency in Internal Auditing, Structures and Methodology.* Altamonte Springs, FL: The Institute of Internal Auditors Research Foundation.

Buffett, W. (2014, February 24). Buffett's annual letter: What you can learn from my real estate investments. *Fortune.* http://finance.fortune.cnn.com/2014/02/24/warren-buffett-berkshire-letter.

Deming, W. E. (1986). *Out of the Crisis.* Cambridge: Massachusetts Institute of Technology Center for Advanced Engineering Study.

Didis, S. K. (1990). Kaizen. *Internal Auditor* 47(4): 66.

Drake, D., J. S. Sutterfield, and C. Ngassam. (2008). The Revolution of Six Sigma: An analysis of its theory and application. *Academy of Information and Management Sciences Journal* 11(1): 29–44.

Edmund, M., and J. M. Juran. (2008). The architect of quality: Joseph M. Juran, 1904–2008. *Quality Progress* 41(4): 20–25.

Goldman, H. H. (2005). The origins and development of quality initiatives in American business. *TQM Magazine* 17(3): 217–225.

Gray, G. R. (1993). Quality circles: An update. *S.A.M. Advanced Management Journal* 58(2): 41.

Hawkes, L. C., and M. B. Adams. (1994). Total quality management: Implications for internal audit. *Managerial Auditing Journal* 9(4): 11.

Heavey, C., and E. Murphy. (2012). Integrating the balanced scorecard with Six Sigma. *TQM Journal* 24(2): 108–122.

The Institute of Chartered Accountants in Australia. (2006). *Extended Performance Reporting: An Overview of Techniques.* Sydney: The Institute of Chartered Accountants in Australia.

Kaplan, R. S., and D. P. Norton. (2007). Using the balanced scorecard as a strategic management system. *Harvard Business Review.* http://hbr.org/2007/07/using-the-balanced-scorecard-as-a-strategic-management-system/ar/1.

Kartha, C. P. (2002). ISO9000: 2000 quality management systems standards: TQM focus. *Journal of American Academy of Business* 2(1): 1–6.

Lampe, J. and S. G. Sutton. (1994). *Developing Productivity in Quality Measurement Systems for Internal Auditing Departments.* Altamonte Springs, FL: The Institute of Internal Auditors Research Foundation.

Landesberg, P. (1999). In the beginning, there were Deming and Juran. *Journal for Quality and Participation* 22(6): 59–61.

McIntosh, E. (1992). *Internal Auditing in a Total Quality Environment.* Altamonte Springs, FL: The Institute of Internal Auditors Research Foundation.

Nugent, P. (2013). The shape of things to come: A look at the new ISO form standards. *Quality* 52(9): 33–36, 38.

Paterson, J. (2012). The lean audit advantage. *Internal Auditor*, December 2012. http://www.theiia.org/intauditor.

Ratliff, R. L., W. A. Wallace, G. E. Sumners, W. G. McFarland, and H. Nieuwlands. (2006). *Sustainability and Internal Auditing.* Altamonte Springs, FL: The Institute of Internal Auditors Research Foundation.

Retna, K. S., and Pak Tee Ng. (2011). Communities of practice: Dynamics and success factors. *Leadership & Organization Development Journal* 32(1): 41–59.

Rezaee, Z. (1996). Improving the quality of internal audit functions through total quality management. *Managerial Auditing Journal* 11(1): 30–34.

Rosenfeld, M. (2013). Framework for excellence. *Internal Auditor*, February 2013. http://www.theiia.org/intauditor.

Sharma, S., and A. R. Chetiya. (2012). An analysis of critical success factors for Six Sigma implementation. *Asian Journal on Quality* 13(3): 294–308.

Stace, R. (1994). TQM and the role of internal audit. *Australian Accountant* 64(6): 26.

Venkatraman, G., and M. Gering. (2000). The balanced scorecard. *Ivey Business Journal* 64(3): 10–13.

Wetzler, S. (1995). Industry circles. *Internal Auditor* 52(1): 46.

W. K. Kellogg Foundation. (1998). *Logic Model Development Guide.* http://www.wkkf.org/knowledge-center/resources/2006/02/wk-kellogg-foundation-logic-model-development-guide.aspx.

PART II

Developing the Quality Assurance and Improvement Program

CHAPTER 3

Developing a Quality Framework

Measurement is the first step that leads to control and eventually to improvement. If you can't measure something, you can't understand it. If you can't understand it, you can't control it. If you can't control it, you can't improve it.

—H. James Harrington

Chief audit executives should embed a structured approach to quality into internal audit operations. Often called a quality assurance and improvement program (QAIP), formalized internal audit quality programs should focus on demand-based drivers of quality rather than compliance drivers. Quality should be pursued based on stakeholder expectations and as a means of delivering value, rather than for the sake of conforming with standards.

A demand-based approach to quality considers the outputs and outcomes the chief audit executive is working toward delivering. It utilizes performance measures that examine the adequacy of inputs to the internal audit function as well as the efficiency and effectiveness of the function.

Internal audit quality is driven by various stakeholders. Although the chief audit executive retains primary responsibility for quality, other stakeholders—including senior management, the audit committee, internal audit staff, and service providers—all have a role to play in ensuring that the internal audit function optimizes its outputs and outcomes.

The Link between Quality, Performance, and Value

Internal auditors should deliver value to their stakeholders, and assist organizations to increase productivity and quality. Value will be unique to each organization, and chief audit executives should determine what is perceived as both value and quality for their own organization.

Determining value requires a thorough understanding of the organization—its objectives and priorities and its definition of success. Once the chief audit executive has a clear vision of the organization's strategic objectives, he or she is better placed to determine how the internal audit function can contribute to these objectives.

Rosenfeld (2013) describes the linkage between internal audit and organizational quality:

> *Ultimately, an audit department can only be as advanced as the board and senior management want it to be. If the overall organization strives to be operationally excellent and provides appropriate support for internal audit, then audit leaders are well positioned to advance their department to world-class levels. Without sufficient support and encouragement, however, audit departments will struggle to go beyond a basic level of performance. If the organization has limited or low expectations for the audit function, then world-class status cannot be achieved even if the audit department fully meets those limited expectations. Moreover, a CAE who cannot get support to improve a lagging audit function is assuming high professional risk.*

The focus on delivering value is a recognized element of the IIA Standards, articulated in Standard 2000.

Standard 2000—Managing the Internal Audit Activity

The chief audit executive must effectively manage the internal audit activity to ensure it adds value to the organization.

Paterson (2012) warns that there can be misconceptions among some audit committees and senior executives regarding the potential value that internal audit can offer. In particular, he warns that audit committees and senior management may unrealistically expect internal audit to find frauds in the areas it audits, even when the scope of audit work and the resources available mean that this is not going to be possible. He also cautions that audit committees may perceive internal audit's primary role as being to support a particular stakeholder over and above the needs of others, resulting in a tendency to dismiss or downplay the extent to which it should accommodate other stakeholder needs. This often can be seen in tension between key stakeholder views about the role of internal audit in terms of which risk areas the plan focuses on, and the balance of audit time between assurance and consulting work.

The chief audit executive should reconcile any discrepancies in the value being sought by different stakeholders to avoid the creation of misaligned expectations. Creating an internal audit strategy can help to do this.

Drivers of Quality

Some chief audit executives' desire for quality is primarily motivated by their aspiration to achieve conformance with prescribed standards. However, the key to developing sustainable quality is cementing practices on demand-based quality drivers rather than compliance drivers. Compliance drivers can initiate the path to quality but demand drivers are needed to embed the process.

Demand-based drivers should be linked to the outputs and outcomes the internal audit function is planning to achieve. Inherent in this approach is a need to fully understand internal audit's goals and strategies, as these will determine internal audit's outputs and outcomes. A formally documented internal audit strategy and charter are important elements in identifying key drivers of quality.

Understanding the inputs necessary to deliver internal audit engagements and the value the internal audit function hopes to deliver in terms of outputs and outcomes both form part of the internal audit program logic illustrated in Figure 3.1.

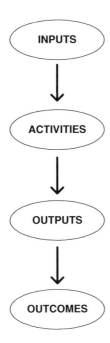

FIGURE 3.1 Inputs and Outcomes

Internal Audit Inputs

The **inputs** to the internal audit function are the resources required to deliver results. Most internal audit functions share a number of common inputs or elements, including:

- Operating budget
- Staffing
- Management structure and supervisory processes
- Operating plans (typically referred to as an internal audit plan)
- Human resources processes such as recruitment, induction, and performance management
- Policies and procedures
- Reporting processes

Grouping each of the key inputs can assist internal auditors to manage and measure quality. While there are various ways to group inputs, one approach is to thinks of an internal audit function in terms of its strategy and budget, staffing, and professional practices (see Figure 3.2).

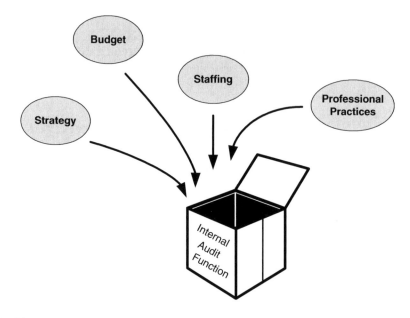

FIGURE 3.2 Internal Audit Inputs

The key features of each of these elements or groups are described in the following sections, and further detail is provided throughout this book.

STRATEGY AND BUDGET   The strategy binds together the internal audit function. Key components include the internal audit vision and value proposition, risk management and resource planning, articulation of key responsibilities, and the internal audit charter. These are each described in Figure 3.3.

When complemented by an adequate budget, a well-developed internal audit strategy will be a key driver of quality and value.

INTERNAL AUDIT STAFFING   The staffing element describes the human resources arrangements implemented by the chief audit executive and the processes used to manage and develop staff. The staffing element includes the sourcing model used by the internal audit function including the decisions to insource, out-source, or co-source activities. Figure 3.4 describes the key inputs to the staffing element.

PROFESSIONAL PRACTICES   The professional practices adopted by internal auditors are the methodologies, systems, and processes used to deliver results. They define the entity as a professional internal audit function distinct from external audit, evaluation, or quality assurance activities.

The high-level professional practice inputs are described in Figure 3.5.

FIGURE 3.3 Strategy Inputs

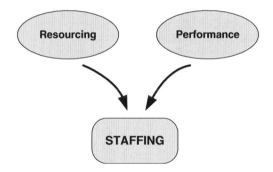

FIGURE 3.4 Staffing Inputs

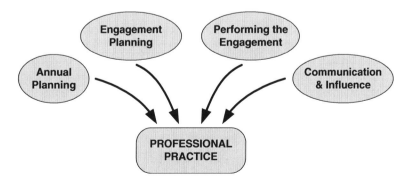

FIGURE 3.5 Professional Practice Inputs

Activities

Internal auditors can undertake a range of activities, including assurance and consulting engagements. These engagements are described in further detail throughout the book. Chief audit executives should determine the types of activities they will undertake in consultation with key organizational stakeholders.

Outputs and Outcomes

Outputs are the products or services that the internal audit function produces. Outcomes are the effects of these products or services on the organization and stakeholders—the longer-term benefits or changes that result from the outputs.

It is sometimes easier to measure internal audit outputs than internal audit outcomes. While the outcomes are what the internal audit function is ultimately trying to achieve, and should link back to the internal audit mission and vision, there will be a range of intermediary outputs that internal audit functions deliver that ultimately contribute to these outcomes. For example, internal auditors should strive to support an organization to deliver its strategy and objectives. Short-term, this will be achieved by high-level stakeholder engagement, value-adding assurance and consulting engagements, and continuous improvement of internal audit processes.

A Structured Approach to Quality

Thinking about quality in a systematic and logical manner ensures that it is built into every day practices. There are many models that can be used for measuring performance, including logic models, balanced scorecards, and maturity models and the use of each of these models is discussed further in the following sections. Generally, a chief audit executive would select one of these approaches as part of their quality assurance and improvement program. Nonetheless, all three are complementary.

Program Logic

Using program logic allows the chief audit executive to determine the types of inputs that are required to deliver specific outputs and outcomes. A typical logic-based, input-outcome representation of an internal audit function is shown in Figure 3.6.

In developing the logic model, chief audit executives should link the measurement of internal audit quality to their inputs, activities, outputs, and outcomes. Measuring results at each of these levels supports quality as a foundational element, rather than an optional extra, and helps determine whether inputs are appropriate and optimized, activities are undertaken in a professional manner, outputs meet the needs of stakeholders, and outcomes link to the value required by the organization.

Internal Audit Balanced Scorecards

Balanced scorecards can be usefully applied to measure internal audit performance and quality, as they consider a broader range of attributes than traditional financial-based reporting. Figure 3.7 provides a sample internal audit balanced scorecard.

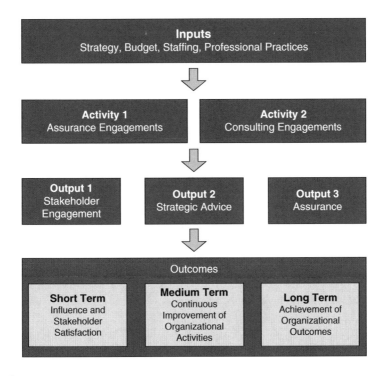

FIGURE 3.6 Internal Audit Logic Model

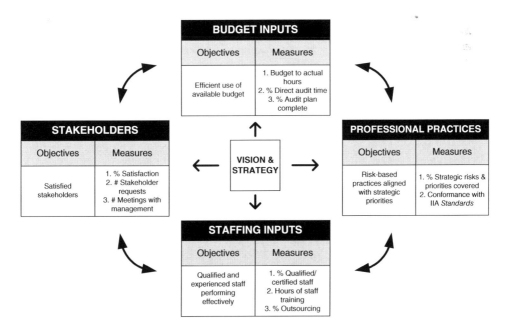

FIGURE 3.7 Sample Internal Audit Balanced Scorecard

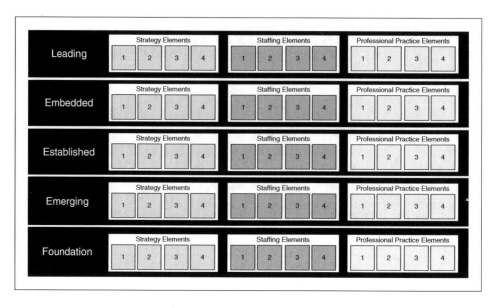

FIGURE 3.8 Internal Audit Maturity Model Extract

Internal Audit Maturity Model

The value of a maturity model is the recognition that an internal audit function should continually evolve and mature. Achieving conformance with professional standards should not be the ultimate aim of chief audit executives. Instead, they should strive to constantly grow and develop their internal audit function to meet stakeholder expectations and the strategic needs of their organization.

Figure 3.8 provides an extract from an internal audit maturity model.

Developing Performance Measures for Internal Audit

As assurance experts, internal auditors will appreciate that monitoring performance is an important internal control providing assurance that outcomes have or will be achieved. It also provides feedback on the effectiveness of other controls. To this end, the Committee of Sponsoring Organizations of the Treadway Commission (COSO) recognized *monitoring activities* as a key element of internal control. Monitoring activities also support an additional element within the COSO *Internal Control—Integrated Framework* (2013), *information and communication*, allowing management to make informed decisions regarding organizational activities and performance.

Chief audit executives should undertake their own monitoring activities to generate management information allowing them to continuously improve the internal audit function, and to provide transparency regarding internal audit's performance.

Monitoring activities should include both ongoing monitoring and periodic assessments as required under IIA Standard 1310.

Standard 1310—Requirements of the Quality Assurance and Improvement Program

The quality assurance and improvement program must include both internal and external assessments.

Common Quality Issue

Studies undertaken by the IIA at a global level, as well as national institutes such as IIA–Australia, have found that a large number of internal audit functions fail to undertake health checks or other periodic internal assessments against recognized standards or better practice.

Metrics, Measures, and Performance Indicators

Effective monitoring of the internal audit function demands the development of balanced indicators of performance, preferably with input from the audit committee and management. By promoting continuous improvement internal audit can also be a powerful aid in improving other processes within the organization. Chief audit executives should be proactive in this respect to set a better practice example. This will enhance internal audit's credibility and provide greater assurance to stakeholders that it is operating effectively.

Articulating internal audit's value proposition in the internal audit strategy will help determine internal audit performance measures because the strategy should cover:

- The environment in which the internal audit function is operating (its strategic context), including supporting legislation, regulations, and policies
- Key internal and external stakeholders
- The internal audit vision and mission
- The internal audit function's mandate, purpose, and authority (possibly articulated through a charter)
- Guiding values
- Categories of activities to be undertaken and the nature of these activities
- Consideration of risks impacting the internal audit function
- Resourcing

A key to effective performance measurement is to focus on the areas that matter. Spending time collecting data and populating metrics when the collected information is not used creates, rather than addresses, inefficiencies. For performance measurement to be relevant, it needs to form part of the continuous improvement cycle.

PERFORMANCE METRICS   Performance metrics are the specific indicators of achievement that allow managers to measure the outputs and outcomes of their activities. Performance metrics can help managers determine if activities are operating efficiently and effectively and if they are delivering value for money.

Internal auditors expect management to develop and implement appropriate performance metrics. Similarly, chief audit executives should develop performance metrics to measure the success of the internal audit function.

Performance metrics send a message about what the organization values most. Well-defined and utilized metrics target the areas of greatest importance for the organization or internal audit function.

Effective performance metrics should be specific to each internal audit function and should cover the following:

- *The adequacy of inputs to the internal audit function.* Examples of adequacy metrics are:
    - Internal audit staff numbers compared to benchmarks
    - Internal audit budget compared to benchmarks
    - Staff audit experience
    - Percentage of staff with qualifications and certifications
- *The efficiency of critical activities undertaken by the internal audit function.* Examples of efficiency metrics are:
    - Average cost per audit
    - Average cost per organizational staff
    - Average cost per internal auditor
    - Budget to actual hours
    - Percent administrative time
    - Percent "direct" audit time
    - Average audit cycle time
    - Percent of time by activity
    - Percentage of audit plan completed
- *The effectiveness of critical activities undertaken by the internal audit function.* Examples of effectiveness metrics are:
    - Hours of professional development
    - Quality assurance and improvement activities undertaken
    - Number of repeat findings
    - Percent recommendations implemented
    - Number of management requests
    - Timeliness of responses to management requests (e.g., responses within one to two working days)
    - Engagement of client satisfaction
- *The outputs delivered by the internal audit function.* Examples of output metrics are:
    - Number of meetings with senior management

- Annual/summary reports prepared
- Number of completed audits
- Number of assurance engagements
- Number of consulting engagements
- *The outcomes (impact) delivered by the internal audit function and the extent to which these are meeting organizational expectations regarding quality and value.* Examples of outcome metrics are:
  - Audit committee and senior management satisfaction
  - Proportion of organization with audit coverage
  - Percent of strategic risks audited
  - Percent of operational risks audited

Performance metrics should also take into account key stakeholders, historical and growth elements (lead and lag indicators) covering what has occurred to date and how current activities are likely to affect future performance, and qualitative and quantitative elements.

The metrics should be appropriately balanced to avoid undue emphasis on one element of the internal audit function at the expense of other elements. The metrics should also be restricted to the smallest number possible that provides the chief audit executive with the necessary information to maximize operations.

Capturing information takes time and effort and is a direct cost to an organization. The value gained from collecting information needs to exceed the cost of collection, as well as the cost of any perverse behaviors that data collection may encourage. For example, measuring the acceptance of recommendation may encourage internal auditors to opt for more easily implemented solutions, regardless of their potential effectiveness. Likewise, requiring a minimum amount of time to be spent on particular types of auditing, such as IT auditing, may discourage time to be spent in other areas, even if these are higher risk.

Knowing what to measure is one thing. More important, however, is knowing what success will look like. For example, many chief audit executives measure elements such as "the percentage of audits finished within agreed time frames." While this may be a useful metric to use, it provides no information on what success, or value, looks like. The associated measure, or performance indicator (or target), may be "completing 90 percent of audits within agreed time frames."

The IIA's *Practice Guide: Measuring Internal Audit Effectiveness and Efficiency* (2010) identifies the following steps the chief audit executive should undertake to establish effective performance indicators (metrics and measures):

1. Identify critical performance categories such as stakeholder satisfaction, internal audit processes, and innovation and capabilities.
2. Identify performance category strategies and measurements. Pursue strategies in compliance with IIA *Standards*, other applicable professional standards, and applicable laws and regulations, to ensure stakeholder satisfaction. Performance measures can be an element of the internal audit function's internal assessment process to comply with IIA *Standards*.
3. Routinely monitor, analyze, and report performance measures.

TIME RECORDING   There is some debate within the internal audit profession over whether to record hours spent on internal audit engagements. While it is relatively incontrovertible that professional services firms will record their time spent on individual engagements to determine fees to be charged to clients, in-house internal audit functions often avoid time recording. Some chief audit executives argue that time recording can be a disincentive to attracting good staff.

Chief audit executives who consider introducing time recording will need to balance the value of this management information with potential morale implications that time recording may have. However, choosing not to record time spent on engagements limits the chief audit executive's ability to monitor performance against the internal audit budget, to determine the efficiency of individuals and the team as a whole, and to justify the need for additional resources.

Recording Time: An Interview with Dr. Sarah Blackburn, Audit Committee Chair and Past President of the Chartered Institute of Internal Auditors (IIA UK and Ireland)

Recording time spent on internal audit engagements provides chief audit executives with valuable management information.

Any concerns staff may have with recording time can be alleviated through reassurance that they will not be rewarded or punished on hours alone, and by explaining that the data will be used for resource planning and allocation. Once an internal audit function collectively regards time as an input, and accepts that performance will be judged on outcomes, every team member can share in understanding how time is currently used and can be further maximized.

The key to effective time recording lies in the level of detail required. Ideally, the approach should be high level and strategic and should include time on each audit engagement, time spent on audit support work, professional development, and administration and staff absences. Conversely, recording detailed information for the stages of each engagement can create inefficiencies—the pursuit of precision makes accuracy less attainable and wastes resources in irrelevance.

It is important that chief audit executives also record their time, as this sets the tone for the internal audit function. If their team is accountable for their time, so should the chief audit executive. While it is unlikely that chief audit executives will be actively engaged in running test programs, their time should still be used wisely and to good effect.

Overall, we need to understand where our time should go and does go. We should aim for simple time records that are not onerous, but are honest and have a clear purpose understood and shared by all.

"SMART" PERFORMANCE MEASURES   Chief audit executives can consider past performance, or the performance of other similar entities, when developing performance measures or indicators. However, for newly established internal audit functions, it may be necessary to set preliminary indicators, which are then refined over the first year or so of operations to ensure that they are realistic and useful for the internal audit function.

A commonly accepted management practice is to develop SMART measures.

S—Specific (a single, simple measure—versus a combination of items—that explicitly states expected results)

M—Measurable (indicators that are measurable with existing data or with data that can be produced at a reasonable cost)

A—Action-oriented (measures that have the potential to lead to continuous improvement)

R—Relevant (measures related to the overall internal audit strategy)

T—Timely (measures that establish realistic expectations within achievable time frames)

KEY RULES FOR PERFORMANCE MEASURES For performance measures to be effective, they must follow some key rules:

- Ensure that measures and indicators are aligned with the internal audit strategy and organizational objectives.
- Ensure that measures focus on important elements of performance, rather than what is easily assessed.
- Keep measures and indicators as simple as possible and ensure that all stakeholders understand them.
- Use SMART measures and indicators.
- Ensure measures can be objectively assessed.
- Ensure measures are cost-effective to administer.
- Consult with stakeholders, including the audit committee, regarding their perceptions of value and associated measures.
- Ensure that the audit committee endorses the measures.
- Implement a process for periodically reviewing measures for ongoing relevance.

Responsibility for Internal Audit Quality

Responsibility for internal audit quality will vary depending on the nature of the organization, the sourcing model used for internal audit, and the types of activities undertaken. However, in every instance, the organization itself, through a nominated chief audit executive, retains overall responsibility for quality. This responsibility cannot be outsourced (see Figure 3.9).

Every internal auditor has a responsibility for delivering a quality product. Regardless of whether particular standards are mandated, as professionals, internal auditors have an obligation to deliver services in accordance with commonly accepted practices. Each internal auditor should strive to deliver the highest-quality product and should endeavor to operate in a way that maximizes quality and value for the organization.

The audit committee and management also share some responsibilities for internal audit quality. Depending on the structure of the organization, the chief audit executive may be accountable to both the audit committee and a senior executive. In this instance, both the audit committee and management will have an oversight role concerning the manner in which the chief audit executive operates.

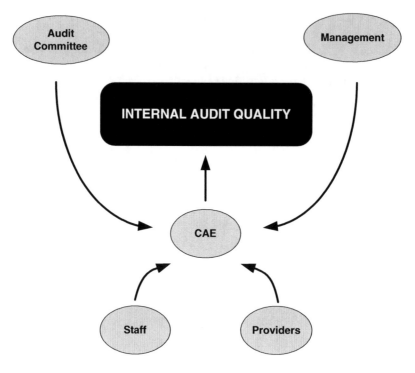

FIGURE 3.9 Responsibility for Internal Audit Quality

Board/Audit Committee

Whether internal audit is accountable to a board or audit committee will vary across organizations. However, where an audit committee exists, it will have a range of possible responsibilities for internal audit quality:

- Approving the internal audit charter
- Approving the internal audit risk assessment and related plans
- Approving decisions regarding the appointment, performance management, and remuneration of the chief audit executive
- Communicating with the chief audit executive regarding both individual engagements and overall performance against the internal audit plan

The responsibilities of an audit committee are organizationally and jurisdictionally dependent. For example, in the public sector in some countries it is the responsibility of the chief executive officer, or the appropriate government minister, to approve the appointment, performance management, and remuneration of the chief audit executive.

Audit committees will vary significantly in their nature and composition, particularly between the public and private sectors. These differences reflect general differences in internal audit between different countries and organizations.

The chair of the audit committee can have a significant influence on the quality of internal audit. The chief audit executive has a symbiotic relationship with the chair, as the chair relies on internal audit to provide assurance over the effective management of risks across the organization. The quality of this assurance will depend on the extent, nature, and standard of work undertaken by internal audit. Simultaneously, the chief audit executive relies on the audit committee to approve the extent and nature of work to be undertaken, and the standard of this work will be influenced to a large extent by the resources available to internal audit and approved by the audit committee. Without this cooperation between the chief audit executive and the audit committee, the internal audit cannot be optimized.

Senior Management

Senior management support internal audit quality both directly and indirectly. Directly, senior management may have oversight responsibilities for internal audit, including the recruitment, day-to-day management, and performance review of the chief audit executive. Senior management may also have a significant influence over the nature of the annual audit plan, the position of internal audit in the organization, and the available budget.

Indirectly, senior management has a role in setting the tone for internal audit—demonstrating their support for the activity and encouraging internal audit's involvement in strategic areas.

Chief Audit Executive

Regardless of the sourcing model, the chief audit executive retains overall responsibility for quality. Under the IIA Standards, the role of chief audit executive cannot be outsourced. Even when internal audit is fully outsourced, an officer within the organization must be nominated to oversee the quality of the service provider.

Standard 1300 is the primary quality standard within the IIA *Standards*.

Standard 1300—Quality Assurance and Improvement Program

The chief audit executive must develop and maintain a quality assurance and improvement program that covers all aspects of the internal audit activity.

Some mid- to large-size internal audit functions allocate responsibility for the quality assurance and improvement program to a single person or team. Rather than assuming responsibility for ensuring that all staff members operate in a quality manner, the quality officer or team is generally accountable for developing and implementing a quality framework that staff can operate within.

Proving the Professionalism of Internal Audit

"Quality is the basis for acceptable performance, and is the foundation from which internal auditing can strengthen its services, thereby meeting stakeholders' increased demands," says J. Graham Joscelyne, former Auditor General of the World Bank and current Audit and Ethics Committee Chair of the Global Fund.

"For institutions that rely on public trust for their very existence, the chief audit executive plays a crucial role in assuring and reassuring a wide range of stakeholders. It's only possible if the chief audit executive makes quality the cornerstone of internal auditing and develops its professional competence and impact to the level now demanded by stakeholders."

To understand what is required of internal auditing, Joscelyne believes internal audit must be integral to strategic discussions at both the board and management levels, but notes, "Its voice will only be heard and advice heeded if it can prove the quality of its professionalism—as a routine rather than as an event."

Internal Audit Staff

Every professional has a responsibility for maintaining professional standards. Internal auditors are required to demonstrate proficiency and due professional care in their work. However, beyond this, internal audit staff should play an active role in ensuring the quality of work produced by the internal audit function.

Internal Audit Service Providers

Many organizations rely on internal audit service providers to deliver part, or all, of their internal audit plan. Service providers form an important component of the internal

Common Quality Issue

Common quality issues associated with internal audit service providers include:

- Promising senior staff for the engagement but providing junior staff
- Being overly optimistic about their ability to meet deadlines
- Failing to maintain staff continuity or build in appropriate succession planning within the service provision team
- Inadequate corporate knowledge
- Inadequate technical experience

audit service delivery process, and considerations for using external service providers are discussed in greater detail later in the book.

The potential for service to operate at a consistently high standard is optimized when there are open and frank channels of communication between providers and the organization. It is incumbent on both parties to maintain an ongoing dialogue. Finding opportunities to transfer knowledge between the service provider and any in-house staff has the potential to significantly add to the quality of internal audit.

Creating a Quality Assurance and Improvement Program

Chief audit executives should formally integrate a quality program into their operations to ensure they are focused on delivering expected value, and are positioned to continuously improve and evolve. Under the IIA Standards, the internal audit quality program is referred to as a *Quality Assurance and Improvement Program* (QAIP). The concept draws on the work of Deming around continuous improvement and quality. It is consistent with the TQM approach and, similarly to ISO 9000, incorporates an independent assurance element to the program.

An internal audit function can maximize its quality by utilizing both internal and external reviews of quality. Viewed from an internal audit lens, operational managers are expected to ascertain the quality and effectiveness of their operations prior to internal audit providing independent assurance. Good managers do not wait for internal auditors to arrive before they start measuring their performance. Ideally, internal auditors should find that managers are operating effectively and have managed their key risks appropriately.

So, too, should the internal audit function measure its own quality. Chief audit executives should be extremely familiar with their operations and have a good understanding of what quality looks like. They should monitor quality in their daily activities through standardized procedures built on professional standards, effective oversight, and periodic assessment of these processes.

From time to time, the internal audit function should undertake "health checks" of its operations. These periodic assessments examine the appropriateness and adequacy of policies and procedures, and the extent to which embedded quality processes are supporting the internal audit function to deliver value to the broader organization.

Similar to the way in which internal audit provides independent assurance, chief audit executives should also receive an impartial review of the quality of their operations. This occurs through external assessment.

The IIA has developed a model quality assurance and improvement program in the *Practice Guide: Quality Assurance and Improvement Program* (2012). The model is illustrated in Figure 3.10.

Internal Processes for Assessing Quality

Measuring quality is something internal auditors should do on an ongoing basis. Although periodic health checks are extremely valuable, unless quality is part of everyday tasks, the internal audit function will need to continuously retrofit outputs to meet quality standards. Instead, internal auditors should embed and measure quality through operational processes, which is a requirement under IIA Standard 1311.

Standard 1311—Internal Assessments

Internal assessments must include:

- Ongoing monitoring of the performance of the internal audit activity; and
- Periodic self-assessments or assessments by other persons within the organization with sufficient knowledge of internal audit practices.

External Processes for Measuring Quality

IIA Standard 1312 promotes the value of independent review through its requirement for an external quality assessment.

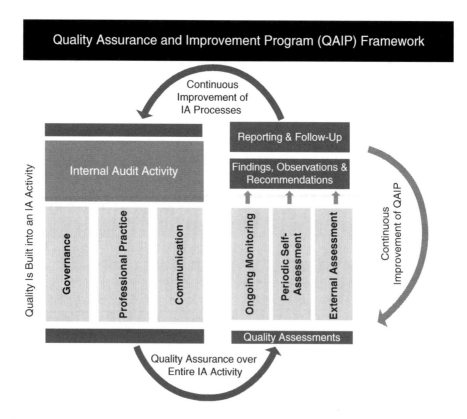

FIGURE 3.10 Quality Assurance and Improvement Program

Source: IIA *Practice Guide: Quality Assurance and Improvement Program* (2012).

Standard 1312—External Assessments

External assessments must be conducted at least once every five years by a qualified, independent assessor or assessment team from outside the organization. The chief audit executive must discuss with the board:

- The form and frequency of external assessment; and
- The qualifications and independence of the external assessor or assessment team, including any potential conflict of interest.

Reporting on Quality

Chief audit executives should report on internal audit's performance against its strategy as well as performance against its quality program. Although interrelated, there are distinct requirements associated with both that are reflected in two different IIA *Standards*.

Standard 1320 specifically relates to reporting against the quality program.

Standard 1320—Reporting on the Quality Assurance and Improvement Program

The chief audit executive must communicate the results of the quality assurance and improvement program to senior management and the board.

Standard 2060 is a broader requirement for reporting against internal audit's strategy.

Standard 2060—Reporting to Senior Management and the Board

The chief audit executive must report periodically to senior management and the board on the internal audit activity's purpose, authority, responsibility, and performance relative to its plan. Reporting must also include significant risk exposures and control issues, including fraud risks, governance issues, and other matters needed or requested by senior management and the board.

Chief audit executives could use an internal audit balanced scorecard or maturity model to assist in their interpretation and reporting of internal audit quality. These could be further supported by a quality assurance dashboard or audit trends report for senior management and the board.

QAIP Hint

Quality assurance and improvement activities can be reflected in a balanced scorecard or internal audit maturity model.

Maturity Model

The *quality assurance and improvement program* could be a key process area within the maturity model, with its existence being a requirement for the achievement of level 3 of a five-stage maturity model.

Balanced Scorecard/KPI

Internal audit functions could develop a performance indicator around the existence and implementation of a quality assurance and improvement program.

Questions about the Quality Framework

Asking questions about the quality of the internal audit function can test performance levels and ensure that internal audit is meeting stakeholder expectations. Questions can be formally incorporated into a quality assurance and improvement program, or, less formally, into ongoing assessment activities. Questions may be variously posed to the chief audit executive, internal auditors, or audit stakeholders. Table 3.1 provides a range of questions about the adequacy of the quality assurance and improvement program.

TABLE 3.1 Quality Questions

Questions	Evidence of Quality
Do stakeholders clearly understand their roles and responsibilities with regard to internal audit quality?	Position descriptions Outsourced provider contracts Stakeholder interviews
Do internal audit staff members understand their responsibilities for internal audit quality?	Internal audit staff interviews
Are quality considerations part of the ongoing dialogue between the chief audit executive, senior management, and the audit committee?	Senior management and audit committee interviews
Are there regular discussions regarding internal audit quality between the chief audit executive and the outsourced providers?	Outsourced provider interviews Records of meetings
Does the internal audit function have a documented approach to monitoring quality and performance?	Documented quality assurance and improvement program
Has a quality assurance and improvement program been developed and documented?	Documented quality assurance and improvement program
Does the quality assurance and improvement program include both internal and external assessments?	Documented quality assurance and improvement program

Does the chief audit executive consider the drivers of quality in its quality program?	Documented quality assurance and improvement program
Does the chief audit executive consider inputs, outputs, and outcomes in the consideration of quality?	Documented quality assurance and improvement program
How does the chief audit executive determine whether the internal audit function has been successful?	Assessment processes and measures Documented quality assurance and improvement program
Can the chief audit executive articulate what success looks like?	Success statement
How do senior managers and the audit committee define success for the internal audit function?	Senior management and audit committee interviews
Does the internal audit function's approach to monitoring quality and performance include health checks, self-assessments, or assessments by another person within the organization with sufficient knowledge of internal audit practices?	Reports and documentation of internal assessments including any relevant action plans

Conclusion

Responsibility for internal audit quality is shared among various stakeholders, although the chief audit executive must bear ultimate responsibility for quality. Even within fully outsourced internal audit functions, this responsibility cannot be devolved to a service provider.

The audit committee, senior management, internal audit staff, and service providers all support the internal audit function to embed quality. Each stakeholder has a role to play in maximizing the value of internal audit.

References

Committee of Sponsoring Organizations of the Treadway Commission. *Internal Control—Integrated Framework Executive Summary*. Accessed at http://www.coso.org/documents/990025P_Executive_Summary_final_may20_e.pdf.

Heavey, C., and E. Murphy. (2012). Integrating the balanced scorecard with Six Sigma. *TQM Journal* 24(2): 108–122.

Innovation Network. *Logic Model Workbook*. http://www.innonet.org/client_docs/File/logic_model_workbook.pdf.

The Institute of Internal Auditors. (2013). *International Professional Practices Framework*. Altamonte Springs, FL: The Institute of Internal Auditors.

The Institute of Internal Auditors. (2010). *Practice Guide: Measuring Internal Audit Effectiveness and Efficiency*. Altamonte Springs, FL: The Institute of Internal Auditors.

The Institute of Internal Auditors. (2012). *Practice Guide: Quality Assurance and Improvement Program*. Altamonte Springs, FL: The Institute of Internal Auditors.

The Institute of Internal Auditors. (2009). *Quality Assessment Manual,* 6th ed. Altamonte Springs, FL: The Institute of Internal Auditors Research Foundation.

The Institute of Internal Auditors Research Foundation. (2009). *Internal Audit Capability Model (IA-CM) for the public sector.* Altamonte Springs, FL: The Institute of Internal Auditors Research Foundation.

McIntosh, E. (1992). *Internal Auditing in a Total Quality Environment.* Altamonte Springs, FL: The Institute of Internal Auditors Research Foundation.

Paterson, J. (2012). The lean audit advantage. *Internal Auditor.* http://www.theiia.org/intauditor.

Ratliff, R. L., W. A. Wallace, G. E. Sumners, W. G. McFarland, and H. Nieuwlands. (2006). *Sustainability and Internal Auditing.* Altamonte Springs, FL: The Institute of Internal Auditors Research Foundation.

Rezaee, Z. (1996). Improving the quality of internal audit functions through total quality management. *Managerial Auditing Journal* 11(1): 30–34.

Rosenfeld, M. (2013). Framework for excellence. *Internal Auditor*, February 2013. http://www.theiia.org/intauditor.

W. K. Kellogg Foundation. (1998). *Logic Model Development Guide.* http://www.wkkf.org/knowledge-center/resources/2006/02/wk-kellogg-foundation-logic-model-development-guide.aspx.

CHAPTER 4

Internally Assessing Quality

Man is a goal-seeking animal. His life only has meaning if he is reaching out and striving for his goals.

—Aristotle

Effective managers have a deep understanding of their organization and staff and measure performance to determine how well they are delivering against their objectives. They celebrate successes while embracing failings as opportunities to improve performance.

Chief audit executives should develop a suite of tools for assessing internal audit quality. This will often include ongoing processes for determining quality as part of daily activities, as well as processes for measuring performance on a periodic basis.

Internal quality assessments can be linked to performance processes such as maturity models or program logic. They may incorporate benchmarking, and can be used as a precursor to an external quality assessment.

Ongoing Internal Monitoring and Maturity Models

Ongoing monitoring processes are not unique to internal audit. Good managers should have in place different processes for ensuring they achieve their business objectives. These should cover strategy, risk management, resourcing, staff management and performance, and operational processes. Assessments should include both conformance with professional standards (compliance drivers of quality) and delivery of value (demand drivers of quality), and incorporate the identification and implementation of better practice.

Thinking about internal audit quality through the lens of a maturity model, differing levels of quality can be built in to different levels of maturity. The chief audit executive, in collaboration with key stakeholders, can then determine the level of maturity that they aspire to.

The concept of maturity models was introduced earlier in the book. In general, a maturity model will incorporate five levels of maturity. While the levels can be defined in different ways, the author proposes the five levels as illustrated in Figure 4.1.

1. *Foundation.* Standards have not been established; routine professional practices are absent; services are not routinely provided; staff are unqualified or inexperienced.

2. *Emerging*. Standards are recognized but not routinely adhered to; professional practices are ad hoc or individualized; service provision is ad hoc; staff have some qualifications and/or experience, but knowledge is not systematically shared.
3. *Established*. Professional practices conform to professional standards and are routinely applied; staff members collectively have the skills and experience required to perform services.
4. *Embedded*. Service provision meets stakeholder expectations and is focused on strategic priorities; staff are provided with structured and systematic development; services include a range of consulting and assurance engagements.
5. *Leading*. Service provision represents better/leading practice; collectively, staff members are highly skilled and experienced; professional practices utilize leading technologies and processes.

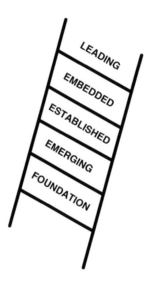

FIGURE 4.1 **Levels of Maturity**

Key process areas within the proposed maturity model are grouped within the categories of *strategy elements, staffing elements*, and *professional practices*. Figure 4.2 includes an extract relating to professional practices from the sample maturity model introduced in Chapter 3.

The key process areas identified in Figure 4.2 (*annual planning, engagement planning, conduct,* and *reporting*) are for illustrative purposes only. It is likely that an internal audit maturity model would include more detailed or specific process areas.

Different indicators of quality would be assigned to each of the key process areas at specific maturity levels. For example, indicators of annual audit planning quality at the *established* level could be the existence of risk-based plans and consultation with stakeholders during planning. Other potential indicators of quality are included in Figure 4.3.

Agreeing on different levels of quality requires a good understanding of stakeholder expectations, and ideally forms part of the strategic planning process. Once the chief audit executive and stakeholders have agreed on the level of maturity being aspired to, the chief audit executive should determine the inputs required to achieve this level. This can then feed into planning processes, such as budget planning and staff capability planning. Examples of inputs are described in Figure 4.4.

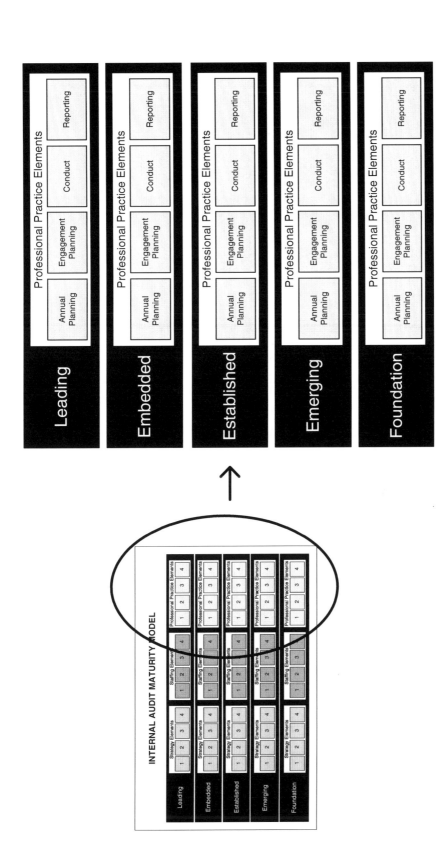

FIGURE 4.2 Key Process Area Categories within a Maturity Model

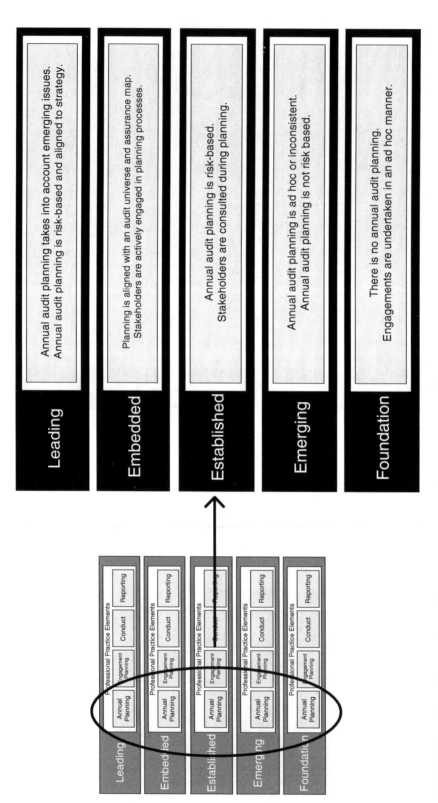

FIGURE 4.3 Quality Indicators for Each Key Process Area within a Maturity Model

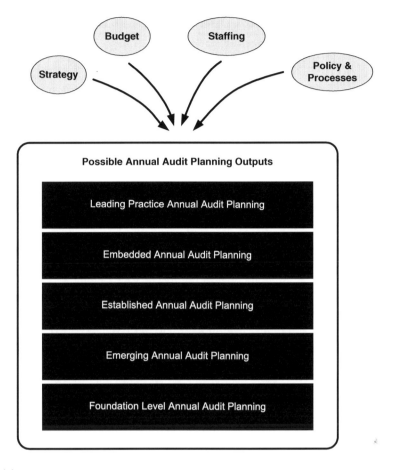

FIGURE 4.4 Inputs to Achieve Key Process Areas

Internal audit functions can only be as mature as the organization in which they operate. For instance, it may be inappropriate for an internal audit function to undertake a large number of governance audits in a new organization with immature governance arrangements. Similarly, an organization that is strongly focused on achieving compliance with a range of legislative provisions may require its internal auditors to undertake a higher than normal number of compliance audits.

Chief audit executives might not always target the highest level of maturity for their internal audit function as this level may require an excessive level of inputs. The chief audit executive will need to determine, in consultation with key stakeholders, whether they aspire to good practice, better practice, or leading practice, taking into consideration the cost benefit of each.

Processes for Embedding Quality

Developing policies and procedures that align with professional standards is fundamental to embedding quality in internal audit practices. In addition, policies and procedures can incorporate specific practices that will allow quality to be monitored on an ongoing basis. These practices can be high-level and strategic, such as articulating the requirement for internal audit staff to follow professional standards within their positions/job descriptions. Conversely, they can be at a more operational level.

The processes used to monitor quality should be aligned to the outputs and outcomes required from the internal audit function, the level of quality being aspired to, and the performance metrics incorporated into measurement tools such as a balanced scorecard. Typical, operations-based processes for embedding quality include the following:

- Checklists/quality checks to identify key tasks and processes and ensure these are being followed.
- Completion of working papers to ensure that the approved engagement plan and program have been performed and that audit findings are adequately supported by relevant and sufficient evidence.
- Ongoing supervision to ensure that work is being conducted in an efficient and effective manner.
- Report review to ensure that conclusions and recommendations/agreed management actions are accurate, objective, clear, concise, and timely.
- Timekeeping systems to measure the efficient use of staffing inputs.
- Regular (weekly to monthly) staff meetings to discuss emerging issues and share better practices.
- Regular (monthly) interviews with senior management and the audit committee chair.

Developing a structured approach to internal audit operations need not limit innovation or creativity.

Effective management and supervision helps ensure the quality of internal audit engagements. Management and supervision support the effective and efficient use of internal audit inputs to undertake agreed activities.

IIA Standard 2340 recognizes the importance of effectively managing engagements.

Standard 2340—Engagement Supervision

Engagements must be properly supervised to ensure objectives are achieved, quality is assured, and staff is developed.

Management and Supervision Better Practices

Better practices relating to *management* and *supervision* include the following:

- Document audit roles and responsibilities—audit manager/supervisor, quality reviewer, team member, and peers (for peer review).
- Document key review points for audit managers and supervisors.

- Develop a standard checklist to support engagement review and enhance communication/report quality.
- Mandate the review of engagement programs prior to the commencement of fieldwork, to validate risks and identify any key areas that may have been overlooked in the proposed methodology.
- Mandate the review of working papers prior to issue of the draft report.
- Introduce a peer review process to ensure consistent quality across the internal audit function.
- Introduce a random working-paper review process to ensure consistent documentation standards are established and embedded.
- Require service providers to demonstrate appropriate supervisory review of their own engagements.

Periodic Internal Assessments: Health Checks

Building quality into standard practices provides assurance that internal audit functions will perform to expectations. However, sometimes standards are not met. Resource constraints or time pressures may result in compromises to quality, staff may be unaware of prescribed procedures, or staff may consciously choose to not follow agreed processes. In these circumstances, the internal audit function will benefit from periodic internal quality assessments, otherwise known as self-assessments or health checks.

Maximizing the Value of Internal Assessments

"There is significant variation in the value to be obtained from internal assessments," cautions Mike Lynn, IT Audit Director at a major global financial services company and vice chairman of the IIA's Professional Issues Committee. Chief audit executives should consider the scope and nature of their internal assessments before embedding their quality program.

Lynn believes that chief audit executives should begin by looking at their budget, staff, and the maturity of their organization, as he thinks this will drive internal audit outcomes. "Quality programs don't give enough consideration to the maturity of the three lines of defense," says Lynn.

Effort should then be placed on examining the process used by internal auditors to identify risks associated with the area being reviewed, as this will have a major impact on the overall quality of the internal audit work. "Sometimes people can focus on the minutiae in the internal assessment—rather than determining the overall quality of the work performed, they concentrate on areas such as how well documentation occurred," says Lynn.

"It is also important to speak with stakeholders as part of the internal assessment," advises Lynn. In cases where internal audits are co-sourced, this should include the service providers as well as the audit clients.

(continued)

(*continued*)

    The key to a successful internal assessment is to embed continuous improvements. Lynn believes it is not the individual findings from the assessment that are important, but how the internal audit function responds to these findings.

Key Elements of a Periodic Internal Assessment/Health Check

These key elements include:

- Whether internal audit engagements are consistent with the internal audit charter and mandate
- The extent to which the internal audit function is meeting management expectations
- The value being delivered by the internal audit function
- The level of effectiveness and efficiency within the internal audit function
- How well the internal audit function is performing against its own policies and procedures
- How well the internal audit function is performing against professional standards
- Benchmarking against other similar organizations
- Opportunities for continuous improvement

Health checks can cover the entire internal audit function or may be limited to specific areas. Examples of limited, or focused, health checks include:

- Conformance with engagement documentation policies through selection of a sample of working papers
- Conformance with the IIA's Performance Standards
- Assessment of training undertaken by internal audit staff and the extent to which this meets their professional development requirements

Using the logic model approach, health checks could be performed against specific inputs, activities, or outputs. For instance, the health check could involve budget monitoring (input), review of assurance engagements (activity), or quality of engagement reports (output).

What Separates a High-Quality Internal Audit Activity from an Average Internal Audit Activity—An Interview with Gibby Armstrong, Chief Audit Executive (Canada) and Member of the IIA Professional Issues Committee

A high-quality internal audit function has insight and foresight; an average one focuses on hindsight. This is, of course, easier to achieve if the chief audit executive is involved in senior management governance committees—so they have timely access to understand the key decisions that are being made and the thought process that went into them. Insight is seeing any discrepancies in information provided for decision making—being "big picture" and strategic about what senior management requires. Foresight is about knowing the risks associated with new strategies and activities—and helping management proactively address them in implementation.

Chief audit executives should focus on developing high-quality infrastructure, undertaking high-quality engagements, and developing a high-quality team.

Develop high-quality infrastructure

- Build respect for the IIA *Standards* and good practices into operations processes and file management systems so that even before objective QA activities are undertaken, it can be reasonably assumed that professional standards have been followed.
- Continuously train staff on how best to document audit work, and encourage staff to learn from each other.
- Integrate QA processes throughout the audit cycle, not just at the end.
- Use a proprietary audit management tool to increase efficiency or develop customized approaches using existing and readily available software.
- Use client surveys that ask meaningful questions, and are followed through with measurable improvement plans.
- Maintain consistency in deliverables that are seen outside the audit shop so time is not spent explaining the audit process versus the key risks or findings.

Undertake high-quality engagements

- Make stakeholder requirements clear to everyone—your audit team and stakeholders: what they need from you and what you commit to giving them.
- Recognize the priority of stakeholders to help target audit objectives and criteria to meet their needs at all levels in development of risk-based audit plans and individual audit plans. Know what matters to your key stakeholders, and why.
- Understand the impact of other assurance providers—and be clear why this does/does not impact audit planned activities and understand when leveraging is an option. This can be achieved through assurance mapping.

Build a high-quality team that

- Listens to and understands the perspectives of others.
- Genuinely wants to understand the challenges in the operating environment.
- Has the necessary skills/competencies and outsources when this is not in-house.
- Is supportive of management excellence in the organization in which they work.
- Is objective and independent.

Quality Teams

There are mixed views as to whether the creation of teams to assess quality represents better practice or whether this removes responsibility for quality from individual staff members.

Those advocating quality teams see them as a valuable tool for delivering a consistent internal audit product, particularly for large internal audit functions. Quality teams could comprise volunteers from the internal audit function, similar to Ishikawa's *quality circles,* or could be selected by the chief audit executive.

If a chief audit executive chooses to establish a quality team, the team can then periodically assess conformance with internal audit policies and procedures. Quality teams should be led by senior internal auditors with a thorough knowledge of professional standards and deep experience in the application of policies and procedures. The quality team could also include less experienced staff as both a development experience and to encourage consideration of different approaches and ideas.

The quality team may be responsible for measuring conformance with a specific policy, procedures, or professional standard. Depending on the size of the internal audit function, this may only require a short, finite effort (possibly over one or two days). The results of this assessment could then be shared with the broader internal audit team to promote continuous improvement.

Health Checking before an External Quality Assessment

Health checking before a full external quality assessment reduces the risk of negative surprises and allows the chief audit executive to be as prepared as possible for the external assessment.

More information regarding external assessments is provided in Chapter 5.

Using the Health Check as a Self-Assessment to Be Independently Validated

A comprehensive health check can also be used as a self-assessment that can be independently validated to meet the requirements of an external quality assessment.

Client Satisfaction

Client satisfaction can be increased by active involvement through audit planning, and by internal auditors providing regular, honest, and transparent feedback during the engagement process. Being responsive to client requests regarding the engagement timing and scope, while maintaining appropriate independence, can support positive working relationships. So, too, can responding to management requests for assistance in a timely manner.

For modern internal audit functions, measuring the level of client satisfaction with internal audit provides insight regarding the value that the internal audit function is providing. Client satisfaction may also be considered an output or outcome from the internal audit logic model, and would therefore be an appropriate element to measure.

Moving from a Good to a Great Function—Ana Figueiredo, Chief Audit Executive Portugal Telecom

Ana Figueiredo, Chief Audit Executive at Portugal Telecom, believes there are four key elements separating a good internal audit function from a great internal audit function.

First, a great internal audit function needs to reflect knowledge of the business. Although internal audit is primarily an assurance activity, the internal audit function needs to understand business trends, the structure of the organization, and both the formal and informal elements of the organization.

Second, the internal audit function needs to communicate well with the entire organization. Although internal auditors report to the audit committee and CEO, they need to know how to interact with the whole organization in a 360-degree manner. They should appreciate that as soon as they deliver a report, they will be evaluated themselves by the business based on the quality and accuracy of the audit report.

Third, internal auditors need to be independent but also need to know where the business is heading. They should be fully aligned with the business objectives.

Finally, great internal auditors need to have the right skills. Collectively, the internal audit function needs staff with business curiosity and a strong commitment to the organization and internal auditing. Internal auditors need to be driven in their pursuit of organizational improvement. Ideally, the team should have staff from a variety of backgrounds.

Ana Figueiredo has some advice for all new internal auditors:

> *Know the process and the business area you are auditing. Undertake research, have intellectual curiosity, and learn from your peers. Be very keen to identify risks that the company faces. Find the hidden spots in terms of operational improvement—the efficiencies that can be brought to the company. Also, for first-time auditors, check everything—don't accept the first information you receive, but cross check this with other evidence and look for the holes in narratives.*

She also cautions: "Quality is not a sprint—it is a marathon."

Benchmarking the Internal Audit Function

Health checks provide useful data for benchmarking the quality of the internal audit function against its peers.

Benchmarking through IIA's GAIN Benchmarking Study

Benchmarking an internal audit function against other internal audit functions provides the chief audit executive, audit committee, and senior management with insight into the appropriateness of the resources available to internal audit, as well as understanding of their efficiency and effectiveness compared with other operations.

Benchmarking can occur informally through comparison with other known organizations, or more formally through established benchmarking criteria. Larger service providers often undertake benchmarking, and many of these have produced publications on internal audit benchmarks. The Institute of Internal Auditors also offers benchmarking information though its *Common*

(continued)

(continued)
Body of Knowledge series of publications (IIA April 2014a). Each of these allows the chief audit executive to compare their own structure, resources, and types of engagements against standard professional practices.

The Institute of Internal Auditors also offers a more formalized benchmarking process through its *Global Audit Information Network* benchmarking study (IIA May 2014b). The study is a rolling benchmarking program that compares responses to analogous internal audit functions based on industry, location, and/or size of organization and internal audit function.

The benchmarking service is available to chief audit executives on a fee-for-service basis and chief audit executives are provided with a detailed report comparing their internal audit function to other organizations across metrics such as:

- Organizational metrics such as revenue, employees, location, and industry type
- Internal audit staffing, including numbers, cost, training, and travel
- Outsourcing
- Oversight, including audit committee information
- Operational measures, including audit lifecycles, number and type of audits, and tools and techniques used
- Risk assessment and audit planning information

QAIP Hint

Internal assessment can be reflected in a balanced scorecard or internal audit maturity model.

Maturity Model

The *internal assessment* or *health check* could be a key process area within the maturity model, with its existence being a requirement for the achievement of level 3 of a five-stage maturity model.

Balanced Scorecard/KPI

Internal audit functions could develop performance indicators around internal assessments or health checks such as:

- Periodic assessments and/or health checks performed on a biannual basis
- All policies and procedures covered through health checks
- General conformance with policies and procedures
- Professional standards covered through health checks
- General conformance with professional standards
- Number of improvements embedded (include target)
- Proportion of engagement working papers reviewed through health checks (include target)
- Level of management satisfaction (include target)
- Level of audit committee satisfaction (include target)

Questions about Internal Assessments

Table 4.1 provides a range of questions about the quality of internal assessment process. These can be formally incorporated into a quality assurance and improvement program, or, less formally, into ongoing assessment activities. Questions may be variously posed to the chief audit executive, internal auditors, or audit stakeholders.

TABLE 4.1 Quality Questions

Questions	Evidence of Quality
Has the internal audit function built quality checkpoints into policies and procedures?	Policies and procedures
Are supervision processes formalized?	Policies and procedures
Has the internal audit function formalized its processes for internal assessments and health checks?	Policies and procedures Documented quality assurance and improvement program
Does the internal audit function undertake periodic assessments and health checks?	Results of periodic assessments and health checks
Do internal assessments include the level of adherence to professional standards?	Scope or terms of reference of assessments
Do internal assessments include the adequacy and appropriateness of the internal audit charter, vision, and mission?	Scope or terms of reference of assessments
Do internal assessments include the adequacy, appropriateness, and level of adherence to internal audit policies and procedures?	Scope or terms of reference of assessments
Do internal assessments consider stakeholders' perspectives regarding the value of the internal audit function?	Scope or terms of reference of assessments
Do the internal auditors have a clear understanding of the internal audit function's level of conformance with professional standards?	Internal audit staff interviews
Do the internal auditors have a clear understanding of the internal audit function's level of efficiency and effectiveness?	Internal audit staff interviews
Is client, management, and audit committee satisfaction considered as part of internal assessments and health checks?	Satisfaction surveys
Is the maturity of the internal audit function formally assessed?	Results of maturity assessment
Has the internal audit function been formally benchmarked against industry data?	Benchmarking results
Does the chief audit executive provide the audit committee with periodic benchmarking on audit capability including experience, average years, qualifications, and professional certifications?	Minutes of audit committee meetings
Are the results of quality activities such as periodic assessments and health checks reported to the audit committee?	Minutes of audit committee meetings

Conclusion

Internal quality assessments are critical to delivering audit quality. They are central to adopting a "Deming-style" continuous improvement process and drawing on Juran's quality improvement approach. Internal assessments should measure and respond to levels of client satisfaction or dissatisfaction. Often, chief audit executives use benchmarking to determine how the internal audit function compares to those in other organizations.

Internal assessment can assist a chief audit executive to identify areas of high performance as well as opportunities for improvement. They allow the internal audit function to continuously respond to changes in organizational priorities and stakeholder expectations. Internal assessments can also prepare the chief audit executive to effectively meet the requirements of an external assessment.

References

Dixon, G., and G. Goodall. (2007). The Quality Assurance Review: Is your internal audit function effective? *Internal Auditing* 22(2): 3–6.

Galloway, D. (2010). *Internal Auditing: A Guide for the New Auditor*. Altamonte Springs, FL: The Institute of Internal Auditors Research Foundation.

Heeschen, P. E., and L. B. Sawyer. (1984). *Internal Auditor's Handbook*. Altamonte Springs, FL: The Institute of Internal Auditors.

The Institute of Internal Auditors. (April 2014a). *CBOK Survey*. Accessed at https://na .theiia.org/iiarf/Pages/Common-Body-of-Knowledge-CBOK.aspx.

The Institute of Internal Auditors. (May 15, 2014b). *GAIN Benchmarking*. Accessed at https://na.theiia.org/services/gain/Pages/GAIN-Benchmarking.aspx.

The Institute of Internal Auditors. (2013). *International Professional Practices Framework*. Altamonte Springs, FL: The Institute of Internal Auditors.

The Institute of Internal Auditors. (2010). *Practice Guide: Measuring Internal Audit Effectiveness and Efficiency*. Altamonte Springs, FL: The Institute of Internal Auditors.

The Institute of Internal Auditors. (2012). *Practice Guide: Quality Assurance and Improvement Program*. Altamonte Springs, FL: The Institute of Internal Auditors.

The Institute of Internal Auditors. (2009). *Quality Assessment Manual,* 6th ed. Altamonte Springs, FL: The Institute of Internal Auditors Research Foundation.

Kinsella, D. (2010). Assessing your internal audit function. *Accountancy Ireland* 42(2): 10–12.

Ridley, J., and K. Stephens. (1996). *International Quality Standards: Implications for Internal Auditing*. Altamonte Springs, FL: The Institute of Internal Auditors Research Foundation.

Sawyer, L. B., M. A. Dittenhofer, and J. H. Scheiner (2005). *Sawyers Internal Auditing,* 5th ed. Altamonte Springs, FL: The Institute of Internal Auditors Research Foundation.

CHAPTER 5

Externally Assessing Quality

Be a yardstick of quality. Some people aren't used to an environment where excellence is expected.

—Steve Jobs

Good managers are not afraid to be critiqued. They understand that an independent person or agency might identify issues that were overlooked, or processes that are undertaken more efficiently in other organizations. External assessments provide that review. Internal auditing bears some similarity to external review, and internal auditors often play the role of a form of external reviewer. To this end, internal auditors should understand the external assessment process. While this does not necessarily make it easier for internal auditors when it comes to having their own activities reviewed, they should at least gain insight into how auditees normally feel.

As assurance professionals, internal auditors should embrace the process of external assessment. Chief audit executives should build external assessments into their quality assurance and improvement program. However, external assessments should complement internal assessments rather than replace these processes. Internal and external assessments should be complementary and support the continuous improvement on the internal audit function.

What Is an External Assessment?

External assessments answer the question *Who audits the auditor?* They are to the internal audit function what internal audit is to the rest of the organization—an independent and impartial review of operations.

Effective managers recognize the value of external review. They appreciate the accountability and knowledge that an external assessor can bring to the process.

The IIA recognizes the value of external assessments through its Standard 1312.

Standard 1312—External Assessments

External assessments must be conducted at least once every five years by a qualified, independent assessor or assessment team from outside the organization. The chief audit executive must discuss with the board:

- The form and frequency of external assessments; and
- The qualifications and independence of the external assessor or assessment team, including any potential conflicts of interest.

External assessments have been mandatory for internal audit functions under the IIA Standards since they were first released in 1978. However, from 2002 there has been a requirement for these external assessments to be conducted at least every five years. The assessments are designed to measure the efficiency and effectiveness of the internal audit function, conformance with professional standards, and to identify opportunities for improvement. To this end, they incorporate the principles of continuous improvement first proposed by Deming.

Dixon and Goodall (2007) recognize that although the primary purpose of an external assessment is to determine compliance with professional standards, they believe that many stakeholders, including audit committee members and C-suite executives, are paying attention to the external assessments: "They are using them to confirm alignment of internal audit with their priorities and expectations, identify opportunities to significantly improve internal audit departments, and optimize the level of convergence of internal audit with other risk functions in the organization."

The IIA *Practice Guide: Quality Assurance and Improvement Program* (2012) identifies two possible approaches for external assessments:

1. A full external assessment would involve the use of a qualified, independent assessor or assessment team to conduct the assessment.
2. A self-assessment with independent (external) validation would involve the use of a qualified, independent assessor or assessment team to conduct an independent validation of the self-assessment completed by the internal audit function.

Why Have an External Assessment?

The value of external assessments is widely recognized. Giard and Cecere (2008) see the value as including:

- An opportunity to validate the internal audit function's proficiency and professionalism with the audit committee and shareholders
- Enhancing the internal audit function's credibility with management and business units
- Motivating internal auditors to aim for the highest-quality standards
- Obtaining an independent opinion on the quality of the internal audit function

Kinsella (2010) adds to this: "Benchmarking internal audit against its peers allows the function to see how its performance compares and provides the opportunity for development."

Kinsella believes that a quality assessment can provide answers to the audit committee regarding:

- Whether internal audit is effective and focusing on the *right* areas
- Whether internal audit is as efficient as possible
- Whether internal audit is adding value
- Whether internal audit is well respected and influential
- Whether internal audit understands stakeholder needs and expectations, and is meeting them
- Whether internal audit practices reflect leading practices of the profession
- Whether internal audit has the right strategies for future success
- Whether internal audit is appropriately structured and resourced
- Whether there a good relationship between internal audit and other assurance functions
- Whether internal audit is playing an active role in relation to risk management

Manchanda and MacDonald (2011) consider there is strategic value in having an external assessment. When referring to an external assessment of their own internal audit function, they noted that the results can "be used tactically and as a starting point for reflecting on how the internal audit function can be enhanced to achieve maximum impact for the organization." In terms of their own function, it "led to the initial conceptualization of a model for the next generation of audits."

The Benefits of an External Assessment

Max Häge, Vice President, Corporate Audit, at Deutsche Bahn AG, Berlin, speaks about the value of external quality assessments. "I have had the privilege of managing several external assessments over the last 10 years through my role as responsible manager for quality at several companies. My conviction has never been stronger that an external assessment is an indispensable tool for the chief audit executive and executive management if performed thoroughly, professionally, and on a regular basis."

Among the numerous benefits, Häge cites the following as the most important:

- Creating or strengthening a true quality culture in the internal audit function.
- Valuable insights for the auditors through the inherent role change that the external assessment generates—after an external quality assessment, they will be better auditors.
- Walking the talk of "no blind spots" and answering the question of "who audits the auditor"—this results in better acceptance by corporate management.
- Unvarnished feedback from inside and outside the organization may unveil important improvement potentials.
- Last but not least, it helps to achieve conformance to professional standards.

Häge believes, "If you are serious about internal auditing, an external quality assessment demonstrates how good you really are."

Types of Assessments

There are different options for undertaking an external assessment. The most independent option is to have the assessment completely undertaken by a reviewer from outside the organization. Alternatively, an external reviewer can be used to validate the findings of an internal assessment. Finally, the organization could engage in a peer review process, working with a group of other internal audit functions to mutually assess quality.

Targeting a Maturity Level

"When undertaking an external quality assessment, internal audit should target a particular maturity level," says Mike Lynn, IT Audit Director at a major global financial services company and vice chairman of the IIA's Professional Issues Committee. Just like management has a risk appetite or target level of risk acceptance, Lynn believes internal audit activities need to look at their industry, risk maturity level, and culture in determining the type of department they aim to be. "After all, quality is always a function of people, time, and resources and, depending on what you invest, the level of quality is a result—it is not an absolute."

Choosing a Reviewer

The IIA *Standards* require that external assessments be conducted by a qualified, independent assessor or assessment team from outside the organization. In general, a reviewer is considered qualified having completed training in quality assessments provided by the IIA, and is considered impartial if not employed or engaged by the organization.

Choosing the right reviewer can have a major impact on the quality of the external assessment. Effective reviewers should have:

- Broad and deep experience in internal auditing
- Experience in undertaking external assessments
- Industry experience relevant to the internal audit function

---

Common Quality Issue

It is not uncommon for service providers to offer reviewers for external assessments with limited internal audit experience—although they may have extensive external audit experience—and/or limited expertise and understanding of internal auditing standards. To avoid this possibility, chief audit executives and/or the audit committee should request specific information regarding the proposed reviewer for an external assessment, rather than relying on the overall experience of the service provider.

Full External Assessment

A full external assessment is the most independent approach to a quality review. It involves a reviewer, or review team, from outside the organization undertaking the assessment. Generally, the reviewer will be selected by the chief audit executive in consultation with the audit committee to avoid any perception of conflict or bias. Figure 5.1 describes a typical process for undertaking an external assessment.

A full external assessment is usually regarded as the most valuable of the external assessment approaches, as it provides a completely impartial view over the efficiency and effectiveness of the internal audit function. It also allows for the identification of improvement opportunities by having the internal audit function benchmarked against other, similar functions.

Listening to Customers

"The quality of products and services is generally developed through competition," says Takuya Morita, General Manager Quality, for the Institute of Internal Auditors-Japan. "Competition allows customers to choose from a range of products and services based on quality and costs. However, internal audit functions do not have competitors in their organizations. Customers of internal audit have no choice, so it's important that internal audit takes the time to listen to their customers."

Morita explains that in Japan people usually work for one company throughout their life, which prevents internal auditors from seeing other companies' audit practices. "However, internal audit functions need to be aware of common practices to determine a baseline for quality. This creates real difficulties for internal auditors."

"External quality assessments can provide a systematic solution," says Morita. "External quality assessments use surveys and interviews to hear the voices of stakeholders and can recommend common or successful practices for enhancing internal audit quality."

JUSTIFYING THE EXPENSE OF AN EXTERNAL ASSESSMENT   A common argument against having a full external assessment is that it is prohibitively expensive. This is a short-sighted attitude, as the cost of an external assessment is usually less than the cost of an average internal audit, and the risks mitigated through an external assessment—that internal audit does not operate efficiently or effectively—are significant.

Senior management and the audit committee expect that internal auditors provide assurance over significant risks across an organization. Therefore, the internal audit function should form a standard part of the audit universe and receive the same level of attention that the rest of the organization receives.

As would be expected for other areas over which the chief audit executive has management responsibility, assurance over the internal audit function should be provided independently and reported to senior management and the audit committee.

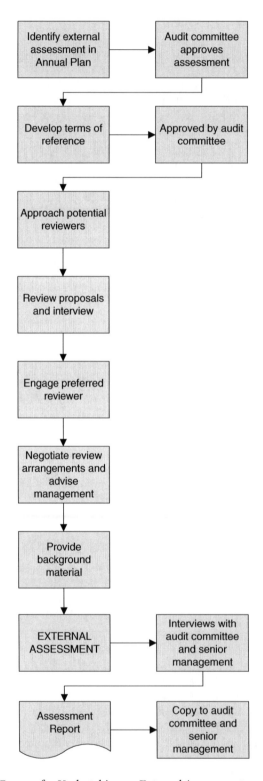

FIGURE 5.1 Typical Process for Undertaking an External Assessment

Checking the Health of the Internal Audit Function: A Conversation with an Experienced External Assessor

Judy Grobler, owner of IA Professionals in South Africa, is an experienced external quality assessor. She talks about the value that chief audit executives can receive from an external assessment.

"After completing a quality review, it is best practice to have an exit presentation, and usually I have it with the whole internal audit staff with the chief audit executive's agreement. After one particular review, the chief audit executive commented to his staff that for him, an external quality assessment was like going to the doctor for a regular health check. He believed it was a privilege to know if something is wrong and how to treat it."

Since that experience, Grobler has explained to chief audit executives that "a thorough check-up will determine your *state of health*, and even if you were not aware of something that may be wrong, the *scan* will pick it up. If all looks good, preventative measures will be prescribed, and if the way that was followed before gets outdated, better practices are recommended." Grobler advises, "What is important is that if you do not perform the *thorough check-up* on a regular basis, the chances are that the 'patient may die'! External quality assessment being performed at least on a three- to five-year basis, is the *health check* for all internal audit activities, whether they are big or small."

Self-Assessment with Independent Validation

A self-assessment with independent validation is a type of external assessment that involves part of the work being undertaken by the internal audit function. Typically, the internal audit function will assess its own efficiency, effectiveness, and conformance with standards, and an independent assessor will then validate this.

The self-assessment with independent validation approach was originally developed to cater to smaller internal audit functions for which a full external assessment might have been considered cost-prohibitive.

Although originally viewed a less-mature approach than full external assessments, when undertaken well, the validation of a self-assessment can add value beyond the full external assessment.

In organizations with mature quality assurance and improvement programs, the internal audit function should be assessing conformance with professional standards on a regular basis, as this should form part of the ongoing internal assessments. The assessment should be supported by appropriate evidence, which can be provided to an external validator with minimal additional work required by the internal audit function. This then allows the external validator to focus on efficiency and effectiveness issues beyond conformance issues.

A secondary value of the self-assessment approach is the opportunity it provides to internal audit staff to develop a deep understanding and insight into the professional standards used by the internal audit function. It also allows the internal audit function to embed continuous improvements into internal audit operations as part of the self-assessment process. In this way, the self-assessment approach is highly reflective of the *kaizen* philosophy and Ishikawa's quality circles, discussed in Chapter 2.

Common Quality Issue

Many internal audit functions focus on conformance with professional standards in their self-assessment, rather than the overall efficiency and effectiveness of the internal audit function. This limits the value of the self-assessment with independent validation approach, as conformance with standards should be considered a basis for operating, rather than an ultimate performance goal.

CONSIDERATIONS FOR SMALL AUDIT SHOPS WHEN CHOOSING A SELF-ASSESSMENT   Small audit shops often use self-assessments with independent validation as their form of external assessment. When deciding whether to use this type of approach, chief audit executive for these smaller functions should consider:

- The time it will take to complete the self-assessment, particularly if they do not have in place a well-established quality assurance and improvement program
- The availability of appropriately experienced staff to complete an internal assessment
- The benefit that a full external assessment might bring to their function, as two of the biggest challenges facing a small audit shop are their isolation and access to a range of professional perspectives.

Peer Review

Strictly speaking, peer reviews are simply a variation on an external assessment, and organizations need to fully meet the requirements for an external assessment when selecting this approach. These requirements include:

- *Ensuring that the reviewers are appropriately experienced and qualified.* This requires the reviewer to have had previous experience in undertaking an external assessment and to be qualified in the external assessment process. For organizations using the IIA *Standards*, this would typically involve the reviewer undertaking IIA training in the quality assessment process.
- *Ensuring that reviewers meet independence requirements.* This prevents two organizations from mutually reviewing each other, or internal audit functions from within one organization reviewing each other. Appropriate reciprocal arrangements involve three or more organizations reviewing one another in a round robin approach as shown in Figure 5.2.

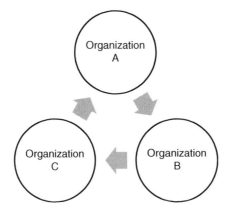

FIGURE 5.2 Peer Review Round Robin

Example 5.1 Quality Assurance Validation Group

The Singapore Economic Development Board, along with another eight member organizations, are part of an ISB QAV Inter-statutory Board Quality Assurance Validation Group. The group, which started in 2004, provides peer reviews between members within the group. The first review was conducted in 2007.

Each member organization undertakes their own internal assessment, which is then validated by two other members from the Inter-statutory Board. The group has formal terms of reference, and its procedures and mandate ensure that confidentiality is maintained.

To date, the group has completed two rounds of peer review across all the member organizations.

Providing an Opinion on the Assessment

External assessments should provide an opinion on the efficiency and effectiveness of the internal audit function, as well as conformance with professional standards.

Common Quality Issue

Beware the service provider who is not prepared to provide an opinion on conformance with professional standards, as this is an essential part of an external assessment.

Usually, an external assessment will utilize a rating scale identifying the level of conformance with professional standards. The internal audit function can determine the nature of this rating scale, or can rely on that offered by the external assessor.

Examples identified in the IIA *Practice Guide*: *Quality Assurance and Improvement Program* (2012) include:

- IIA Quality Assessment Manual Scale—*Does Not Conform/Partially Conforms/ Generally Conforms*
- IIA Capability Model for the Public Sector—*Initial/Infrastructure/Integrated/ Managed/Optimizing*
- DIIR (IIA Germany) Guideline for Conducting a Quality Assessment—*3 = Satisfactory/2 = Room for Improvement/1 = Significant Improvement Needed/0 = Unsatisfactory or Not Applicable*

QAIP Hint

External assessment can be reflected in a balanced scorecard or internal audit maturity model.

Maturity Model

The *external assessment* could be included as a key process area within the maturity model. The conduct of an external assessment could be a requirement for the achievement of level 3 of a five-stage maturity model.

Balanced Scorecard/KPI

Internal audit functions could develop performance indicators around external assessments, such as the completion of an external assessment within five years.

Questions about External Assessments

Table 5.1 provides a range of questions about the quality of the external assessment process. These can be formally incorporated into a quality assurance and improvement program, or, less formally, into ongoing assessment activities. Questions may be variously posed to the chief audit executive, internal auditors, or audit stakeholders.

TABLE 5.1 Quality Questions

Questions	Evidence of Quality
Have external assessments been performed (either a full external assessment or a self-assessment with independent validation)?	External quality assessment report Board minutes
Was the last external assessment performed within the last five years?	External quality assessment report Board minutes
Did a qualified and independent assessor perform the external assessment?	List of competencies for the assessor leader and assessment team
Does the external assessment include an opinion on the level of conformance with the standards and the effectiveness of the internal audit function?	Results of external assessment

| Is the audit committee actively involved in the external assessment of the internal audit function, including the frequency and scope of review as well as the selection of the reviewer? | Chief audit executive interview Audit committee interviews |
| Have the results of the external assessment been reported to senior management and the audit committee? | Audit committee minutes Senior management and audit committee interviews |

Conclusion

There are many ways that a chief audit executive can undertake an external quality assessment. Choosing the best way will depend on the size and nature of the internal audit function, although generally the chief audit executive will select a full external assessment, a self-assessment with independent validation, or a peer review. Ideally, the chief audit executive will consult with senior management and the audit committee regarding the most appropriate approach for their organization.

References

Deutsches Institut für Interne Revision e.V. (2007). *Guidelines for Conducting a Quality Assessment (QA): Addendum to DIIR Standard Number 3 ("Quality Management"),* 2nd. rev. ed. Frankfurt am Maim, Germany.

Dixon, G., and G. Goodall. (2007). The Quality Assurance Review: Is your internal audit function effective? *Internal Auditing* 22(2): 3–6.

Galloway, David. (2010). *Internal Auditing: A Guide for the New Auditor.* Altamonte Springs, FL: The Institute of Internal Auditors Research Foundation.

Giard, Y., and M. Cecere. (2008). Role reversal. *CA Magazine* 141(7): 61–62.

Heeschen, Paul E., and Sawyer, L. B. (1984). *Internal Auditor's Handbook.* Altamonte Springs, FL: The Institute of Internal Auditors Research Foundation.

The Institute of Internal Auditors. (2013). *International Professional Practices Framework.* Altamonte Springs, FL: The Institute of Internal Auditors.

The Institute of Internal Auditors. (2010). *Practice Guide: Measuring Internal Audit Effectiveness and Efficiency.* Altamonte Springs, FL: The Institute of Internal Auditors.

The Institute of Internal Auditors. (2012). *Practice Guide: Quality Assurance and Improvement Program.* Altamonte Springs, FL: The Institute of Internal Auditors.

The Institute of Internal Auditors. (2009). *Quality Assessment Manual,* 6th ed. Altamonte Springs, FL: The Institute of Internal Auditors Research Foundation.

The Institute of Internal Auditors Research Foundation. (2009). *Internal Audit Capability Model (IA-CM) for the Public Sector.* Altamonte Springs, FL: The Institute of Internal Auditors Research Foundation.

Kinsella, D. (2010). Assessing your internal audit function. *Accountancy Ireland* 42(2): 10–12.

Manchanda, A., and C. B. MacDonald. (2011). External assessments as tactical tools. *Internal Auditor.* http://www.theiia.org/intauditor.

Ridley, J., and K. Stephens. (1996). *International Quality Standards: Implications for Internal Auditing.* Altamonte Springs, FL: The Institute of Internal Auditors Research Foundation.

Sawyer, L. B., M. A. Dittenhofer, and J. H. Scheiner. (2005). *Sawyers Internal Auditing,* 5th ed. Altamonte Springs, FL: The Institute of Internal Auditors Research Foundation.

PART III

Internal Audit Governance Structures

CHAPTER 6

Internal Audit Strategy and Planning

Perception is strong and sight weak. In strategy it is important to see distant things as if they were close and to take a distanced view of close things.
Miyamoto Musashi

Internal audit functions exist to ask the difficult questions and to challenge the pervading wisdom. They offer the safety and comfort of an internal assurance activity—providing management and the audit committee with an early warning that things may not be tracking as desired or assurance when things are working well.

Chief audit executives walk the tightrope between management and the board, working collaboratively with both groups to provide assurance over risks at an operational, strategic, financial, and regulatory level. Ultimately, internal audit functions support management to maximize organizational value.

The internal audit strategy is the glue that binds the internal audit function and defines its vision and purpose. The strategy articulates what success will look like for internal audit and identifies the opportunities, risks, and resource implications of internal audit's planned approach.

Strategic Planning as a Key Input of the Internal Audit Function

Internal Audit Strategy

Internal audit strategy is the first of three key sets of inputs to a quality internal audit function; the other elements are staffing and professional practices.

Managing Expectations and Being Part of the Strategic Conversations

"Quality is about managing expectations, and high quality service delivery has to exceed expectations," says Trygve Sørlie, former Chief Audit Executive at Gjensidige in Norway and current member of the International Internal Audit Standards Board. "For an internal audit activity to deliver a quality product it needs to be able to manage expectations. It needs to define its mission—which meets these expectations—and document its strategy in a business plan or strategic plan."

(continued)

(*continued*)

Sørlie believes that internal audit needs to be part of the strategic conversations within an organization—at the board and senior management meetings. Otherwise it risks becoming an operational area focused on control effectiveness, rather than a strategic area that supports the organization to achieve its objectives.

"You need to have the right resources and be appropriately positioned in the organization to be part of this strategic conversation. Otherwise, it doesn't matter how good the chief audit executive is, they won't be in a position to be part of the conversation. A good chief audit executive is respected and has valuable dialogue with the audit committee. This makes the people skills of the chief audit executive and internal auditors more important than ever."

The Institute of Internal Auditors, in its *Practice Guide: Developing the Internal Audit Strategic Plan* (2012) defines strategy as follows:

> *Strategy is a means of establishing the organization's purpose and determining the nature of the contribution it intends to make while predefining choices that will shape decisions and actions. Strategy for the internal audit activity enables the allocation of financial and human resources to help achieve these objectives as defined in the activity's vision and mission statements (which contribute to the achievement of the organization's objectives). This benefits the internal audit activity through its unique configuration of resources aimed at meeting stakeholder expectations.*

The key inputs to the strategy were described earlier in the book as the internal audit vision and value proposition, risk management and resource planning, articulation of key responsibilities and types of work to be undertaken, and the internal audit charter. These inputs are further elaborated in Figure 6.1.

The strategy itself may include key success factors, or other measures of success, or these may be included in the quality assurance and improvement program or other quality process. In addition, the charter may include strategies and action steps, or these may be separately defined in an annual audit plan.

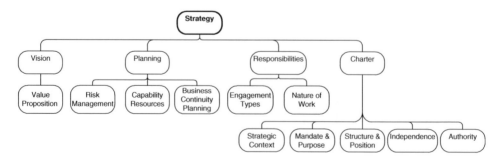

FIGURE 6.1 Strategy Elements

The chief audit executive prepares the internal audit strategy in consultation with the chief executive, board, audit committee, and senior management. The strategy is based on the risks facing the organization and the business improvement opportunities available to the organization, and describes how the internal audit function will contribute to the improvement of organizational objectives. Senior management and the audit committee should approve the strategy.

Occasionally, the chief audit executive needs to play an educative role with senior management in relation to internal audit and help them to establish appropriate expectations. There may be times when senior management does not fully recognize the potential that internal audit offers and/or has expectations regarding internal audit that will not maximize its value to the organization.

Improving Management's Understanding of Internal Audit

Takeshi Shimizu is a *kansayaku* (statutory auditor in Japanese companies) with more than 15 years' experience as an internal auditor and is a member of IIA's Professional Issues Committee. He suggests that internal auditors need to have a good understanding of their management's expectations (and knowledge) of internal audit and believes that without this understanding, it will be difficult for internal auditors to be strategically aligned with the needs of the organization. He warns that at times, management may not fully understand the role of internal audit and how this relates to other governance and assurance functions. In these situations internal auditors need to also advocate on behalf of internal audit—helping set the expectations management has for the function.

The IIA's *Practice Guide: Developing the Internal Audit Strategic Plan* (2012), describes the internal audit strategy as being "fundamental to remaining relevant—playing an important role in achieving the balance between cost and value, while making meaningful contributions to the organization's overall governance, risk management, and internal controls."

A well-developed internal audit strategy will be a key driver of quality. It will help ensure that internal audit is appropriately structured and resourced to deliver value, and that activities are focused on areas of greatest need. Appropriate performance measures should be developed to determine the extent to which the strategy is realized, and these should be embedded within, or linked to, the quality assurance and improvement program.

Internal Audit Stakeholders

Determining the internal audit function's major stakeholders allows the strategy to be focused on their specific needs. According to Rezaee (1996), internal audit stakeholders have varied over the last 60 to 70 years. In the late 1940s, Rezaee considers that internal audit functions were primarily focused on serving the needs of management. However, by 1990, this had changed to a focus on the organization as a whole.

Vision

The vision statement should identify what the desired future would look like if the internal audit function achieves its objectives. It outlines the philosophy behind the internal audit function and its proposed contribution to the organization. A vision statement might be as short as one sentence, or could incorporate a number of points.

Example 6.1 Sample Vision Statement

Our vision is to be a professional and relevant internal audit function that provides value-adding assurance and consulting services supporting better practice, innovation, and continuous improvement across the organization.

Internal Audit's Value Proposition

Determining Value

An internal audit function must exist for a purpose beyond conformance with mandatory requirements, if it is to deliver quality outputs and outcomes. It should be seen as a respected business partner that delivers value. It must be focused on key risks to the achievement of organizational objectives rather than "easily manageable stuff." To deliver value, the internal audit function should reflect what is valuable to the organization.

Definitions of value will vary across, and even within, organizations. These differences will be particularly noticeable in organizations that incorporate a wide range of cultures, business units, or geographic locations. The internal audit function should adopt an approach that best meets the value sought from the organization, bearing in mind that this role may well need to evolve as the organization changes.

Abdolmohammadi and colleagues (2013) recognize there can sometimes be an expectation gap between the chief audit executive and senior management. They contend that there is a need for more shared goals to allow for a mutual understanding of what value internal audit can provide. Abdolmohammadi and colleagues argue that there is a need for increased shared knowledge to ensure that the internal audit function represents the business. There should be mutual respect between each party and high-quality communications between the internal audit function and the business.

The roles adopted by the internal audit function may also vary—the internal audit function may adopt a particular approach for some areas of the organization and a different approach to others. A continuum of internal auditing roles is illustrated in Figure 6.2.

FIGURE 6.2 Continuum of Internal Auditing Roles

Although some organizations will view internal audit's role as that of an impartial observer, others will seek different value from their internal auditors—looking at them more as a "critical friend." It is the responsibility of the chief audit executive to determine what the organization's expectations are.

Neighborhood Policemen

Goh Thong, Chief Audit Executive at SPRING Singapore, describes internal auditors as the "friendly neighborhood policemen." He believes that their role is to check, provide warnings when *doors are not locked*, and advise how to *be safe*.

Stakeholders' expectations may also extend beyond specific internal audit work to incorporate other requirements. Stakeholders may also view internal auditors as the:

- "Controls champion"
- Sarbanes-Oxley coordinator
- Business continuity coordinator
- Risk management facilitator and/or assurance provider
- Regulatory compliance assurance provider
- Strategic adviser
- External audit coordinator
- Risk and controls trainer

Some of these activities may start to merge into management responsibilities. The chief audit executive should determine which of these expectations can be met, and whether there is a need to reconcile management expectations with professional independence obligations.

Showing People What They Need

"Quality is what your clients and stakeholders want. But there is a twist— internal audit has an opportunity, and responsibility, to educate their clients on what they need (or should want)" suggests Archie R. Thomas, Consulting Internal Auditor in Canada. "When you're educating organizations on what they need from internal audit, the simplest, most straightforward way is to tie in to strategy. Internal audit should assess strategy execution and related risks across the organization. Value in an internal audit activity is an inextricable link between internal audit strategy and that of the organization."

Historically, the internal audit profession was primarily focused on individual controls. Changing expectations now require internal audit functions to be more focused on how the controls work together to achieve outcomes for their organization. This new perspective offers enhanced value to organizations.

The IIA *Standards*, and in particular Standard 2000, recognize the importance of adding value to the organization.

Standard 2000—Managing the Internal Audit Activity

The chief audit executive must effectively manage the internal audit activity to ensure it adds value to the organization.

The Australian National Audit Office, in its *Public Sector Internal Audit: Better Practice Guide* (2012), identifies a number of features of value-adding internal audit functions. These are listed in Example 6.2.

Example 6.2 Features of a Better Practice Internal Audit Function Identified by the Australian National Audit Office

A better practice internal audit function:

- Has the confidence and visible support of key stakeholders, including the chief executive, the board (where applicable), the audit committee, and senior management.
- Is operationally independent; that is, internal audit is independent from the activities subject to audit.
- Has a well-developed strategy that clearly identifies internal audit's role and responsibilities and contribution to the entity's broader assurance arrangements.
- Has sufficient financial resources, staff, and access to contractors when appropriate, with the necessary skills, experience, and personal attributes to achieve the contribution expected of internal audit.

Operationally, the function:

- Is business-focused and has audit plans that are comprehensive and balanced, and are aligned to the entity's risks.
- Undertakes all audits in accordance with specified professional standards.
- Provides an annual assessment, based on internal audit work undertaken, of the effectiveness of the entity's system of internal controls.
- Advises the audit committee and entity management of patterns, trends, or systemic issues arising from internal audit work.
- Disseminates lessons learned from its work, and from external audit, to relevant areas of the entity to contribute to organizational learning.
- Regularly informs the audit committee of progress in the implementation of agreed internal and external audit and other relevant report recommendations.
- Facilitates communication between external audit and entity management where appropriate.

Common Quality Issue

Many internal audit functions fail to adequately consider the strategic objectives of the organization in their annual audit planning processes. This can lead to the internal audit function focusing on operational control effectiveness and compliance issues at the expense of more valuable engagements.

Providing Value to the Audit Committee

The audit committee is a primary stakeholder of internal audit. As such, chief audit executives should ensure they have a comprehensive understanding of the needs and expectations of their audit committee.

The ABCs of a Professional Audit Practice—Delivering What the Audit Committee Really Needs

Bruce Turner has over 30 years of internal auditing experience, including chief audit executive roles within transport and energy corporations, and government departments in the public sector. He retired as the Chief Internal Auditor at the Australian Taxation Office in 2012 and now serves as the independent chair of several audit committees.

Turner believes there are significant opportunities for chief audit executives to add value to audit committees, and says, "It's as simple as ABC—being attuned, balanced, and credible."

Attuned

"Internal auditors are expected to be in tune with what's really going on in the business," says Turner. "The role of internal auditors will continue to expand. They should already be involved in activities beyond what some see as traditional areas."

Turner's top 10 tips for internal auditors to become more attuned are:

1. Get into the business to see what really goes on.
2. Understand the environment in which the organization is operating.
3. Know the entity's strategic direction and emerging risks.
4. Establish a constructive, trusted partnering relationship with the audit committee.
5. Keep abreast of audit committee expectations through regular discussions.
6. Establish a structured stakeholder relationship program.
7. Develop a risk-based and strategically focused forward work program.
8. Establish high-level audit themes within the work program to facilitate future reporting on trends and systemic issues.

(continued)

(continued)

9. Assist the organization to value independent scrutiny—embed internal auditors early in major projects.
10. Strive to always deliver excellence in what, when, and how internal auditors do their work.

Balanced

Turner recommends that internal auditors develop a balanced approach to annual audit planning that incorporates the main organizational risk areas. "Whilst most internal audit activities have always had a plan, these days there's a need to sharpen the strategic focus," suggests Turner. "A blended approach is desirable, so there is sufficient coverage of the traditional compliance areas, coupled with coverage of performance and strategic areas."

Turner's top 10 tips for a balanced internal audit approach are:

1. Tap into organizational health for the audit committee by:
   - Accessing information independently.
   - Reducing reliance on management perspective of entity risks.
2. Achieve balanced coverage in work programs, blending traditional areas of financial audit coverage with efficiency, effectiveness, and ethics elements—incorporating deep dives and spot checks.
3. Position internal audit as a provider of advice and consultancy services.
4. Showcase internal audit's contribution in a comprehensive annual report.
5. Deliver crisp reports that really matter and are:
   - Pitched in a manner that aligns to critical business drivers.
   - Short, sharp, and succinct.
6. Enhance reporting through a high-level, themes-based report.
7. Write balanced reports that tell it as it is.
8. Monitor and report effectively on open audit recommendations.
9. Expand involvement in activities that may be beyond traditional coverage:
   - Work with business leaders on areas like business continuity, risk management, and compliance until they reach a reasonable level of maturity.
10. Undertake effective monitoring and reporting of the status of audit recommendations.

Credible

Turner challenges that nothing less than professional excellence should be acceptable to a high-performing audit committee. He recommends that chief audit executives create a well-balanced team with the skills and capacity to meet the demands placed on the internal audit function. He considers it important for internal auditors to come from a variety of backgrounds and have relevant industry experience.

Turner's top 10 tips for creating a credible internal audit function are:

1. Review the internal audit charter, so it remains relevant, consistent with better practice models, and complements the audit committee charter.

2. Maintain stakeholder communication strategies to ensure consistency in dealings with stakeholders.
3. Establish recruitment and retention strategies that deliver a well-balanced team with a professional culture and complement strategies with a professional development plan.
4. Maintain honesty and fairness in all reporting relationships.
5. Comply with professional auditing standards: Deliver an overarching quality assurance assertion each year.
6. Provide the audit committee with periodic benchmarking on audit capability: experience, average years, qualifications, and professional certifications.
7. Maintain effective functional and administrative reporting lines.
8. Showcase internal audit in the organization's published annual report.
9. Pursue positive trends in management's perception of internal audit: value add and ensure the usefulness of recommendations.
10. Tailor a balanced scorecard reporting approach.

Guiding Values

The IIA's Code of Ethics requires internal auditors to apply and uphold the principles of integrity, objectivity, confidentiality, and competency. Each of these principles should be embedded into the culture and values of the internal audit function.

Internal audit functions with strong, shared positive cultures often distinguish themselves as being higher performing than activities without shared, positive cultures. Adamec and colleagues (2009) identify key cultural pillars as being trust, emotional intelligence, performance focus, courage, support, and shared learning. Their work recognizes that by sharing a strong, positive culture, internal audit functions are less likely to conform to negative client values.

Internal audit functions can embed the principles within the IIA's Code of Ethics by actively supporting and encouraging a range of cultural traits or values among staff. Examples of these are provided in Table 6.1.

TABLE 6.1 Alignment of Values with the Code of Ethics

Integrity	Objectivity	Confidentiality	Competency
Honesty	Lack of bias	Prudence	Professionalism
Diligence	Open-mindedness	Privacy	Skill
Responsibility	Transparency	Discretion	Experience
Ethics	Courage	Collaboration	Acumen
Trust	Constructive criticism	Caution	Continuous improvement
Respect	Consistency	Empathy	Shared learning
Candor	Neutrality	Maturity	Commitment
Incorruptibility	Impartiality	Thoughtfulness	Outcome focused

Embedding a set of shared values requires the active support of the chief audit executive and commitment from internal audit staff. Creating a positive and supportive culture requires time and effort.

Values Statement

Include a *value statement* in the internal audit charter or strategic plan to highlight the values shared across the internal audit function.

Example 6.3 is a value statement created by the internal audit activity within Deakin University in Australia and promoted within its internal audit strategy.

Example 6.3 Internal Audit Values at Deakin University

Internal audit values:

- Be committed to the pursuit of excellence (meet or exceed expectations every time).
- Maintain professional, collaborative relationships with stakeholders, which are built on mutual respect and trust.
- Be an active and positive member of, and advocate for, the internal audit activity.
- Be committed to continuous improvement and professional development.
- Lead by example in all behaviors, especially those relating to ethics and integrity.
- Be honest, accountable, and transparent in all actions.
- Be environmentally responsible.

An alternative values statement is provided in Example 6.4.

Example 6.4 Sample Values Statement

Our values are:

- To be customer-focused and to provide value-added assurance and consulting services to assist in the achievement of the organization's strategic objectives. We believe in respecting our customers, listening to their requests, understanding their expectations, and delivering products and services in an efficient and effective manner.
- To be regarded as an essential service by the organization and audit committee.

- To be seen as a critical friend—able to be trusted with sensitive and confidential matters while having the integrity and objectivity to ask difficult questions and raise matters that require attention.
- To operate as a supportive team encouraging innovation, diversity, and personal excellence, and providing the professional opportunities and a work environment necessary for the professional development of staff.
- To be committed to continuous improvement of our systems and processes and be at the forefront of emerging risk areas.

Chief audit executives should consider reinforcing the internal audit function's shared values with marketing collateral (such as an internal audit pamphlet) or through an internal audit intranet site. These provide transparency and promote the professionalism of internal audit. Further discussion regarding internal audit marketing opportunities is included in Chapter 16.

Planning to Deliver Value

Effective planning is essential to the good governance of the internal audit function. Planning should extend beyond individual audit engagements and include other elements essential to developing and sustaining a quality internal audit function such as risk management planning, capability planning, and business continuity planning.

Memorandum of Understanding/Service Level Agreement

The chief audit executive, chief executive officer, audit committee chair, and other senior executives can each sign a memorandum of understanding or service level agreement that specifies their respective roles and responsibilities in relation to internal audit. For instance, this could include:

- Minimum notice periods from internal auditors before commencing an engagement
- Allocation of internal audit liaison officers within the business for internal auditors to use as a first point of contact
- Maximum periods for the business to respond to information requests
- Maximum lapsed time from completion of fieldwork to issue of draft report
- Maximum periods for management responses to draft reports

Schwartz (2013) identifies the following four steps that chief audit executives can take to achieve strategic alignment, increase their relevance, and create a more mature risk management environment:

1. Leverage the organizational strategy.
2. Develop a well-aligned internal audit strategy.

3. Employ critical enablers throughout the audit life cycle.
4. Run internal audit operations like a business.

Assessing Risks Associated with the Internal Audit Function

The internal audit function plays a key role in supporting organizational risk management that includes:

- Providing assurance over the effectiveness of the organization's risk management processes
- Aligning audit planning to the organization's goals and giving due consideration to the risks that may impact these goals
- Undertaking risk assessments as part of individual engagement planning

In addition, internal auditors should consider the risks associated with delivering against the strategic plan.

Internal Audit Risk Assessment

Internal audit's responsibilities for assessing and contributing to organizational risk management are commonly accepted. However, many internal audit functions do not formally address the risks associated with their own activities with the same vigilance that they do for other areas of the organization.

Similar to other business units, the internal audit function should identify, assess, and appropriately mitigate the risk associated with the delivery of internal audit services. These should include the risks associated with the overall management of the function, as well as the risks related to individual engagements.

Typical risks associated with the management of the internal audit function are identified in Table 6.2.

TABLE 6.2 Risks Associated with Management of the Internal Audit Function

Risk Area/Source of Risk	Consequence
Changing strategic priorities	The internal audit function does not focus on key organizational issues.
Changing management expectations	The internal audit function does not meet stakeholder expectations.
Changing regulatory environment	The internal audit function does not conform to regulatory requirements and/or does not adequately assess conformance of the organization against new requirements.
Inadequate leadership support/"tone at the top"	The internal audit function is not effectively supported in its operations and its impact is reduced.
Inappropriate reporting lines	The internal audit function is not seen as independent and/or internal audit's role is restricted.
Lack of awareness of internal audit	The internal audit function is not seen as a strategic partner and/or is not called on to assist management.

Inadequate coverage of regional and remote areas	The internal audit function may not address key strategic priorities and associated risks.
Inadequate or inappropriate recruitment and retention processes	The internal audit function is unable to attract and retain competent, experienced professionals reducing its capacity for value-adding engagements.
Inadequate working arrangements/flexibility	The internal audit function is unable to attract and retain competent, experienced professionals reducing its capacity for value-adding engagements.
Unsafe work environment	Internal auditor health or well-being is impacted.
Inadequate resources	The internal audit function is unable to deliver on its audit plan, and its value to the organization is diminished.
Inadequate contractor management	Loss of audit quality and/or reputational damage for internal audit.
Inadequate procurement of audit resources and/or inadequate contractor management	Fraud, nepotism, reputational damage, and/or loss of audit quality for internal audit.
Inadequate knowledge management	Loss of key corporate knowledge and diminished value for the organization.
Inadequate or inappropriate use of information technology	Loss of efficiency and/or effectiveness in undertaking audit engagements and diminished value for the organization.

Engagement Risk Assessments

Internal auditors should undertake specific risk assessments for larger internal engagements, in addition to a risk assessment of the entire internal audit function. These engagement risk assessments provide additional assurance that the audit will add value to the organization.

Resource Planning

Knowing what adds value is the foundation of an effective internal audit function. However, the right staff and resources are essential to delivering this value.

Internal Audit Structure

Internal audit functions may be centralized (typically with staff located at the head office or corporate office), be decentralized (with staff located within organizational areas), or utilize a hybrid model (combining elements of centralization and de-centralization). Advantages and disadvantages of each of the models are provided in Table 6.3.

The model used for internal audit should be aligned to strategic priorities across the organization and should be built in to the internal audit strategy.

TABLE 6.3 Advantages and Disadvantages of Operating Models

Model	Advantage	Disadvantage
Centralized	Responsive to senior executives Process consistency Increased control by chief audit executive Training consistency	Isolation from business Travel time associated with visiting sites Reduced responsiveness to operational management Reduced understanding of regulatory environments in geographically dispersed business units Cultural isolation (language or culture barriers) Lower levels of staff autonomy
Decentralized	Responsive to operational management Culturally responsive Responsive to regulatory environment Knowledge of operations Travel efficiencies Empowers staff	Potential for process inconsistency Reduced control by chief audit executive Training inefficiencies Reduced responsiveness to senior executives
Hybrid	Responsive to senior executives and operational management Culturally responsive Responsive to regulatory environment Knowledge of operations Travel efficiencies	Potential for process inconsistency Reduced control by chief audit executive Training inefficiencies

Capability Planning

Capability planning allows the chief audit executive to determine the collective skills and experience required to deliver against proposed activities, and identify ways to recruit, procure, or develop this capability. Capability planning can be undertaken during the strategic planning process, or more commonly, as a separate exercise.

Further information about capability planning is provided in Chapter 9.

Sourcing Model

There are many different approaches to resourcing an internal audit function—from a fully insourced model, with in-house internal auditors, to a fully outsourced model.

The chief audit executive should consider the appropriate sourcing model for internal audit during internal audit strategic planning. Decisions about sourcing should be made in consultation with senior management and the audit committee.

Burch (2011) identifies a number of considerations when selecting an appropriate sourcing model:

- Size of the organization—current and projected revenues and the number of employees the organization has

- Complexity of operations—the diversity of the organization in terms of business units, functions, processes, products, and services
- Specialized skill set—the need for specialized knowledge or skills to conduct audits
- Global reach—the countries in which the organization operates and the regulatory and cultural environment in these locations

There are advantages and disadvantages associated with outsourcing internal audit services. Fitzpatrick (2001) identifies some of these advantages:

- Increased ability for in-house staff to focus on core activities
- Access to leading practices and specialized skills
- International coverage

However, Burch also recognizes that there may be a cost to outsourcing—both in financial terms as well as in corporate knowledge. He warns of the impact on objectivity by outsourced providers who share the internal and external auditor roles.

Internal Audit Budget

The internal audit budget should ideally be set after the development of the annual audit plan. This allows the budget to reflect the requirements for specific engagements, and takes into account any co-sourcing that may be required with external service provides. The internal audit budget is discussed further in Chapter 12.

Business Continuity Planning

The internal audit function should consider the need for business continuity planning. In the event of a natural disaster or other major disruption to business, what will internal audit do? The business continuity plan should identify processes—both preventative and retrospective—that reduce the consequences of an adverse event for the internal audit function.

In some organizations, creating the business continuity plan will be undertaken at the corporate level, and internal audit will be considered alongside other organizational areas. However, if a plan is not developed at a corporate level, it should be considered as a stand-alone exercise.

QAIP Hint

Strategy elements can be reflected in a balanced scorecard or internal audit maturity model.

Maturity Model

Strategy could be included as a key process area within the maturity model, with the existence of an internal audit strategy being a requirement for the achievement of level 3 to 4 of a five-stage maturity model.

(continued)

(*continued*)
Balanced Scorecard/KPI

Internal audit functions could develop performance indicators around the internal audit strategy, such as:

- Annual review of the internal audit strategy
- Endorsement of the strategy by the audit committee
- Endorsement of the internal audit values by the audit committee
- Level of management satisfaction with strategy (include target)
- Level of audit committee satisfaction with strategy (include target)
- Internal audit risk assessments conducted annually
- Capability and resource planning undertaken annually
- Business continuity planning undertaken annually

Questions about the Internal Audit Function's Strategy and Planning Processes

Table 6.4 provides a range of questions about the quality of the internal audit function's strategy and planning processes assessment process. These can be formally incorporated into a quality assurance and improvement program, or, less formally, into ongoing assessment activities. Questions may be variously posed to the chief audit executive, internal auditors, or audit stakeholders.

TABLE 6.4 Quality Questions

Questions	Evidence of Quality
Has the internal audit function developed a formal strategy or strategic plan?	Internal audit strategy Strategic plan
Is the internal audit strategy aligned to the strategic risks and priorities of the organization?	Linkages between audit plan and strategic risks
Does the strategy effectively support key organizational initiatives?	Linkages between audit plan and key organizational initiatives Senior management and audit committee interviews
Is there a documented vision for the internal audit function?	Documented vision statement
Is this vision shared and understood by all internal audit staff members?	Staff interviews
Have senior management and the audit committee been consulted about, and do they support, the vision statement?	Senior management and audit committee interviews
Does the vision meet the strategic objectives of the organization?	Linkages between vision and strategies objectives Senior management and audit committee interviews

Has consideration been given to how the internal audit function can be a proactive driver of value and innovation rather than a reactive reviewer?	Senior management and audit committee interviews Inclusion of value-adding engagements in the audit plan
Can the chief audit executive articulate what the organization sees as value from the internal audit function?	Chief audit executive interview Senior management and audit committee interviews
Does the chief audit executive understand the value requirements of different stakeholders?	Chief audit executive interview Senior management and audit committee interviews
Can the chief audit executive articulate what the organization needs the internal audit function to focus on to maximize organizational success and to deliver on the organization's quality expectations?	Chief audit executive interview Senior management and audit committee interviews
Does the chief audit executive actively engage senior management in discussion regarding what stakeholders see as the internal audit function's value?	Chief audit executive interview Records of interviews and conversations
Does the internal audit function add value to the organization?	Senior management and audit committee interviews Audit coverage and alignment with strategic objectives and priorities
What capacity does the internal audit function have to adapt to changing business priorities?	Assessment of staff capabilities and resourcing
Do stakeholders demonstrate trust of, and respect for, the internal audit function?	Management-initiated engagements
Does the internal audit function display courage in its review and analysis of difficult or sensitive areas and its dealings with challenging clients?	Senior management and audit committee interviews Post-audit surveys
Is constructive criticism of the internal audit function welcome?	Senior management and audit committee interviews Post-audit surveys
Does the internal audit function deal with sensitive issues discretely?	Senior management and audit committee interviews Post-audit surveys
Does the internal audit function have the confidence of the audit committee and senior management?	Senior management and audit committee interviews
Does the chief audit executive undertake risk assessments (at least annually) of the internal audit function?	Internal audit risk assessment and/or risk management plan (prepared or updated in previous 12 months)
Has the internal audit function undertaken capability and resource planning?	Capability and resource plans (prepared or updated in previous 12 months)
Does the internal audit function have a detailed, documented budget?	Budget
Is the internal audit plan used to drive the resource requirements for the internal audit function?	Budget Staffing analysis and annual operating plans Internal audit plan

(*continued*)

TABLE 6.4 (*continued*)

Questions	Evidence of Quality
Do the current internal audit resourcing levels allow sufficient audit coverage of higher risk areas?	Budget Risk management plan Senior management and audit committee interviews
Has the chief audit executive discussed resourcing models with senior management and the audit committee?	Records of interviews/conversations
Has the internal audit function undertaken business continuity planning for its own activities?	Business continuity plans (prepared or updated in previous 12 months)

Conclusion

Undertaking effective strategic planning helps ensure the success of the internal audit function. Strategic planning assists the chief audit executive in understanding the expectations of both senior management and the audit committee. It provides an opportunity for these stakeholders to articulate what they see as value from the internal audit function, and engages stakeholders in the process of defining the type of role that internal auditors will play across the organization.

Chief audit executives can work with senior management and the audit committee during the strategic planning process to articulate the vision for internal audit and the guiding values that the internal audit function will adopt.

Strategic planning processes should incorporate an internal audit risk assessment as well as capability and resource planning. Chief audit executives should consider the risks associated with the management of the internal audit function as well as individual engagement risks.

Dedicating time to strategic planning maximizes the potential for internal audit functions to achieve stakeholder expectations.

References

Abdolmohammadi, M. J., S. Ramamoorti, and G. Sarens. (2013). *CAE Strategic Relationships—Building Rapport with the Executive Suite*. Altamonte Springs, FL: Institute of Internal Auditors Research Foundation.

Adamec, B., L. M. Leincke, and J. A. Ostresky. (2009). Six cultural pillars of successful audit departments. *Internal Auditor*. http://www.theiia.org/intauditor.

Australian National Audit Office. (2012). *Public Sector Internal Audit: An Investment in Assurance and Business Improvement—Better Practice Guide, September 2012*. Commonwealth of Australia.

Baker, N. (2011). A stronger partnership. *Internal Auditor*. http://www.theiia.org/intauditor.

———. (2010). Know your business. *Internal Auditor*. http://www.theiia.org/intauditor.

Boritz, J. E. (1983). *Planning for the Internal Audit Function*. Altamonte Springs, FL: Institute of Internal Auditors Research Foundation.

Burch, S. (2011). Building an internal audit function. *Internal Auditor*. http://www
.theiia.org/intauditor.

Cathcart, R., and G. Kapor. (2010). An internal audit upgrade. *Internal Auditor*. http://
www.theiia.org/intauditor.

Chambers, A. D., G. M. Selim, and G. Vinten. (1994). *Internal Auditing*, 2nd ed.
London: Pitman Publishing.

Chen, Jiin-Feng, and Wan-Ying Lin. (2011). *Measuring Internal Auditing's Value—
CBOK Report III*. Altamonte Springs, FL: Institute of Internal Auditors Research
Foundation.

Fitzpatrick, G. (2001). Outsourcing internal audit: Good mix or all mixed up? *Accountancy Ireland* 33(4): 12–14.

Galloway, D. (2010). *Internal Auditing: A Guide for the New Auditor*. Altamonte
Springs, FL: Institute of Internal Auditors Research Foundation.

Heeschen, P. E., and L. B. Sawyer. (1984). *Internal Auditor's Handbook*. Altamonte
Springs, FL: The Institute of Internal Auditors.

HM Treasury. (2010, July). *Good Practice Guide: Audit Strategy*. Available at www.hm-
treasury.gov.uk.

Holt, J. E. (2012). A high-performing audit function. *Internal Auditor*. http://www
.theiia.org/intauditor.

The Institute of Internal Auditors. (2012). *Practice Guide: Developing the Internal
Audit Strategic Plan*. Altamonte Springs, FL: The Institute of Internal Auditors.

The Institute of Internal Auditors. (2013). *International Professional Practices Framework*. Altamonte Springs, FL: The Institute of Internal Auditors.

Loebbecke, J. K. (1996). *Internal Auditing: Principles and Techniques*. Altamonte
Springs, FL: The Institute of Internal Auditors.

Martin, A. G. (2013). A refocused internal audit function adds value through the
organization. *Internal Auditor* 28(1): 25–34.

Reding, K. F., P. J. Sobel, U. L. Anderson, M. J. Head, S. Ramamoorti, M. Salamasick,
and C. Riddle. (2009). *Internal Auditing: Assurance and Consulting Services*.
Altamonte Springs, FL: The Institute of Internal Auditors Research Foundation.

Rezaee, Z. (1996). Improving the quality of internal audit functions through total quality
management. *Managerial Auditing Journal* 11(1): 30–34.

Ridley, J., and A. Chambers. (1998). *Leading Edge Internal Auditing*. Hertfordshire,
England: ICSA Publishing Limited.

Ridley, J., and K. Stephens. (1996). *International Quality Standards: Implications
for Internal Auditing*. Altamonte Springs, FL: The Institute of Internal Auditors
Research Foundation.

Roth, J. (2002). *Adding Value: Seven Roads to Success*. Altamonte Springs, FL: The
Institute of Internal Auditors Research Foundation.

Sawyer, L. B., M. A. Dittenhofer, and J. H. Scheiner. (2005). *Sawyers Internal Auditing*,
5th ed. Altamonte Springs, FL: The Institute of Internal Auditors Research
Foundation.

Schwartz, B. M. (2013). Risk management focus brings opportunities for internal audit.
RMA Journal 95(6): 11, 16–21.

CHAPTER 7

Areas of Responsibility and Nature of Work

A desk is a dangerous place from which to view the world.

—John Le Carré

The *look and feel* of the internal audit function will vary considerably between organizations. High-priority areas in some organizations may have little or no relevance in others. Similarly, the types of engagements undertaken will change between organizations. Ultimately, areas of responsibility and the nature of internal audit's work must link back to the organization's strategic priorities and risks. To understand these drivers, the chief audit executive must first have a thorough understanding of the organization, and this is best achieved by talking with management and viewing operations firsthand.

Internal audit engagements are generally divided into assurance and consulting engagements. While better practice requires that internal audit functions undertake both these types of engagements, there is a tendency for some internal auditors to focus on assurance engagements at the expense of consulting engagements. This reduces the potential value that internal audit can provide to an organization.

Types of Engagements

The IIA defines internal audit as "an assurance and consulting activity." Responsibilities of each internal audit function will vary considerably, depending on the size, nature, and maturity of both the internal audit function and the organization in which it operates and the resources available to the internal audit function. However, the activities undertaken by internal audit can generally be classified into either assurance or consulting (sometimes called advisory) engagements.

Internal audit engagements can include:

- Financial audits
- Information technology (IT) audits
- Compliance audits (sometimes mandatory such as payroll and petty cash)
- Internal control reviews

- Operational/performance/value for money audits
- Environmental audits
- Fraud investigations and forensic auditing
- Follow-up audits
- Management initiated reviews
- Consulting activities including
  - Facilitated control self-assessments
  - Risk management training
  - Facilitated risk assessments
  - Business process reviews
  - Advice regarding systems under development
  - Fraud control activities
  - Evaluations of policies and procedures

Internal audit engagements can be undertaken on a program basis or a functional basis. They can utilize a single type of auditing—for example, a focused financial audit—or can be undertaken as an integrated engagement that includes a number of different types of auditing, such as financial, IT, and compliance.

Program-Based Engagements

Program-based engagements are focused on a range of activities that collectively lead to a particular outcome. For example, they could include the activities associated with an organizational program such as human resources management, or, in the government sector, the delivery of a specific health or education program.

Program-based engagements may incorporate elements of a number of individual functional engagements.

Functional Engagements

Functional engagements are associated with a specific activity or process, and usually assess the entire life cycle of the activity or process. For example, staff recruitment processes could form the basis of a functional engagement.

Integrated Auditing

Integrated engagements incorporate a range of auditing types and techniques to provide assurance over a program or activity.

QAIP Hint

The internal audit function could reflect the types of engagements it undertakes in an internal audit maturity model or a balanced scorecard.

Maturity Model

Types of engagements undertaken could be a key process area within the maturity model with functional engagements being a requirement for the achievement of level 3 of a five-stage maturity model, program-based engagements being a requirement for level 4, and integrated auditing being a requirement for level 5.

Balanced Scorecard/KPI

Internal audit functions could include a performance indicator such as the relative proportions of time spent on functional engagements, program-based engagements, and integrated auditing.

Assurance

The IIA (2013a) defines assurance services as "an objective examination of evidence for the purpose of providing an independent assessment on governance, risk management, and control processes for the organization. Examples may include performance, compliance, system security, and due diligence engagements."

There are many different types of assurance activities that internal audit can undertake, which are described in the following sections.

The chief audit executive should document the types of assurance activities the internal audit function will provide, based on identification of organizational needs and appropriate stakeholder engagement. Before embarking on particular types of engagements, the chief audit executive should ensure that the internal audit function is appropriately resourced with access to competent and experienced internal auditors.

IIA Standard 1000.A1 requires that assurance services are defined in the internal audit charter.

Standard 1000.A1

The nature of assurance services provided to the organization must be defined in the internal audit charter. If assurances are to be provided to parties outside the organization, the nature of these assurances must also be defined in the internal audit charter.

Financial Audits

Financial audits assess the financial aspects of an organization, including the integrity of financial and operating information and the accuracy of what is reported. They can include examination of controls providing assurance over the integrity of financial information, compliance with legislative and regulatory requirements, and the prevention of fraudulent public financial reporting. Often, financial audits are focused on historical events.

Financial audits may be driven by external requirements, and are ideally coordinated with external audit. In some cases, the external auditor will place significant reliance over internal audit's financial audits.

Information Technology (IT) Audits

Information technology (IT) audits assess the controls within an organization's IT systems and processes. IT audits can include:

- Efficiency and effectiveness of new or ongoing IT and related systems
- Adequacy of controls supporting systems under development
- Adequacy of general computer controls design, documentation, implementation, testing, and remediation
- Adequacy of application controls design, documentation, implementation, testing, and remediation
- System design
- Pre- and post-implementation reviews
- Data conversion, interface, and database reviews

IT audits should cover the full breadth of operating systems within an organization—for example, mainframe, client/server technologies, and UNIX. They should also cover each of the application systems (e.g., SAP, banking systems) and involve the use of automated audit tools and data analysis tools.

Common Quality Issue

The specialist nature of IT auditing can often lead to these audits being considered in isolation from the rest of the annual audit plan, and many organizations assess potential risk exposures associated with the failure or inadequacy of IT controls differently to other controls. However, like other forms of internal audit, IT auditing should be based on an adequate assessment of risk, and IT audits should be prioritized alongside other prospective internal audits.

Compliance Audits

Compliance audits assess operating controls to determine conformance with mandatory requirements such as laws, legislation, regulations, internal and external policies, operating plans, documented procedures, and contract provisions. Elements of compliance audits can merge with financial auditing and IT auditing.

Common Quality Issue

Compliance audits continue to form the bread and butter of some traditional, and/or less mature, internal audit functions. This may be due to internal auditors, or audit committees, being unduly influenced by the historical predominance of this type of auditing, or it may reflect a lack of understanding of the nature of modern internal auditing.

Often, these internal audit functions continue to undertake a majority of compliance audits without any real consideration of whether engagements reflect the risk priorities of their organization.

Operational/Performance/Value for Money Audits

Operational audits (also known as performance audits, value for money audits, or 3 Es audits—referring to efficiency, effectiveness, and economy—in the public sector) assess the extent to which business objectives are achieved, or goods and services are delivered, in an efficient, effective, and/or economical manner.

According to the European Court of Auditors (2008):

A performance audit is an audit of sound financial management, namely of the economy, efficiency and effectiveness with which the Commission and/or other audited entities have used Community funds in carrying out their responsibilities.

Efficiency refers to the use of financial, human, physical, and information resources such that output is maximized for any given set of resource inputs, or input is minimized for any given quantity and quality of output.

Example 7.1 Efficiency Considerations in a Government Performance Audit

An efficiency consideration for a performance audit examining the contribution of an internal evaluation team to a government department would be whether the procurement processes for engaging contractors to conduct evaluations of departmental projects minimize the level of staff resources involved. An example of an efficient procurement process would be the establishment of a panel of contractors, which would alleviate the need to approach the market for each separate procurement engagement.

Example 7.2 Efficiency Considerations in a Financial Services Operational Audit

An efficiency consideration for a performance audit relating to project management within a financial institution would be whether project milestones are fully achieved within the project budget.

Effectiveness refers to the achievement of the objectives or other intended effects of activities (such as the delivery of a product or service to specification).

Example 7.3 Effectiveness Considerations in a Government Performance Audit

An effectiveness consideration for a performance audit examining the contribution of an internal evaluation team to a government department would be the degree to which evaluation reports address evaluation objectives.

Example 7.4 Effectiveness Considerations in a Financial Services Operational Audit

An effectiveness consideration for a performance audit relating to project management within a financial institution would be the degree to which projects are successfully implemented.

Economy refers to the acquisition of the appropriate quality and quantity of financial, human, physical, and information resources at the appropriate times and at the lowest cost.

Example 7.5 Economy Considerations in a Government Performance Audit

An economy consideration for a performance audit examining the contribution of an internal evaluation team to a government department would be the cost of undertaking evaluations compared with other departments.

Example 7.6 Economy Considerations in a Financial Services Operational Audit

An economy consideration for a performance audit relating to project management within a financial institution would be the appropriate acquisition of project management expertise at the lowest cost.

Not all operational audits will assess all three Es for every engagement.

Common Quality Issue

Some internal audit functions do not adequately incorporate operational and performance auditing as part of the annual audit plan. This may be due to:

- A lack of understanding of the value of operational auditing;
- Inadequate capability among staff to undertake operational audits; and/or
- A lack of support from management for operational audits.

The key differences between operational/performance audits and financial audits have been described by the European Court of Auditors (2008) and are summarized in Table 7.1.

TABLE 7.1 Differences between Financial and Operational/Performance Audits

Aspect	Operational/Performance Audit	Financial Audit
Purpose	Assesses whether public funds have been used with economy, efficiency, and effectiveness	Assesses whether financial operations have been legally and regularly executed and accounts are reliable
Focus	Policy, program, organization, activities, and management systems	Financial transactions, accounting, and key control procedures
Academic Base	Vary from auditor to auditor	Accountancy
Methods	Vary from audit to audit	Standardized format
Criteria	More open to the auditors' judgment. Unique criteria for the individual audit	Less open to the auditors' judgment. Standardized criteria set by legislation and regulation for all audits

Source: European Court of Auditors (2008)

Fraud Investigations and Forensic Auditing

Fraud investigations can be undertaken by the internal audit function, or by a special fraud investigation team, to assist management in detecting or confirming the presence of fraudulent activities. Forensic auditing is a specialized field of auditing, often used as part of, or following, a fraud investigation to collect evidence suitable for a court of law.

Internal auditors are not expected to be expert fraud investigators or forensic auditors, although all internal auditors should be able to identify the indicators of fraud.

In Chapter 3, Paterson (2012) warned that audit committees and senior executives might have unrealistic expectations of internal auditors as identifiers of fraud. They may unrealistically expect the internal audit function to find fraud in all audit engagements, even when the scope of work and resources available would not support this. In these situations, the chief audit executive needs to work with the audit committee and senior management to ensure that their expectations are realistic and do not lead to misconceptions regarding value and quality.

Follow-Up Audits

The chief audit executive should schedule follow-up audits as part of the annual audit plan to review the manner in which management has addressed significant findings from previous audit reports.

Management-Initiated Reviews

Management-initiated reviews (MIRs) are engagements commissioned, and sometimes funded, by operational or senior management to assess a specific issue, operation, or process.

Internal audit's involvement in management-initiated reviews reflects well on the internal audit function, as a sign that management is supportive of the role of internal audit and values its opinion. Mature internal audit functions should dedicate a proportion of their annual audit plan (possibly 10 to 20 percent) to this type of engagement. This allows the chief audit executive to assess the importance and appropriateness of each management request, and undertake the work without impacting other planned audits.

Value-Added Assurance

Regardless of the types of assurance engagements undertaken by the internal audit function, value is achieved when assurance moves beyond the adequacy of individual controls to the overall adequacy of systems and processes.

Thematic Auditing

Vanessa Johnson, Group Manager, Corporate Risk and Assurance, at New Zealand Inland Revenue, believes the key driver of quality and value for internal audit is the ability to move beyond simple transactional auditing to thematic auditing. She challenges internal audit functions to ask the question *What does it mean?* when presented with a range of internal audit findings.

Combining Assurance

Chief audit executives can maximize the assurance provided to their organization by combining their assurance with that of other assurance providers. Sarens and colleagues (2012) view combined assurance as intending "to provide effective and compete assessment of risk, control and governance process for organizations." This concept is discussed further in Chapter 12.

QAIP Hint

Internal audit functions could incorporate *assurance activities* into an internal audit maturity model or balanced scorecard.

Maturity Model

Assurance activities undertaken could be a key process area within the maturity model, with compliance auditing being a requirement for the achievement of level 3 of a five-stage maturity model and operational/performance audits being a requirement for level 4.

Balanced Scorecard/KPI

Internal audit functions could include performance indicators such as:

- Total number of engagements completed by the internal audit function (include target)

- Number of assurance engagements completed by the internal audit function (include target)
- Number of assurance engagements performed by the internal audit function as a proportion of the overall plan (include target)
- Number of compliance audits, operational/performance audits, IT audits, management initiated reviews, and consulting engagements completed (include target)
- Number of compliance audits, operational/performance audits, IT audits, management initiated reviews, and consulting engagements as a proportion of the overall plan (include target)
- Time spent on compliance audits, operational/performance audits, IT audits, and consulting engagements as a proportion of the overall plan (include target)
- Time spent on fraud investigations as a proportion of the overall plan (include target)
- Time spent on management-initiated reviews as a proportion of the overall plan (include target)
- Time spent on follow-up audits (include target)
- Time spent on audit support activities (include target)

Consulting

The IIA (2013a) defines consulting services as "advisory and related client service activities, the nature and scope of which are agreed with the client, are intended to add value and improve the organization's governance, risk management, and control processes without the internal auditor assuming management responsibility. Examples include counsel, advice, facilitation and training."

The chief audit executive should define the types of consulting activities undertaken by their internal audit function, as these can take many forms:

- Facilitated control self-assessments
- Risk management training
- Facilitating the development of the organization's risk management plan (in the absence of a specialized risk management activity)
- Advice regarding systems under development
- Advice regarding the adequacy of control design
- Fraud-control activities
- Evaluating policies and procedures

Internal auditors have the opportunity to work with management to improve systems, processes, and methods of operating. Internal auditors are well placed to detect control weaknesses in projects and systems under development, prior to these going live. Recognizing loopholes and strengthening systems during development is desirable, as it is more cost-effective than trying to change the system at a later date. It will also allow for the controls to be fully tested prior to implementation and can reduce delays in project implementation.

Transitioning from Advice to Assurance

Archie R. Thomas, a consulting internal auditor in Canada, recommends that internal auditors formalize their processes for providing advice. He further suggests that an internal audit function develop a formal policy for any such work that could be perceived as management activities, which clearly defines the *exit strategy* for withdrawing from this management involvement and ultimately auditing the area.

The distinction between consulting and assurance activities is not always clear, as there are times that assurance activities may incorporate an element of consulting, or consulting activities provide a level of assurance. Nonetheless, the IIA's *International Professional Practices Framework* (IPPF) includes both Assurance and Consulting Standards that specify requirements for each type of engagement. To this end, there are a number of standards relevant to consulting activities. Some of the key standards are included here.

Standard 1000.C1

The nature of consulting services must be defined in the internal audit charter.

Standard 1210.C1

The chief audit executive must decline the consulting engagement or obtain competent advice and assistance if the internal auditors lack the knowledge, skills, or other competencies needed to perform all or part of the engagement.

Standard 2010.C1

The chief audit executive should consider accepting proposed consulting engagements based on the engagement's potential to improve management of risks, add value, and improve the organization's operations. Accepted engagements must be included in the plan.

Standard 2201.C1

Internal auditors must establish an understanding with consulting engagement clients about objectives, scope, respective responsibilities, and other client expectations. For significant engagements, this understanding must be documented.

Chief audit executives should work with their audit committee and senior management to determine the extent and nature of any consulting services they provide.

Common Quality Issue

Some internal audit functions are excessively focused on providing assurance at the expense of undertaking consulting engagements. This may be due to a perception by management that consulting engagements impair the independence of the internal audit function, or because of inadequate internal auditor expertise. It can also result from inadequately defining consulting services within the internal audit charter.

To ensure that consulting engagements are conducted efficiently and effectively, chief audit executives should allocate specific resources to consulting activities within the annual audit plan to avoid compromising the completion of agreed assurance engagements.

Example 7.7 Typical Consulting Engagement—Systems under Development

This type of engagement can provide advice regarding the proposed control environment associated with systems under development. These consulting engagements maximize the potential for effective systems implementation and provide value to the organization in terms of minimizing future rework.

QAIP Hint

Consulting engagements can be reflected in a balanced scorecard or internal audit maturity model.

Maturity Model

Completion of consulting engagements could be a key process area within the maturity model, with their completion being a requirement for the achievement of level 3 to 4 of a five-stage maturity model.

Balanced Scorecard/KPI

The internal audit activity could include a performance indicator such as the relative proportion of time spent on consulting versus assurance engagements.

Nature of Work

The nature of work undertaken by internal auditors will depend on both the maturity of the internal audit function and the organization as a whole. Less mature internal audit functions or internal audit functions in less mature organizations may be focused on control processes through compliance and financial auditing. As the internal audit function and/or organization starts to mature, the scope of internal auditing should be extended to include governance and risk management processes in accordance with IIA Standard 2100.

Standard 2100—Nature of Work

The internal audit activity must evaluate and contribute to the improvement of governance, risk management, and control processes using a systematic and disciplined approach.

Chief audit executives should define their scope of work in the internal audit charter, as this then provides internal auditors with the authority to operate in each area.

Common Quality Issue

Some internal auditors are excessively focused on providing assurance over controls and give inadequate consideration to governance and risk management issues. However, an effective internal audit function should support the organization to improve governance, risk management, and control processes.

Taking into Account the Operating Environment

The nature of internal audit's work should give consideration to the environment in which the internal audit function is operating. For example, many corporations in Japan have adopted the *kansayaku*, or statutory auditor, model. For these organizations, the *kansayaku*, rather than the internal audit function, will be responsible for assessing the performance of the chief executive officer and the board.

Governance

Internal auditors should provide assurance over governance processes within an organization. The IIA (2013a) defines governance as "the combination of processes and structures implemented by the board to inform, direct, manage, and monitor the activities of the organization towards the achievements of its objectives." Other definitions of governance are the "set of relationships between a company's management, its board, its shareholders, and other stakeholders. Corporate governance provides the structure through which the objectives of the company are set and the means of attaining those objectives and monitoring performance are determined" (OECD 2004) and "the system by which companies are directed and controlled" (Financial Reporting Council 2012).

Governance influences how objectives are set and achieved, how risk is monitored and assessed, how decisions are made, and how performance is optimized. Effective governance supports the following:

- Clear strategy and direction setting
- Informed and transparent decision making
- Alignment of activities to formal objectives
- Conformance with internal and external requirements

In recent years, there have been numerous major failures of governance leading to significant corporate losses, reputational damage, and, in some cases, the ultimate demise of organizations. These failures have not been restricted to particular geographical areas or types of organizations. They have encompassed both the public and private sectors in most countries. Spencer Pickett (2012) identifies a number of examples, some of which include:

- Barlow-Clowes (1988)
- Polly-Peck International (1989)
- BCCI (Bank of Credit and Commerce International [1991])
- Baring Futures (1995)
- (London) Metropolitan Police (1995)
- Sumitomo Corporation (1996)
- Enron (2001)
- WorldCom (2002)

RESPONSIBILITY FOR GOVERNANCE   Responsibility for governance rests with a broad range of stakeholders—the board, board committees, senior executives, organizational committees, and operational management.

IIA Standards 2110 and 2130.A1, among others, relate to assurance over governance processes.

Standards 2110—Governance

The internal audit activity must assess and make appropriate recommendations for improving the governance process in its accomplishment of the following objectives:

- Promoting appropriate ethics and values within the organization;
- Ensuring effective organizational performance management and accountability;
- Communicating risk and control information to appropriate areas of the organization; and
- Coordinating the activities of and communicating information among the board, external and internal auditors, and management.

Standard 2130.A1

The internal audit activity must evaluate the adequacy and effectiveness of controls in responding to risks within the organization's governance, operations, and information systems regarding the:

- Achievement of the organization's strategic objectives;
- Reliability and integrity of financial and operational information;
- Effectiveness and efficiency of operations and programs;
- Safeguarding of assets; and
- Compliance with laws, regulations, policies, procedures, and contracts.

The IIA also has three specific practices advisories relating to governance: 2110–1 (Governance: Definition), 2110–2 (Governance: Relationship with Risk and Control), and 2110–3 (Governance: Assessing the Adequacy of the Risk Management Process).

Auditing governance processes provides assurance to stakeholders that an organization is operating as intended, within the laws and expected standards, in an open and accountable manner, and with full regard to prudent and clear decision making. Figure 7.1 provides a model of the different types of governance audits that can be undertaken.

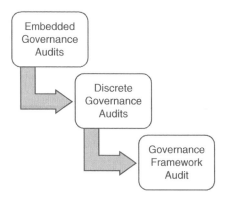

FIGURE 7.1 Types of Governance Audits

The role of internal audit in improving organizational governance will vary, depending on the maturity of the organization's processes. An organization with low maturity may require internal auditors to take an advisory role to help build the governance processes. Often, this role will be of a more informal, rather than formal, nature. However, as organizational maturity increases, the role of the internal audit function can become more formalized, moving from advice to audits of governance elements as part of other engagements, through to formalized audits of governance frameworks.

EMBEDDED GOVERNANCE AUDITS At a minimum, internal auditors should consider aspects of governance as part of other engagements. For example, engagement plans could include questions such as:

- Have the objectives for individual activities been appropriately identified and communicated?
- Are the project or activity objectives consistent with the organization's strategic objectives?
- Have the risks associated with the activity been appropriately identified and managed?
- Has responsibility and/or accountability for activities and risks been clearly identified?
- Is there an appropriate monitoring and reporting framework to ensure the efficiency and effectiveness of the activity?
- Have stakeholders for the activity or project been identified and appropriately engaged?

Example 7.8 Embedded Governance Objectives in a Human Resources Audit

The overall objective is to determine whether HR processes are operating efficiently and effectively. Subobjectives are to:

- Determine whether regulatory and policy obligations have been defined and appropriately delegated.
- Determine whether HR policies and procedures are appropriately documented and disseminated to staff.
- Determine whether HR processes conform to policies and procedures and result in the efficient and effective recruitment and retention of staff.

DISCRETE GOVERNANCE AUDITS Mature internal audit functions, in mature organizations, might consider incorporating discrete governance audits as part of the annual plan. However, these should always be risk based and be supported by the audit committee. Typical governance audits include:

- Strategic and Business Planning Processes
- Risk Management Framework and Activities
- Performance Reporting Processes
- Integrated Reporting
- Alignment of Performance Monitoring with Strategic Objectives
- Ethics and Culture
- Fraud Control Processes
- Whistleblower Processes

- Executive Remuneration
- Conflicts of Interests/Registers of Interest
- Committee Operations and Performance
- Financial Governance
- IT Governance

Example 7.9 Sample Objective for a Discrete Governance Audit

The overall objective is to assess whether the governance arrangements supporting the School Councillor Program facilitate effective service delivery. Specifically,
the audit will:

- Determine whether roles and responsibilities associated with the program
  have been clearly defined.
- Assess whether risks associated with program delivery have been identified,
  assessed, and treated.
- Determine whether effective monitoring and review processes have been
  established that support decision making and continuous improvement.

GOVERNANCE FRAMEWORK AUDITS   There are many frameworks highlighting the key
elements typical of good governance. These include the OECD Principles of Corporate
Governance (2004), the UK Corporate Code (2012), ASX Corporate Governance
Principles (2010), and King III (2010).

These frameworks provide high-level, credible criteria against which internal
auditors can assess the adequacy and effectiveness of governance frameworks, as
well as individual governance elements (in an embedded or discrete governance
audit).

No one framework will fit all organizations, and even within an organization, the
framework may require modification to meet stakeholder and organizational needs.
Internal auditors, therefore, need to be mindful in choosing a framework that is
appropriate for the organization, and in some cases, the organization itself might
have predetermined a framework, or iteration of a framework, it intends to adopt.

Auditing the entire governance framework is a large and sophisticated engagement that combines a number of the elements of discrete governance audits. This type
of auditing requires a high level of maturity within both internal audit and the
organization as a whole.

If an audit of the entire governance framework is conducted, the internal auditors
first need to determine the nature of the framework that exists within the organization.
To do this, they should identify each of the key governance elements within the
organization (e.g., a risk management framework, code of conduct, delegations)
without drawing any conclusions regarding the adequacy of these elements. Internal
auditors can also undertake interviews with senior management and the board to
determine their approach to governance.

Example 7.10   Governance Framework Audit Sample Objective 1

The overall objective is to assess the alignment of governance arrangements within the organization, and to determine whether these arrangements are effective in supporting expected service delivery outcomes. Subobjectives are to:

- Assess whether governance arrangements align with the needs of both internal and external stakeholders.
- Determine whether governance arrangements are appropriate for effective decision making.
- Examine the processes used to monitor and review governance arrangements.

Example 7.11   Governance Framework Audit Sample Objective 2

The overall objective is to assess the adequacy and effectiveness of the organization's governance framework. Specifically, the audit will assess whether the framework will do the following:

- Support alignment with the organization's mandate and priorities.
- Support the development of, and promote, the organization's strategic direction.
- Articulate and fairly represent the organization's decision-making processes and accountability structures.
- Promote continuous improvement across the organization.

Planning to Assess Governance   There are eight steps that an internal audit function should follow prior to embarking on governance audits:

1. Review all relevant documents relating to governance. This should include the strategic plan, annual report, board and committee terms of reference, policies, and procedures.
2. Discuss governance with senior management and the audit committee to clarify the organizational approach to governance and expectations regarding internal audit's role in assurance over governance.
3. Develop a broad framework of the organization's governance structure and define governance for the organization.
4. Compare the organization's approach to established governance models, or determine if an explicit model has been used (or is required to be used).
5. Define internal audit's role in governance in the internal audit charter.
6. Discuss potential governance topics with other stakeholders, including external audit, legal, compliance, and risk management.

7. Consider governance as part of the annual audit planning process and when planning individual audits.
8. If new to auditing governance, consider performing a pilot audit or use an embedded approach.

Questions That Can Be Considered during a Governance Audit   The following governance questions have been adapted from better practice guidance from the Australian National Audit Office (2003).

Governance and the Board

- Are governance arrangements clearly documented and articulated?
- Is the board structured to avoid conflicts of interest?
- Do members have the authority, qualifications, experience, and attributes to perform effectively?
- Does the board include nonexecutive directors?
- Is there diversity among board directors?
- Is the board and audit committee appropriately independent?
- Are the objectives, roles, and accountabilities of the board, management, and other committees clearly documented?
- Does the board receive adequate, timely information?
- Are board meetings appropriately structured and managed?
- Are there appropriate, functioning board committees, including a specific audit and risk committee?
- Is board and committee performance monitored?

Leadership, Ethics, and Performance Culture

- Is there a clear statement regarding the handling of conflicts of interest?
- Is there a clear statement regarding ethical and professional behavior?
- Do leaders drive good governance structures and processes?
- Do leaders walk the talk?
- Are there ethics and whistleblower processes?
- Does ethical behavior form part of the staff selection, training, and evaluation scheme?
- Is remuneration appropriately and fairly determined?

External Conformance and Accountability

- Are the role, vision, mission, and strategies clearly articulated?
- Are governance arrangements clearly documented and articulated?
- Is the external reporting framework built into the annual planning cycle and organizational processes?
- Is communication with stakeholders timely, complete, and interactive?
- Is there a risk-based audit program?

Internal Conformance and Accountability

- Is there a performance planning and review process?
- Is there a clear and robust financial planning and budgeting system, overseen by a properly constituted committee?

- Do the chief executive officer and chief financial officer sign off on financial reports to the board, confirming accuracy and fairness?
- Is there appropriate oversight by management and effective internal controls?
- Is the internal audit function appropriately resourced and positioned?
- Is there a fraud control plan and process?
- Are there appropriately documented delegations?

Risk Management

- Does the board take a structured, integrated, and detailed approach to risk management?
- Are appropriate risk management procedures in place to allow the board and other committees to consider levels of ongoing organizational risk as well as risks associated with particular functions or projects?
- Do managers take responsibility for managing risks?

Planning and Performance Monitoring

- Does the organizational structure support the achievement of objectives?
- Is there effective corporate and business planning, including individual performance plans, aligned with organizational objectives?
- Is there a standard set of strategic and operational plans?
- Do the operational plans link directly to the strategic aims and objectives of the organization?
- Is there a structured and regular performance monitoring system, aligned with organizational outcomes and outputs?

Common Quality Issue

Many internal audit functions avoid governance audits because of:

- Concerns regarding internal auditor competence
- Inadequate appreciation of the value of governance audits
- Lack of support from senior management and the audit committee

---

Risk Management

Internal audit's role in risk management is closely aligned to its governance role. As with assurance over governance, the internal audit function can provide overall assurance regarding risk management systems and processes, or can embed its assurance over risk management into other engagements.

Having responsibility for risk management impacts internal audit's ability to provide independent assurance over risk management. However, for some less-mature organizations, the internal audit function takes on this responsibility in the absence of an alternative. In this case, assurance should still be provided over risk management activities, although this assurance may need to be outsourced to an external service provider.

IIA Standards 2120, 2120.A1, and 2120.C3, among others, relate to assurance over risk management processes.

Standard 2120—Risk Management

The internal audit activity must evaluate the effectiveness and contribute to the improvement of risk management processes.

Standard 2120.A1

The internal audit activity must evaluate risk exposures relating to the organization's governance, operations, and information systems regarding the:

- Achievement of the organization's strategic objectives;
- Reliability and integrity of financial and operational information;
- Effectiveness and efficiency of operations and programs;
- Safeguarding of assets; and
- Compliance with laws, regulations, policies, procedures, and contracts.

Standard 2120.C3

When assisting management in establishing or improving risk management processes, internal auditors must refrain from assuming any management responsibility by actually managing risks.

ENTERPRISE RISK MANAGEMENT   Enterprise risk management (ERM) is the application of risk management approaches across an organization in a structured and disciplined manner. Sobel and Reding (2012) see ERM monitoring as being important:

> *It provides assurance that the ERM system continues to operate effectively over time. Monitoring helps ensure that deficiencies in design adequacy or operating effectiveness are identified and rectified in a timely manner. It also facilitates timely identification of changes in the organization's external and internal context, performance objectives, strategies, and risks, and expedites appropriate ERM alterations in response to the changes identified. Ensuring that the ERM system continues to perform as expected, especially during periods of significant change, is important because it provides assurance that the organization's strategic, operations, reporting, and compliance objectives continue to be achieved.*

Not all organizations will have established an effective ERM system. However, for those that have, internal audit should look to provide assurance over this framework.

Example 7.12 Risk Management Framework Audit Sample Objective 1

The objective is to assess the extent to which the enterprise risk management framework has been embedded within the organization.

Example 7.13 Risk Management Framework Audit Sample Objective 2

The objective is to assess the adequacy and effectiveness of the organization's risk management framework.

Common Quality Issue

Some internal audit functions fail to provide adequate assurance over risk management. They do not include the risk management framework, or ERM, within their audit universe, or do not include consideration of risk as an embedded part of other audits.

FRAUD RISKS Fraud is a significant risk for all organizations, and internal auditors have a responsibility to assist organizations to effectively mitigate this risk. Although internal auditors are not expected to be fraud experts, they should be alert to indicators of fraud and have a sound understanding of fraud risk. This is highlighted in IIA Standard 2120.A2.

Standards 2120.A2

The internal audit activity must evaluate the potential for the occurrence of fraud and how the organization manages fraud risk.

Martin (2013) argues that internal auditors should maintain a leadership role in initiating fraud prevention and detection measures. This could include the use of data analytics to identify suspicious transactions that might have escaped scrutiny in previous transaction sampling practices. Martin believes that if internal auditors adopt a more proactive approach to identifying fraud risks, they can reduce the potential for massive or widespread fraud.

Common Quality Issue

There is a common misconception among managers that an effective internal audit function will prevent fraud from occurring. This is simply not true. While some researchers, including Coram and colleagues (2006), have identified a positive relationship between the existence of internal audit and fraud detection, there is no evidence to support the prevention of fraud by effective internal audit.

Assurance over Controls

Providing assurance over the adequacy, effectiveness, efficiency, and/or appropriateness of controls is a fundamental tenet of internal auditing, and there are a number of IIA standards relating to this. The most important of these is Standard 2130.

Standard 2130

The internal audit activity must assist the organization in maintaining effective controls by evaluating their effectiveness and efficiency and by promoting continuous improvement.

Controls assurance is often described as the bread and butter of internal auditing. However, internal audit does not have a unique responsibility for assuring the adequacy and effectiveness of controls—this responsibility is shared with management and a range of other internal and external assurance providers.

Three Lines of Defense

The IIA, in its position paper *Three Lines of Defense in Effective Risk Management and Control* (2013b), identifies different roles and responsibilities across an organization for effective coordination of risk management and control oversight. These are shown in Figure 7.2.

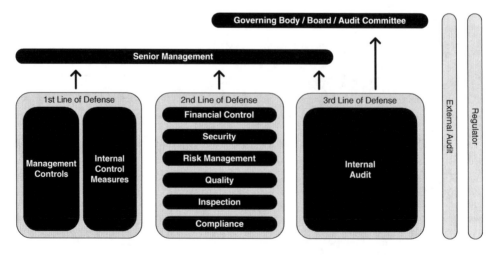

FIGURE 7.2 Three Lines of Defense

Within the first line of defense, management has a responsibility for providing assurance over its controls. The second line of defense incorporates other internal assurance providers such as compliance and quality functions, and internal audit is positioned as the third line of defense. Internal auditors can consider the roles of each assurance provider through assurance mapping, which is discussed further in Chapter 12.

QAIP Hint

Internal audit's assurance over governance, risk management, and control can be reflected in a balanced scorecard or internal audit maturity model.

Maturity Model

Assurance over governance, risk management, and control could be a key process area within the maturity model, with control assurance, and integrated governance and risk management assurance being a requirement for the achievement of level 3 of a five-stage maturity model. Discrete governance and risk management engagements could be a requirement for level 4.

Balanced Scorecard/KPI

Internal audit functions could include performance indicators such as:

- Relative proportions of time spent on governance, risk management, and control assurance (include target)
- Number of engagements incorporating governance, risk management, and control elements (include target)
- Number of engagements focused exclusively on governance, risk management, or control assurance (include target)

Audit Support Activities

Better practice internal audit functions allocate specific resources to audit support activities. These types of activities include:

- Marketing the internal audit function to ensure that the organization has a sound understanding of it roles and responsibilities
- Assisting the audit committee to discharge its responsibilities through the provision of induction and ongoing training
- Providing secretarial support to the audit committee
- Monitoring the implementation of agreed recommendations
- Disseminating better practice and lessons learned across the organization
- Providing mentoring and professional development to internal audit staff
- Managing outsourced and co-sourced providers
- Managing the audit function, including implementing the quality assurance and improvement program and maintaining audit policies and procedures

Questions about the Internal Audit Function's Areas of Responsibility and Nature of Work

Table 7.2 provides a range of questions about the internal audit function's areas of responsibilities and nature of work. These can be formally incorporated into a quality assurance and improvement program, or, less formally, into ongoing assessment activities. Questions may be variously posed to the chief audit executive, internal auditors, or audit stakeholders.

TABLE 7.2 Quality Questions

Questions	Evidence of Quality
Does the internal audit charter define the nature of assurance services provided to the organization?	Internal audit charter
Does the internal audit charter specifically define consulting activities?	Internal audit charter
Are compliance audits based on identified, prioritized risks?	Internal audit plan Details of engagements completed
Are any compliance audits undertaken because they always have been (without considering risk)?	Internal audit plan Details of engagements completed Senior management and audit committee interviews
Are operational or performance audits undertaken?	Internal audit plan Details of engagements completed
Does the internal audit function undertake integrated auditing?	Internal audit plan
Does the internal audit function undertake consulting activities?	Internal audit plan Details of engagements completed
Is there any evidence that the internal audit function has undertaken consulting engagements in areas beyond its expertise?	Internal audit plan Details of engagements completed Post-engagement surveys
Is there evidence that the internal audit function has considered the potential value of a consulting engagement to the organization before accepting the engagement?	Evidence of discussions with management requesting consulting engagements
Do planned consulting engagements appear in the annual audit plan?	Internal audit plan
Does the internal audit function respond appropriately to management requests for consulting or assurance engagements?	Senior management interviews Post-engagement surveys
Do internal auditors consider risks as part of consulting engagements?	Evidence of risk assessment Post-engagement surveys
Is knowledge of controls gained through consulting engagements incorporated back into an evaluation of control processes?	Internal audit staff interviews Senior management and audit committee interviews

Is there evidence that internal auditors plan consulting engagements with engagement clients?	Planning documentation Evidence of discussions with stakeholders Post-engagement surveys Senior management interviews
Have internal auditors documented their mutual understanding (with clients) for significant consulting engagements?	Planning documentation Post-engagement surveys
Does the internal audit function undertake engagements that evaluate and contribute to the improvement of governance?	Internal audit plan Details of engagements completed Senior management and audit committee interviews
Does the internal audit function undertake engagements that evaluate and contribute to the improvement of risk management?	Internal audit plan Details of engagements completed Post-engagement surveys
Does the internal audit function undertake engagements that evaluate and contribute to the improvement of control processes?	Internal audit plan Details of engagements completed Post-engagement surveys
Does the internal audit function assess and make appropriate recommendations for improving governance processes?	Internal audit working papers and reports Post-engagement surveys Senior management and audit committee interviews
Does the internal audit function evaluate the design, implementation, and effectiveness of the organization's ethics-related objectives, programs, and activities?	Internal audit plan Details of engagements completed
Does the internal audit function assess whether IT governance supports the organization's strategies and objectives?	Annual audit plan Details of engagements completed Engagement working papers
Does the internal audit function assess the adequacy and effectiveness of governance controls?	Annual audit plan Details of engagements completed Engagement working papers
Do internal audit engagements include an assessment of risk management practices within the engagement subject area?	Engagement working papers Post-engagement surveys
Does the internal audit function periodically review the organization's risk management framework?	Details of engagements completed
Is there a mechanism for the internal audit function to input risks from individual engagements back into the risk management framework?	Internal audit staff interviews

Does the internal audit function evaluate operational risks such as:
  • Reliability and integrity of financial and operational information
  • Effectiveness and efficiency of operations and programs
  • Safeguarding of assets
  • Compliance with laws, regulations, policies, procedures, and contracts
	Annual audit plan
	Details of engagements completed
	Engagement working papers
	Senior management and audit committee interviews

(*continued*)

TABLE 7.2 (*Continued*)

Questions	Evidence of Quality
Does the internal audit function evaluate strategic risks that can impact the achievement of strategic objectives?	Annual audit plan Details of engagements completed Engagement working papers
Does the internal audit function have any operational responsibility for managing risks beyond those specifically connected to internal audit activities?	Senior management and audit committee interviews Internal audit charter
Does the internal audit function evaluate the potential for the occurrence of fraud and how the organization manages fraud risk?	Annual audit plan Details of engagements completed Engagement working papers
Does the internal audit function evaluate the adequacy and effectiveness of controls?	Annual audit plan Details of engagements completed Engagement working papers
Does the internal audit function offer recommendations to support the continuous improvement of controls?	Internal audit reports Senior management and audit committee interviews Post-engagement surveys
Does the internal audit function feed knowledge gained of controls through consulting engagements back into a broader evaluation of controls?	Internal audit staff interviews Senior management and audit committee interviews

Conclusion

In determining the areas of responsibility and nature of work for an internal audit function, chief audit executives must have a comprehensive understanding of the needs and expectations of their organization. This understanding can be achieved through effective strategic planning, and by maintaining an open and ongoing dialogue with senior managers, operational managers, and the audit committee.

Ideally, an internal audit function will incorporate a combination of assurance and consulting engagements, covering governance, risk management, and control. Engagements may be program-based or functionally based. Alternatively, they may incorporate an integrated approach covering a range of auditing types and techniques.

When considering the types of assurance and consulting activities to be undertaken, chief audit executives should consider the three lines of defense model. Doing so will allow them to take into account the assurance provided by other lines of defense, such as operational managers and other assurance providers. This will help to maximize the use of scarce resources across the organization.

References

Anderson, R. J., and J. C. Svare. (2011). *Imperatives for Change: The IIA's Global Internal Audit Survey in Action—CBOK Report V*. Altamonte Springs, FL: The Institute of Internal Auditors Research Foundation.

Asian Development Bank (2010). *Corporate Governance and the Role of Internal Audit in Asia*. China: Asia Development Bank.

ASX Corporate Governance Council. (2010). *Corporate Governance Principles and Recommendations with 2010 Amendments*. ASX Corporate Governance Council. http://www.asx.com.au/documents/asx-compliance/cg_principles_recommen dations_with_2010_amendments.pdf.

Australian National Audit Office. (2003). *Public Sector Governance: Volume 1: Framework, Processes and Practices—Better Practice Guide*. Commonwealth of Australia. http://www.anao.gov.au~/media/Files/Better%20Practice%20Guides/ Public%20Sector%20Governance.pdf.

Bahrmam, P. D. (2011). *Advancing Organizational Governance: Internal Audit's Role*. Altamonte Springs, FL: The Institute of Internal Auditors Research Foundation.

Boritz, J. E. (1983). *Planning for the Internal Audit Function*. Altamonte Springs, FL: Institute of Internal Auditors Research Foundation.

Burch, S. (2011). Building an internal audit function. *Internal Auditor*. http://www .theiia.org/intauditor.

Cathcart, R., and G. Kapor. (2010). An Internal Audit Upgrade. *Internal Auditor*. http:// www.theiia.org/intauditor.

Chambers, A. D., G. M. Selim, and G. Vinten. (1994). *Internal Auditing*, 2nd ed. London: Pitman Publishing.

Chen, Jiin-Feng, and Wan-Ying Lin. (2011). *Measuring Internal Auditing's Value— CBOK Report III*. Altamonte Springs, FL: The Institute of Internal Auditors Research Foundation.

Coram, P., C. Ferguson, and R. Moroney. (2006). *The Value of Internal Audit in Fraud Detection*. http://www.theage.com.au/ed_docs/Fraud_paper.pdf (accessed November 18, 2013).

European Court of Auditors. (2008). *Performance Audit Manual, 2008*. http:// audit-network.wikispaces.com/file/view/CourtOfAuditors+Manual.pdf (accessed November 17, 2013).

Financial Reporting Council. (2012). *The UK Corporate Governance Code*. http://www. slc.co.uk/media/78872/uk-corporate-governance-code-september-2012.pdf.

Galloway, D. (2010). *Internal Auditing: A Guide for the New Auditor*. Altamonte Springs, FL: The Institute of Internal Auditors Research Foundation.

Glover, H. D., and J. C. Flagg. (1997). *A Decade of Model Internal Audit Case Summaries*. Altamonte Springs, FL: The Institute of Internal Auditors.

Gray, G. L. and M. J. Gray. (1994). *Business Management Auditing, Promotion of Consulting Auditing*. Altamonte Springs, FL: The Institute of Internal Auditors Research Foundation.

HM Treasury. (2010, July). *Good Practice Guide: Audit Strategy*. http://www.hm-treasury.gov.uk.

Institute of Directors in Southern Africa. (2010). *King Report on Governance*. http:// www.iodsa.co.za/?kingIII.

The Institute of Internal Auditors. (2013a) *International Professional Practices Framework*. Altamonte Springs, FL: Institute of Internal Auditors.

The Institute of Internal Auditors. (2013b). *IIA Position Paper—The Three Lines of Defense in Effective Risk Management and Control,* January 2013. https://www .iia.org.au/sf_docs/default-source/member-services/thethreelinesofdefenseineffec tiveriskmanagementandcontrol_Position_Paper_Jan_2013.pdf?sfvrsn=0.

The Institute of Internal Auditors. (2010). *Internal Auditing—A Glance at the Future of the Profession*. Mexico City: Montecito, 38.

The Institute of Internal Auditors. (2013). *The Value of Internal Auditing for Stake-holders*. http://www.theiia.org/theiia/about-the-profession/value-proposition/?sf1473960=1 (accessed November 28, 2013).

Leung, P., B. J. Cooper, and P. Robinson. (2004). *The Role of Internal Audit in Corporate Governance and Management*. Melbourne: RMIT University.

Loebbecke, J. K. (1996). *Internal Auditing: Principles and Techniques*. Altamonte Springs, FL: The Institute of Internal Auditors.

Martin, A. G. (2013). A refocused internal audit function adds value through the organization. *Internal Auditor* 28(1): 25–34.

OECD. (2004). *Principles of Corporate Governance*. http://www.oecd.org/corporate/ca/corporategovernanceprinciples/31557724.pdf.

Paterson, J. (2012). The lean audit advantage. *Internal Auditor*. http://www.theiia.org/intauditor.

Reding, K. F., et al. (2009). *Internal Auditing: Assurance and Consulting Services*. Altamonte Springs, FL: The Institute of Internal Auditors Research Foundation.

Sarens, G., L. Decaux, and R. Lenz. (2012). *Combined Assurance: Case Studies on a Holistic Approach to Organizational Governance*. Altamonte Springs, FL: The Institute of Internal Auditors Research Foundation.

Sawyer, L. B., M. A. Dittenhofer, and J. H. Scheiner. (2005). *Sawyers Internal Auditing*, 5th ed. Altamonte Springs, FL: The Institute of Internal Auditors Research Foundation.

Schwartz, B. M. (2013). Risk management focus brings opportunities for internal audit. *RMA Journal* 95(6): 11, 16–21.

Sobel, P. J., and K. F. Reding. (2012). *Enterprise Risk Management—Achieving and Sustaining Success*. Altamonte Springs, FL: The Institute of Internal Auditors Research Foundation.

Soh, Dominic S. B., and N. Martinov-Bennie. (2011). The internal audit function. *Managerial Auditing Journal* 26(7): 605–622.

Spencer Pickett, K. H. (2012). *The Essential Guide to Internal Auditing*, 2nd ed. West Sussex, England: John Wiley & Sons.

CHAPTER **8**

Internal Audit Charter

The higher we report, the more valuable our work. The earlier we get involved when the organization undergoes strategic decision making, the better. We want to provide solutions, not just find problems. And we need to present those solutions in a way that makes it more likely they will be accepted and implemented.

—Phil Tarling, IIA Chairman of the Board, 2012

The internal audit charter defines internal audit's mandate and purpose. It is a subset of the overall internal audit strategy—articulating the professional and organizational authority of the internal audit function.

The charter should identify the strategic and organizational context in which internal audit operates. It defines the structure and position of the internal audit function and should confirm the independence of internal audit within the organization.

Internal Audit Mandate and Purpose

In order for any organization or activity to operate at a consistently high standard, there must be a clear, shared understanding of its mandate or purpose. Internal audit functions are no different. Their mandate, or purpose, should be well understood, and this understanding should be shared across the organization. The documented mandate should provide the organization with a clear understanding of what the internal audit function is (its raison d'être).

The IIA's (2013) definition of internal auditing provides a useful basis for creating a mandate or purpose statement:

Internal auditing is an independent, objective assurance and consulting activity designed to add value and improve an organization's operations. It helps an organization accomplish its objectives by bringing a systematic, disciplined approach to evaluate and improve the effectiveness of risk management, control, and governance processes.

Burch (2011) identifies a key step for chief audit executives building or transforming an internal audit function as understanding the expectations of key stakeholders of the function. She believes the chief audit executive needs to understand how the organization wants to engage with, and benefit from, internal audit. These expectations should help to define internal audit's mandate, which should be articulated in a charter and approved by senior management and the audit committee.

Strategic Context

The internal audit function requires a clear understanding of its organizational and strategic context.

Organizational Context

In order to deliver value, internal auditors must understand and reflect the environment in which their organization operates. This includes:

- The regulatory and policy environment
- The political environment
- Key business drivers and/or strategic objectives
- Major competitors
- Emerging markets and issues
- Customer and client demographics

These contextual elements determine the activities that internal audit should undertake, as well as the types of outcomes and outputs expected of the function.

Internal Audit's Strategic Context

The internal audit function is affected by both the broad organizational context (e.g., the regulatory, political, and competitive environment) and its own strategic context. Internal audit's strategic context can include the motivation behind internal audit's existence (e.g., any legislated requirements for internal audit), key challenges that the internal audit function faces, and what value it provides to stakeholders.

SUPPORTING LEGISLATION, REGULATION, AND POLICY Some organizations will voluntarily establish internal audit functions, recognizing the benefits that internal audit can offer management and the board. For other organizations, internal audit is established to meet legislative and regulatory requirements. For instance, the *Federal Accountability Act* (2006) in Canada requires federal departments to establish appropriate internal audit capacity and audit committees.

In situations where the internal audit function is required to meet external requirements, the chief audit executive should be fully conversant with the nature of these requirements and their implications for internal audit. Requirements should be articulated in the internal audit charter and embedded into standard operating procedures.

Structure and Position

The structure and position of the internal audit function will have a significant bearing on its independence and authority. Without effective independence, management is unable to rely on internal audit engagements, and without adequate authority, internal auditors may be impeded in their ability to provide assurance.

IIA Standard 1110 requires that chief audit executives report to a level within the organization that allows them to fulfill their responsibilities. The intention is that management should not adversely affect the engagements selected for the annual plan, or the outcomes of individual engagements. Ideally, internal audit should report functionally to the audit committee and administratively to the chief executive officer, as described in Figure 8.1.

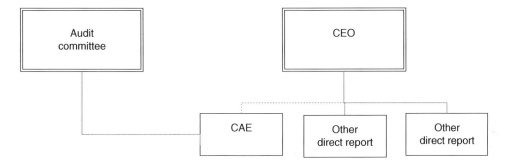

FIGURE 8.1 Internal Audit Reporting Lines

Reporting to the chief executive officer enhances the authority of the internal auditors and sets the tone regarding the perceived importance of the internal audit function. It also avoids potential hindrances to independence that could result if the chief audit executive reports to the chief financial officer or other line manager.

The IIA has two standards specifically relating to the position of the chief audit executive—Standards 1110 and 1111.

Standard 1110—Organizational Independence

The chief audit executive must report to a level within the organization that allows the internal audit activity to fulfill its responsibilities. The chief audit executive must confirm to the board, at least annually, the organizational independence of the internal audit activity.

Standards 1111—Direct Interaction with the Board

The chief audit executive must communicate and interact directly with the board.

The functional reporting line between the chief audit executive and the audit committee is specifically reinforced in IIA Standard 1111.

Common Quality Issue

It is not uncommon in organizations for the chief audit executive to report administratively to the chief financial officer or other line manager.

This may occur in smaller organizations for practical reasons. Some organizations consider themselves too small to justify employing a chief audit executive with the authority and experience to report administratively to the chief executive officer.

It is arguable that, as the nature of internal auditing evolves, there can be as many independence issues associated with the chief audit executive reporting administratively to the chief executive officer as there are in reporting to the chief financial officer.

Historically, when much of internal audit's work was of a financial nature, there were significant independence issues associated with a reporting line between the chief financial officer and chief audit executive. This reporting line increased the potential for the chief financial officer to limit the scope of the internal audit plan as well as the scope and findings of individual engagements.

However, with internal auditors increasing their focus on governance and strategy, the risk of interference from chief executive officers who are directly responsible for internal audit also increases. Nonetheless, the value of the chief audit executive reporting directly to the chief executive officer is the prominence this can give to internal audit.

The IIA's Practice Advisory 1110–1 describes the board's (or audit committee's) role in relation to the internal audit function as typically including:

- Approving the internal audit charter
- Approving the internal audit risk assessment and related audit plan
- Receiving communications from the chief audit executive on the results of the internal audit engagements or other matters that the chief audit executive determines are necessary, including private meetings with the chief audit executive without management present, as well as annual confirmation of the internal audit function's organizational independence
- Approving all decisions regarding the performance evaluation, appointment, or removal of the chief audit executive
- Approving the annual compensation and salary adjustment of the chief audit executive
- Making appropriate inquiries of management and the chief audit executive to determine whether there is audit scope or budgetary limitations that may impede the ability of the internal audit function to execute its responsibilities

There may be instances where the audit committee is unable to fulfill all of these roles. For instance, some government organizations have legislated requirements for the chief executive officer, ministerial delegate, or an external body to appoint the chief audit executive.

Regardless of the specific requirements within each organization, the relationship between the audit committee and the internal audit function should be formalized in the internal audit charter. This ensures that there is a clear understanding of the interactions between the audit committee and the internal audit function, and the areas where the audit committee will rely on internal audit.

Focusing on Organizational Objectives

According to Trygve Sørlie, former Chief Audit Executive at Gjensidige in Norway and current member of the International Internal Audit Standards Board, "Internal audit's product is influence." He encourages chief audit executives to spend time interacting directly with the chief executive officer and senior management. "Once a month, have an hour with the chief executive officer to discuss current and emerging issues. This influence is extremely important and allows internal audit to help support the organization to achieve its objectives."

QAIP Hint

Internal audit functions could incorporate *lines of reporting* into an internal audit maturity model or a balanced scorecard.

Maturity Model

Internal audit functions could include *lines of reporting* as a key process area in its maturity model. For example:

- Level 2 of a five-stage maturity model could identify that the chief audit executive reports to operational management
- Level 3 could identify that the chief audit executive reports functionally to the audit committee and administratively to the chief executive officer

Balanced Scorecard/KPI

Internal audit functions could include performance indicators such as:

- The number of times the chief audit executive meets privately with the chief executive officer and other senior management (include target)
- The number of times the chief audit executive meets privately with the audit committee (include target)

Independence

> Think of strawberries and cream, or apple pie and custard. Each is fine on its
> own, but it's the combination of the two that really makes the mouth water.
> There is a similar relationship between audit committees and internal auditors.
> In isolation, each can do a good job. But when they work together, when they
> have a mutually supportive relationship, they can achieve amazing things for
> their organizations.
>
> —*Neil Baker (2011)*

A key principle of internal auditing is that it is independent from management.
This independence is essential to internal audit's effectiveness and allows the internal
audit function to provide objective assurance, while also supporting management to
add value to the organization. This tightrope can often be difficult to walk.

Rezaee (2010) believes that the independence and objectivity of internal auditors
can be strengthened when they report their findings and opinions directly to the audit
committee.

The chief audit executive should determine the most appropriate communication
pathway for their internal audit function in consultation with the audit committee.
Usually, this will involve reporting findings directly to the engagement client, as well as
to the audit committee. However, depending on the size and structure of the
organization and the number of audit engagements undertaken, the committee may
prefer to receive executive summaries of internal audit reports rather than the full
report. The right approach will vary between organizations, and the chief audit
executive should find a model that best meets their stakeholders' needs.

IIA Standards 1100, 1110.A1, and 1130.A2 are relevant to independence.

Standards 1100—Independence and Objectivity

The internal audit activity must be independent, and internal auditors must be
objective in performing their work.

Standard 1110.A1

The internal audit activity must be free from interference in determining the scope
of internal auditing, performing work, and communicating results.

Standard 1130.A2

Assurance engagements for functions over which the chief audit executive has
responsibility must be overseen by a party outside the internal audit activity.

Key independence principles associated with quality internal audit functions include the following:

- The internal audit function should be independent of the activities audited.
- The internal audit function should be independent from operational management and organizational internal control process excepting those that specifically relate to internal audit.
- The chief audit executive should have direct access to the audit committee.
- The chief audit executive should have direct access to the chief executive officer.
- The internal audit function should be subject to an independent external quality assessment when directed by the audit committee and at least once every five years.

Conflicts of Interest

Internal auditors have various roles and responsibilities relating to conflicts of interest. First and foremost, they should ensure that any conflicts of interest impacting the internal audit function are identified, managed appropriately, and formally documented. They should also ensure that conflicts of interest for the audit committee and any co-sourced providers are appropriately managed and documented.

Internal auditors should consider potential conflicts of interest as part of governance engagements. In some organizations, internal auditors may be responsible for managing an interests register for the organization.

The Australian Independent Commission Against Corruption (2004) cautions that conflicts of interest cannot always be avoided or prohibited. Instead, unavoidable conflicts of interest need to be identified, disclosed, and effectively managed. The commission recognizes that "there is nothing unusual or necessarily wrong in having a conflict of interest" and provides a framework (Example 8.1) for managing conflicts of interest.

Example 8.1 Framework for Managing Conflicts of Interest

The Australian Independent Commission Against Corruption (2004) has released the following framework for managing conflicts of interest:

- Identify the different types of conflicts of interest that typically arise in organizations.
- Develop appropriate conflicts of interest policies, management strategies, and responses.
- Educate staff, managers, and the senior executive and publish conflicts of interest policies across the organization.
- Lead the organization through example.
- Communicate the organization's commitment to its policies and procedures for managing conflicts of interest to stakeholders, including contractors, clients, sponsors, and the community.
- Enforce conflicts of interest policies.
- Review conflicts of interest policies regularly.

Management Responsibilities

The chief audit executive needs to effectively manage the internal audit function to ensure that it provides value to the organization. Ideally, the chief audit executive should not be responsible for managing other activities within the organization. While this separation of responsibilities can sometimes be challenging for small audit shops, it preserves the independence and objectivity of internal audit.

Ratliff and colleagues (1996) recognize:

> *Most internal auditing departments will likely, at some time, be assigned tasks outside their auditing function. It is not that internal auditors should not perform these duties. Rather, when they do, they (and management) must recognize the nature of the differences in the duties in order to perform them in a way that minimizes conflict with the primary responsibilities of the internal auditing function.*

FRAUD AND RISK MANAGEMENT RESPONSIBILITIES   In some organizations, chief audit executives are unable to avoid management responsibilities. The two operational areas they most commonly have responsibility for are fraud investigations and risk management. However, reasons for avoiding these responsibilities include:

- Impairment of independence when providing assurance over the quality of these important functions.
- Challenges associated with accurately predicting the level of resourcing required for fraud and other investigations, and the potential risk this has on diverting resources from internal audit engagements.
- Potential impacts on the relationship between internal auditors and the organization by blurring the line between audit and investigation. Management are likely to be less open and transparent with internal audit if they fear they may face formal investigation by internal audit.
- The need for different skill sets between internal auditors and investigators.

Managing the Conflict Associated with Management Responsibilities

It is not uncommon, especially in small audit shops, for the chief audit executive to have administrative responsibilities for governance or risk management. This presents a risk that the internal audit function will provide inadequate assurance over these processes.

This risk can be managed through outsourcing the assurance over these management functions, and having the outsourced providers present these engagement reports directly to the person to whom the chief audit executive reports and/or the audit committee.

QAIP Hint

Internal audit functions could include *management responsibilities* as a key process area in its maturity model. For example:

- Level 2 of a five-stage maturity model could identify that the chief audit executive has management responsibilities and that there are no arrangements to provide independent assurance over these.
- Level 3 could identify that the chief audit executive has management responsibilities but that there are specific assurance arrangements in place to manage this potential conflict.
- Level 4 could identify that the chief audit executive has no management responsibilities.

Authority

It is important that the authority of the internal audit function be clearly established. This authority should allow internal auditors to undertake their professional responsibilities with appropriate support from management and with minimal interference. Ideally, this authority will be formally documented in the internal audit charter in accordance with the IIA *Standards*.

Standards 1000—Purpose, Authority, and Responsibility

The purpose, authority, and responsibility of the internal audit activity must be formally defined in an internal audit charter, consistent with the Definition of Internal Auditing, the Code of Ethics, and the Standards. The chief audit executive must periodically review the internal audit charter and present it to senior management and the board for approval.

Example 8.2 provides an extract from an internal audit charter relating to authority.

Example 8.2 Authority Extract from an Internal Audit Charter

Internal auditors are authorized to have full, free, and unrestricted access to all organizational departments, activities, premises, assets, personnel, records, and other documentation and information relevant to the performance of audit engagements. Except where limited by law, the work of the internal audit function is unrestricted. The internal audit function is free to review and evaluate all policies, procedures, and practices for any organizational program, activity, or function.

All records, documentation, and information accessed in the course of undertaking internal audit engagements are to be used solely for the conduct of these engagements. The chief audit executive is responsible for maintaining the confidentiality of the information received during an internal audit engagement.

In undertaking engagements, the internal audit function has no direct responsibility for any of the activities reviewed.

Executive Support

An effective internal audit function requires the support of the organization's senior management and line management. The attitude of management to the internal audit function can significantly influence the behavior of staff toward internal auditors, and can ultimately strengthen or hamper the role of internal audit.

Surviving as a Chief Audit Executive for over 25 Years

Bill Middleton, Chief Audit Executive at the New South Wales Department of Education in Australia, shares his secrets to surviving as a chief audit executive for over 25 years:

- *Become a trusted adviser.* You must build a strong relationship with your key customers, especially the audit committee and the chief executive officer.
- *Tell it like it is.* You must be able to give full and frank advice and opinion even when you don't have all the evidence. For the big-ticket items, providing opinion early is the key to making a difference—there's no point waiting until it's all over before you tell them there's a problem.
- *Maintain a customer focus.* You must know the customers and their business to be able to give valuable advice.

Internal audit's authority can be reinforced through executive support. Cathcart and Kapoor (2010) identify a number of ways in which management can support the internal audit's function:

- Allowing senior auditors to participate on key management and governance committees
- Making the chief audit executive a member of the executive committee
- Championing the importance of internal audit
- Taking immediate and proactive action on audit findings
- Holding senior executives accountable for unsatisfactory results
- Supporting the internal audit function when its findings are unpopular
- Defining the internal audit function's role and management's expectations
- Providing appropriate talent and authority to the function
- Monitoring audit performance and providing feedback regularly

Holt (2012) recognizes that top-performing internal audit functions have visibility across the various operational areas and business units, allowing for a holistic view of the organization. He believes internal audit should reflect a sound understanding of business strategy and the associated risks to the achievement of the strategy. Internal auditors should be willing to challenge the control environment and infrastructure supporting the strategy, and need to be more than an organization's police force, focused solely on compliance functions. Holt argues that senior management and others across the organization need to recognize internal audit as a function that provides a quality challenge.

Executive Support

There is significant value to be gained from the chief executive officer and other senior management providing strong, demonstrable support to the internal audit function. This support could be through reference to positive outcomes on internal audit engagements at staff meetings, and positive commentary on internal audit in memorandum to staff.

QAIP Hint

Internal audit functions could incorporate *executive support* into a balanced scorecard by including performance indicators such as the number of strategic committees that internal auditors are involved in.

Internal Audit Charter

The internal audit charter is a key element of the internal audit strategy and its value is acknowledged through IIA Standard 1000.

Although some internal audit functions may not have a formal charter, instead articulating their purpose in a strategic or operational plan, the formalized charter helps to define the professional nature of the internal audit function. Unlike the broader strategy, which will vary significantly between internal audit functions, charters should share a number of common elements regardless of the size or nature of the internal audit function or the organization in which it is operating.

Developing a formalized charter provides an opportunity to share the purpose and authority of internal audit with staff across the organization. It affords senior management and the audit committee visibility to the role of internal audit, and reinforces the professionalism of the internal audit function.

In addition to the mandate or purpose, the charter should include the types of engagements that internal audit will undertake, the nature of its work, its authority to operate, and its guiding values. These points are shown in Figure 8.2.

IIA Standard 1010 requires that the internal audit charter recognizes the IIA's Definition of Internal Auditing and the mandatory nature of the IIA's Code of Ethics and Standards.

Standard 1010—Recognition of the Definition of Internal Auditing, the Code of Ethics, and the Standards in the Internal Audit Charter

The mandatory nature of the Definition of Internal Auditing, the Code of Ethics, and the Standards must be recognized in the internal audit charter. The chief audit executive should discuss the Definition of Internal Auditing, the Code of Ethics, and the Standards with senior management and the board.

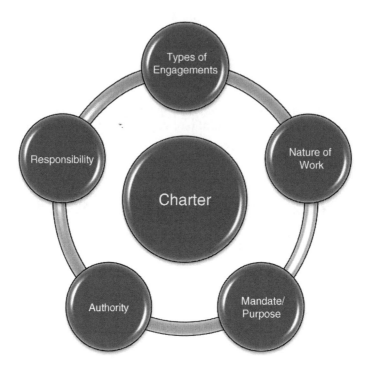

FIGURE 8.2 Internal Audit Charter

REVIEW OF THE CHARTER   The chief audit executive should review the charter at least annually to ensure that it continues to reflect internal audit practices and the needs and expectations of the organization.

Common Quality Issue

It is not uncommon for internal audit functions to have an incomplete, outdated, or missing charter. Other quality issues can include the following:

- Failure to have the audit committee or senior management approve the charter
- Inadequate engagement of senior management and the audit committee in determining the mandate or purpose of the internal audit function
- Lack of recognition of the IIA's definition of internal auditing in the charter

QAIP Hint

Internal audit functions could incorporate an *internal audit charter* into a balanced scorecard by including performance indicators such as:

- Annual review of the internal audit charter
- Compliance with internal audit charter as demonstrated through an internal or external quality assessment

Questions about the Quality of the Internal Audit Charter

Table 8.1 provides a range of questions about the quality of the internal audit charter. These can be formally incorporated into a quality assurance and improvement program, or, less formally, into ongoing assessment activities. Questions may be variously posed to the chief audit executive, internal auditors, or audit stakeholders.

TABLE 8.1 Quality Questions

Questions	Evidence of Quality
Is there an internal audit charter defining the purpose of the internal audit function?	Internal audit charter
Has the internal audit charter been approved by senior management and the audit committee?	Evidence of consultation and/or approval
Has the internal audit charter been reviewed and endorsed by the audit committee in the last 12 months?	Evidence of review and/or endorsement
Does the internal audit charter define the internal audit function's purpose?	Internal audit charter
Does the internal audit charter define the internal audit function's authority?	Internal audit charter
Does the internal audit charter define the internal audit function's responsibilities?	Internal audit charter
Does the internal audit charter recognize the mandatory nature of the IIA's Code of Ethics (if the IIA *Standards* are used)?	Internal audit charter
Does the internal audit charter recognize the mandatory nature of the definition of "internal audit" in the IIA's *Standards* (if the IIA *Standards* are used)?	Internal audit charter
Has the internal audit function documented any legislation, regulation, or policy that it is required to conform with?	Formal internal audit documentation
Does the internal audit charter establish the position of internal audit within the organization?	Internal audit charter
Does the internal audit charter or other formal document specify the nature of the chief audit executive's reporting relationship to the audit committee?	Internal audit charter Organization charts demonstrating the internal audit function's reporting lines
Does the chief audit executive report functionally to the audit committee?	Internal audit charter Organization charts demonstrating the internal audit function's reporting lines
Does the audit committee approve the appointment, removal, and remuneration of the chief audit executive?	Internal audit charter Audit committee interviews
Is the audit committee actively involved in the performance management of the chief audit executive?	Chief audit executive interview Audit committee interviews
Does the audit committee approve the internal audit budget, scope, and resource plan?	Internal audit charter Audit committee interviews Audit committee minutes

(continued)

TABLE 8.1 (*continued*)

Questions	Evidence of Quality
Does the chief audit executive attend audit committee meetings in person and interact directly with audit committee members?	Audit committee interviews
Does the chief audit executive have direct and unrestricted access to senior management and the audit committee?	Internal audit charter Organization charts demonstrating the internal audit function's reporting lines Chief audit executive interview Senior management and audit committee interviews
Does the audit committee contribute to setting the tone at the top by having its chair meet one-on-one at least quarterly with the chief audit executive?	Chief audit executive interview Senior management and audit committee interviews
Is the internal audit function structured to maintain independence and objectivity, while also allowing a close enough relationship with the business to build understanding and networks?	Chief audit executive interview Senior management and audit committee interviews
Does the organization perceive the internal audit function as being independent?	Senior management interviews
Does the audit committee perceive the internal audit function as being independent?	Audit committee interviews
Is the internal audit function considered to be a critical friend or an impartial observer?	Senior management and audit committee interviews
Is there any evidence that the internal audit function has been restricted in audit planning?	Senior management and audit committee interviews Unsupported changes to audit planning
Is there any evidence that the internal audit function has provided assurance over activities for which the chief audit executive is responsible?	Record of engagements undertaken
Does the chief audit executive have a process for obtaining external assurance over activities for which he or she is responsible?	Documented process (possibly in the internal audit charter) Chief audit executive interview
Does the internal audit charter authorize access to records, physical property, and personnel relevant to the performance of engagements?	Internal audit charter
Is the internal audit function involved in key organizational committees, either as an active participant or as an observer?	Committee participant lists Committee minutes Senior management and audit committee interviews
Do senior managers actively encourage internal audit involvement in key organizational committees?	Senior management interviews Chief audit executive interview
Are internal auditors' opinions heard and valued?	Senior management and audit committee interviews Chief audit executive and internal audit staff interviews
Do senior management and the audit committee regularly seek the chief audit executive's perspective on trends in risk and control issues?	Senior management and audit committee interviews Chief audit executive interview

Conclusion

An effective internal audit function has a clear mandate and purpose. It operates independently of management and undertakes its activities in an objective manner. The internal audit function's authority should be explicitly articulated in an internal audit charter as well as being implicitly promoted through the actions and behaviors of senior management and the audit committee.

References

Australian National Audit Office. (2011). *Public Sector Audit Committees: Independent Assurance and Advice for Chief Executives and Boards—Better Practice Guide.* http://www.anao.gov.au/Publications/Better-Practice-Guides/2011-2012/Public-Sector-Audit-Committees.

Baker, N. (2011). A stronger partnership. *Internal Auditor.* http://www.theiia.org/intauditor.

Burch, S. (2011). Building an internal audit function. *Internal Auditor.* http://www.theiia.org/intauditor.

Canadian Federal Accountability Act. 2006. http://laws-lois.justice.gc.ca/eng/acts/F-5.5/page-1.html.

Cathcart, R., and G. Kapor. (2010). An internal audit upgrade. *Internal Auditor.* http://www.theiia.org/intauditor.

Galloway, D. (2010). *Internal Auditing: A Guide for the New Auditor.* Altamonte Springs, FL: The Institute of Internal Auditors Research Foundation.

Holt, J. E. (2012). A high-performing audit function. *Internal Auditor.* http://www.theiia.org/intauditor.

The Institute of Internal Auditors. (2013). *International Professional Practices Framework.* Altamonte Springs, FL: The Institute of Internal Auditors.

The Institute of Internal Auditors. (2009). *Model Internal Audit Activity Charter.* unpublished.

Ratliff, R. L., W. A. Wallace, G. E. Sumners, W. G. McFarland, and H. Nieuwlands. (2006). *Sustainability and Internal Auditing.* Altamonte Springs, FL: Institute of Internal Auditors Research Foundation.

Reding, K. F., et al. (2009). *Internal Auditing: Assurance and Consulting Services.* Altamonte Springs, FL: The Institute of Internal Auditors Research Foundation.

Rezaee, Z. (2010). The importance of audit opinions. *Internal Auditor.* http://www.theiia.org/intauditor.

Sawyer, L. B., M. A. Dittenhofer, and J. H. Scheiner. (2005). *Sawyers Internal Auditing,* 5th ed. Altamonte Springs, FL: The Institute of Internal Auditors Research Foundation.

Spencer Pickett, K. H. (2012). *The Essential Guide to Internal Auditing,* 2nd ed. West Sussex, England: John Wiley & Sons.

Tarling, P. (2012, August). Say it right. *Internal Auditor.* http://www.theiia.org/intauditor.

PART IV

Internal Audit Staffing

CHAPTER 9

Internal Audit Staffing

The best executive is the one who has sense enough to pick good men to do what he wants done, and self-restraint to keep from meddling with them while they do it.

—Theodore Roosevelt

Internal auditing is essentially a knowledge-based activity. It is highly reliant on quality internal auditors to produce quality outcomes. Appropriate staffing of the internal audit function is therefore critical.

Effective people management requires a considered approach to resourcing as well as ongoing performance management. Key elements of resourcing will include capability planning, recruitment and retention processes, and consideration of the service delivery model. These elements will be discussed in depth in this chapter. Performance management, including performance and development processes at both the team and individual level, is discussed further in Chapter 10.

Capability planning requires identification of current capabilities and consideration of those that will be needed into the future. Professional activities like internal auditing will have both proficiency and competency elements to capability planning. The specific skills and expertise required for high-value engagements need to be identified and addressed.

In addition to technical competencies, effective internal auditors require a range of characteristics and attributes that allow them to work productively and collaboratively across an organization. An effective team will have a range of personality types, and chief audit executives will need to determine how to best achieve this balance.

Chief audit executives must determine which service delivery model would best meet the needs of their organization. Some may choose to adopt a fully insourced model. Others may select a fully outsourced model, or a co-sourced model, which includes a combination of both in-house staff and service providers. Depending on the model selected, recruitment and procurement processes will play varying roles in ensuring the internal audit function has access to an appropriate pool of suitably qualified and experienced internal auditors.

Overview of the Staffing Element

Internal audit staffing is the second of three key sets of inputs to a quality internal audit function, the other elements being *strategy* and *professional practices*. The specific elements in internal audit staffing are shown in Figure 9.1.

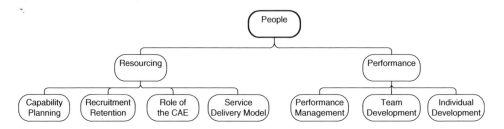

FIGURE 9.1 **Staffing Elements**

Committed and Strategic Staff

Constance Ng-Yip Chew Ngoh, Chief Audit Executive at a statutory board in Singapore, believes that internal auditors need to be strategic and have the conviction of what they say—they cannot feign the commitment, passion, or belief that is required to operate effectively.

The importance of good staff and good leadership for internal audit functions has been recognized for some time. In 2005, the Auditor General of Alberta in Canada stated:

> *Successful internal audit departments are led by well-trained business orientated internal audit professionals who understand the need to focus on key risks of the organization. These professionals determine and guide the entire internal audit department with respect to direction, focus, and internal audit processes. Internal audit professionals may not come with traditional internal audit backgrounds.*

Key considerations in effectively staffing an internal audit function are the sourcing model to be used, recruitment practices, staff capacity and capability, and the financial resources available. Additional elements include job design and retention practices.

Capability Planning for the Internal Audit Workforce

Effective chief audit executives optimize the mix of skills, experience, and personalities within the internal audit function. They strategically plan for the capabilities the team needs both now and into the future. This process is shown in Figure 9.2.

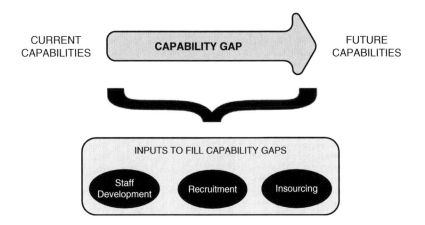

FIGURE 9.2 Capability Planning

Capability planning looks to maximize the skills and experience of the internal audit function as a collective, rather than focusing on individual positions or people. Effective capability planning will ensure a close link between the internal audit strategy and staffing practices. Strategic and resource planning activities actively consider questions related to future capabilities and whether a develop or acquire strategy is best suited to meeting these needs.

While recruiting talent is important in creating a quality internal audit function, it does not in itself guarantee success. Chief audit executives also need to develop a structure in which staff can work effectively, people are developed and supported, and additional skills can be insourced as required. These issues are discussed further in Chapter 10.

Chief audit executives should be mindful of their team as a whole in considering appropriate staffing structures and in recruitment processes. Team composition should take into account personalities as well as skills. Cole (2010) suggests that the most effective teams have a mix of:

- Dominant directors—these people set the pace for the group and tend to drive it along.
- Conscientious thinkers—these are the detail people; they produce accurate information, carefully check things, dot the *i*'s, and cross the *t*'s.
- Interacting socializers—these people provide the energy, enthusiasm, and fun for the group.
- Steady relaters—these are the patient, willing, cooperative, and reliable team members.

For insourced and co-sourced internal audit functions, determining an appropriate staffing strategy and undertaking effective workforce planning help ensure that the function will have staff members with appropriate skills and experience, who are able to work together in a supportive team.

Holt (2012) recognizes that effective chief audit executives must have the vision for medium- and long-term staffing strategies that stay ahead of growth areas and on top of new and emerging risks, while also fostering an environment to attract talent.

Maximizing Value through Staff Resources

Tan Peck Leng, Head of Internal Audit at Defence Science and Technology Agency in Singapore, believes chief audit executives are likely to maximize the value of internal audit through effectively managing staff resources. She argues that it is critical to have staff members who really want to be there—that internal auditors need to be passionate about their role. She considers the ideal internal auditor to be highly strategic, with excellent interpersonal communication skills and an ability to interact well with people.

Many organizations will choose to employ in-house resources to undertake internal audit engagements. In these circumstances, it is imperative that the chief audit executive has in place a planned approach for engaging these resources, and an understanding of the specific skills required to deliver different outputs and outcomes.

Proficiency and Competency

The internal audit function should collectively possess the knowledge and skills both essential for the delivery of engagements and specific to the needs of their organization. This will require clear understanding of the organization's expectations of internal audit and the types of engagements to be delivered. Although there will be times when a specific set of skills or experience may be required for an engagement that lies beyond those available to the internal audit function, having in place effective planning will help the chief audit executive to determine what sourcing model will best fit the organization.

Utilizing a structured approach to capability planning helps ensure that internal auditors demonstrate proficiency and due professional care in their work in accordance with IIA Standard 1200.

Standard 1200—Proficiency and Due Professional Care

Engagements must be performed with proficiency and due professional care.

This proficiency requirement is identified in IIA Standard 1210.

Standard 1210—Proficiency

Internal auditors must possess the knowledge, skills, and other competencies needed to perform their individual responsibilities. The internal audit activity collectively must possess or obtain the knowledge, skills, and other competencies needed to perform its responsibilities.

Staff should have professional proficiency, including a comprehensive understanding of internal auditing. This can be obtained both on the job and through formal training. Ideally, professional proficiency should be consolidated through attainment of specific professional certifications or qualifications such as the IIA's Certified Internal Auditor, ISACA's Certified Information System Auditor, IIA-Australia's Graduate Certificate in Internal Auditing, or the Chartered Institute of Internal Auditors' (IIA-UK's) IIA Diploma and IIA Advanced Diploma.

Internal audit functions should also collectively have sufficient knowledge to be able to understand events or activities occurring within the organization without extensive recourse to technical research and assistance. This may require an appreciation of the fundamentals of subjects such as accounting, public administration, law, finance, and information technology as well as more detailed knowledge of disciplines specific to the organization. To this end, staff would normally have either a formal qualification in a generalist field (such as accounting, liberal arts, or law) or specific qualifications relevant to the nature of the organization (such as engineering, public policy, health sciences, or environmental sciences).

Both the IIA and IIA-Australia have identified the core competencies required for internal auditors. The IIA has established a competency framework consisting of 10 core competencies:

1. Professional ethics: Promotes and applies professional ethics
2. Internal audit management: Develops and manages the internal audit function
3. IPPF: Applies the *International Professional Practices Framework (IPPF)*
4. Governance, risk, and control: Applies a thorough understanding of governance, risk, and control appropriate to the organization
5. Business acumen: Maintains expertise of the business environment, industry practices, and specific organizational factors
6. Communication: Communicates with impact
7. Persuasion and collaboration: Persuades and motivates others through collaboration and cooperation
8. Critical thinking: Applies process analysis, business intelligence, and problem-solving techniques
9. Internal audit delivery: Delivers internal audit engagements
10. Improvement and innovation: Embraces change and drives improvement and innovation

Often competency frameworks are related back to the different roles within a team. For an internal audit function, this could be graduate internal auditors, senior internal auditors, audit managers, and the chief audit executive. The specific competencies required at each level are identified, assisting management to recruit against specific competencies and highlighting for staff members any development needs they may have to progress within the organization.

Developing a Competency Framework

Develop a skills and competency framework based on key competencies such as leadership, management, interpersonal skills, knowledge areas, and internal audit standards to target training effort and enhance staff capability.

Job Designs

Chief audit executives should ensure that in-house internal auditor jobs are designed in a way that optimizes value delivery. Job designs will vary between internal audit functions, with larger functions generally supporting more specialized jobs and smaller functions requiring internal auditors able to perform a variety of tasks.

Developing effectively designed jobs requires the chief audit executive to examine what the position involves, the specific skills required, the level of experience required, and what sort of person would likely be the best fit for the position and for the internal audit function.

CLEARLY ARTICULATED ROLES AND RESPONSIBILITIES   Chief audit executives should ensure that internal audit staff have clearly articulated roles and responsibilities. Doing so promotes increased accountability among staff members and can support greater empowerment.

Account Executives/Client Liaisons

Chief audit executives sometimes formally identify senior internal audit staff as *account executives* or *client liaisons,* with responsibility for specific areas of the organization. This has a number of positive outcomes:

- Allowing the internal auditor and/or internal audit team to develop a greater knowledge and understanding of a particular organizational area
- Providing a single point of contact for the area with the internal audit function
- Supporting greater responsiveness to client needs

The account executive approach is often formally supported through an accountability framework that articulates the roles and responsibilities for individual staff and their level of authority.

DELEGATION   Delegating tasks allows for greater use of resources, as well as providing for individual and team development. Chief audit executives need to decide what activities should be delegated and should recognize the capability, experience, and development needs of the team in deciding to whom to delegate tasks. Murdock (2011) provides the following advice when choosing to delegate activities:

- Allocate time to explain the tasks.
- Provide people with training to undertake the tasks.
- Establish clear accountability standards when delegating.
- Provide feedback on the delegated tasks without micromanaging, and be available to provide support.
- Get feedback on the delegation process.

QUALIFICATIONS VERSUS EXPERIENCE   While not strictly necessary, employing staff with professional qualifications reinforces the professional status of internal audit. However, it is important that internal audit staff members also have, or gain, a good understanding of operational processes. Employing some professional staff from fields other than accounting and finance, and supporting them to obtain relevant internal audit knowledge, will add to the credibility of the internal audit function. This can help promote a culture among the internal audit team of thinking about operations in terms of what should go right rather than what could go wrong.

Creative and Innovative Staff

Many organizations have traditionally recruited internal audit staff from within the internal audit or accounting professions. However, this approach to recruitment has started to change.

More organizations are looking for internal audit staff with operational experience specific to the nature of their organization. This could include engineers in resource companies and medical professionals in the health care industry. Increasing numbers of chief audit executives consider it critical to have staff that can adapt to change, and who are creative and innovative. While they value professional certifications, they recognize that these don't always guarantee success as an internal auditor.

Larger internal audit functions will require a variety of staff with differing skills and experience. As the seniority of the staff increases, their required experience will also increase. However, this experience need not be restricted to internal auditing—some highly effective chief audit executives have broad management and organizational experience, rather than being career internal auditors. Staff will tend to move from requiring a reasonably high level of technical competence to requiring higher-level communication and strategic skills.

Personal Qualities

The personal qualities and attributes required from internal auditors continue to evolve as the nature of internal auditing changes. There is increasing demand on internal auditors possessing excellent interpersonal and communication skills while retaining their analytical and conceptual abilities. Chief audit executives face the challenge of deciding which qualities and attributes they require in new recruits and which of these they can develop.

CHARACTERISTICS OF EFFECTIVE INTERNAL AUDITORS   Effective internal auditors demonstrate a range of characteristics, including:

- The ability to align internal audit engagements to the strategy and risks of the organization

- Strong interpersonal skills, including an ability to build and maintain strategic relationships
- Performance-focused service delivery capabilities, including consistency in approach and delivery
- Highly developed people management skills, including the ability to build and develop a quality internal audit team
- The ability to juggle multiple priorities
- A high level of technical competence
- Good understanding of the business of the organization

Identifying the Great Internal Auditor

Bob McDonald, OAM, Chief Governance Officer at the Queensland Department of Health in Australia, believes that some people have an innate ability to be an internal auditor but that it is very, very difficult to identify this quality in people. He also challenges that this innate ability cannot be taught. He considers the key qualities and attributes for internal auditors to be the ability to communicate verbally and in writing and, most important, excellent listening skills.

McDonald sees a common fault of chief audit executives as only looking for internal auditors from the finance profession. He believes that great internal auditors will understand that they don't have all the answers themselves and will look to the client to help identify issues and find solutions. Going through this process often means they then start resolving the problem before the process is finished.

McDonald offers the following tips for chief audit executives:

- Staff the internal audit function with both operational managers and traditional internal auditors to provide a good blend of internal audit and business skills.
- Staff the internal audit function with a blend of experienced and junior staff in accordance with the size of the function (small internal audit functions may require staff with a minimum level of experience).
- Engage internal audit staff with operational experience relevant to the organization.

USING THE CAPABILITY PLAN TO DRIVE STAFF DEVELOPMENT The capability plan provides a valuable resource for supporting individual and team development. Having determined the capabilities required across the internal audit function, chief audit executives can then assess the skills and experience of individual staff against those articulated in the capability plan. The chief audit executive can work with individuals to determine how capability gaps will be addressed, or whether the internal auditor is, in fact, an appropriate fit for the emerging needs of the organization.

The Value of Variety

Having internal auditors with homogenous backgrounds can make it easier to induct them into internal auditing processes. However, the value of having people with various backgrounds can often outweigh the challenges this brings, as it leads to a richer workforce. Although training people without accounting or financial backgrounds in internal auditing practices can present increased challenges, this is often balanced by their analytical skills and ability to produce high-quality reports.

QAIP Hint

The internal audit function could incorporate *capability planning* into an internal audit maturity model or a balanced scorecard.

Maturity Model

Internal audit functions could include *capability planning* as a key process area in its maturity model. For example, level 4 could identify that the internal audit function has in place a capability plan that identifies the skills and experience required by the internal audit function, and recruitment and development are tied to the capability plan.

Balanced Scorecard/KPI

Internal audit functions could include performance indicators such as:

- Capability plan reviewed on an annual basis
- Proportion of capabilities identified within the plan met by current staff (include target)
- Number of internal auditors per 1,000 staff average, compared to sector average
- Number of internal auditors as a percentage of total corporate staff (include target)
- Average years of staff experience (include target)
- Number of years of internal audit experience (include target)
- Number of years in area of current audit (include target)
- Proportion of internal auditors with degree and postgraduate qualifications (include target)
- Number of professional certifications/percentage of staff certified (include target)
- Absenteeism rates (include target)
- Level of internal audit staff turnover (include target)
- Number of new hires versus total number of staff on audit team (include target)
- Levels of internal audit staff satisfaction (include target)
- Levels of internal audit staff grievances (include target)

Flexible Work Practices

Providing flexible work practices can help to attract and retain quality staff. It can also support diversity in the workplace and enhance staff morale. Flexibility promotes organizations as an employer of choice, fostering loyalty and reducing absenteeism. The need for, and approach to, flexibility will be determined by each organization and its particular employee needs. These needs may change over time, based on both team and individual requirements.

Some jurisdictions have a legislative requirement to offer employees flexible work practices to avoid indirect discrimination arising from factors such as gender and family responsibilities. The State of Victoria, in Australia, has an *Equal Opportunity Act* (2010) that provides that indirect discrimination occurs if a person imposes, or proposes to impose, a requirement, condition, or practice:

- That has, or is likely to have, the effect of disadvantaging persons with an attribute; and
- That is not reasonable.

Women with family responsibilities and disabled people have successfully argued that, under this legislation, they should be entitled to flexible work arrangements.

The provision of flexible work arrangements is best supported by a formalized policy to ensure that all staff members are treated consistently and transparently. The policy should take into account any legislative requirements or industrial arrangements that may impact the provision of flexible arrangements.

Attracting Staff through Flexible Working Arrangements

Goh Thong, Chief Internal Auditor at SPRING Singapore, is an advocate of flexible working arrangements. While he acknowledges that there are some issues with having part-time staff, he believes these issues are balanced by attracting high-quality people who may not otherwise be interested in a particular position. From his staff, he is primarily looking for good communicators with high integrity, an ability to view things from a different perspective, and an ability to analyze issues holistically. He concedes that it is difficult to find people with these skills, and especially to attract people to the public sector with the remuneration offered, but flexible working arrangements make the positions more attractive.

Flexible work practices that chief audit executives could consider include:

- Flexible working hours, including flexible start and finish times
- Part-time work
- Job sharing
- Home-based work or telework to attract people otherwise unable to be employed, such as people with disabilities or those living in rural or regional areas
- Flexible leave arrangements, including both paid and unpaid leave to cover medical and family commitments

---

The key to providing appropriate flexibility is through ongoing negotiations with staff, including those for whom flexible arrangements are offered as well as other staff that may be impacted by these arrangements. Discussions will need to occur regarding:

- Health and safety issues associated with home-based or telework
- Communication processes for staff working outside the corporate office

- Supervision processes for staff working outside the corporate office
- Attendance at staff meetings and other activities set for a specific time or venue
- Information management processes, including the need to file information on a central repository as soon as possible, adoption of adequate version control practices, and maintenance of data security
- The time period for the flexible arrangements and whether there is to be a trial period and/or whether the arrangements will cease at a particular point
- A process for reviewing the arrangements to determine whether it is mutually beneficial for all parties

QAIP Hint

Internal audit functions could incorporate *flexible work practices* into an internal audit maturity model or a balanced scorecard.

Maturity Model

Internal audit functions could include *flexible work practices* as a key process area in its maturity model. For example:

- Level 2 of a five-stage maturity model could identify that flexible work practices are not provided.
- Level 3 could identify that flexible work practices are provided on an individual basis.
- Level 4 could identify that flexible work practices are provided and utilized by staff and are supported by a formal policy.

Balanced Scorecard/KPI

Internal audit functions could include performance indicators such as:

- Existence and annual update of a flexible work policy
- Flexible work practices offered to all staff
- Proportion of staff utilizing flexible work practices (include target)

Recruitment and Retention

Implementing effective recruitment processes gives an internal audit function a competitive advantage. Chief audit executives are more likely to recruit *star performers* to their team when processes support effective recruitment and selection, and candidates are attracted to the position. Once recruited, however, the chief audit executive needs to ensure that staff are appropriately inducted and retained.

Recruitment Processes

Recruitment and selection of internal audit staff is a critical element in the ultimate deliverables of quality outputs and outcomes, and staffing is a key input to the internal audit function.

Various recruitment and selection techniques are available to the chief audit executive. Louw (2013) contends that "the decision to use recruitment and selection methods differ from country to country and region to region. Such decisions are dictated by labour legislation and the source of recruitment that may be available from within or outside the organisation." To this end, recruitment within internal audit functions will vary between organizations and jurisdictions. Ultimately, however, the aim is to maximize the pool of potential candidates from which to select a suitable person.

Initial steps in the recruitment process will include verifying the vacancy and writing a job description. These should be aligned with the capability plan to the extent that the need for the internal recruitment is justified in accordance with the longer-term sourcing model for the internal audit function, and the job description addresses the competencies required for immediate effect and longer-term planning. Having completed these tasks, the chief audit executive should instigate a process to produce a pool of candidates.

Suitable candidates can be generated through various methods, including:

- Personal contacts and networking (including social networking)
- Newspaper advertising
- Internet-based recruitment websites
- Social media
- Job postings on organizational recruitment pages
- Careers fairs/expos
- Direct contact of potential candidates by recruitment firms

Selection processes are designed to choose the best possible candidate from the pool available. According to Louw (2013) this will involve two aspects—the extent to which the job provides rewards that meet the candidate's needs and the extent to which the applicant's skills, abilities, and experience meet the needs of the employer. Selection processes will generally include at least some of the following:

- Formal written applications
- Interviews
- Ability and aptitude testing
- Psychometric testing
- Medical testing
- Reference checking

CULTURAL CONSIDERATIONS IN RECRUITMENT PROCESSES Recruiting in a cross-culturally appropriate manner is not always easy. Falconer (2008), in discussing recruitment in New Zealand, warns, "It's curious how something 'normal' in one culture is considered offensive in another. Recruitment and selection processes are no exception."

Falconer cautions that candidates who appear overly deferential in some cultures are simply polite in others. Societal expectations in particular countries may encourage candidates to focus extensively on educational attainment, whereas in other countries candidates would focus on skills and experience. Some candidates may make religious references in their application—for example, "I pray to God that you'll consider my application"—that are uncommon across all cultures. And some cultures will require the inclusion of personal information in applications, such as age and marital status, which are not commonly acccpted, or even legislatively permissible, in others.

Taking into account these cultural differences during the recruitment and selection process will ensure that quality candidates are not inadvertently overlooked.

INDUCTION Optimizing staff induction, or onboarding, reduces the time required for staff to become conversant with organizational practices and supports staff morale. Moreover, it sets the tone for the new recruit's attitude and approach to internal auditing, as the induction program should be centered on the internal audit strategy.

An effective induction program recognizes that staff members will not always be recruited with the full set of competencies demanded of a position. Some chief audit executives will recruit based on attitude and attributes over and above technical competencies, knowing that it is often easier to teach technical skills than change someone's personality. To this end, these technical gaps will need to be acknowledged, and appropriate training provided through the induction process to meet these requirements.

Some internal audit functions will assign buddies or mentors to new recruits. This can often assist the new recruit to feel engaged; however, care should be taken in selecting mentors to ensure that they induct the recruit in accordance with the internal audit strategy and values.

Retention and Separation Strategies

Retaining talented staff is critical to the long-term success of the internal audit function. Losing staff can involve significant costs to the organization, including:

- Costs associated with the administration of the resignation and recruitment processes
- Any payouts associated with early contract terminations
- Direct costs associated with the recruitment and selection, including advertising, travel, and testing
- Costs associated with temporary staffing
- Costs associated with induction and training
- Productivity losses during the early employment period

While recognizing the cost of recruitment, chief audit executives need to find the balance between excessive and inadequate staff turnover. There are times that having a staff member in a position for too long is as damaging as having them for too short a period. Similarly, the expectations of the internal audit function may change over time, resulting in some staff not having the competencies to meet these new demands.

Exit Interviews

Undertake exit interviews with departing staff members to determine whether there is a need for increased flexibility in the workplace and/or whether current practices are considered fair and reasonable.

Succession Planning

Good management requires consideration of both current and future staffing requirements. Larger internal audit functions have the advantage over smaller activities of
enabling a structure that provides staff with the opportunity to develop in different
areas, including supervisory and management skills. When combined with appropriate, formal professional development, staff members are then well positioned to take
on higher-level roles when these become available. This succession planning can be
further supported by secondment and rotation policies.

Reducing Staff Turnover

Karen Chia, Director (Audit) at the Agency for Science, Technology, and Research
in Singapore, recommends trying to reduce staff turnover to ensure the retention
of corporate knowledge and to avoid continually training new staff. She sees this
as ultimately improving audit quality and the value offering to the organization.

Elements that could be considered in reducing staff turnover and increasing
retention include the following:

- Considering the appropriateness of management styles and whether these
  meet the needs of the workforce. This can be particularly important if there
  are age, gender, ethnicity, or educational differences between management
  and the workforce.
- Examining communication styles. Consider whether these support open and
  shared communication between management and staff.
- Remuneration and reward processes that recognize the individual contributions of staff.
- Appropriate job design and allocation. Allocate roles and responsibilities
  commensurate with staff skills and experience.
- Professional development and mentoring.

Secondment and Rotation Policies

Effective secondment and rotation practices can dramatically increase the collective pool
of skills and experience within the internal audit function. Transferring staff from the
organization into internal audit provides these people with a greater appreciation of the
role of the internal auditor, while also allowing them to share their operational experience
with the internal audit team. Likewise, internal auditors seconded to other parts of the
organization can act as ambassadors for the internal audit function, while gaining a depth
of experience in operations that they would not be privy to within internal audit.

The chief audit executive may choose to use guest auditors for some audit
engagements. These people provide specific operational expertise, and are usually
partnered with an internal auditor who can provide technical auditing expertise.

When using secondment, rotations, or guest auditors, chief audit executives should
be mindful of the potential for conflicts of interest. These should be actively managed to
ensure that the integrity of the internal audit function is maintained.

Guest Auditors

Utilize guest auditors from other parts of the organization. In doing so:

- Ensure they are independent from the area being audited.
- Require them to sign confidentiality agreements.
- Provide an adequate induction to the internal audit function.
- Support them to utilize the internal audit methodology.

QAIP Hint

Internal audit functions could incorporate *recruitment and retention* into an internal audit maturity model or a balanced scorecard.

Maturity Model

Internal audit functions could include *recruitment and retention* as a key process area in its maturity model. For example:

- Level 2 of a five-stage maturity model could identify that recruitment and retention processes are informal or ad hoc.
- Level 3 could identify that recruitment and retention processes have been formalized in internal audit or organization policies.
- Level 4 could include that recruitment and retention processes are aligned to capability planning.
- Level 5 could include the use of guest auditors, secondment, and rotations.

Balanced Scorecard/KPI

Internal audit functions could include performance indicators such as:

- Candidate satisfaction with recruitment and/or induction processes (include target)
- Time taken to successfully recruit to fill a vacant position (include target)
- Cost of recruitment/cost per hire (include target)
- Completion of induction by all new recruits
- Number of times guest auditors utilized on engagements (include target)
- Number of internal audit staff seconded to other parts of the organization (include target)
- Number of staff rotated into internal audit (include target)

Service Delivery Models

Given that internal audit functions can range from a single internal auditor working in one location to many hundreds (or even thousands) of internal auditors working around the globe, the sourcing models available are similarly diverse.

At the highest level, internal audit functions can be insourced, co-sourced, or outsourced. Insourced activities are permanent in-house functions that may be fully staffed by permanent, full-time employees or may include part-time, casual, or contract staff. A co-sourced activity has a combination of in-house staff and outsourced providers. This can include outsourcing to various providers for individual engagements, depending on the requirements of each audit, or working with a single outsourced provider. Fully outsourced activities usually involve a single outsourced provider, but may include different providers for different types of audits.

As described in Chapter 6, Burch (2011) identifies a number of considerations for chief audit executives when selecting an appropriate sourcing model, including the size of the organization, complexity of operations, requirements for a specialized skill set, and global reach.

Some internal audit functions in selected jurisdiction will be required to adopt a particular sourcing model based on their regulatory environment. For example, banks within a number of jurisdictions are required to utilize an in-house model.

There are advantages and disadvantages associated with each of the sourcing models. These are described in Table 9.1.

Outsourcing and co-sourcing provide organizations with access to internal audit resources without the associated effort of recruiting staff. They also provide for the delivery of internal audit services in organizations where it may not be feasible or economical to engage in-house resources.

Procuring external skills allows the organization to target its resources appropriately, and fulfill its requirements under its capability planning. This is reflected in IIA Standard 1210.A1.

Standards 1210.A1

The chief audit executive must obtain competent advice and assistance if the internal auditors lack the knowledge, skills, or other competencies needed to perform all or part of the engagement.

Procurement Processes and Contract Management

Organizations should engage and manage internal audit service providers in the same manner that they would undertake other procurement and contractual processes. Undertaking a formal procurement process ensures fairness, transparency, and value for money, and avoids any perceptions of nepotism. Effective contract management provides assurance regarding the delivery of a quality internal audit engagement. Figure 9.3 outlines a typical procurement/contract management process.

DETERMINING RESOURCING NEEDS The chief audit executive should consider the resourcing model for internal audit as part of the strategic planning and capability planning processes. They should have an understanding of the scope of services required before going to the market. A preliminary consideration should be the relative risks and benefits of procuring internal audit services, rather than employing internal auditors.

The costs, benefits, and risks associated with an in-house function should be weighed against those associated with engaging external service providers. A key risk

TABLE 9.1 Advantages and Disadvantages of Sourcing Models

Model	Advantage	Disadvantage
Insourced	Familiarity with senior executives and operational management Understanding of strategy and operations Process consistency Increased control Training consistency Knowledge transfer—corporate knowledge Enhanced succession planning	Isolation from business Travel time associated with visiting sites Reduced responsiveness to operational management Cultural isolation (language or culture barriers)
Outsourced	Specialization and access to leading practices Flexible resource allocation—coverage of peak workloads International coverage—potential travel efficiencies Potential for increased cultural responsiveness with use of local providers	Cannot outsource role of CAE—ownership of QAIP Reduced familiarity with senior executives and operational management Reduced understanding of strategy and operations Potential for process inconsistency Reduced control Potential for increased cost Inconsistent training Reduced responsiveness to senior executives Reduced succession planning Impairments to independence with other consulting activities
Co-sourced	Familiarity with senior executives and operational management Understanding of strategy and operations Specialization and access to leading practices Flexible resource allocation—coverage of peak workloads International coverage—potential travel efficiencies Potential for increased cultural responsiveness with use of local providers Knowledge transfer—corporate knowledge	Reduced familiarity with senior executives and operational management Reduced understanding of strategy and operations Potential for process inconsistency Reduced control

that should be considered in this stage includes the failure to obtain senior management and/or audit committee support for the preferred model.

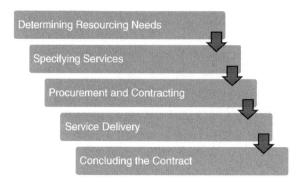

FIGURE 9.3 **Typical Contract Management Processes**

SPECIFYING SERVICES   The procurement of internal audit services may range from a single engagement (usually for co-sourced arrangements) to an entire multiyear program of services (usually for a single provider, fully outsourced arrangement). These variations are shown in Figure 9.4.

The chief audit executive should determine whether to procure an entire suite of internal audit services from a single provider or multiple providers, whether to preselect service providers for a panel arrangement, or whether to procure individual engagements separately.

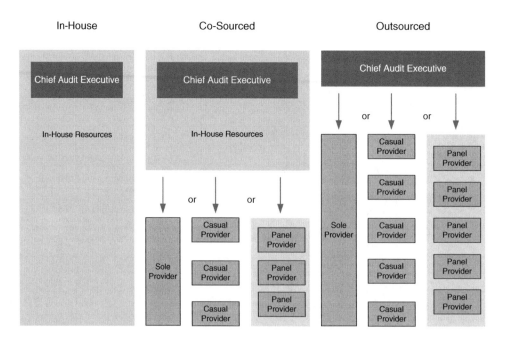

FIGURE 9.4 **Sourcing Models**

Risks that should be considered in this stage include the failure to obtain senior management and/or audit committee approval for individual procurement activities and allocating insufficient time to complete procurement tasks.

Choosing the Right Number of Co-Sourced Providers

Co-sourcing provides a range of benefits to chief audit executives. It ensures the retention of some skills and experience in-house, while also allowing for the procurement of special skills that may not be required on a full-time basis. Co-sourcing can support the resourcing of internal audit functions that have experienced unexpected staff turnover, and can provide additional resources during high-demand periods. Nonetheless, the chief audit executive, in consultation with the audit committee, should predetermine the number of co-sourced providers that will be used.

PROCUREMENT AND CONTRACTING Chief audit executives should establish transparent procurement processes and develop formal contracts for the engagement of service providers. They should consider the costs and benefits of a fully open and actively marketed procurement process against a selective tendering process.

Formal contracts with external providers will generally specify the nature of the engagement(s) or service(s) to be delivered, including milestones and deliverables. The need to conform to professional standards, such as the IIA *Standards*, should be included as a contractual requirement, and appropriate performance measurements should be agreed as part of the contract.

Effective contract performance measurements will allow the chief audit executive to assess performance over the life of the contract—whether it is for a single engagement or a collection of services over a number of years. The performance indicators should specify the area and frequency of measurement as well as the indicators or targets that will be used. The chief audit executive may need to revisit these measures for an extended contract.

HM Treasury (2011) recommends that contracts with service providers make clear that any information they collect or generate as part of any review undertaken is the property of the organization that appointed them. The contract should ensure that the information is fully accessible, handed over at an appropriately agreed point, and retained in accordance with information management policies. Similarly, any papers generated by the audit process must be made available for quality review purposes.

Table 9.2 identifies a number of standard contract provisions recommended by the Australian National Audit Office. Although initially developed in relation to public-sector contracts, the elements could be similarly applied to contracts with external service providers.

Risks that should be considered in the procurement and contracting stage include:

- Inability to attract suitable service providers to participate in the procurement process
- Inability to obtain, or retain, resources through the selected model
- Failure to obtain approval for selected service provider(s)
- Service deliverables described in vague or ambiguous terms
- Failure to specify service standards

- Failure to establish cost-effective performance monitoring
- Failure to link payment to effective delivery
- Failure to cap contract expenditure

TABLE 9.2 Common Contract Provisions

Access and disclosure	Key personnel
Assistance provided to the contractor	Liabilities and indemnities
Confidential information	Payments
Conflict of interest	Penalties and incentives
Contract variations	Securities and guarantees
Disclosure of information (confidentiality)	Subcontracting
Dispute resolution	Termination and contract end dates
Insurance	Transition arrangements
Intellectual property rights	Warranties and fitness for purpose

Source: Australian National Audit Office (2012).

Working Papers and Professional Standards

Contracts with internal audit service providers should specify that the internal audit function will retain ownership of any engagements' working papers. This will ensure the chief audit executive has access to working papers as required for quality purposes.

In addition, contracts should specify service providers conform with IIA *Standards*.

SERVICE DELIVERY   The chief audit executive is responsible for the effective delivery of internal audit services regardless of the sourcing model used. This will include providing an effective induction for in-house and outsourced internal auditors and developing an quality assessment process (these are discussed further later in the chapter).

In accordance with IIA Standard 2201.A1, the chief audit executive should ensure that outsourced providers are provided with a written understanding regarding the engagement and their responsibilities.

Standard 2201.A1

When planning an engagement for parties outside the organization, internal auditors must establish a written understanding with them about objectives, scope, respective responsibilities, and other expectations, including restrictions on distribution of the results of the engagement and access to engagement records.

Risks that should be considered in the service delivery stage include:

- Failure to provide adequate induction into organizational procedures and activities
- Lack of clarity in respective roles of the outsourced provider and the chief audit executive

- Failure to monitor service standards and performance measures
- Failure to link payment to effective delivery

CONCLUDING THE CONTRACT In general, the outsourced provider's contract will conclude when an engagement is completed or when the duration of the contract is achieved. However, there may also be times that a contract needs to be terminated due to poor performance or other unforeseen circumstances. In these cases, the chief audit executive should seek appropriate legal advice as to the implication of an early termination.

Risks that should be considered in this stage include:

- Extension of existing contract without determining value for money
- Inadequate time to effectively transition to new outsourced provider
- Failure to provide working papers or other material within the agreed time frame
- Disruption to the provision of ongoing services
- Early termination, leading to litigation by the service provider

ENSURING THE QUALITY OF A FULLY OUTSOURCED INTERNAL AUDIT FUNCTION There are challenges associated with measuring the quality of fully outsourced internal audit functions, as responsibility for activities is shared between both the organization and the provider. However, regardless of the sourcing model used for internal audit, the organization itself retains overall responsibility for delivering effective internal audit services. In other words, the organization cannot outsource the role of chief audit executive. Even with a fully outsourced function, the organization must nominate one of its people to undertake the responsibilities of chief audit executive. Whether this role will require a dedicated officer, or the role is but one of a number of responsibilities the officer has, will depend on the size and nature of the organization.

Advantages of Co-Sourcing and Outsourcing

Research by Desai and colleagues (2008) found that co-sourcing and outsourcing arrangements for internal audit were rated as significantly more objective, competent, skillful, and independent (measured by assessed risk and likelihood of acquiescing to management) than in-house arrangements. However, they also found that there has been a significant shift in preference toward the co-sourcing arrangement from the outsourcing arrangement, indicating that managers recognize the co-sourcing arrangement as a superior alternative to the outsourcing arrangement. They describe the key advantages of co-sourcing as being (1) access to professionals' skills, knowledge, and expertise; (2) a new point of view that may improve the internal audit function; and (3) being able to cover unexpected staffing needs.

Challenges Associated with Co-Sourcing and Outsourcing

There are a range of challenges associated with co-sourced and outsourced internal audit functions. These include:

- Balancing the (potential) additional costs associated with the delivery of an individual outsourced or co-sourced engagement with the administrative cost savings on using an in-house resource.

- Balancing the costs in buying expertise versus building expertise and the potential loss of this expertise at the end of each engagement.
- Managing the potential loss of tacit knowledge at the end of each engagement.
- Understanding specific organizational cultures and whether there is a pre-disposition toward outsourcing versus in-house activities.
- Finding service providers that have the expertise and experience in different sectors.
- Finding service providers able to deliver services for organizations operating in remote, isolated, or globally diffuse areas.
- Ensuring the quality of the internal auditors actually undertaking the engagements, rather than those who sold the service (i.e., being given junior staff when senior staff were originally proposed).
- Managing the loss of the ability to use internal audit as a future talent source for the organization.
- Ensuring that service providers have appropriate access to organizational systems and tools while managing confidentiality and information management issues.
- Providing appropriate clarity of roles in the internal audit charter, including specific demarcation of responsibilities.
- Managing the risk of the outsourced provider leveraging their time within the organization to upsell other services.

Assuring the Quality of the Service Provider

"It is extremely important to work collaboratively with your service provider to help produce quality internal audit reports destined for the Audit Committee," says Dr. Len Gainsford, Chief Audit Executive at the Victorian Department of Transport, Planning and Local Infrastructure in Australia.

Dr. Gainsford recommends the following strategies for assuring the quality of service providers:

- Key performance indicators for the service provider specified in the contract or service level agreement. This includes KPIs around knowledge transfer.
- Post-audit surveys completed by auditees. The questionnaire responses must then be correctly analyzed and acted upon.
- Scheduled weekly meetings involving internal audit practitioners, the service provider, and relevant stakeholders.
- Defined responsibilities for establishing and maintaining stakeholder relationships. This includes relationships with the external auditor.
- Identifying a point of contact for both the internal audit function and the service provider. This is usually the chief audit executive and the provider's line partner.
- Physical co-location of internal audit practitioners and provider teams to help promote dialogue and professional respect for the quality of work performed.
- Defined criteria around disclosure and the provider undertaking other consulting or advisory work in the organization.

QAIP Hint

Internal audit functions could incorporate *sourcing arrangements* into a balanced scorecard with performance indicators such as:

- Relative proportions of the internal audit plan insourced and outsourced (include target)
- Turnover of staff within the service provider allocated to engagements for the organization (include target)
- Years of relevant experience among service provider staff allocated to engagements for the organization (include target)
- Time allocated by external providers to share learnings with in-house staff (include target)
- Number of better practices recommended by the service provider (include target)
- Number of systemic issues identified by the service provider (include target)
- Proportion of time spent by the service provider in meeting with management (include target)

Role of the Chief Audit Executive

Regardless of the sourcing model used for internal audit, the role of chief audit executive should always be retained in-house. This is reinforced through IIA Standards 1300 and 2070.

Standard 1300—Quality Assurance and Improvement Program

The chief audit executive must develop and maintain a quality assurance and improvement program that covers all aspects of the internal audit activity.

Standard 2070—External Service Provider and Organizational Responsibility for Internal Auditing

When an external service provider serves as the internal audit activity, the provider must make the organization aware that the organization has the responsibility for maintaining an effective internal audit activity.

Retaining the role of chief audit executive in-house offers three advantages:

1. It provides assurance that the service provider is delivering a quality internal audit function in accordance with a set of professional standards.
2. It provides assurance that internal audits are risk based, align with strategic priorities, and meet the needs and expectations of the organization.
3. It allows for effective contract management.

Characteristics of the Chief Audit Executive

The chief audit executive has a critical role in determining the overall success of the internal audit function. He or she sets the expectations regarding quality and determines the value that the internal audit will deliver to the organization.

Audit committees and CEOs are under increasing pressure to steer organizations on a legal, ethical, and risk-aware course—while at the same time containing costs and increasing growth and profits. Not surprisingly, they are looking to the CAE for unprecedented leadership and contribution to overarching strategy. Old-line CAEs who have been entrenched solely in internal auditing may no longer fit the profile that corporate boards seek; over the past several years, many have been the victims of attrition. Today, it's estimated that within the Fortune 500, new CAEs are recruited from outside internal auditing almost half the time. Simply put, a new set of skills is required.

Chambers, Eldridge, and Park (2010)

Regardless of whether the chief audit executive is a full-time professional role or a senior officer with other responsibilities, the chief audit executive has primary responsibility for the oversight of internal audit quality. Under the IIA *Standards,* quality is managed through the development and implementation of a quality assurance and improvement program, which was discussed in Chapter 3.

The quality assurance and improvement program provides assurance that the quality of the internal audit function is adequate and that the audit plan addresses the needs and risks of the organization. The organization itself must have a process to assess whether outsourced providers are operating in a professional and appropriate manner.

Anderson (2009) recognizes key chief audit executive skills as being adaptability, continuous learning, judgment, and diversity management. Chambers and colleagues (2010) identified seven key attributes essential for chief audit executive success:

1. Superior business acumen
2. Dynamic communication skills
3. Unflinching integrity and ethics
4. Breadth of experience
5. Excellent grasp of business risks
6. Gift for developing talent
7. Unwavering courage

The Makings of a Good Chief Audit Executive

Dr. Sarah Blackburn, Audit Committee Chair and past President of the Chartered Institute of Internal Auditors (IIA UK and Ireland), believes good chief audit executives are able to bridge the gap between the top and the bottom of an organization. They are strategic and confident communicators able to relate well to people across the organizational hierarchy. Effective chief audit executives are also able to consolidate volumes of information for the audit committee, to allow members to focus on the question of *why.*

EFFECTIVE LEADERSHIP OF THE INTERNAL AUDIT FUNCTION   Effective leadership is critical to the internal audit function delivering quality outcomes. Requiring the internal audit function to meet the challenges of constant change and undertake increasingly complex engagements, sometimes with diminishing resources, will often depend on the ability of the chief audit executive to inspire and motivate the team. Great leadership will allow the internal audit function to achieve more as a group than they could as individuals.

Example 9.1 Leadership and Motivation

A key aspect of enabling highly effective teams is the ability of the team leader to motivate team members. Put simply, motivation is the degree to which a person is willing to invest time and effort into achieving a goal.

Where team members are motivated and engaged, performance, productivity, morale, and retention soar. Effective leaders motivate, engage, and inspire their teams by understanding and tapping in to the things that are important to their team members.

Different people are motivated by different things, and in order to motivate their teams and team members effectively, leaders need to understand what motivates the individuals. They also need to be able to understand and discern the difference between intrinsic motivation and extrinsic motivation.

Essentially, intrinsic motivation comes from within the person rather than being driven by an external force (e.g., reward). Typically, intrinsic motivation is characterized by a desire to do a job well because of factors such as personal self-esteem, enjoyment of the job itself, and wanting to do the right thing.

Extrinsic motivation is characterized by a desire to do the job well because of external factors that would typically include some sort of reward structure, such as money, promotion, recognition, or acceptance.

Whether a person is motivated by intrinsic or extrinsic factors (or a combination of both), an effective leader will be able to understand what that person's basic needs are and how work can be structured to deliver those needs in a manner that also contributes most effectively to overarching team goals.

Source: Excerpt from *IIA-Australia Graduate Certificate in Internal Auditing Module 4.*

Questions about the Quality of Internal Audit Staffing Practices

Table 9.3 provides a range of questions about the quality of internal audit staff management processes. These can be formally incorporated into a quality assurance and improvement program, or, less formally, into ongoing assessment activities. Questions may be variously posed to the chief audit executive, internal auditors, or audit stakeholders.

TABLE 9.3 Quality Questions

Questions	Evidence of Quality
Do internal audit staff members have the skills and experience to deal with challenging or contentious issues?	Assessment of staff capabilities and resourcing

(continued)

TABLE 9.3 (*continued*)

Questions	Evidence of Quality
Do job descriptions exist and do they clearly articulate the roles and responsibilities of the chief audit executive and internal audit staff members?	Job descriptions/position descriptions Internal audit staff interviews
Are internal audit staff accountabilities clearly defined?	Job descriptions/position descriptions Accountability framework Internal audit staff interviews
Can internal audit staff members clearly articulate their respective accountabilities?	Internal audit staff interviews
Do job descriptions reflect the qualifications and experience necessary for undertaking the position's requirements?	Job descriptions
Do internal audit staff have appropriate qualifications and experience for the position they occupy?	Details of staff qualifications and experience Internal audit staff interviews
Do internal audit staff collectively possess the knowledge, skills, and competencies necessary for the internal audit function to operate effectively?	Details of staff qualifications and experience
Are the skills, knowledge, and competencies of internal audit staff aligned to the resource requirements of the internal audit plan?	Details of staff qualifications and experience Internal audit plan
Do internal audit staff possess the attributes necessary to operate effectively?	Performance reviews Staff interviews Post-engagement surveys
Does the chief audit executive provide the audit committee with periodic benchmarking of audit capability, including experience, average years, qualifications, and professional certifications?	Minutes of audit committee meetings
Does the chief audit executive have structured and documented retention strategies in order to maintain an appropriate level of staff turnover?	Human resources policies or documentation
Has the chief audit executive undertaken succession planning to retain important corporate knowledge?	Succession plan Capability plan
Does the chief audit executive have structured and documented secondment and rotation strategies in order to develop staff and import organizational knowledge into the team?	Succession plan Capability plan
Are internal audit staff offered flexible work practices?	Internal audit staff interviews Documentation formalizing flexible work practices
Are internal audit staff provided with an appropriate balance of travel in order to attract and retain high-performing staff?	Internal audit staff interviews
Has the chief audit executive considered staff location in terms of the potential to attract and retain high-performing staff?	Internal audit staff interviews Capability plan

Does the budget reflect the sourcing model and include capacity for purchasing additional resources or special resources as required?	Staffing plans make provisions for the knowledge, skills, and other competencies required to perform the internal audit responsibilities
Has the chief audit executive considered the cost/benefit of alternative sourcing models?	Chief audit executive interview Senior management interviews
Has the chief audit executive discussed resourcing models with senior management and the audit committee?	Senior management and audit committee interviews
Has the internal audit function followed organizational procurement processes for sourcing capacity?	Contract documentation
Does the chief audit executive have processes in place for assessing the quality of external service providers and feeding this assessment into the quality assurance and improvement program?	Quality assurance and improvement program Key performance indicators Policies and procedures Feedback from outsourced providers demonstrating an understanding of the policies and procedures
Does the quality assurance and improvement program specify quality assessment activities specific to external service providers?	Quality assurance and improvement program
Do contracts for external service providers specify performance standards and performance indicators?	Service provider contracts
Are performance requirements for external service providers cost-effective for both parties?	Service provider performance measures Service provider interviews
Do performance requirements for external service providers encourage performance over the life of their contract?	Service provider performance measures Service provider interviews
Are there specific policies and procedures for external service providers to ensure the quality of their work?	Policies and procedures Service provider interviews
Are outsourced providers given a written understanding for engagements about objectives, scope, respective responsibilities, and other expectations, including restrictions on distribution of the results of the engagement and access to engagement records?	Engagement memorandum Service provider interviews

Conclusion

Effectively staffing the internal audit function relies on an appropriate sourcing model, targeted recruitment or procurement practices, adequate internal auditor capacity and capability, and sufficient financial resources.

Approaches to internal audit resourcing will vary across organizations. At times, decisions around staffing may be dictated by the general attitude or approach of the parent organization. Other times, chief audit executives may be given the flexibility to develop their own staffing model. Regardless, these models are often dynamic, responding to changes in organizational structures and the demands of the organization.

References

Adams, A. (2010). Changing role of HR. *Human Resources*, 45–48.

Anderson, R. J. (2009). Critical skills for CAE success. *Internal Auditor*. http://www
.theiia.org/intauditor.

Auditor General of Alberta. (2005). *Examination of Internal Audit Departments*.
http://www.oag.ab.ca/files/oag/Examination_IAD.pdf.

Australian National Audit Office. (2012). *Developing and Managing Contracts—Better
Practice Guide*. http://anao.gov.au/~/media/Files/Better%20Practice%20Guides/
2012%202013/BPG_ContractManagement/31856%20WNAODeveloping%20%
20Managing%20ContractsBPGTextWeb.pdf.

Bailey, J. A. (2010). *Core Competencies for Today's Internal Auditor—CBOK Report III*.
Altamonte Springs, FL: The Institute of Internal Auditors Research Foundation.

Burch, S. (2011). Building an internal audit function. *Internal Auditor*. http://www
.theiia.org/intauditor.

Chambers, A. D., G. M. Selim, and G. Vinten. (1994). *Internal Auditing*, 2nd ed.
London: Pitman Publishing.

Chambers, R. F., C. B. Eldridge, and P. Park. (2010). *License to Lead: Seven Personal
Attributes That Maximize the Impact of the Most Successful Chief Audit Executives*.
Korn Ferry Institute and The Institute of Internal Auditors Audit Executive Centre.

Cole, K. (2010). *Management Theory and Practice*, 4th ed. Australia: Pearson.

Desai, N. K., G. J. Gerard, and A. Tripathy. (2008). *Co-sourcing and External Auditor's
Reliance on the Internal Audit Function*. Altamonte Springs, FL: The Institute of
Internal Auditors Research Foundation.

Falconer, T. (2008). Recruitment: Dealing with difference—A diverse workforce. *New
Zealand Management*.

HM Treasury. (2010). *Good Practice Guide: Audit Strategy*. http://www.hm-treasury.gov.uk.

Holt, J. E. (2012). A high-performing audit function. *Internal Auditor*. http://www.theiia.org/
intauditor.

The Institute of Internal Auditors. (2013). *International Professional Practices Framework*. Altamonte Springs, FL: The Institute of Internal Auditors.

The Institute of Internal Auditors. (2014). *Internal Audit Competency Framework*. https://global.theiia.org/about/about-internal-auditing/Pages/Competency-
Framework.aspx.

Institute of Internal Auditors–Australia. (2013). *Graduate Certificate in Internal Audit
Module 4 Unit 2*. Unpublished.

Louw, G. J. (2013). Exploring recruitment and selection trends in the Eastern Cape in
South Africa. *Journal of Human Resource Management* 11(1): 1–10.

Mosher, R., and D. Mainquist. (2011). The outsourcing relationship. *Internal Auditor*.
http://www.theiia.org/intauditor.

Murdock, H. (2011). *10 Key Techniques to Improve Team Productivity*. Altamonte
Springs, FL: The Institute of Internal Auditors Research Foundation.

Parliament of Victoria (Australia). (2010). *Equal Opportunity Act 2010*. http://www
.legislation.vic.gov.au/Domino/Web_Notes/LDMS/PubStatbook.nsf/f932b66241ecf1b7
ca256e92000e23be/7CAFB78A7EE91429CA25771200123812/$FILE/10-016a.pdf.

Sangeetha, K. (2010). Effective recruitment: A framework. *IUP Journal of Business
Strategy* 7(1): 93–107.

Sawyer, L. B., M. A. Dittenhofer, and J. H. Scheiner. (2005). *Sawyers Internal Auditing*, 5th
ed. Altamonte Springs, FL: The Institute of Internal Auditors Research Foundation.

CHAPTER 10

Managing and Measuring Staff Performance

The companies that look after their people are the companies that do really well. I'm sure we'd like a few other attributes, but that would be the most important one.

—Richard Branson

The quality of the internal audit staff will determine the overall quality of the internal audit function. Chief audit executives should develop structured processes for managing and measuring staff performance. These processes should be designed around optimizing the existing skills and experience of the internal auditors, as well as developing skills aligned with the internal audit function's capability needs.

The internal audit staff performance regime should be closely aligned to its overall quality assurance and improvement program. Staff performance should be managed on an ongoing basis to provide the internal auditor with an opportunity to continuously improve the manner in which they undertake their audit engagements. Periodically, the chief audit executive should also find time to review the overall performance of internal auditors to determine how well his or her performance aligns with the needs of the internal audit function.

Performance management processes should be structured in such a way that development needs can be readily identified. Both team and individual development opportunities should be built into the process. Resources allocated to internal auditor development are an investment in the longer-term success of the internal audit function.

Professional Attributes

Internal auditing requires more than technical competence. Superior internal auditors possess a range of professional and personal attributes that allow them to work effectively with stakeholders and add value in each of their engagements.

Due Professional Care

Due professional care is the care and skill that a reasonably prudent and competent internal auditor would apply in performing his or her duties. This requirement is reflected in IIA Standard 1220.

> ### Standard 1220—Due Professional Care
>
> Internal auditors must apply the care and skill expected of a reasonably prudent and competent internal auditor. Due professional care does not imply infallibility.

In conducting engagements, internal auditors can demonstrate due professional care through:

- Retaining an open and unbiased mindset while demonstrating appropriate professional skepticism
- Being alert to the possibility of intentional wrongdoing, errors and omissions, inefficiency, waste, ineffectiveness, and conflicts of interest
- Being aware of fraud risks
- Identifying absent or inadequate controls and recommending improvements to promote compliance with acceptable procedures and practices

Exercising due professional care implies competence and thoroughness, rather than infallibility. Due professional care requires professional judgment, as the level of care may vary depending on the objectives, complexity, nature, and materiality of the engagement being performed. It requires consideration of the sufficiency and appropriateness of audit evidence and its degree of persuasiveness.

In accordance with IIA Standard 1220.A1, demonstrating due professional care in relation to specific engagements will require regard to the:

- Extent of work needed to achieve the engagement's objectives
- Relative complexity, materiality, or significance of matters to which assurance procedures are applied
- Adequacy and effectiveness of governance, risk management, and control processes
- Probability of significant errors, fraud, or noncompliance
- Cost of assurance in relation to potential benefits

Ethical Practice

The IIA has a Code of Ethics, which was introduced earlier in this book. Internal audit functions may also develop their own ethics or values as part of their internal audit strategy.

Example 10.1 Ethical Decision Making

It is likely that internal auditors will be faced with circumstances where they either need to judge the ethics of decisions made or their own ethical decision making. To determine the ethics of a decision, it can be useful for internal auditors to consider the following questions:

- What are the facts, and what assumptions am I making?
- How do the facts impact my personal values, and what specific values are being impacted?
- Would I be happy for the decision to appear on the front page of the newspaper?
- Would I be happy if my family and close friends knew about the decision?
- Will the decision negatively impact my individual or personal reputation?
- What would happen if everybody made the same decision?
- Would I make the same decision if it directly impacted my family or close friends?
- Do the ends justify the means?

Objectivity

Objectivity is central to internal auditing. Internal auditors need to demonstrate objectivity in the work—avoiding bias and ensuring that work is undertaken in a transparent and impartial manner. Requirements around objectivity are articulated in IIA Standards 1100, 1120, 1130, 1130.A1, and 1130.C2.

Standard 1100—Independence and Objectivity

The internal audit activity must be independent, and internal auditors must be objective in performing their work.

Standard 1120—Individual Objectivity

Internal auditors must have an impartial, unbiased attitude and avoid any conflict of interest.

Standard 1130—Impairment to Independence or Objectivity

If independence or objectivity is impaired in fact or appearance, the details of the impairment must be disclosed to appropriate parties. The nature of the disclosure will depend upon the impairment.

Standard 1130.A1

Internal auditors must refrain from assessing specific operations for which they were previously responsible. Objectivity is presumed to be impaired if an internal auditor provides assurance services for an activity for which the internal auditor had responsibility within the previous year.

Standard 1130.C2

If internal auditors have potential impairments to independence or objectivity relating to proposed consulting services, disclosure must be made to the engagement client prior to accepting the engagement.

Performance Management Processes

Effective staff performance management begins with understanding the role and purpose of the internal audit function, identifying the outputs desired from the function, and linking these to individual staffing expectations. Ideally, there is clear alignment between the internal audit strategy, capability plan, annual audit plan, and individual staff responsibilities.

Performance management provides for transparent planning and monitoring of staff performance. It also ensures that job expectations and goals are focused and directly aligned with business goals. Designed well, performance management processes can improve employee morale and retention. However, poor performance management can expedite the loss of talented staff or entrench undesirable values and nonperformance.

Performance Reviews/Appraisals

Although staff may welcome performance feedback, performance reviews can still be challenging and create anxiety for both the supervisor and the staff member involved. Nonetheless, periodic performance appraisals are an effective way to influence staff performance. They can establish an agreed set of performance standards, motivate staff to reach these standards, create an environmental for mutual feedback, and help assess development needs. They also provide an objective and legally defensible basis for human resources decisions.

POST-ENGAGEMENT REVIEWS   Some chief audit executives formally review internal auditor performance after each engagement. The appraisals generally cover the actions taken by the engagement team and individual internal auditors, as well as the results of the engagement.

Post-engagement reviews provide an opportunity for identifying any issues associated with the audit methodology, as well as any systemic issues that may affect other audits. The reviews can incorporate engagement client feedback and provide a process for continuous improvement of the internal audit function. Ideally, post-engagement reviews should be formally recognized as an ongoing internal assessment process within the quality assurance and improvement program.

ANNUAL STAFF APPRAISALS   Many organizations have formal requirements for annual staff appraisals, and, where these exist, the internal audit function should utilize the organization's model. In the absence of an organization-wide process, chief audit executives should undertake annual staff appraisals aligned to the internal audit capability plan, the annual audit plan, and individual staff job descriptions.

360-Degree Processes   Three hundred sixty–degree processes are formal appraisal systems where feedback is provided to individuals from their subordinates, peers, managers, and sometimes clients. A questionnaire is usually used, and feedback is provided anonymously. The process is designed to engender opinions from a broad group of stakeholders, on the premise that a supervisor will not have complete oversight of the work undertaken by a subordinate.

Three hundred sixty–degree processes lend themselves to internal audit functions, where much of the work is undertaken by internal auditors working alone or in a small team, engaging directly with clients.

Peer Reviews   Peer reviews are a condensed version of a 360-degree process, where feedback is provided by colleagues. Peer reviews can be incorporated into a quality team approach, where the chief audit executive uses a group of staff members to develop and implement standard practices across the internal audit function.

Staff Satisfaction Surveys   Staff satisfaction surveys can provide useful information regarding the climate or culture of larger internal audit functions. These surveys could be undertaken on an annual basis or as part of a periodic internal assessment.

QAIP Hint

Internal audit functions could incorporate *performance management processes* into a balanced scorecard with performance indicators such as:

- Proportion of internal audit staff performance evaluations completed on an annual basis (include target)
- Development and review of a capability plan on an annual basis
- Proportion of budget allocated to professional development (include target)

The Australian Government's Fair Work Ombudsman (2013) has developed a best practice guide to performance management that identifies the following key steps in managing underperformance:

1. Identify the problem—in particular, identify the key drivers of performance or underperformance and ensure the performance problem is clearly identified.

2. Assess and analyze the problem—collect information on the nature of the problem, its seriousness, how long it has gone on, and how wide the expectation gap is.
3. Meet with the employee and discuss the problem—explain what the problem is, why it is a problem, and how it impacts the workplace. Have an open (two-way) discussion and encourage the employee to identify all matters impacting on the situation.
4. Jointly devise a solution—work with the employee to identify solutions to the problem (thus increasing buy-in in the solution) and develop a clear (and agreed) plan of action.
5. Monitor performance—provide ongoing feedback (formal or informal) and have a follow-up meeting to review the situation.

Team Development

Researchers Yamoah and Maiyo (2013) argue that the provision of efficient services by any organization depends on the quality of its workforce. They state, "Employee training and development is not only desirable but it is an activity which management must commit human and fiscal resources to if it is to maintain skilled and knowledge-able personnel. Personnel training and development is a process of altering employee's behaviour to further organizational goal."

Effective Teams

Effective teamwork is a critical element of quality internal auditing. The IIA recognizes this in its paper *7 Attributes of Highly Effective Internal Auditors* (2013), which states, "The highly integrated nature of the business processes internal audit examine requires intensive collaboration among internal auditors with different areas of technical expertise."

When performed well, teamwork creates synergy among internal audit staff—leading to greater outcomes than could be achieved by each team member in isolation. In contrast, poor teamwork can result in reduced quality of outcomes, inefficiencies, low morale, performance management issues, and increased staff turnover.

Effective internal audit teams are built by their chief audit executive over time. Tuckman (1965) first identified the typical process for team building and described five stages that teams move between during their life cycle. He described these as *forming, storming, norming, performing,* and *adjourning.* Each stage has different characteristics and imposes different imperatives on the chief audit executive, whose primary task is to move the team from its current stage to a higher one, taking into account that *adjourning* is generally restricted to temporary teams created for a specific project.

Often, teams operate a continuum between the different stages, and at times will regress to a lower stage. Nonetheless, the chief audit executive should remain vigilant in recognizing the dynamics operating within the team and, where necessary, adopt a hands-on approach to enhance these dynamics.

Motivation and Morale

"Motivation and morale are very important to building an effective internal audit team," says Ana Figueiredo, Chief Audit Executive at Portugal Telecom. Figueiredo believes it is hard at times to be an internal auditor. "Generally, auditors are not the most popular person, and they sometimes have to deliver bad news, which can lower morale."

Chief audit executives need to work hard to maintain team morale. Some strategies that Figueiredo has adopted include sharing any praise from the chief executive officer for specific pieces of work with the responsible team, as well as the entire internal audit team.

Figueiredo believes in working closely with the team. She recommends letting teams know they are respected and valued and recognizing when individuals, or the team as a whole, need attention. "Sometimes we may be in a rush and don't always have time; however, you need to make the effort to speak with people and let them know you understand what they are going through." Providing support to people facing professional or personal challenges will engender trust and enable effective leadership.

Not all organizations will have the luxury of providing staff with financial rewards for high levels of performance. In these cases, it is necessary to identify other opportunities for nonfinancial rewards. Part of this will be reinforcing the particular role each person has to play in the team. As Figueiredo says, "You don't need a team full of stars. There will be a place for rising stars—but you also need people who are happy to avoid the limelight and are prepared to do the less interesting work."

The chief audit executive needs to identify the strengths and weaknesses of everyone in the team and leverage this. A highly analytical person might not be the quickest to complete their tasks, and a person with excellent interpersonal skills might not always have first-rate written communication skills. Ultimately, there is a need to balance the team with the right people in the right place.

Team Training

The capability plan is a valuable resource for supporting individual and team development. Having determined the capabilities required across the internal audit function, chief audit executives can assess the skills and experience of individual staff against those articulated in the plan. The chief audit executive can then work with the team to determine how these gaps will be addressed, or whether individual internal auditors are an appropriate fit for the emerging needs of the organization.

Team-Wide Competency Planning and Skills Assessment

The internal audit function should collectively possess the skills, expertise, and experience to deliver high-quality internal audit engagements. According to Cole (2010), team-based planning needs to consider individual needs, task needs, and team needs.

Aligning Training to the Competency Framework

Chief audit executives can maximize the value that staff members generate from professional development activities by aligning training to an internal audit capability plan or competency plan. Ideally, this plan should be developed by the chief audit executive as part of the process to determine internal audit resourcing.

If a chief audit executive has not developed a competency plan, they could instead choose to align staff training requirements against an established (publicly available) competency framework such as that developed by the IIA.

Eileen Tay, former Head of Internal Audit at Singapore's Central Provident Fund Board, encourages chief audit executives to put in place a training and competency plan for staff to ensure that they are competent to do their work. She believes there is often a need to develop the competencies of new recruits, and this best occurs through a structured approach.

Team training is an efficient way of providing professional development to the entire internal audit function. It ensures that staff receive a consistent message, and affords staff an opportunity to interact away from the demands of their everyday work.

Various approaches can be taken for team training, from sending the team offsite for a focused development exercise, attending conferences together, or bringing in subject-matter experts.

Novel Approaches to Team Training

Team training needn't follow traditional classroom-based approaches. Some novel approaches include:

- Using newspaper reporters to talk to staff about how they can analyze small pieces of information, connect the dots, and write a story in a very limited time frame
- Having scientists talk to staff about how failed experiments can actually lead to the creation of a whole new product—encouraging internal auditors to use unexpected findings to identify unanticipated issues
- Developing case studies based on major issues faced by other organizations to identify the cause of adverse events and consider what internal audit could do to support these organizations to respond appropriately
- Modeling a graduate auditor intern program on the intern approach used by the medical profession

Mentoring

Mentoring provides an opportunity for a more experienced person to impart knowledge and expertise to a less experienced person. In an internal audit function, this could involve the chief audit executive or other senior internal audit manager working individually with one or more staff members. It could also involve internal audit staff, including the chief audit executive, working with senior managers from the broader organization.

Sarros and Butchatsky (1996) interviewed a number of well-recognized leaders and from these discussions identified the following principles of effective mentoring:

- Mentors develop and nurture their protégés.
- Mentors reveal and remediate weaknesses, and reinforce strengths.
- Mentoring is hard work, requiring honesty and a caring attitude.
- Mentors teach skills in clear thinking and management of complex projects.
- Mentors enrich a person's appreciation of many elements of the job.
- Mentors take a multifaceted approach—always seeing the big picture.
- Mentors provide a balance between ambition (individualistic) and self-actualization (individual and organizational focus).
- Patience and persistence are key attributes identified and reinforced by mentors.
- Mentors can challenge mentees to adopt a new lens through which to view challenging situations.

Team Meetings

Team meetings play an important role in facilitating the sharing of information and better practice. They support coordination and provide an opportunity for team training.

Keyhoe and Bentley (1989) discuss the importance of effective team meetings. Here are some of their tips for making meetings more productive:

- Restrict objectives to an achievable number and circulate them in advance.
- Set and maintain a start and finish time for the meeting.
- Rotate the role of meeting chair and appoint someone to record minutes.
- Control the discussion while still encouraging participation:
  - Ask questions of noncontributors.
  - Ensure that all discussion is relevant to objectives.
  - Ask talkative members to clarify the relevance of their comments.

QAIP Hint

Internal audit functions could incorporate *team meetings* into a balanced scorecard with a performance indicator such as the regularity of staff meetings.

Individual Professional Development

Individual staff should take on a level of personal responsibility for their own professional development, as this development will ultimately benefit their career.

However, there are advantages to both the internal audit function and broader organization in supporting individual professional development. Doing so helps to maximize staff contribution to the internal audit function, as well developing skills and experience that can be transferred throughout the organization.

Many professional associations, including the IIA, have a requirement for continuing professional development.

Standard 1230—Continuing Professional Development

Internal auditors must enhance their knowledge, skills, and other competencies through continuing professional development.

Professional Development Days

Allow each staff member a minimum number of development days per annum (e.g., 10 days). This can include time spent on formal training programs, at conferences or workshops, and on professional networking.

Individual Training

Individual staff training should be aligned to the broader internal audit capability plan and the specific requirements of each position. Training needs should be recognized through performance management processes and appropriate support provided to allow training requirements to be met.

Internal auditor training can cover technical issues, interpersonal skills, or management areas. Linking training needs to a specific capability plan or competency framework (such as those developed by the IIA and IIA–Australia) helps to determine commonly accepted capabilities for different levels within the internal audit function. For example, IIA–Australia (2010) identifies four different competency groupings for internal auditors—*interpersonal skills, technical skills, standards*, and *knowledge areas*.

TECHNICAL SKILLS   Within the technical skills group, IIA–Australia identifies six key competencies:

1. Research and investigation
2. Business process and project management
3. Risk and control
4. Data collection and analysis
5. Problem-solving tools and techniques
6. Computer aided auditing techniques (CAATs)

For each of these key competencies, the IIA–Australia competency framework identifies the key attributes or skills that would be expected of an internal auditor with varying levels of seniority and experience.

INTERPERSONAL SKILLS Communication and influence are critical elements of effective internal auditing. These rely on superior interpersonal skills, and staff may require specific training to achieve an appropriate skill level.

IIA–Australia identifies four key interpersonal skills in its competency framework:

1. Influence and communication
2. Leadership and teamwork
3. Change management
4. Conflict resolution

Chief audit executives should provide appropriate development opportunities to support staff in acquiring and maintaining the requisite level of interpersonal skills.

Management Training

Organizations should not assume that internal auditors who are very good at managing engagements will also be good at managing people and operations. The two skills sets intersect, but also have very different elements, as shown in Figure 10.1.

Management skills can be acquired through formal qualifications such as MBAs and other post-graduate degrees, short courses as well as through on-the-job training, mentoring, and coaching.

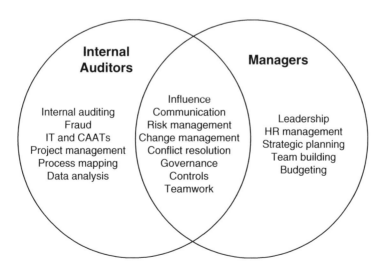

FIGURE 10.1 Internal Audit and Management Competency Sets

Professional Membership and Involvement

The value of professional membership and involvement in professional associations should not be underestimated. Professional associations such as the IIA provide an opportunity to network with peers, gain professional insight, and discover new and emerging practices.

Professional associations also provide an opportunity to market an internal audit function and to identify leading internal audit practitioners. This provides a mechanism for identifying and attracting potential new recruits to the internal audit function.

QAIP Hint

Internal audit functions could incorporate *professional development* into an internal audit maturity model or balanced scorecard.

Maturity Model

Internal audit functions could include *professional development* as a key process area in its maturity model. For example:

- Level 2 of a five-stage maturity model could identify that the professional development is not provided or is provided inconsistently.
- Level 3 could identify that professional development is provided based on individual requirements.
- Level 4 could identify that professional development is provided based on an activity-wide training plan.
- Level 5 could identify that professional development is provided based on a formal capability plan developed from a recognized competency framework.

Balanced Scorecard/KPI

Internal audit functions could develop performance indicators such as:

- Proportion of individual training/development plans implemented (include target)
- Average training hours per internal auditor (include target)
- Attendance at professional meetings
- Number of internal audit staff involved as volunteers in professional associations (include target)
- Number of internal audit staff involved in mentoring activities (include target)

Questions about the Quality of Internal Audit Staff Development Processes

Table 10.1 provides a range of questions about the quality of the internal audit staff development processes. These can be formally incorporated into a quality assurance and improvement program, or, less formally, into ongoing assessment activities. Questions may be variously posed to the chief audit executive, internal auditors, or audit stakeholders.

TABLE 10.1　Quality Questions

Questions	Evidence of Quality
Do staff management practices provide assurance that engagements are conducted with proficiency and due professional care?	Engagement supervision Post-engagement surveys
Do internal audit staff members demonstrate proficiency through their internal audit work?	Engagement supervision Working paper review Post-engagement surveys
Do internal audit staff members demonstrate due professional care through their internal audit work (including both consulting and assurance engagements) by considering the following?	Working paper review Engagement supervision Post-engagement surveys
■ Needs and expectations of clients, including the nature, timing, and communication of engagement results; ■ Relative complexity and extent of work needed to achieve the engagement's objectives; and ■ Cost of the consulting engagement in relation to potential benefits?	
Do internal audit staff members undertake their work professionally and cause minimal disruption to organizational activities?	Senior management and audit committee interviews Post-engagement surveys
Have internal audit staff members considered the extent of work needed to achieve the engagement's objectives?	Working paper review Engagement plan
Have internal audit staff members demonstrated consideration of the relative significance and materiality of findings?	Working paper review Post-engagement surveys
Is senior management confident that the internal audit function can identify the root causes of control breakdowns?	Senior management interviews
Have internal audit staff members demonstrated consideration of the cost of assurance versus the potential benefits?	Working paper review
Do the chief audit executive and audit managers have a strategic mindset?	Chief audit executive interview Internal audit staff interviews Senior management and audit committee interviews Post-engagement surveys
Do internal audit staff members sign a code of conduct or code of ethics?	Internal audit staff code of conduct/code of ethics
Does the code of conduct or code of ethics refer to the IIA's Code of Ethics?	Internal audit staff code of conduct/code of ethics
Do internal audit staff members maintain an objective, unbiased mindset when undertaking engagements?	Working paper review Senior management interviews Post-engagement surveys
Do internal audit staff members avoid any conflicts of interest in undertaking engagement?	Chief audit executive interview

(continued)

TABLE 10.1 (*continued*)

Questions	Evidence of Quality
Is there evidence that any impairment to objectivity is appropriately documented for assurance engagements?	Working paper review
Do internal audit staff members avoid providing assurance over areas they have been involved in in the previous 12 months?	Chief audit executive interview
Is there evidence that consulting engagement clients are advised of any impairment to independence or objectivity prior to the engagement being accepted?	Engagement client feedback
Has the chief audit executive developed a strategic capability plan to allow for strategic human resources (HR) management?	Capability plan
Has the chief audit executive considered the availability of external service providers as part of its capability planning?	Chief audit executive interview
Are internal audit staff members provided with regular, formal performance evaluations?	Chief audit executive interview Internal audit staff interviews
Does the internal audit function utilize 360-degree feedback as part of its internal performance processes?	Chief audit executive interview Staff interviews
Does the internal audit function adopt peer review processes, particularly with regard to completed engagements?	Chief audit executive interview Internal audit staff interviews Report from peer reviews
Does the internal audit function utilize staff satisfaction surveys as part of its HR management and internal quality processes?	Internal audit staff satisfaction surveys
Have internal audit staff members demonstrated proficiency through the attainment of professional certifications?	Internal audit staff training register Lists of staff certifications
Is professional development offered to internal audit staff?	Training register Chief audit executive interview Internal audit staff interviews
Is there a clear career continuum for internal audit staff, outlining expected skills, knowledge, and attributes across the different levels within the internal audit function?	Internal audit staff interviews Capability plan
Is professional development targeted appropriately to provide internal audit staff with the proficiency necessary to undertake engagements?	Internal audit staff training plans and records
Do processes exist to feed back development needs identified through internal audit engagements into individual training plans?	Chief audit executive interview
Does the chief audit executive maintain a training register for individual staff members?	Training register
Are internal audit staff members offered the opportunity to attend external courses as required and in accordance with a structured professional development plan?	Internal audit staff training plans and records Internal audit staff interviews

Are external courses assessed to ensure that they meet professional development requirements and offer value for money?	Chief audit executive interview
Do internal audit staff members participate in professional or industry conferences?	Internal audit staff training plans and records
	Internal audit staff interviews
Do internal audit staff members attend in-house training?	Internal audit staff training plans and records
	Internal audit staff interviews
Do internal audit staff members utilize online training?	Internal audit staff training plans and records
	Internal audit staff interviews
Does team-wide competency planning include consideration of fraud awareness?	Internal audit staff training plans and records
Does team-wide competency planning include consideration of technology-based audit techniques?	Internal audit staff training plans and records
Are regular team meetings held to allow for professional development and knowledge sharing?	Chief audit executive interview
	Internal audit staff interviews
	Meeting minutes
Has the chief audit executive developed a formal communication strategy for sharing information among internal audit staff members?	Internal audit communication strategy
Are internal audit staff members provided opportunities to attend training that supports team building?	Internal audit staff training plans and records
	Internal audit staff interviews
Has the chief audit executive adopted formal or informal mentoring strategies for staff members?	Chief audit executive interview
	Internal audit staff interviews
Are internal audit staff members supported to obtain or retain professional membership?	Records of professional membership
	Internal audit staff interviews
Do internal audit staff members attend professional meetings?	Internal audit staff interviews
Does the chief audit executive actively support the IIA or other relevant professional associations?	Chief audit executive interview
Are the chief audit executive and/or senior internal audit staff office bearers within the IIA or other relevant professional associations?	Chief audit executive interview
	Internal audit staff interviews
Does the internal audit budget make allowance for professional development?	Internal audit budget
Are internal audit staff members committed to continuous learning?	Internal audit staff interviews
	Records of professional development

Conclusion

Internal audit functions need to remain abreast with emerging trends and practices to continue to add value to an organization. Internal auditors must have an understanding of the business in which they are operating. They also need to be experts in governance, risk management, and control. All internal auditors, regardless of their years of experience, need to undertake continuous professional development. This should be tailored to the specific skills and experience of each internal auditor and should relate back to the overall capability needs of the internal audit function.

References

Australian Government Fair Work Ombudsman. (2013). *Best Practice Guide—Managing Underperformance.* http://www.fairwork.gov.au/BestPracticeGuides/09-Managing-underperformance.pdf.

Birkett, W. P., M. R. Barbera, B. S. Leithead, M. Lower, and P. J. Roebuck. (1999). *Assessing Competency in Internal Auditing, Structures and Methodology.* Altamonte Springs, FL: The Institute of Internal Auditors Research Foundation.

Cole, K. (2010). *Management Theory and Practice,* 4th ed. Australia: Pearson.

Godbehere, S. (2005). Measuring staff performance. *Business Credit* 107(10): 49–50.

The Institute of Internal Auditors. (2013). *International Professional Practices Framework.* Altamonte Springs, FL: The Institute of Internal Auditors.

The Institute of Internal Auditors. (2013). *7 Attributes of Highly Effective Internal Auditors.* https://na.theiia.org/news/Documents/7%20Attributes%20of%20Highly%20Effective%20Internal%20Auditors.pdf.

Institute of Internal Auditors–Australia. (2010). *Internal Audit Competency Framework.* Unpublished.

Keyhoe, D., and M. Bentley. (1999). *Tips for Managers.* Perth, Australia: Bentley Keyhoe Consulting Group.

Sarros, J. C., and O. Butchatsky. (1996). *Leadership: Australia's Top CEOs—Finding Out What Makes Them the Best.* Sydney: HarperCollins.

St. James Ethics Centre. (2013). Ethical Decision Making. http://www.ethics.org.au/content/ethical-decision-making.

Tuckman, B. (1965). Developmental sequence in small groups. *Psychological Bulletin* (63): 384–399.

Verschoor, C. C. (2007). *Ethics and Compliance—Challenges for Internal Auditors.* Altamonte Springs, FL: Institute of Internal Auditors Research Foundation.

Yamoah, E. E., and P. Maiyo. (2013). Capacity building and employee performance. *Canadian Social Science* 9(3): 42–45.

PART V

Internal Audit
Professional Practices

CHAPTER 11

Internal Audit Professional Practice

Organizing is what you do before you do something, so that when you do it,
it is not all mixed up.

—A.A. Milne

The key to high quality internal auditing is finding the right blend of intuition, intelligence, insight, planning, flexibility, and creativity. Great internal auditors need to be strategic influencers while at the same time being empathic listeners. Chief audit executives need to strike a balance between being responsive and being proactive.

Internal auditors need to adopt a systematic and disciplined approach to their work to ensure their independence and objectivity. This is most likely to occur when the internal audit function has adopted formalized procedures that are understood and adhered to by all staff members.

Elements of Internal Audit Professional Practice

Professional practice is the third of the three sets of inputs to a quality internal activity. The other two sets of inputs, *strategy* and *staffing*, have been described previously in this book. The specific elements that comprise professional practice are shown in Figure 11.1.

Building a New Practice

Building a new internal audit practice offers an exciting opportunity to chief audit executives, giving them scope to develop processes in a manner consistent with stakeholder expectations and strategic priorities. Figure 11.2 shows the typical stages the chief audit executive may work through to establish the internal audit function.

Chief audit executives should start by understanding stakeholder needs. Doing so maximizes internal audit's potential to deliver quality and value to the organization. This is a precursor to developing an effective internal audit strategy—both of which are discussed further in Chapter 6. The strategy sets the direction for the internal audit function and allows it to focus on priority areas.

Once the strategy is developed, the chief audit executive can consider the risks associated with delivering on the strategy as well as developing a capability plan that identifies the skills and experiences required to deliver against the types of

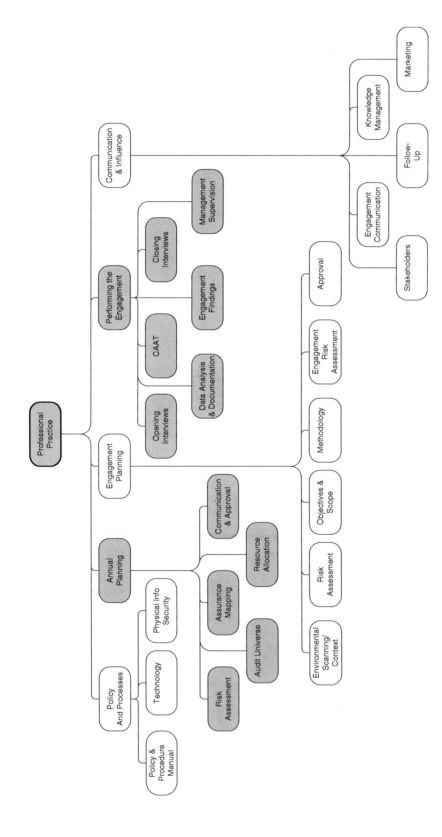

FIGURE 11.1 Elements of Internal Audit Professional Practice

Understand stakeholder expectations.

Develop a strategy.

Plan for capabilities and manage risks.

Develop methodologies and quality practices.

Source staff.

FIGURE 11.2 Steps in Establishing a New Internal Audit Professional Practice

engagements planned for the internal audit function. Chapter 6 provides further information about assessing these risks and Chapter 9 discusses capability planning.

Chief audit executives should next develop policies and procedures that provide guidance for the particular activities they will undertake, and put in place a quality program to ensure that the policies and procedures are effective, being implemented, and produce the required outputs and outcomes. Finally, once the internal audit function is fully established, the chief audit executive can look to source internal auditors to undertake internal audit engagements that meet the organization's requirements.

Reinventing an Internal Audit Practice

An effective internal audit function that is being continuously enhanced through a quality assurance and improvement program is unlikely to need dramatic change unless the organization itself experiences significant change. In this event, chief audit executives should consider how they can best provide assurance within the shifting operating environment. There may be times, however, that a new chief audit executive is faced with the challenge of reinventing an internal audit function that has been allowed to degrade, or that does not meet the needs of stakeholders.

Tips for Modernizing an Internal Audit Practice

Ana Figueiredo, Chief Audit Executive at Portugal Telecom, has a number of tips for modernizing an internal audit function:

- Ensure the organizational structure of the internal audit activity is appropriate and aligned with the corporate structure.
- Look at the physical office structure, and if necessary move people from individual offices into an open plan environment to promote communication and information sharing.

(continued)

(*continued*)
- Develop an audit manual with standardized templates and work with staff to embed these practices.
- Assess staff competency and determine whether the skill sets meet the needs and expectations of a modern internal audit activity.
- Determine whether staff members are aligned with a new operating approach, whether they are willing to change their styles, and whether they should ultimately remain in the internal audit activity.
- Recruit new staff as required that fit the revised culture and operations and complement existing staff.
- Introduce IT tools to support data analysis.
- Align reports with the operating style of the organization—where necessary, change formats (including reducing the length of reports) and consider using PowerPoint as a presentation tool.
- Implement a quality assurance and improvement program; introduce internal assessments and have an external assessment performed.
- Revisit the strategy on an annual basis.
- Last but not least, communicate, communicate, and communicate.

Stages in the Internal Audit Process

There are typical stages in the internal audit process. These have been summarized by the Institute of Internal Auditors–Australia in its Graduate Certificate in Internal Audit (2013) and are illustrated in Figure 11.3.

Internal audit professional practices should cover each of the audit stages, and ensure that the stages combine to deliver the outputs and outcomes described in the internal audit strategy.

Internal Audit Policies and Procedures

Developing formalized policies and procedures helps ensure consistency and professionalism within internal audit functions. The level of formalization will vary depending on the size of the internal audit activity, but even single auditor functions need to ensure that the auditors are approaching each engagement in a structured and systematic manner.

IIA Standard 2040 recognizes the need for formal policies and procedures.

Standard 2040—Policies and Procedures

The chief audit executive must establish policies and procedures to guide the internal audit activity.

Policies and procedures should define the standards expected of internal auditors and the methodology to be adopted by the internal audit function.

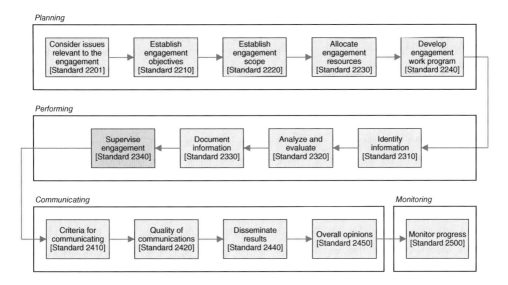

FIGURE 11.3 Internal Audit Stages

Source: Institute of Internal Auditors–Australia (2013).

Diagram does not include all IPPF Performance Standards.
Supervision (Standard 2340) is undertaken throughout an engagement.

Policies and procedures should be developed that apply to specific internal audit professional practices such as annual planning and engagement planning, as well as to broader management areas such as staffing. The range of potential policies and procedures is shown in Figure 11.4.

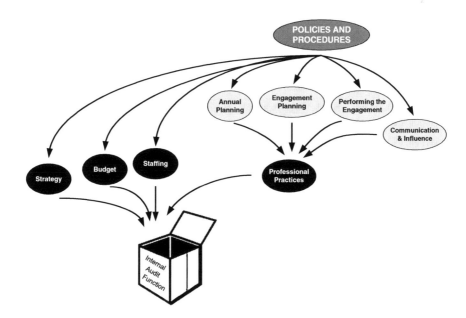

FIGURE 11.4 Types of Policies and Procedures and Their Link to Internal Audit Inputs

Although dependent on the size of the internal audit function, common policies and procedures cover:

- Conformance with regulatory and policy requirements
- Professional standards
- Development and maintenance of the internal audit strategy and charter
- Development and maintenance of the quality assurance and improvement program, including supervisory processes and performance metrics
- Development and maintenance of the internal audit risk management plan
- Development and maintenance of the internal audit business continuity plan
- Development and maintenance of the internal audit capability and resource plan, including:
  - Organizational structure
  - Internal audit delegations and responsibilities
  - Performance management
  - Professional development
- Annual planning, including development and maintenance of the audit universe and assurance mapping
- Engagement planning processes, including:
  - Risk assessment
  - Methodology, including sampling criteria
- Engagement conduct processes, including:
  - Fieldwork practices, including audit evidence requirements
  - Working papers
- Communication processes, including:
  - Communication and stakeholder engagement planning
  - Engagement reporting, including reporting formats and rating scales
  - Staff communication, including team meetings
  - Marketing
- Follow-up processes, including recommendations monitoring and follow-up audits
- Information management and security
- Physical security
- Audit committee support processes

Using Graduates/Interns to Map Processes

Graduate/interns can be provided with on-the-job training in undertaking an audit by systematically walking them through the engagement process. Concurrently, the graduates/interns can be mapping the engagement process. This can help to identify opportunities for improvement in the engagement's process, can subsequently form part of the internal audit policies and procedures, and can be used to induct guest auditors.

Policies and procedures should be updated regularly, based on lessons learned through the quality assurance and improvement program. Chief audit executives should make time to discuss with staff whether the policies and procedures support them to deliver a quality product, and, where necessary, modify the approach to better meet the needs of the internal audit function and broader organization.

Common Quality Issue

Common quality issues related to *policies and procedures* include:

- Policies and procedures are not formally documented.
- Policies and procedures are poorly aligned to the size and nature of the internal audit function (for instance, the chief audit executive may have adopted policies and procedures from a large internal audit function into a small audit shop).
- Policies and procedures are incomplete and do not cover the necessary elements
- Policies and procedures do not reflect intended work practices.
- Policies and procedures have not been implemented.
- Policies and procedures are not followed by all internal audit staff.
- Policies and procedures are not reviewed.

Internal Audit Manual

Some internal audit functions will document their policies and procedures in an internal audit manual, although this is not always necessary. For smaller internal audit functions, standardized templates and checklists, rather than detailed and structured manuals, might be adequate. The chief audit executive will need to determine what documents provide the greatest value for money for their function.

Example 11.1 provides a sample table of contents from an internal audit manual, reflecting one approach (typically for a larger internal audit function). However, chief audit executives should adopt an approach that meets their individual circumstances.

Example 11.1 Internal Audit Manual Table of Contents

Foreword

Version Control
Maintenance of the Manual

Internal Audit Governance

Internal Audit Strategy
- Internal Audit Vision
- Internal Audit Values
- Regulatory Context

(continued)

(*continued*)

Internal Audit Risk Management Plan
Internal Audit Business Continuity Plan
Internal Audit Charter
- Structure of Internal Audit
- Reporting Lines
- Independence
- Authority
- Areas of Responsibility
- Nature of Work
Audit Committee
- Audit Committee Charter
- Conflicts of Interest

Relationships with Other Assurance Providers

Quality Assurance and Improvement Program

QAIP Structure
Key Performance Indicators
Ongoing Internal Monitoring
- Quality Checklists
- Peer Reviews
- Post-Engagement Surveys
Periodic Health Checks
- Periodic Assessment of Standards
- Client Surveys
- Staff Surveys
External Quality Assessments
QAIP Reporting

Internal Audit Staffing

Internal Audit Capability Plan
- Roles and Accountabilities
- Job Descriptions
- Proficiency and Due Professional Care
HR Policies
- Recruitment
- Induction
- Code of Conduct
- Conflicts of Interest
- Confidentiality
- Health and Safety
- Travel
- Time Recording
Performance Management
- Post-Engagement Reviews
- Annual Staff Appraisals

Training and Development
- Competency Framework
- Training Plans
- Continuing Professional Development
- Support of Professional Memberships
Sourcing Strategies
- Managing External Service Providers

Annual Audit Planning

Key Dates and Milestones
Audit Universe
Assurance Map
Alignment with Risk Management Processes
Annual Audit Plan
Internal Audit Budget
Responding to Management Requests

Engagement Planning

Client Engagement
- Engagement Memorandum
Environmental Scanning
Assessing Risks and Controls
- Process Mapping
- Considering Fraud Risks
Engagement Objectives
- Engagement Criteria
- Engagement Scope
- Methodology
- Sampling and Data Analytics
- CAATs
- Interviewing
Timing of Reviews
Resourcing and Milestones
Assessment of Engagement Risks
Approval of the Engagement Plan

Performing the Engagement

Opening Interviews
Audit Evidence
- Requesting Information
Analyzing Information
- Referral for Fraud or Other Investigation
Information Management and Confidentiality
- Use and Storage of Documents and Other Evidence
- File Conventions
- Use of Portable Devices and USBs

Supervision

Communication

Stakeholder Mapping
Engagement Communications
- Agreed Reporting Periods
- Draft Report Structure and Approvals
- Final Report Structure and Approvals
Recommendations and Agreed Management Actions
Report Ratings
Monitoring of Agreed Management Actions
- Communicating the Acceptance of Risks
Audit Committee Communications
Annual Reporting
Knowledge Management Processes
- Capturing Lessons Learned
- Handover of Client and Engagement Information

Marketing Processes

Appendices
- Appendix A: Process Map of Engagement Process
- Appendix B: Audit Process Templates
- Appendix C: Quality Checklists

Elements of Better Practice Policies and Procedures

Elements of better practice policies and procedures include:

- Policies and procedures aligned with IIA *Standards*
- Inclusion of process maps in the internal audit manual
- Web-based internal audit manuals that avoid version control issues and are easily accessible for both in-house and outsourced staff

Quality Assessment Policies

Policies and procedures to support internal audit quality are typically captured in the quality assurance and improvement program. This should outline the specific requirements around internal and external assessments and include guidance for measuring quality throughout the internal audit cycle. The quality assurance and improvement program is discussed further in Chapter 3.

Human Resources Policies

Subject to the size of the internal audit function, it may have in place its own human resources (HR) policies or it may rely on those of the broader organization. Usually, these policies would include elements such as the following:

- Recruitment
- Induction
- Remuneration
- Leave and entitlements
- Code of conduct
- Conflicts of interest
- Workplace health and safety
- Official travel
- Performance management
- Training and development

Information Security Policies

Confidentiality is an important tenet of internal auditing, and appropriately safeguarding client information prevents inappropriate disclosures, which could be damaging to both the internal audit function and the broader organization. Chief audit executives should recognize that information is an asset that requires securing.

HM Treasury in the United Kingdom in its 2011 guidance, *Internal Audit Records Management*, identifies three elements of information security:

- Protecting information from unauthorized access or disclosure (confidentiality)
- Ensuring that systems and information are complete and free from unauthorized change or modification (integrity)
- Ensuring that information and associated services are available to authorized users when and where required (availability)

The need for information security is reflected in IIA Standards 2330.A1, 2330.A2, 2330.C1, and 2440.A2, among others.

Standard 2330.A1

The chief audit executive must control access to engagement records. The chief audit executive must obtain the approval of senior management and/or legal counsel prior to releasing such records to external parties, as appropriate.

Standard 2330.A2

The chief audit executive must develop retention requirements for engagement records, regardless of the medium in which each record is stored. These retention requirements must be consistent with the organization's guidelines and any pertinent regulatory or other requirements.

Standard 2330.C1

The chief audit executive must develop policies governing the custody and retention of consulting engagement records, as well as their release to internal and external parties. These policies must be consistent with the organization's guidelines and any pertinent regulatory or other requirements.

Standard 2440.A2

If not otherwise mandated by legal, statutory, or regulatory requirements, prior to releasing results to parties outside the organization, the chief audit executive must:

- Assess the potential risk to the organization;
- Consult with senior management and/or legal counsel as appropriate; and
- Control dissemination by restricting the use of the results.

Chief audit executives should develop an information retention and disposal policy that is consistent with the organization's guidelines and any relevant legislation.

HM Treasury (2011) identifies the following typical objectives for an internal audit information management policy:

- Adequate records of information are maintained to account fully and transparently for all actions and decisions, and demonstrate due professional care.
- The legal and other rights of staff or those affected by internal audit actions are protected.
- Records are relevant, complete, and accurate, and the information they contain is reliable and authentic.
- Information can be efficiently retrieved by those with a legitimate right of access, for as long as the information to support audit decisions and conclusions needs to be held.
- Information is secure from unauthorized and accidental alteration or erasure, access and disclosure is properly controlled, and audit trails track usage and changes.
- Information is held in a robust format that remains readable for as long as it is required.
- There are consistent and documented retention and disposal procedures to include provisions for permanent preservation of archival material and secure disposal of information at the end of its life.
- Staff members are made aware of their information handling and keeping responsibilities through learning or awareness programs and guidance.

Chief audit executives should determine whether electronic communications (emails) are to be included in the information management policy.

Staff Safety and Physical Security Policies

Chief audit executives should consider staff safety as part of their policies and procedures, particularly in situations where internal auditors may be exposed to an unsafe working environment during fieldwork.

Chief audit executives should ensure the physical security of assets to avoid financial losses, as well as the potential loss of confidential information stored on portable assets.

QAIP Hint

Internal audit functions could incorporate *policies and procedures* into an internal audit maturity model or balanced scorecard.

Maturity Model

The internal audit function could include *policies and procedures* as a key process area in its maturity model. For example:

- Level 2 of a five-stage maturity model could identify that professional practices are undocumented and performed in an ad hoc manner.
- Level 3 could identify that policies and procedures are formally documented.
- Level 4 could identify that processes exist to ensure ongoing conformance with policies and procedures.

Balanced Scorecard/KPI

Internal audit functions could include performance indicators such as:

- Existence of policies and procedures
- Annual review of policies and procedures
- Extent to which policies and procedures are being applied by internal audit staff

Questions about Internal Audit Policies and Procedures

Table 11.1 provides a range of questions about policies and procedures. These can be formally incorporated into a quality assurance and improvement program, or, less formally, into ongoing assessment activities. Questions may be variously posed to the chief audit executive, internal auditors, or audit stakeholders.

TABLE 11.1 Quality Questions

Questions	Evidence of Quality
Are there internal audit policies and procedures in place that are appropriate to the size of the internal audit function?	Policies and procedures

(continued)

TABLE 11.1 (*continued*)

Questions	Evidence of Quality
Are internal audit staff aware of the policies and procedures?	Internal audit staff interviews
Do policies and procedures include key audit stages (engagement planning, fieldwork, etc.)?	Policies and procedures
Does the internal audit function have adequate policies and procedures for annual audit planning?	Policies and procedures
Do policies and procedures reflect contemporary audit practice?	Policies and procedures
Does the internal audit function have communication protocols (including report distribution, timing, etc.) that have been approved by management and the audit committee?	Communication protocols
Do standardized processes/templates exist for engagement reports/communications?	Standardized processes and templates
Does the internal audit function use contemporary, or leading-edge, audit processes and tools?	Assessment of internal audit processes, including the use of CAATs
Do policies and procedures cover the use of technology-based audit and data analysis techniques?	Policies and procedures
Are there specific policies regarding potential conflicts or impairments to objectivity?	Policies and procedures
Do policies and procedures cover access to engagement records?	Policies and procedures
Do policies and procedures include retention requirements for engagement records consistent with organizational guidelines and any regulatory requirements?	Policies and procedures
Do policy requirements provide for internal audit personnel to ensure security of engagement documents and information?	Policies and procedures
Do policies and procedures exist for dissemination of results with external parties?	Policies and procedures
Are policies and procedures updated on a regular (at least annual) basis?	Evidence of review
Does the chief audit executive discuss the need for changes to policies and procedures with staff?	Internal audit staff interviews

Conclusion

When reviewing operational areas, internal auditors will often look for the existence of policies and procedures, and determine the extent to which these are being applied. Internal auditors realize that policies and procedures form a key directive control for the organization.

Internal audit policies operate similarly. They help guide the internal auditor to operate in a consistent and professional manner. Policies and procedures provide assurance to audit clients that they are being treated fairly and impartially, and set a benchmark against which internal auditors can operate.

Policies and procedures should be developed to maximize the efficiency and effectiveness of the internal audit function, and their complexity and form should be relative to the size of the internal audit function.

References

HM Treasury. (2013, April). *Good Practice Guide: Audit and Risk Assurance Committee Handbook.* https://www.gov.uk/government/uploads/system/uploads/attachment_data/file/206978/audit_and_risk_assurance_committee_handbook.pdf.

HM Treasury. (2011, June). *Internal Audit Records Management.* https://www.gov.uk/government/uploads/system/uploads/attachment_data/file/207215/Internal_Audit_Records_Management.pdf.

The Institute of Internal Auditors. (2013). *International Professional Practices Framework.* Altamonte Springs, FL: The Institute of Internal Auditors.

The Institute of Internal Auditors–Australia. (2013). *Graduate Certificate in Internal Audit Module 1 Unit 1.* Unpublished.

New South Wales Treasury. (2012). *Internal Audit Manual.* Unpublished.

Reding, K. F., et al. (2009). *Internal Auditing: Assurance and Consulting Services.* Altamonte Springs, FL: The Institute of Internal Auditors Research Foundation.

Sawyer, L. B., M. A. Dittenhofer, and J. H. Scheiner. (2005). *Sawyers Internal Auditing,* 5th ed. Altamonte Springs, FL: The Institute of Internal Auditors Research Foundation.

CHAPTER 12

Annual Audit Planning

When I started out in business, I spent a great deal of time researching every detail that might be pertinent to the deal I was interested in making. I still do the same today. People often comment on how quickly I operate, but the reason I can move quickly is that I've done the background work first, which no one usually sees. I prepare myself thoroughly, and then when it is time to move ahead, I am ready to sprint.

—Donald Trump

Effective annual planning maximizes the internal audit function's potential to deliver high quality, value-added services. It provides an opportunity to align internal audit engagements with key organizational priorities and strategic risks, and creates an opportunity for engaging with organizational stakeholders.

Chief audit executives should consider the organization's strategic priorities and key risks as part of the annual audit planning process. In mature and established organizations they can draw on strategic documentation, including enterprise risk management planning, to inform the annual audit plan. However, where these do not exist, the chief audit executive should undertake some of this preliminary planning work before embarking on the annual planning process.

Value-Added Planning

Chief audit executives are required to undertake audit planning to ensure that the internal audit function maximizes its value to the organization. This requirement is reflected in IIA Standard 2000.

Standard 2000—Managing the Internal Audit Activity

The chief audit executive must effectively manage the internal audit activity to ensure it adds value to the organization.

The annual audit plan is a schedule of engagements that take into account key organizational priorities and strategic risks, and includes a clear assessment of the audit universe. Annual plans should reflect the nature of work described in the internal audit strategy and charter and reconcile budgetary and resource constraints. Quality plans incorporate a balanced portfolio of internal audit engagements and respond to changes in organizational conditions as well as internal audit focus, process, or strategy. They give due consideration to the materiality of potential auditable areas and factor in the work of other assurance providers in the organization.

Effective audit planning takes significant time and resources. Chief audit executives should have a clear understanding of the lead time required to produce their annual audit plan and ensure they commence planning sufficiently early to deliver the draft plan to the audit committee for approval or endorsement.

Applying an Objectives-Based Approach to Audit Planning

Internal auditors often describe better practice internal auditing as being risk-based. Although this is true, excessive focus on risks can prevent the internal audit function from appropriately considering strategy, and has the potential to cast the internal audit function in a negative light.

Internal audit should be focused on both strategic risks and the achievement of strategic objectives. This provides an opportunity for internal audit to operate in partnership with senior management, and moves the discourse from "What can go wrong?" to "What do we need to do right?"

Focusing on Organizational Objectives

"Ultimately, internal audit should be able to provide assurance on the organization achieving its objectives—which is not just risk-based," says Trygve Sørlie, former Chief Audit Executive at Gjensidige in Norway and current member of the International Internal Audit Standards Board. Sørlie believes that internal audit functions should look at both risks and enablers.

"Looking at enablers to achieving objectives may be better accepted by management because it is positive, rather than a negative risk-based approach." According to Sørlie, internal audit needs to stay slightly ahead of the business— seeing where the business is heading and ensuring that the business's approach reflects good practice.

Understanding the Organization's Business

Critical to the ability to add value through the annual audit plan is the need to fully understand the organization's business. While this might appear self-evident to experienced internal auditors, the risk of misunderstanding the operating environment is that the internal audit function reverts to traditional, often generic, internal audit engagements. Although these engagements may be of some value, they may not be focused on critical areas.

Baker (2010) identifies five questions that chief audit executives can ask to determine their level of organizational knowledge:

1. Do you know what the business is here for?
2. Do you know how the business is positioned in its sector?
3. Do you know what the business model is?
4. Do you know how each business line or support unit contributes to the bigger picture?
5. Do you know how each process within that line or unit aids that contribution?

If the chief audit executive is able to readily answer these questions, he or she will be well positioned to commence the audit planning process.

Common Quality Issue

Some internal audit functions develop annual audit plans that are not aligned to the organization's objectives, strategies, and risks. Instead, they may have drawn heavily on historical audits, or focused on lower-level operational or financial controls. Understanding the business well enough to focus on strategic areas is challenging for fully outsourced internal audit functions, particularly if the outsourced provider is not actively engaged in senior management discussions.

Applying a Risk-Based Approach to Audit Planning

While it is critical that internal audit functions support the achievement of organizational objectives, a key premise of quality internal auditing is that engagements also focus on the key risks impacting an organization. Adopting a risk-based approach to audit planning provides rigor and transparency to the selection of auditable areas.

Consideration of the level of risk forms the basis for prioritizing and selecting audit topics for inclusion in the annual plan for the forthcoming financial year plus out years. The need for risk-based panning is reflected in IIA Standards 2010 and 2010.A1.

Standard 2010—Planning

The chief audit executive must establish a risk-based plan to determine the priorities of the internal audit activity, consistent with the organization's goals.

Standard 2010.A1

The internal audit activity's plan of engagements must be based on a documented risk assessment, undertaken at least annually. The input of senior management and the board must be considered in this process.

Different Approaches to Identifying Risks

The risk assessment establishes a link between the proposed internal audit engagements and the operational and strategic risks of the organization. The risk assessment should take account of feedback received from operational managers, senior management, and the board.

Ideally, the internal audit function will draw on established risk management plans from across the organization to identify risks. These can be further supported by internal audit's own assessment of risk. The chief audit executive may choose to identify these risks through risk assessment questionnaires, facilitated risk assessments, stakeholder interviews, and/or audit committee input. In addition, the chief audit executive can review key corporate documents, such as the organization's strategic plan and business plan, and the findings of previous internal and external audit reports.

Common Quality Issue

Not all organizations will have an established, formalized risk management process that the chief audit executive can draw on in developing the annual audit plan. The IIA *Standards* anticipates this situation in the interpretation for Standard 2010. "If a (risk management) framework does not exist, the chief audit executive must use his/her own judgment of risks after consideration of input from senior management and the board (Audit Committee)."

APPROACH 1: IDENTIFYING RISKS AT THE ACTIVITY, ORGANIZATIONAL, AND EXTERNAL LEVELS
In the absence of an organization-wide risk management process, the chief audit executive could consider risks in relation to the organizational structure. This can be facilitated by considering risks at each of three distinct levels—activity risks, organizational risks, and external risks.

Activity Risks Activity risks relate to specific activities, projects, or programs. They include the strategic, staffing, and operational risks that exist within a project or program area and for which the individual manager is responsible. Examples of these activity, project, or program risks include:

- Failure to establish effective project or program governance
- Failure of a project or program to achieve its objectives
- Failure to comply with legislative or policy requirements
- Inadequate recruitment and retention of skilled and experienced staff to meet operational requirements
- Inadequate budget and financial management arrangements to deliver agreed outputs and outcomes

Organizational Risks Organizational risks are relevant across the business and include the strategic, staffing, and operational risks for which senior management is responsible. Examples of organizational risks include:

- Failure to achieve strategic objectives across the organization

- Failure to establish effective governance arrangements across the organization
- Failure to comply with legislative or policy requirements
- Inadequate financial management arrangements to achieve efficient, effective, and economical outputs and outcomes

External Risks   External risks relate to interactions between the organization and external parties. They result from collaborations with other organizations, such as through joint ventures in the private sector or whole-of-government activities in the public sector. External risks will generally be managed at the interorganizational level through an oversight or steering group. Examples of external risks include:

- Failure to establish effective oversight arrangements between entities
- Failure to establish appropriate contractual arrangements or terms of reference to ensure accountability and risk management
- Failure to establish consistent work practices across organizations
- Failure to effectively manage financial or budgetary arrangements

APPROACH 2: IDENTIFYING RISKS AT THE ENVIRONMENT, PEOPLE, AND ORGANIZATIONAL LEVELS   Chief audit executives could also consider risks by separating them into environmental, people, and organizational risks. Environmental risks are typically those external to the organization that impact the context in which the organization operates. People risks relate to those risks impacting employees within an organization, and organizational risks relate to all elements of the organization other than employees.

Types of risk areas that would normally be considered under each of these elements are provided in Table 12.1.

The chief audit executive should define the specific risks associated with each of these categories.

TABLE 12.1 Risk Areas

Environmental Risk Areas	People Risk Areas	Organizational Risk Areas
Regulatory conformance	Workforce planning	Governance structure and processes, including internal control systems
Global financial stability and sovereign debt	Accountabilities and responsibilities	Organizational structure, including growth and downsizing
Conservation and heritage	Sourcing processes, including outsourcing and recruitment	Strategic and business planning
Environmental sustainability and pollution	Succession planning and retention	Budget and financial management, including financial systems
Natural hazards and disasters	Staff capability and competency	Corporate information and information management
Geographical isolation and economies of scale	Leadership skills, including integrity of leadership	Information technology, including recent changes and existence of legacy systems

(continued)

TABLE 12.1 (*continued*)

Environmental Risk Areas	People Risk Areas	Organizational Risk Areas
Government stability and politics	Management skills and competence of management	Project management
Globalization and emerging markets	Social and interpersonal skills	Asset management and liquidity of assets
Customers and client base	Professional liability	Business continuity and disaster recovery
Marketing	Performance management	Legislative compliance and legal
Public relations	Professional development	Occupational health and safety
Stakeholder relationships and external knowledge sharing	Organizational culture, including tone at the top and employee morale	Security
Third-party providers	Industrial relations and working arrangements	Contracts and procurements

Rating Risks

Where an organizational risk framework exists, internal auditors should use this to classify and rate risks. Ideally, this will take account of the organization's risk appetite. Where no such framework exists, the internal audit function will need to use its own process, which should be articulated within internal audit policies and procedures.

Usually, risks will be rated according to the likelihood of the risk occurring and the consequence of the risk occurring. Combined, these will then generate an overall risk rating. Typical likelihood and consequence ratings are provided in Tables 12.2 and 12.3.

TABLE 12.2 Risk Likelihood Ratings

Rating	Likelihood of Risk Occurring	Indicative Frequency
Almost certain	It is expected to occur multiple times during the term of the corporate/strategic plan. A regular event.	5+ times (during the term of the corporate/ strategic plan)
Likely	Expected to occur at some time during the term of the corporate/strategic plan.	1 to 5 times
Possible	If risk is not controlled, likely to occur at some point during the term of the corporate/ strategic plan. Risk has been previously realized within the organization or is known to have been realized within other, similar organizations.	1
Unlikely	May occur in some circumstances, especially if risk is left uncontrolled. A particular set of circumstances would need to eventuate for the risk to be realized.	<1
Rare	Very unlikely to occur and, if so, only would occur once.	<0.5

TABLE 12.3 Risk Consequence Ratings

Rating	Budgetary Consequences	Service Delivery Consequences	Reputational Consequences	Strategic Consequences
Severe	Significant additional funding/budget required to fund mitigation actions; impacts other services or production	Indeterminate, prolonged disruption to key or essential services or production	Negative publicity occurs in national media or extensively on social media	Organization's mission and/or strategy not achieved
Major	Significant additional funding/budget required to fund mitigation actions	Prolonged (3–10 days) disruptions to services or production	Negative publicity occurs in local media or moderately on social media	Organization cannot demonstrate achievement of all its objectives
Moderate	Additional funding/budget required to fund mitigation actions	Short to medium term (1–3 days) disruption to services or production within a division	Concerns raised with board regarding effectiveness of organization	Operational objectives not achieved
Minor	Funding/budget within organizational area needs to be reallocated to fund mitigation actions	Short term (<1 day), temporary disruption to nonessential services or production	Concerns raised with CEO regarding effectiveness of division	One or more operational objectives need to be amended
Insignificant	No additional funding required	Only impacts upon timing of delivery of existing services and production; no critical deadlines affected	No impact on how organization is perceived	One or more operational KPIs are not achieved

Determining the significance of each risk should also include consideration of materiality, or the impact and significance of the activity or program to the overall organization. This should extend beyond financial considerations and encompass social, cultural, environmental, and well-being impacts to the organization and its external clients, customers, and stakeholders.

Considering materiality and impact will require an assessment of the following:

- Economic or financial impact of the activity or program on the organization as a whole. This should take account of the relative expenditure or income within and generated from the activity or program.
- Social and cultural materiality, including the number of external stakeholders, customer base, or broader public likely to be affected by the activity or program.
- Environmental and well-being impacts of the activity or program, including the potential benefits or damage to the environment as well as any associated impacts on public health and well-being.
- Importance of the activity or program to achieving the organization's objectives
- Nature, size, and complexity of the activity or program relative to the entire organization

---

Conversations with Senior Management

Matt Tolley, National Manager, Audit, Commonwealth Department of Human Services in Australia, recommends that in situations where the organization's risk management framework is still evolving, chief audit executives consider implementing a strategic dialogue with the organization's executives about risk. Chief audit executives should consider:

- When and with whom they will have those conversations
- The specific nature of each conversation, recognizing that different stakeholders might require different conversations
- How to draw their own conclusions about risk across the organization from those conversations
- How to present conclusions

Tolley warns that it is unlikely that simply approaching executives and asking them to discuss their risks in general terms will be effective. He believes that, first, such a discussion is likely to be premised on executives' current understanding of the organization's strategic risks, which may not necessarily be accurate. Second, in the absence of a consistent conversational framework, the discussion is likely to range across strategic and operational risks and vary markedly between executives, generating a large quantity of information of inconsistent quality.

He also recommends that the increased use of analytics during the development of a strategic audit plan could focus these conversations in a manner that will reduce the quantity and improve the quality of information gathered, while also helping the internal audit function to meet its other planning and reporting obligations under the IIA's *Standards*.

Internal auditing provides assurance over the adequacy and effectiveness of control within an organization. However, the internal audit function itself operates as a detective control—identifying errors, abuse, and inefficiencies. It also acts as a deterrent, discouraging deliberate mismanagement and abuse through the *threat* of being discovered. Both of these attributes—deterrence and detection—need to be balanced in the creation of the annual audit plan.

Auditable Areas and the Audit Universe

The IIA's practice advisories supporting the Standards, and in particular PA2010–1, recognize the value in chief audit executives developing an audit universe as a precursor to the development of the audit plan.

Practice Advisory 2010–1: Linking the Audit Plan to Risks and Exposures

In developing the internal audit activity's plan, many CAEs find it useful to first develop or update the audit universe. The audit universe is a list of all the possible audits that could be performed. The CAE may obtain input on the audit universe from senior management and the board.

The audit universe can include components from the organization's strategic plan. By incorporating components of the organization's strategic plan, the audit universe will consider and reflect the overall business objectives.

In developing the audit universe, chief audit executives should consider (and potentially map) all major processes and operations within the organization. This can be a complex and time-consuming process, and chief audit executives should allocate appropriate resources (both in terms of time and experience) to map the universe. Nonetheless, in undertaking this task, chief audit executives will be rewarded with a comprehensive insight into their organization's activities and processes. Conversely, the absence of an audit universe and/or a risk-based audit plan limits the potential to determine whether internal audit resources are sufficient and appropriately allocated.

Common Quality Issue

Internal audit functions may not have fully documented their organization's auditable areas. This may be due to the audit team's limited understanding of the organizational environment, overreliance on historical audits as a basis for future audit planning, or limited resources to map the universe. It can result in internal audit resources being expended on providing assurance over areas of low importance to the organization.

(continued)

(*continued*)

The chief audit executive may also decide against developing a complete audit universe because of their focus on identified strategic risks. While this is reasonable, it poses its own risk that significant, material areas or activities within the organization, or strategic objectives, are not provided with adequate assurance. In this case, the chief audit executive needs to strike a balance between auditing identified, strategic risks, and key organizational activities and processes.

Mapping the Audit Universe Using a Matrix Approach

For large organizations, mapping the audit universe can involve a high level of repetition, as similar programs or products may be delivered or produced in multiple locations, and corporate support services may be shared across a number of areas. In these situations, rather than viewing the audit universe as a one-dimensional list of activities, the chief audit executive could develop a three-dimensional universe that recognizes the interplay between a range of different activities across the organization. An example of a three-dimensional model is provided in Figure 12.1.

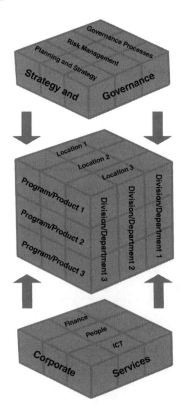

FIGURE 12.1 Three-Dimensional Audit Universe

Using a three-dimensional approach to the audit universe provides the chief audit executive with the ability to undertake specific audits of corporate services (e.g., finance or human resources) or strategy and governance (e.g., risk management, planning, or strategic committees). The chief audit executive can then look at the ways in which these are delivered within different divisions and locations or affect program delivery or production—that is, the selection of the divisions, locations, products, and programs determine the scope, rather than the objective, of the audit.

Assurance Mapping

Internal audit functions work within organizations to support the improvement of governance, risk management, and control processes. Achieving success requires collaboration between internal audit and management, as well as other internal and external assurance providers. It is unlikely that the internal audit function would have sufficient resources to provide assurance over the entire organization. Regardless, there are efficiencies to be achieved in coordinating assurance.

Chief audit executives should have a clear understanding of the assurance provided by other organizational stakeholders to ensure that they deliver value to their organization. This is best achieved through assurance mapping, which supports conformance with IIA Standard 2050.

Standard 2050—Coordination

The chief audit executive should share information and coordinate activities with other internal and external providers of assurance and consulting services to ensure proper coverage and minimize duplication of efforts.

Assurance mapping can help *join the dots* between the activities of each of the different assurance providers, avoiding duplication while maximizing the use of organizational resources.

Assurance providers include:

- Management
- Risk management
- Compliance teams
- Quality assurance
- Evaluation teams
- Internal audit
- External audit
- Other external sources, including:
  - Government reviewers
  - Accreditation providers

- Workplace health and safety inspectors
- Environment protection/monitoring authorities

The Australian National Audit Office (2012) believes that assurance mapping can help an audit committee obtain confidence in the organization's governance, risk management, and control processes by presenting a broad, entity-wide perspective of the assurance *landscape*. It believes internal audit effectiveness can be maximized by considering internal auditing in the context of other elements of the organization's assurance framework.

An assurance map will typically document assurance over the key risks affecting an organization. It provides senior management and the audit committee with visibility over the management of key risks through the associated controls or risk mitigation strategies, and the assurance provided over these controls or mitigations. The process is illustrated in Figure 12.2.

Documenting the assurance map highlights any duplication of assurance, and allows senior management and the audit committee to make an informed decision regarding the desirability of this duplication. The map should also point out any areas lacking assurance coverage, which will assist senior management and the audit committee to determine the appropriateness of the proposed annual audit plan.

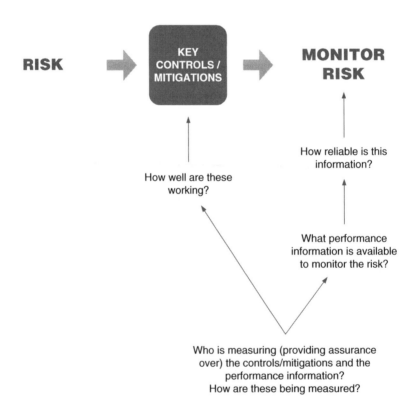

FIGURE 12.2 Assurance Map

Elements within an Assurance Map

There are many different ways to develop an assurance map. An approach used successfully by Pitt Group, an Australian-based provider of internal audit services, involves an Excel-based map that uses separate sheets for each key risk. Key elements that are identified for each risk (on each sheet) in the map include the following:

- The name of the key risk
- The risk owner
- Key controls and/or treatments for the risk
- The process owner for each control or treatment
- First-line assurance activities undertaken by operational management and the owner of these activities
- Second-line assurance activities undertaken by other organizational assurance providers such as Compliance or Quality Assurance, and the area responsible
- The focus of each assurance activity in relation to the control or treatment (i.e., is the activity primarily focused on assurance over the control, or is assurance provided as a secondary focus?)
- The quality of the first- and second-line assurance. This is usually determined by internal or external audit through testing the assurance activity itself. Including this measure provides visibility to management and the audit committee as to whether the assurance can be relied on.

An extract from a model map is provided in Figure 12.3.

Key Risk 1						Risk Owner			
Key control/ treatment	Control Owner	First-line assurance activity	Assurance owner	Level and focus	Second-line assurance activity	Assurance owner	Level and focus	Third-line assurance activity	External audits
Key Control 1									
Key Control 2									
Key Control 3									

FIGURE 12.3 Assurance Map Extract

Combined Assurance

Combined assurance is the coordination of assurance between different providers. Often, this assurance crosses the three lines of defense, incorporating management, second-line providers such as Compliance and Quality Assurance, internal audit, and external audit.

Sarens and colleagues (2012) have identified that combined assurance:

- Helps make better decisions.
- Helps to prioritize actions.
- Brings comfort to senior management and the audit committee.
- Increases the knowledge of the business and risk awareness among managers.
- Eliminates silos.
- Elevates exposure and carries much more weight.
- Increases accountability.
- Increases transparency.
- Promotes better use of assurance resources.
- Increases the quality of internal audit functions.
- Standardizes assurance work.

Coordinating with External Audit

Internal and external auditors should ideally work as collaborators, with distinct but complementary assurance roles. Internal audit functions should not defer to external audit, nor should they exist to simply reduce the level of work needed to be undertaken by external auditors.

Spencer Pickett (2011) describes the ideal interaction between internal and external audit as "interfaced audit planning." He suggests there are three stages of cooperative planning that internal and external auditors can progress through, as demonstrated in Figure 12.4.

Spencer Pickett acknowledges the difficulties in achieving the third stage and suggests this may be more likely to occur in the public, rather than the private, sector. However, he believes a level of harmonization is essential and should be encouraged.

STAGE ONE
Copies of plans are exchanged.

STAGE TWO
A joint meeting is held where plans are discussed and harmonized but plans are issued separately.

STAGE THREE
Regular meetings are conducted where fully integrated plans are issued as one composite document.

FIGURE 12.4 Interfaced Audit Planning
Source: Spencer Pickett (2011).

Resource Allocation

Chief audit executives are usually limited by resource constraints from reviewing the entire audit universe. They then face the challenge of having to determine which internal audit engagements can be undertaken within the finite resources they have.

The production of an annual internal audit budget should occur contiguously with the development of the annual audit plan. This ensures that the plan reflects available resources and the budget reflects the engagements requiring completion. In developing the budget, the chief audit executive should consider salaries of in-house staff, consulting fees for external resources, and costs for travel.

Internal Audit Budget

The budget available for staffing the internal audit function will both drive the decisions made around the sourcing model and be driven by the sourcing model. The resources allocated to the internal audit function will be largely driven by senior management's perceptions of internal audit's value. Being able to demonstrate significant value can often lead to budget increases.

> ## Standard 2030—Resource Management
>
> The chief audit executive must ensure that internal audit resources are appropriate, sufficient, and effectively deployed to achieve the approved plan.

Example 12.1 provides a simplified internal audit budget from the Australian National Audit Office (2012).

Example 12.1 Internal Audit Budget

Budget	Year –1 $	Year 1 $	Year 2 $	Year 3 $
Staff (including overheads)				
Travel and accommodation				
External service provider(s)				
Total				
Human resources	Year –1 Days	Year 1 Days	Year 2 Days	Year 3 Days
Available days: In-house staff				
External service provider(s)				
Total available days				
Less days applied to nonaudit activities				

Total available internal audit days				
Internal audit support activities				
Development of the internal audit strategic business plan and annual work plan				
Monitor audit and other report recommendations				
Prepare annual assessment report				
Service the audit committee				
Manage audit program				
Staff recruitment/training				
External auditor liaison				
Other internal audit support activities				
Total internal audit support activity days				
Total available for annual work plan				

Source: Australian National Audit Office (2012).

Common Quality Issue

There are three common quality issues associated with the internal audit budget—insufficient budget, inadequate linkage to audit planning, and inadequate budget monitoring.

There is a strong correlation between an inadequate internal audit budget and a failure by the internal audit function to demonstrate value to senior management and the audit committee. Organizations are unlikely to commit increased resources to an activity that cannot demonstrate value.

An organization, or chief audit executive, can determine what would be an appropriate level of internal audit resources through benchmarking with like organizations. This can occur informally using professional networks or formally through recognized benchmarking services such as those offered by professional services firms, recruitment firms, and professional associations such as the IIA. However, considerations when benchmarking include:

- Comparative organizations may not be demonstrating better practice.
- Resource requirements need to be linked to the value expected by senior management and the board, and may differ significantly between similar organizations.
- The types of auditing and nature of engagements undertaken will require different levels of skills and experience.
- Variations in expectations between countries and sectors may exist.

Matching Skills and Resources

Chief audit executives need to determine how they will staff individual engagements, matching the complexity and nature of the audit with appropriately skilled and experienced staff. Where appropriate in-house skills are unavailable, the chief audit executive will need to look at insourcing these skills.

Issues around resourcing the internal audit activity are discussed further in Chapter 9.

Flexible Planning

Embedding flexibility within the internal audit plan allows the internal audit function to account for changing organizational priorities, urgent new initiatives, and requests for ad hoc engagements.

Embedding Flexibility in the Audit Plan

To embed flexibility in the audit plan:

- Include scope for management identified reviews and follow-up audits.
- Develop a rolling plan of audits to allow some movement of proposed audits between years.
- Include previous audit coverage in the plan to provide visibility over the time between audits.
- Include specific time for nonaudit activities (such as management and supervision, quality assurance, professional development, review of charters and procedures, attendance at management meetings, audit committee support, etc.).
- Become proactively involved in new projects and initiatives to expedite changes to the audit plan to accommodate these new areas.
- Include a specific allocation within the audit plan for investigations if the internal audit function is responsible for these.

Annual Audit Plan Formats

There are many formats that can be used for an annual audit plan, and the chief audit executive should design an approach that best meets the organization's needs. Nonetheless, typical elements of the annual audit plan will include:

- Name of the program or activity proposed for review
- Links to the audit universe and assurance map if available
- Person responsible for program or activity (engagement client)
- Focus area or high-level objective of engagement
- Link to strategic/operational risks and risk rating
- Link to strategic/operational objectives (if relevant)

- Type of engagement (performance/operational audit, financial audit, IT audit, etc.)
- Estimated days or hours for the engagement
- Proposed time period for the engagement

Rolling Audit Plans

Once chief audit executives have completed all the elements associated with effective audit planning (i.e., assessing risks, mapping the audit universe, factoring in other assurance provided, and estimating the time required for each audit), they are well placed to develop their annual audit plan.

Some chief audit executives will choose to develop a rolling audit plan. This is a complete list of potential audit engagements, prioritized according the risk and materiality of the auditable area. Normally it would identify the time since the last audit and the proposed duration between audits.

A rolling audit plan helps chief audit executives reconcile their inability to audit their entire audit universe. Using the plan, chief audit executives can prioritize potential audits, placing the highest priority audits at the top of the plan. They can then effectively draw a line though the list at the point for which they are resourced. Those audits falling below this line can form supplementary audits in the event a planned audit is unable to be delivered, or could be considered in subsequent years.

Having a list of audits that extend beyond those that can be completed within available resources provides visibility to senior management and the audit committee of the value they are receiving from the allocated internal audit resources. Importantly, it allows stakeholders to make an informed decision regarding the benefit of allocating additional resources in order to receive a greater level of assurance.

Communication and Approval

Ensuring that the audit planning process is rigorous and transparent will help the chief audit executive to build positive relationships with senior management and the audit committee. It is important that the audit committee have ownership of the audit plan through its final approval, as the plan will ultimately determine the level of type of assurance that is provided to them. Effective planning will help embed the internal audit function as a *critical friend* rather that perpetuate an image of an impartial observer.

IIA Standard 2020 requires the chief audit executive to communicate the plan with senior management and the board and to seek approval for its initial development and any subsequent changes.

Standard 2020—Communication and Approval

The chief audit executive must communicate the internal audit activity's plans and resource requirements, including significant interim changes, to senior management and the board for review and approval. The chief audit executive must also communicate the impact of resource limitations.

QAIP Hint

Internal audit functions could incorporate *annual audit planning* into an internal audit maturity model or a balanced scorecard.

Maturity Model

Internal audit functions could include *annual audit planning* as a key process area in its maturity model. For example:

- Level 2 of a five-stage maturity model could identify that no formalized annual planning is undertaken—audits are selected in an ad hoc manner.
- Level 3 could identify that annual audit planning is undertaken, and risks are considered in the planning process.
- Level 4 could identify that annual audit planning is aligned to strategic and operational risks, and strategic priorities. Management is actively involved in the development of the plan.
- Level 5 could identify that annual audit planning is aligned to an audit universe and assurance map and that strategic risks and objectives are routinely addressed through the plan.

Balanced Scorecard/KPI

Internal audit functions could include performance indicators such as:

- Proportion of senior managers consulted as part of the planning process (include target)
- Level of senior management satisfaction with the audit plan (include target)
- Proportion of the organization's strategic priorities addressed in the audit plan (include target)
- Conduct of a periodic, at least annual, comprehensive risk assessment
- Percentage of key risks audited per annum (include target)
- Proportion of audit universe addressed in the audit plan
- Extent of coverage of strategic priorities (include target)
- Extent of coverage of key business activities (include target)
- Proportion of geographic and functional areas addressed in the audit plan (include target)
- Percentage of major projects audited per annum (include target)
- Percentage of major systems audited per annum (include target)
- Percentage of "systems under development" audited per annum (include target)
- Existence of audit committee concerns regarding unaddressed risks
- Completion of audit plan
- Number of management initiated requests (include target)

Questions about Annual Audit Planning

Table 12.4 provides a range of questions about annual audit planning. These can be formally incorporated into a quality assurance and improvement program, or, less formally, into ongoing assessment activities. Questions may be variously posed to the chief audit executive, internal auditors, or audit stakeholders.

TABLE 12.4 Quality Questions

Questions	Evidence of Quality
Do the chief audit executive and internal auditors spend time in the business to develop an understanding of key issues?	Senior management and audit committee interviews
Does the scope of work in the annual audit plan meet the role of internal audit under the internal audit charter?	Annual audit plan
Does the annual audit plan consider an environmental scan of the wider external context of the organization such as legislative compliance requirements, industry risks, and economic factors?	Annual audit plan
Does the annual audit plan align with the strategic and operational risks of the organization?	Annual audit plan
Is the annual audit plan based on a documented risk assessment of the organization's risks?	Annual audit plan Documented risk assessment
Is this risk assessment performed at least annually?	Annual audit plan Documented risk assessment
Does the annual audit plan consider the organization's risk management framework, including any risk appetite set by management?	Annual audit plan Senior management interviews
Does the annual audit plan adequately account for new and emerging risk areas?	Annual audit plan Senior management interviews
Is the annual audit plan dynamic and flexible, adapting as the risk profile of the organization changes (e.g., changes occur to the annual audit plan during the year if the risk profile changes)?	Annual audit plan Senior management interviews
Has the internal audit function identified the auditable areas across the organization?	Audit universe
Does the internal audit function have a process for ensuring optimal budget allocation and adherence for annual planning such as prioritizing projects?	Annual audit plan Chief audit executive interview
Is input to the annual audit plan obtained from senior management and the audit committee?	Documented evidence of input Senior management and audit committee interviews
Has the internal audit function applied a consistent approach to assessing risks and potential auditable areas?	Audit planning methodology Senior management interviews
Does the annual audit plan include an appropriate mix of engagements covering the scope of organizational activity?	Annual audit plan
Are senior management and the audit committee satisfied with the assurance coverage provided through the annual audit plan?	Senior management and audit committee interviews

Are the annual audit plan and any significant changes communicated to senior management and the audit committee for approval?	Documented evidence of input Senior management and audit committee interviews
Is there alignment between the internal audit function and other assurance providers?	Chief audit executive interview Senior management and audit committee interviews
Are there any instances where the internal audit function has unnecessarily duplicated the work of other assurance providers?	Senior management and audit committee interviews
Are other assurance providers consulted during the development of the annual audit plan?	Senior management and audit committee interviews
Does the internal audit function have a formal process for engaging with the external audit team regarding the audit plan?	Chief audit executive interview
Is the annual audit plan shared with other assurance providers?	Documented evidence of input Assurance providers interviews

Conclusion

Undertaking better practice, risk-based audit planning ensures that the chief audit executive is directing resources at areas most likely to add value to the organization. Without adequate planning, the chief auditor executive may not be meeting stakeholder expectations.

However, planning presents significant challenges in today's dynamic organizational environments. Constant structural and operational changes will require chief audit executives to regularly reassess the relevance of their plan to determine if proposed audits should also be adjusted. The organization's risks may be affected by reduced resources or additional activities, and mergers and acquisitions will change the nature of the organization. Each of these will need to be considered in planning future engagements.

References

Abdolmohammadi, M. J., and A. Sharbatouglie. (2005). *Continuous Auditing: An Operational Model for Internal Auditors*. Altamonte Springs, FL: The Institute of Internal Auditors Research Foundation.

Australian National Audit Office. (2012, September). *Public Sector Internal Audit: An Investment in Assurance and Business Improvement—Better Practice Guide*. http://www.anao.gov.au/~/media/Files/Better%20Practice%20Guides/2012%202013/ANAO%20%20Public%20Sector%20Internal%20Audit.pdf.

Baker, N. (2010, June). Know your business. *Internal Auditor*. http://www.theiia.org/intauditor.

The Institute of Internal Auditors. (2013). *International Professional Practices Framework*. Altamonte Springs, FL: The Institute of Internal Auditors.

Reding, K. F., et al. (2009). *Internal Auditing: Assurance and Consulting Services*. Altamonte Springs, FL: The Institute of Internal Auditors Research Foundation.

Sarens, G., L. Decaux, and R. Lenz. (2012). *Combined Assurance: Case Studies on a Holistic Approach to Organizational Governance*. Altamonte Springs, FL: The Institute of Internal Auditors Research Foundation.

Sawyer, L. B., M. A. Dittenhofer, and J. H. Scheiner. (2005). *Sawyers Internal Auditing*, 5th ed. Altamonte Springs, FL: The Institute of Internal Auditors Research Foundation.

Spencer Pickett, K. H. (2012). *The Essential Guide to Internal Auditing*, 2nd ed. West Sussex, England: John Wiley & Sons.

CHAPTER 13

Planning the Engagement

Failing to plan is planning to fail.

—Winston Churchill

Effective audit planning sets the foundation for a quality engagement. It allows the internal audit function to identify the areas in which it will focus its effort, and helps to ensure that the engagement is completed efficiently and effectively.

Planning provides an opportunity for internal auditors to familiarize themselves with the operations and activities of areas under review. It promotes a structured and strategic approach to conducting internal audit engagements, and the success of an engagement often rests on how well planning has been undertaken.

Purpose of Engagement Planning

Internal audit engagements are undertaken for a variety of reasons. Although their overall purpose is to support the organization to improve governance, risk management, and control processes, an individual engagement will have a specific area of focus. This focus will be influenced by management expectations, the type of engagement being undertaken, and the area or activity being reviewed. The chief audit executive should be clear about the purpose of the engagement prior to commencing.

Engagement planning allows the internal auditor to do the following:

- Obtain a comprehensive understanding of the operations and activities of the area under review in order to focus on significant risks.
- Ensure alignment between internal audit engagements, the annual audit plan, and the internal audit charter.
- Ensure alignment between the internal audit function and other assurance activities.
- Ensure that engagement fieldwork conforms with the internal audit function's policies and procedures.
- Develop a methodology that will maximize the potential to address the engagement objectives in an efficient manner.

Spending time on planning will pay dividends in terms of undertaking a focused and value-adding engagement. For this reason, IIA Standards 2200 and 2240 articulate specific requirements around planning.

Standard 2200—Engagement Planning

Internal auditors must develop and document a plan for each engagement, including the engagement's objectives, scope, timing, and resource allocations.

Standard 2240—Engagement Work Program

Internal auditors must develop and document work programs that achieve the engagement objectives.

Each internal audit function should develop its own approach to engagement planning and either document this as part of its policies and procedures or develop standardized templates to support consistency. Typically, an engagement plan will include the following elements:

- Background (including an overview of the operations or activity, how it fits into the broader organization, as well as its budget and staffing)
- Risk assessment/key risks
- Audit objectives (and subobjectives if used)
- Criteria
- Audit scope
- Methodology

It may also include:

- Previous audits conducted
- Resources, including budget and staffing
- Milestones
- Approvals of the plan

For larger engagements, and in particular operational and performance audits, engagement planning can sometimes merge into conduct or fieldwork. Information may be obtained during the planning phase that ultimately supports findings and conclusions. Depending on the proposed duration of the overall engagement, the time taken for planning can range from days to weeks.

Planning a Great Engagement

"A great audit engagement is often defined by the quality of the planning," says Rune Johannessen, Senior Audit Manager and Head of Competence and Development at Nordea Bank AB in Norway, and member of the IIA Professional

Issues Committee. He considers there to be a number of elements that combine together to produce effective planning:

1. The plan needs to make sense and be easy to follow. It needs to reflect business priorities, and demonstrate internal audit's understanding of business objectives.
2. The plan needs to clearly identify business risks and incorporate these in a way that even external parties can understand and can see what part of the process or activity the risks relate to.
3. The plan similarly needs to clearly identify key controls and their relationship to risks.
4. Engagement plans should demonstrate intelligent auditing—incorporating smart ways of providing assurance that are not reliant only on resource intensive audit sampling.

Johannessen believes a good audit is one where people haven't taken short cuts in the planning, resulting in a focus on end-point transactions at the expense of process design. "Great engagement planning will minimize the cost and time of the audit whilst maximizing organizational outcomes," says Johannessen.

Client Engagement

To commence planning, the chief audit executive, possibly through the internal auditor responsible for the engagement (engagement leader), should notify the relevant senior manager (engagement sponsor) of the internal audit function's intention to start planning. The chief audit executive should request an appropriate contact (engagement client) from the area to be reviewed.

Timing of Reviews

The annual audit plan will often identify the time period (month, quarter, etc.) in which an engagement is proposed to be undertaken. Good practice requires the internal audit function to confirm with the engagement sponsor, whether the proposed timing is, in fact, suitable for the area being audited.

There may be times such as end of financial year or during a major change management initiative that are extremely busy for some areas or activities, and are best avoided by internal audit. Doing so demonstrates respect for the pressures already on the engagement client, and also enhances the potential that internal audit will receive an appropriate level of support and *buy-in* from the engagement client.

Initial Meeting with the Engagement Client

The engagement leader should arrange an initial meeting with the engagement client, which should be attended by the engagement team and possibly the chief audit executive. The meeting should be used to do the following:

- Provide a broad outline of the high-level engagement objective, the reason it was selected, and its relationship to the annual audit plan.
- Explain the purpose of the planning phase, which is to conduct background research on the area to be reviewed in order to establish the objectives, scope, and criteria to be applied, leading to the development of an engagement plan.
- Explain the processes and methods the internal audit function will use to plan the engagement and the nature of the information to be collected and/or needed from the engagement client.
- Seek feedback on any areas of potential focus that would assist the engagement client (recognizing the risk of being directed toward areas known to be satisfactory).
- Obtain contact details of key personnel who may assist with any inquiries during the planning phase.
- Identify any concerns of the engagement client regarding the overall engagement process.
- Outline the process for ensuring the engagement client is consulted on the outcomes of the planning phase, including any opportunity they may have to comment on the engagement plan.

The initial meeting can also be a good opportunity to provide an overview of the roles and responsibilities of the internal audit function, and standard processes that it adopts for undertaking engagements. This meeting will set the tone for the engagement, so care should be taken to ensure that the meeting is conducted in a professional, organized, and structured manner.

Avoid Increasing Management's Anxiety

"Be aware that operational management deals with a range of pressures on a daily basis," says Cesar Martinez, member of the IIA Professional Issues Committee.

Commencing an internal audit in an area already facing competing demands and deadlines has the potential to really increase management's stress levels. Martinez cautions internal auditors to be aware of these potential tensions and to understand how an internal audit can really add value for management. Wherever possible, internal auditors should try to reduce, rather than increase, management's concerns.

The internal audit function should emphasize that input into the planning of the engagement is welcomed and that the engagement will be undertaken in an open, fair, and consultative manner.

The engagement leader could use the initial meeting as an opportunity to seek feedback from the engagement client regarding his or her previous experience with internal audit, and to set positive expectations regarding the proposed engagement.

Audit Notification Memorandum

Internal audit functions may choose to issue an engagement notification memorandum (or similar) to engagement clients, advising them of the overall objective of the engagement, its proposed timing, and the need to organize an opening interview.

QAIP Hint

Internal audit functions could incorporate *engagement planning* into an internal audit maturity model or a balanced scorecard.

Maturity Model

Internal audit functions could include *engagement planning* as a key process area in its maturity model. For example:

- Level 3 of a five-stage maturity model could identify that the engagement client is aware of the engagement through the annual audit plan.
- Level 4 could identify that the engagement client is actively consulted about the engagement objective, scope, and criteria prior to the engagement commencing.
- Level 5 could identify that the engagement client is actively consulted about the engagement objective, scope, and criteria prior to the final approval of the engagement plan.

Balanced Scorecard/KPI

Internal audit functions could include a performance indicator such as "the engagement client is always consulted prior to the engagement commencing."

Objectives, Criteria, and Scope

Clear and concise objectives are critical to the success of the engagement. Although the high-level purpose for the engagement will have been determined during annual audit planning, the engagement planning phase provides an opportunity to define the detailed objectives and scope of the engagement and to define the criteria that will be used to determine success.

Objectives

The objectives form the basis of the engagement—determining the key questions to be answered through the engagement and defining what the engagement will achieve. The objectives provide both the internal audit function and the engagement sponsor and client with a clear rationale and road map for the engagement.

The IIA *Standards* covering engagement objectives include Standards 2210, 2201.A2, and 2210.C1.

Standard 2210—Engagement Objectives

Objectives must be established for each engagement.

Standard 2210.A2

Internal auditors must consider the probability of significant errors, fraud, noncompliance, and other exposures when developing the engagement objectives.

Standard 2210.C1

Consulting engagement objectives must address governance, risk management, and control processes to the extent agreed upon with the client.

Internal audit functions can chose their own format for stating engagement objectives.

Example 13.1 Positively Stated Engagement Objective

Determine the adequacy and effectiveness of controls supporting the management of overtime arrangements.

Example 13.2 Question-Based Engagement Objective

Do controls support the adequate and effective management of overtime?

Key considerations with regard to audit objectives include:

- The extent to which objectives cover governance, risk management, and control elements, and whether any key area may be excluded.
- The extent to which objectives cover high-risk areas identified during engagement planning.
- The *auditability* of each objective and the potential to achieve the objective through the engagement.

LEVEL OF ASSURANCE The level of assurance that each engagement will provide is an issue more relevant to external audit than internal audit. In general, *limited* and *reasonable* assurances are accounting terms defined in external auditing standards. Although used by some internal auditors, their use reflects the professional background of the internal auditor (i.e., finance or accounting) rather than accepted practice in internal auditing.

The IIA does not define reasonable or limited assurance, but instead defines assurance services as "an objective examination of evidence for the purpose of providing an independent assessment on governance, risk management, and control processes for the organization" (IIA 2013).

Internal auditors should provide assurance without having to specify whether this is reasonable or limited. If a chief audit executive chooses to define different levels of assurance, they should provide these definitions to their audit committee and senior management for endorsement. The definitions should also be included in the engagement plan and report to provide clarity regarding the scope or intention of the engagement.

Determining the Level of Assurance

Dr. Sarah Blackburn, Audit Committee Chair and past President of the Chartered Institute of Internal Auditors (IIA UK and Ireland), believes that the level of assurance will vary between engagements. However, she sees a role for the audit committee in setting an assurance appetite, based on advice from the chief audit executive.

SUBOBJECTIVES Subobjectives can be used to further refine the engagement objective. The subobjectives should clearly and concisely describe what the engagement is going to achieve and should be specific to a particular program or activity.

Criteria

The internal audit function should include appropriate criteria to determine the extent to which the objective is met. The criteria are the performance standards against which the objective will be assessed (i.e., the criteria will define what success or achievement look like).

Standard 2210.A3

Adequate criteria are needed to evaluate governance, risk management, and controls. Internal auditors must ascertain the extent to which management and/or the board has established adequate criteria to determine whether objectives and goals have been accomplished. If adequate, internal auditors must use such criteria in their evaluation. If inadequate, internal auditors must work with management and/or the board to develop appropriate evaluation criteria.

Considerations for developing appropriate criteria that address the requirements in IIA Standard 2210.A3 include:

- Whether there are preexisting criteria for the entity or activity, such as minimum operating standards or legislative requirements
- The reliability of the criteria—whether they are from a reliable source or whether they are generally accepted good practice
- Whether the criteria are appropriate to the entity or activity
- Whether an individual criterion completely covers the objective or whether multiple criteria will be required
- Whether evidence is available to support each criterion
- Whether the criteria will support findings and opinions regarding the objectives.

The source of the criteria will determine the effort required to determine their suitability and/or acceptance. Criteria based on legislation, regulations, or recognized professional standards are among the most incontrovertible. Generally accepted criteria can also be obtained from sources such as professional associations, recognized bodies of experts, and academic literature. The other main sources of engagement criteria are the standards and measures adopted by the engagement client.

If existing criteria are not available, the internal audit function can focus on performance achieved in comparable organizations, best practices determined through benchmarking or consultation, or standards developed by internal audit through an analysis of activities.

Regardless of their source, criteria must be objective, relevant, reasonable, and attainable. They should be generated from recognized sources and, as far as possible, should be agreed on with the engagement client.

Common Quality Issue

Sometimes internal auditors may fail to obtain management agreement to proposed criteria. This can ultimately result in the engagement client or sponsor disagreeing with findings or conclusions because of their belief that activities have been assessed against inappropriate standards.

Scope

The purpose of the scope is to establish the nature, timing, and extent of engagement procedures required to conduct the engagement. The scope should be sufficiently detailed to provide a clear understanding of the parameters of the work to be completed and defined in such a way as to provide assurance that risks are appropriately mitigated.

IIA Standards 2220 and 2220.A1 specifically cover the engagement scope.

Standard 2220—Engagement Scope

The established scope must be sufficient to achieve the objectives of the engagement.

Standard 2220.A1

The scope of the engagement must include consideration of relevant systems, records, personnel, and physical properties, including those under the control of third parties.

Often, the scope includes a series of statements that collectively describe what will be covered by the engagement. It may also include a statement as to what is specifically excluded from the engagement (often described as *out-of-scope*). Setting the scope correctly is important to ensuring that the engagement is focused but has not inadvertently excluded important elements.

The scope should be as clear as possible so that different parties can come to the same conclusion with respect to what the engagement covers. Examples of engagement scope statements are provided in Examples 13.3, 13.4, and 13.5.

Example 13.3 Sample Scope Statement 1

The scope of the engagement is to cover training provided to operational staff between January 1, 2015, and December 31, 2015.

Example 13.4 Sample Scope Statement 2

The scope of the engagement is to include the performance of each of the formal subcommittees of the board. The scope will not include any operational or tactical committees.

Example 13.5 Sample Scope Statement 3

The engagement includes operations in sites A, B, and C. The engagement will not include coverage of activity 1, 2, or 3.

Common Quality Issue

Common quality issues relating to *objectives, criteria,* and *scope* include the following:

- Insufficient input from engagement clients regarding the engagement objectives

(continued)

(*continued*)
- Failure to obtain management agreement to the criteria used as part of the engagement planning process.
- The scope incorporating activities outside the responsibility of the audited entity

Environmental Scanning

It is important that the internal audit function has a comprehensive understanding of the operations or activities being reviewed, bearing in mind that this understanding will be further developed during the conduct of the audit.

For significant engagements, insight into operations can be gained through environmental scanning—a process of reviewing the internal and external environments of the organization to identify potential threats and opportunities.

Environmental scanning should provide the internal audit function with relevant background material to understand the purpose and rationale for the engagement. It involves gathering information on the operation's or activity's objectives and key processes. However, it will also include elements external to the operation or activity that will influence the way that this operates, such as the regulatory environment, competitors (in the private sector), and other relevant government agencies (in the public sector).

Aligning Engagements to Key Risks

Internal audit engagements should be aligned to the specific risks impacting an operation or activity, as well as the objectives or outputs the operation or activity is hoping to deliver. This ensures that the engagement is focused on areas most likely to influence overall organizational outputs and outcomes.

This requirement is reinforced through IIA Standards 1220.A3, 2201, and 2210.A1.

Standard 1220.A3

Internal auditors must be alert to the significant risks that might affect objectives, operations, or resources. However, assurance procedures alone, even when performed with due professional care, do not guarantee that all significant risks will be identified.

Standard 2201—Planning Considerations

In planning the engagement, internal auditors must consider:

- The objectives of the activity being reviewed and the means by which the activity controls its performance;

- The significant risks to the activity, its objectives, resources, and operations, and the means by which the potential impact of risk is kept to an acceptable level;
- The adequacy and effectiveness of the activity's governance, risk management, and control processes compared to a relevant framework or model; and
- The opportunities for making significant improvements to the activity's governance, risk management, and control processes.

Standard 2210.A1

Internal auditors must conduct a preliminary assessment of the risks relevant to the activity under review. Engagement objectives must reflect the results of this assessment.

Identifying Key Risks

In identifying key risks and objectives, internal auditors should consider:

- What the operation or activity is trying to achieve—its reason for being
- What could go wrong within the operation or activity that would prevent the objectives from being achieved
- What must go right for the operation or activity in order for it to meet its objectives
- What external events could impact the operation or activity
- The relative impact of each of these factors (risks) on the operation or activity
- The likelihood that these risks will occur

This consideration will be enhanced when internal auditors have an understanding of the following:

- Cost or value of the operations or activity
- Lifecycle of the operations or activity
- Political or public interest in the operations or activity
- Consequences of failure
- Executive management interest in the operations or activity
- Stability of the operations or activity, including any recent significant change to operating processes or staffing
- Complexity of the operations or activity
- Length of time the operations or activity has existed, giving consideration to obsolescence, legacy systems, etc.

Considerations regarding risk and materiality were discussed in greater detail in relation to annual audit planning in Chapter 12.

Once the key risks and opportunities have been identified, the engagement team should identify the key controls that exist to mitigate risks and maximize the achievement of opportunities, and determine the effectiveness and adequacy of these controls.

The engagement team should give consideration to the findings of other relevant audit or assurance activities as any previous coverage can alert the internal audit function to areas of potential focus. The team should balance the risk of duplicated assurance coverage with ensuring that previous findings have been addressed.

Considering Fraud Risks

Internal auditors are not expected to be fraud experts; however, engagements should consider the potential for fraud occurring.

Risk-Centric Approaches to Engagement Planning

Cathcart and Kapoor (2010) have identified the need for internal auditors to adopt a risk-centric approach to internal audit. They identify a number of key elements to such an approach, as follows:

- Taking fraud prevention and business ethics from a compliance perspective to a cultural mindset. Auditing these risks requires more than just checking to see whether rules are being followed; auditors must ensure that the spirit of these rules is incorporated into activities at every level.
- Determining key business and fraud risks rather than casting a wide net over numerous risks, many of which may be remote or obscure.
- Identifying emerging risk issues and trends, such as changes in the regulatory environment, and bringing them to the attention of key stakeholders.
- Estimating the significance of each risk and assessing the probability of occurrence based on a deep understanding of the data and sometimes sophisticated statistical analysis.
- Identifying programs and controls designed to prevent and detect risk and testing their effectiveness.
- Coordinating with other risk and control functions, such as compliance, risk management, controllers, and legal, to ensure that the risks are controlled and managed appropriately.

QAIP Hint

Internal audit functions could incorporate *engagement risk assessment* into an internal audit maturity model or a balanced scorecard.

Maturity Model

Internal audit functions could include *engagement risk assessment* as a key process area in its maturity model. For example:

- Level 2 of a five-stage maturity model could identify that risks are not routinely considered.
- Level 3 could identify that risks are considered as part of engagement planning.
- Level 4 could identify that a formal risk assessment is undertaken of the auditable area as part of the engagement planning process.
- Level 5 could identify that a formal risk assessment is undertaken of the auditable area—specifically considering fraud risks—as part of the engagement planning process.

Balanced Scorecard/KPI

Internal audit functions could include a performance indicator such as "Risk assessments are conducted of the auditable areas as part of engagement planning."

Methodology

The internal audit function determines appropriate methodology for undertaking each engagement. The methodology should allow the internal auditors to collect sufficient, relevant, and reliable evidence on which findings can be based.

The methodology is typically described in an engagement work program (or a work plan/test plan). This requirement is identified in IIA Standard 2240.A1.

Standard 2240.A1

Work programs must include the procedures for identifying, analyzing, evaluating, and documenting information during the engagement. The work program must be approved prior to its implementation, and any adjustments approved promptly.

The work program should cover each of the engagement objectives and include procedures for assessing the achievement of each criterion. This will often include the typical evidence that will be gathered to draw conclusions. The methodology should factor in the potential to gather this evidence in the time frames available for fieldwork and whether alternative evidence will be required.

The work program should specify the engagement tasks (tests to be performed), such as:

- Reviews of systems and processes
- Process mapping
- Sampling
- Data analysis
- Interviews
- Questionnaires/surveys
- Direct observation

Common Quality Issue

Sometimes internal auditors fail to develop audit work programs establishing procedures for identifying, analyzing, evaluating, and recording information during an engagement.

Integrated Reviews

Undertake integrated reviews that cover objectives crossing a number of organizational elements and using a variety of audit methods—for example, a combined performance and IT audit that looks at the effectiveness of customer information management.

Process Mapping

Process mapping is a valuable tool that can be used as part of planning to identify key controls and help determine the audit focus, as well as during fieldwork to determine any potential control gaps or control breakdowns.

Process maps generally include the inputs, activities, workflows, and outputs of a particular activity. They can be supported by process narratives, providing additional written information regarding the process flow.

Process mapping is especially useful when the internal auditor is required to look at an activity that involves a set of sequential tasks. The map can be used to identify and record the risks and controls associated with each task. Creating this visual representation is also an effective way of testing whether the current procedures used by staff align with those documented and approved by management.

Process mapping can be a useful tool for clarifying complex procedures with the engagement client and ensuring that the internal auditor correctly understands the procedures used by staff and management.

Process Mapping

Use process maps or narratives during the planning phase of each engagement to describe key controls. Better practice process maps are clear and concise without being oversimplified. Process maps can include brief notes as required, and should include consistent symbols.

Analytical Procedures and Data Analysis

The processes of collecting data and analyzing that data are critical to the fulfillment of the engagement objectives. This is reinforced through IIA Standard 2310.

Standard 2310

Internal auditors must identify sufficient, reliable, relevant, and useful information to achieve the engagement's objectives.

DATA COLLECTION TECHNIQUES Internal auditors are required to use a range of data collection techniques, with the particular technique(s) chosen in a given engagement being dependent on the objectives of that engagement. Common data collection techniques include:

- Interviewing
- Observation
- Sampling
- Questionnaires and surveys

The critical features of each of these data collection techniques are discussed in the following sections.

Interviewing An interview is a professional conversation conducted with a specific purpose or goal in mind. Its intent is the gaining of knowledge and uncovering information useful to the engagement. The characteristics of a typical interview include the following:

- It is conducive to eliciting information in a nonthreatening manner.
- The goal is to gain more information or knowledge about the process/procedure/ area of interest.
- The tone is professional and nonaccusatory.
- The interviewee should be given free rein to explain himself/herself fully.
- It lasts for a relatively short time (often 15 minutes to 1 hour).

Interviewing is discussed in further detail in Chapter 14.

Observation Observation is exactly as the word suggests—it is the process of the internal auditor directly observing people, actions, or processes. Direct observation by the auditor can be more useful than relying on secondhand reports from people in an interview or written submission.

Sampling Sampling involves the testing of less than 100 percent of a given population. Engagement sampling enables internal auditors to obtain and evaluate evidence about some characteristic of the items selected in order to form or assist in forming a conclusion about the population from which the sample is drawn.

The internal audit function should use professional judgment when determining the appropriate amount of testing to be undertaken. In some cases, a statistical sample may be applied, particularly when large volumes of transactions are included in the audit scope. In these circumstances, it may not be possible, practical, or cost-effective to examine the whole population.

The sampling scheme used should be based on the frequency at which a control is performed or by the total population size. The internal audit function must sample in a manner that will allow appropriate conclusions to be drawn, potentially across the whole population being reviewed. Consideration also needs to be given to the confidence level with which conclusions are to be made, and to the margin for error associated with a statement.

Random Sample   Essentially a random sample is chosen in a way such that each member of the total population of prescribed activities has an equal chance of being selected in the sample.

Targeted Sample   Targeted sampling removes an element of randomness by concentrating on specifically identified members of the total population. Such members are usually chosen based on a risk profile and often include high-volume or large-dollar-value activities. Often, targeting will occur after an initial analysis that determines the range of expected results.

Practical considerations with respect to the resources available may also dictate the targeting of a sample. For example, it may be necessary to conduct a number of physical inspections in particular locations to minimize the time and travel requirements on internal auditors.

Where targeted sampling is used, it may not be possible to infer that the results arising are applicable to the entire population.

It is possible to combine random sampling and targeted sampling—for example, identifying the subpopulation of large-dollar-value transactions, then randomly selecting within that subpopulation. In such cases, it may be possible to generalize findings across the entire subpopulation.

Sample Size   Sample size is affected by the level of sampling risk that the internal audit function is willing to accept. The lower the risk the auditor is willing to accept, the greater the sample size will need to be.

The formula used to calculate the sample size contains three key components—population size, confidence interval, and confidence level. While population size is fixed for a given sample, changing either or both of the other two components will result in a change to the required sample size.

Confidence Interval   A confidence interval gives an estimated range likely to include an unknown population parameter. The estimated range is calculated using the observed sample data. The confidence interval is often reported as a plus-or-minus figure.

Example 13.6 Sample Confidence Interval

Determining error rates using a confidence interval of +/−4, and finding 47 percent of a sample with errors, provides a level of certainty that the entire population has an error rate of between 43 percent (47 − 4) and 51 percent (47 + 4). How certain we are of this is described by the *confidence level*.

Confidence Level The confidence level describes the level of certainty associated with a confidence interval. It is expressed as a percentage and represents how often the true population parameter can be expected to lie within the confidence interval if repeated random samples were drawn and analyzed. The 95 percent confidence level indicates 95 percent certainty; the 99 percent confidence level indicates 99 percent certainty. Researchers commonly use the 95 percent confidence level. The lower the level of certainty required, the smaller the sample size required.

Example 13.7 Combined Confidence Level and Confidence Interval

Combining the confidence level and the confidence interval allows a statement such as "There is 95 percent certainty that the true error rate in the population is between 43 percent and 51 percent."

Nonstatistical Sampling It is not always appropriate to use statistical sampling, particularly for performance or operational auditing, or in cases where population is not homogenous and/or contains a small number of large or individually significant transactions. In these circumstances, alternative data collection methods will be required.

In these cases, the internal auditor could choose to use nonstatistical sampling. However, it may not be possible to extrapolate results derived from such a sample to the population as a whole.

In some instances, for example, tests of controls, the auditor may be able to use a nonstatistical sampling approach that allows more latitude with sample selection and evaluation than in the case of statistical sampling. It relies on nonrandom selection techniques to select a sample *expected to be* representative of the population. It may be possible to make inferences about the entire population based on such a sample; however, such inferences should always be issued with the caveat that the auditor has exercised judgment in an attempt to target a representative sample. Another name for nonstatistical sampling is judgmental sampling.

Questionnaires and Surveys Questionnaires and surveys can be useful for collecting large volumes of information using a consistent format. In general, the questionnaire or survey should be as short as possible and the questions should be designed to avoid ambiguity and facilitate analysis.

Questionnaires and surveys can use both open and closed questions. Open questions allow for a free-text response and support qualitative analysis. However, they can be more difficult to analyze than questions characterized by a number of discrete choices. Often, surveys include a number of closed questions supplemented by open, narrative responses. Questionnaires or surveys can be completed in hard copy, as part of a face-to-face or telephone interview, or via web-based programs.

Questionnaires and surveys can also be used to gain an understanding of a process, its associated risks, and established controls.

Internal control questionnaires are a useful way of getting information about what controls are in place and how well the engagement client believes they operate. An internal control questionnaire is a list of questions about the process, its associated risks, and its established internal controls. The level of complexity of an internal control questionnaire can vary significantly; some questionnaires are extremely long and complex, while others are short and simple.

Most internal control questionnaires consist of predominantly closed questions, often requiring a yes/no answer to whether a specific control or feature is in place. It is typical for them to be structured in a way that a no answer serves as a prompt to the auditor to seek an explanation for why a particular control is not in place.

Wed-Based Survey Tools

There are a range of web-based survey tools freely available that can be used for conducting surveys. However, the internal audit function will need to determine whether their use conforms to organizational IT policies.

DATA ANALYSIS Having collected information, the internal auditor needs to assess it with a view to forming findings and conclusions that contribute to achieving the engagement objectives. This is the crux of data analysis.

Analytical Auditing Procedures Analytical auditing procedures are used to obtain an understanding of an entity and its environment by studying and comparing the relationships of information. They highlight unexpected information (such as unexpected differences or the absence of expected differences) and unusual or nonrecurrent transactions or events. This can assist internal auditors in identifying conditions that may need to be addressed during the engagement.

Analytical procedures can be used for both financial and nonfinancial data, can analyze data at a point in time, and can determine trends over a period of time. They include:

- Comparison of current period information with prior periods, budgets, or forecasts
- Study of relationships of financial information with the appropriate operating, economic, and nonfinancial information
- Comparison of information between programs, activities, or personnel

An analytical review of information assists the internal auditor to uncover the relationships and anomalies with collected information. It can also help the auditor decide what areas are most in need of audit and those that may be examples of better practice.

Some common data analysis tools and techniques are described in the following sections.

Trend Analysis Internal auditors can use trend analysis to analyze activities over a period of time. Trend analysis is often used to identify performance indicators, highlight significant changes, and assess how past performance has led to the current position.

Ratio Analysis Ratio analysis is a subset of trend analysis that is used primarily to compare the relationships of information at a point in time. Two methods of ratio analysis are commonly employed by internal auditors—*common size statement* and *financial ratios.*

Benchmarking A benchmark is a standard or point of reference used in measuring and judging quality or value. Benchmarking is the process of continuously comparing and measuring an organization, program, or activity against other comparable organizations, programs, or activities. The purpose of benchmarking is to gain information that will help the entity take action to improve its performance.

Computer Assisted Auditing Techniques

Subject to the nature of the engagement, the methodology may incorporate computer assisted auditing techniques (CAATs). The IIA *Standards*, specifically Standard 1220.A2, require internal auditors to consider the relevance of CAATs as part of the planning process.

Standard 1220.A2

In exercising due professional care internal auditors must consider the use of technology-based audit and other data analysis techniques.

CAATs include automated audit techniques such as generalized audit software, test data generators, computerized audit programs, and specialized audit systems.

Data analytics can be utilized across a population data set extracted from the organization's databases. The analysis can identify any unusual trends or data anomalies that warrant further investigation such as duplicate, unusual, or unauthorized transactions, significant processing errors, system control weakness, and potential fraudulent activities. Exception data analysis results can then be confirmed during the conduct of the engagement.

Not all engagements will lend themselves to technology-based techniques, although where these are relevant they can improve the efficiency and scope of the engagement.

Audit Options Papers

Some internal audit functions develop audit options papers for their large and complex engagements. This allows the internal auditors to evaluate alternative approaches to conducting the engagement and to identify a preferred approach. The options paper provides the chief audit executive with the rationale for selection of a particular option so that further planning work can proceed consistently with the approved option.

QAIP Hint

Internal audit functions could incorporate *engagement methodology* into an internal audit maturity model or a balanced scorecard.

Maturity Model

Internal audit functions could include *engagement methodology* as a key process area in its maturity model. For example:

- Level 2 of a five-stage maturity model could identify that the engagement plan does not specify the methodology to be used.
- Level 3 could identify that the engagement plan specifies the methodology to be used, although the methodology is generally limited to sampling and interviews.
- Level 4 could identify that engagement work programs are developed that specify the methodology to be used. Consideration has been given to the use of various audit methodologies.
- Level 5 could identify that the internal audit function develops audit options papers for larger performance and operational audits to consider the various possible approaches to the audit.

Balanced Scorecard/KPI

Internal audit functions could include a performance indicator such as "Analytical procedures and CAATS are used in a minimum number of engagements (specifying number)."

Resourcing and Milestones

The engagement plan should include the predicted resources required to undertake the engagement—both in-house and outsourced. The allocated resourcing should take account of the proposed methodology and the potential for this to be achieved. If the resources are finite, the methodology may need to be modified to account for this.

Standard 2230—Engagement Resource Allocation

Internal auditors must determine appropriate and sufficient resources to achieve engagement objectives based on an evaluation of the nature and complexity of each engagement, time constraints, and available resources.

Distribution of Resources across the Engagement Process

There is reasonable debate regarding the level of resources that should be applied to the various engagement stages. To a large extent this is dependent on the type of engagement, the nature of the organization, and the approach of each internal audit function. Regardless, appropriate resourcing applied at the audit planning stage will inevitably lead to higher value and greater impact engagements.

Resource utilization should be balanced between having a clear and comprehensive understanding of the activity or program being reviewed, collecting sufficient and appropriate evidence to provide insight, and actively engaging with engagement clients to ensure that influence is maximized.

Stakeholders

The plan may identify specific stakeholders for the engagement. These include the internal auditors responsible for conducting and overseeing the engagement, the engagement sponsor and client (auditee), and sometimes key staff to be interviewed as part of the engagement.

Milestones

Including key milestones in the engagement plan provides transparency to the audit sponsor and accountability to the internal auditor. It also provides a useful performance measure for the chief audit executive.

Assessing Risks to the Audit Engagement

For larger internal audit engagements, the chief audit executive may determine that an individual engagement risk assessment is warranted. This provides assurance that the audit objectives will be achieved in an efficient and timely manner.

The risks typically associated with the management of an internal audit function were described in Chapter 6. Risks that could impact an internal audit engagement are identified in Table 13.1.

TABLE 13.1 Internal Audit Engagement Risks

Risk Area/Source of Risk	Consequence
Inadequate planning—Engagement objectives or scope are not clarified.	The engagement does not fulfill stakeholder requirements and/or meet expectations.
Inadequate planning—Engagement context is not identified.	The engagement does not appropriately consider external influences.
Inadequate planning—Alternative methodologies are not identified at the planning stage.	Inefficiencies or loss of effectiveness in engagement fieldwork.
Inadequate planning—The scope and/or complexity of the engagement are not identified.	The internal audit function is unable to complete the engagement in the planned hours.
Inadequate planning—Overlaps or duplication with other engagements are not identified.	Ineffective use of limited resources.
Inadequate stakeholder/engagement client buy-in	Lack of acceptance of engagement findings and recommendations.

(continued)

TABLE 13.1 (*continued*)

Risk Area/Source of Risk	Consequence
Inadequate capability and experience within assigned audit team	The internal audit function does not focus on key, causal issues and/or provide valuable recommendations.
	The engagement is not completed within the planned hours.
Inadequate management of external contractors.	The engagement does not meet the internal audit function's quality standards.
Inappropriate communicational/ineffective stakeholder management.	Low levels of trust between the internal audit function and organizational stakeholders.
Errors or omissions in engagement findings; the engagement report does not meet quality standards.	Impacts to the internal audit function's reputation and/or litigation against the internal audit function.
The engagement report fails to add value and/or is focused on low-level issues.	Impacts to the internal audit function's reputation.

Approval of the Engagement Plan

Each internal audit function will determine the appropriate person to approve the engagement plan. For small to mid-sized internal audit functions this might be the chief audit executive, but for large internal audit functions this might be an internal audit manager or team leader.

Engagement sponsors and clients need to understand the proposed plan and agree to the audit criteria. There will be advantages and disadvantages of sharing the entire engagement plan with management. For example, sharing the plan promotes transparency and accountability. However, it also presents the risk that management might steer the engagement away from important auditable areas.

QAIP Hint

Internal audit functions could incorporate *engagement risk assessments* into an internal audit maturity model or a balanced scorecard.

Maturity Model

The internal audit function could include *engagement risk assessments* as a key process area in its maturity model. For example:

- Level 4 of a five-stage maturity model could identify that engagement risk assessments are undertaken for all larger performance and operational audits.
- Level 5 could identify that engagements risk assessments are conducted for all engagements.

Balanced Scorecard/KPI

Internal audit could include a performance indicator such as "Engagement Risk Assessments conducted for 100 percent of operational/performance audits."

Questions about Planning the Engagement

Table 13.2 provides a range of questions about planning the engagement. These can be formally incorporated into a quality assurance and improvement program, or, less formally, into ongoing assessment activities. Questions may be variously posed to the chief audit executive, internal auditors, or audit stakeholders.

TABLE 13.2 Quality Questions

Questions	Evidence of Quality
Do plans exist for each internal audit engagement?	Engagement plans
Are work programs developed to support the engagement plan for each internal audit engagement?	Work programs
Are all work programs (and subsequent adjustments) approved in writing by the chief audit executive or designee prior to the engagement commencing?	Electronic/hard copy work program papers reviewed before commencing review
Does the engagement sponsor approve the engagement scope/terms of reference prior to the engagement commencing?	Documented evidence of sponsor approval
Has the internal audit function considered external factors or contemporary best practice when planning each engagement (i.e., are there lessons to be learned from other organizations and are there implications to risks/controls based on external factors)?	Chief audit executive interview Internal audit staff interviews Engagement plans
Do engagement plans and work programs consider significant risks to the function, its objectives, resources, and operations and the means by which the potential impact of risk is kept to an acceptable level?	Engagement plans Work programs
Do engagement plans include an objective?	Engagement plans
Is there evidence that the internal audit function has considered the probability of significant errors, fraud, noncompliance, and other exposures when developing the engagement objectives?	Engagement plans
Does the internal audit function use relevant criteria for evaluating governance, risk management, and control?	Engagement plans
Do consulting engagements address governance, risk management, and control to the extent agreed upon with the engagement client?	Engagement plans
Are consulting engagement objectives consistent with the organization's values, strategies, and objectives?	Engagement plans
Do engagement plans include scopes sufficient to achieve engagement objectives?	Engagement plans
Do engagement plans and/or engagement work programs document the required resources and procedures for identifying, analyzing, evaluating, and documenting information during the engagement?	Engagement plans Work programs
Is there evidence the internal audit function has considered the use of technology-based audit and other data analysis techniques?	Engagement plans Work programs

(continued)

TABLE 13.2 (*continued*)

Questions	Evidence of Quality
Are resources for individual engagements assigned based on an analysis of the scope, complexity, time constraints, and available resources?	Engagement plans Work programs
Are special resources sourced where required?	Engagement plans Work programs
Do engagement plans include milestones?	Engagement plans

Conclusion

During engagement planning, internal audit functions should focus on how they expect engagements will contribute to adding value and improving the organization's operations. At the conclusion of the planning process, internal auditors should be able to clearly demonstrate why the engagement should be undertaken.

References

Australian National Audit Office. (2012, September). *Public Sector Internal Audit: An Investment in Assurance and Business Improvement—Better Practice Guide.* http://www.anao.gov.au/~/media/Files/Better%20Practice%20Guides/2012%202013/ANAO%20%20Public%20Sector%20Internal%20Audit.pdf.

Cathcart, R., and G. Kapoor. (2010). An internal audit upgrade. *Internal Auditor.* http://www.theiia.org/intauditor.

Gibbs, N., D. Jain, A. Joshi, S. Muddamsetti, and S. Singh. (2010). *A New Auditors' Guide to Planning, Performing and Presenting IT Audits.* Altamonte Springs, FL: The Institute of Internal Auditors Research Foundation.

The Institute of Internal Auditors. (2013). *International Professional Practices Framework.* Altamonte Springs, FL: The Institute of Internal Auditors.

Murdock, H., and J. Roth. (2009). *Using Surveys in Internal Audits.* Altamonte Springs, FL: The Institute of Internal Auditors Research Foundation.

Reding, K. F., et al. (2009). *Internal Auditing: Assurance and Consulting Services.* Altamonte Springs, FL: The Institute of Internal Auditors Research Foundation.

Sarens, G., L. Decaux, and R. Lenz. (2012). *Combined Assurance: Case Studies on a Holistic Approach to Organizational Governance.* Altamonte Springs, FL: The Institute of Internal Auditors Research Foundation.

Sawyer, L. B., M. A. Dittenhofer, and J. H. Scheiner. (2005). *Sawyers Internal Auditing,* 5th ed. Altamonte Springs, FL: The Institute of Internal Auditors Research Foundation.

CHAPTER 14

Performing the Engagement

It is easier to do a job right than to explain why you didn't.

—Martin Van Buren

The conduct, or fieldwork, stage of an engagement presents multiple opportunities for an internal audit function to demonstrate its professionalism and maturity. A quality internal audit function is distinguished by established, transparent procedures and a commitment to impartiality. Nonetheless, better practice internal auditing recognizes the need for effective collaboration with engagement clients and the enhanced value that this offers an organization.

Audit Evidence

The internal audit function should undertake fieldwork in accordance with the agreed engagement plan and work program. The work program should identify the specific methodology to be utilized during the engagement.

Internal auditors should collect enough evidence to make an informed opinion against the audit objective. The information required will vary and professional judgment is needed to determine the requisite amount and nature of evidence.

In assessing the adequacy of audit evidence, the internal audit function should consider:

- The nature of the engagement and the program or activity being reviewed
- The degree of risk involved in the program or activity and the adequacy of internal control
- The susceptibility of the program or activity to fraud, manipulation, or misstatement
- The materiality of possible errors or irregularities associated with the information collected

The evidence used should be collected from a variety of sources, including documentation, interviews, and direct observation. The engagement methodology is discussed in detail later in the chapter.

Great Evidence

Great audit evidence often shares a number of key attributes, including:

- The evidence is *credible, authoritative*, and *accurate* and fairly represents a particular condition.
- The source of the evidence is *independent* from the audit client.
- The evidence is in its *original* form.
- *Documentation* is available to support testimonial evidence.
- The evidence has been obtained through *direct observation*.

Sufficient and Appropriate Evidence

The internal audit function should collect sufficient and appropriate evidence to perform the engagement, as noted in IIA Standard 2300.

Standard 2300—Performing the Engagement

Internal auditors must identify, analyze, evaluate, and document sufficient information to achieve the engagement's objectives.

SUFFICIENT EVIDENCE Internal auditors need to collect sufficient evidence to support the engagement findings. Typically, a *reasonable person* test is used to determine sufficiency—there is enough evidence if a reasonable person can be persuaded that the engagement findings are valid. Factors affecting the sufficiency of evidence can include the quantity and completeness of evidence. In general, a sufficient volume of evidence is required that addresses each of the engagement objectives, and covers the scope of the engagement.

Determining the sufficiency of evidence will require a level of professional judgment—inadequate evidence can lead to unsupported findings, whereas excessive evidence can reduce audit efficiency. Considerations in determining sufficiency include the following:

- The significance of the finding arising from the evidence and the risk associated with reaching an incorrect conclusion
- Experience gained in previous audits about the reliability of the evidence
- The degree to which statistical sampling can be utilized
- The degree to which the evidence is sensitive or contentious in nature
- The cost of gathering the evidence relative to the added value that additional evidence would lend to supporting the engagement findings and conclusions
- The persuasiveness of the evidence and the potential for the engagement to lead to further, formalized investigations (such as in a situations of suspected fraud)

DEGREE OF PERSUASIVENESS Gleim (2004) identifies that the ultimate purpose of information gathering is to provide sufficient support for the auditor's observations, conclusions, and recommendations. Accordingly, although the individual items of information may have drawbacks and therefore different degrees of persuasiveness, the internal auditor's task is to assemble a body of information that in the aggregate provides the requisite support.

Gleim suggests that during this process, the internal auditor may determine that particular information justifies full reliance, partial reliance, or no reliance:

- An internal auditor fully relies on information when no additional corroboration is needed. For example, the internal auditor may decide that his or her own physical count of inventory provides sufficient, reliable, relevant, and useful information.
- Most information merits only partial reliance and must therefore be corroborated. For example, testimonial information through interviews ordinarily should be supplemented by other audit evidence. Furthermore, information that at some time has passed through the engagement client's operations ordinarily should be reinforced by obtaining assurances about the adequacy and effectiveness of internal control.

Circumstances may dictate that internal auditors place little or no reliance on certain information. However, such information may be useful in indicating the direction of the engagement. For example, unsupported testimonies provided by the engagement client are likely to be significantly discounted because of their tendency toward self-serving bias. Nevertheless, the information furnished by the engagement client may suggest other sources of information.

APPROPRIATE EVIDENCE The appropriateness of the evidence can be considered in terms of both its relevance and reliability. Relevant evidence specifically addresses the engagement objective.

Reliable evidence has been determined by the internal audit function as being credible, reasonable, and accurate. It accurately represents the observed phenomena and can be independently verified.

Example 14.1 Complete and Relevant Evidence

Vouching journal entries does not support the completeness assertion about reported transactions. Instead, tracing transactions to the accounting records would provide relevant information.

In general, evidence secured from a credible, independent source provides greater assurance than evidence sourced directly from the audit client. However, care should be taken in relying on *hearsay* or secondhand evidence. Original documentation is also considered more reliable than copies of documents.

Written Evidence and Documentation

Documentation is the most common form of evidence used in internal audit engagements. It can include both physical records and electronic information (i.e., databases, operating system software, electronic documents, and email files).

Physical records are usually created by the organization, program, or activity being reviewed and can include strategic and operational planning documents, policies and procedures, review and evaluation reports, and records of complaints and documented disputes and correspondence. They can also include documentation produced externally to the auditable area such as inward correspondence, external reviews, legislation, regulations, industry guidelines, and better practice guides.

In using documentary evidence, internal auditors should determine that evidence is complete and accurate, and that the most recent version has been obtained.

Direct Observation and Physical Evidence

Direct observation can be used to gain a firsthand perspective on the program or activity being reviewed. It can allow internal auditors to observe the operation of processes and controls, and to subsequently map these as part of the planning process (process mapping was discussed in detail in Chapter 13). During fieldwork, direct observation (or *walk-throughs*) can be used to determine whether the documented processes reflect actual practice.

Direct observation can assist in identifying control breakdowns and the reasons behind them.

Example 14.2 Using Direct Observation to Identify Control Breakdowns

A hospital may have introduced an infection control process requiring staff to wash their hands after dealing with each patient. However, through direct observation this control may be observed as being ineffective, as time pressures on staff lead them to move directly from patient to patient.

Direct observation can also be useful for confirming the existence of assets, or the number of staff members involved in specific activities. Evidence from direct observation can be captured through written records or through media such as photos or videos (subject to appropriate privacy considerations if members of the public, customers, or clients are captured electronically).

Interviews

Interviews form a key element of internal auditing. From selecting staff members to identifying risks, collecting audit evidence, and communicating the results of an engagement, internal auditors use interviews on an ongoing basis. For this reason, developing effective interviewing techniques can significantly enhance the performance of both individual internal auditors as well as the overall internal audit function.

Ensuring Quality Interviews

Both structured and semistructured interviews can be used during audit fieldwork. Structured interviews normally have a precise objective, and are used when the internal auditor wishes to obtain specific information. In these instances, the questions are prepared in advance and are sometimes provided to the interviewee. Structured interviews can also be used to gain standardized responses to the same questions from a number of different people.

Semistructured interviews are normally used as an exploratory tool (often during planning or early in fieldwork) to identify issues or further lines of inquiry, or as a device to elicit rich, qualitative information from people. The emphasis of semi-structured interviews may be on exploring the underlying causes, reasons, and effects of issues.

Sawyer (2005) identifies six key steps to a successful interview: preparing, scheduling, opening, conducting, closing, and recording. Craig (1991) recommends a similar approach to audit interviews, with an emphasis on advanced planning; selection of open-ended, unbiased questions; effective conduct; and ending the interview in an appropriate manner.

PREPARING   Except for the shortest interview, internal auditors should spend time understanding the interviewee's roles and responsibilities in relation to the topic of discussion. The internal auditor should have a clear understanding of the purpose of the interview and what they hope to achieve from it—often, this is formally reflected in an agenda or set of interview questions. Ideally, the internal auditor should avoid using leading, biased, or closed questions.

SCHEDULING   Interviews should be scheduled with sufficient lead time to allow for effective preparation and to demonstrate respect of the interviewee's time. The location should be chosen to ensure privacy as well as to provide a nonthreatening environment.

OPENING   Interviews should be opened in a manner intended to develop rapport and to avoid any perceptions of an adversarial relationship. Interviewees should be clear about the purpose of the interview and how the results will be used. The opening can also provide an opportunity to share additional background information about internal audit's role, as well as the purpose of the specific engagement.

CONDUCTING   Interviews should be conducted in an open and transparent manner. They should provide an opportunity for the internal auditor to gain a greater under-standing of a particular program or activity, as well as to obtain an explanation as to why things occur in a particular way.

Interviews should be used to elicit information from an interviewee, rather than being focused on confirming preconceived ideas.

CLOSING   Prior to concluding the interview, internal auditors should summarize the key issues covered to avoid any misunderstandings and to help with recall following the interview. Internal auditors should also provide a final interview opportunity to add any additional, relevant information, or to seek clarification regarding the interview or overall engagement.

RECORDING   Internal auditors should not attempt to fully transcribe the interview—either during or following it. They should make note of key issues during the interview and then provide further clarity or detail as soon as possible afterward.

ACTIVE LISTENING   Internal auditors need to display excellent active listening skills. This requires moving beyond simply hearing what people are saying, to a point where the internal auditor understands both the content and meaning behind what is said. It requires an appreciation of the feelings or sentiments that accompany or underpin verbal statements.

Active Listening

Active listening helps establish a strong connection between an interviewer and interviewee and encourages people to be more open and forthcoming in their responses. It requires that listeners give their undivided attention to the person speaking and demonstrate both listening and understanding. Often, this will involve seeking confirmation through paraphrasing what has been said and, where relevant, demonstrating an understanding of the feelings behind what has been stated through supplementary comments such as, "You must have been feeling very angry when . . ." or, "You must have felt very proud when . . ."

Effective interviewing is an important skill for internal auditors, and Seipp and Lindberg (2012) recognize that "a considerable portion of a successful audit interview deals with human behavior and interpersonal relationships." They believe that interviewing is more of an art than a science, and that to maximize the effectiveness of an interview the "techniques employed should be based on the personal style and the preference of the interviewer." Nonetheless, there are a number of key considerations that can help increase the chance of a successful interview.

Interviewing Tips

- Take appropriate time to plan the interview.
- Be respectful of the interviewee's time and schedule the interview as far in advance as possible.
- Choose a location that helps to put the interviewee at ease.
- Establish and maintain a good rapport with the interviewee and be prepared to overcome the perception of an adversarial relationship between the internal auditor and the interviewee.
- Use a conversational style with open-ended questions—avoid questions that call for a yes or no answer.

- Avoid leading questions that could bias the information obtained or require a self-incriminating reply.
- Recognize when interviewees are intentionally wasting time or steering the interview away from particular issues.
- Avoid preparing verbal responses until the interviewee has completed their answer and be respectful when responding.
- Listen for what is not said. A poor listener tries to absorb the many facts a speaker uses to support the central ideas being conveyed and loses the central concept—the hook on which the facts hang.
- Do not let emotion-laden words get in the way of hearing the facts.
- Summarize the interviewee's responses to ascertain that the issues have been heard correctly.
- Pay attention to avoid losing important facts.
- Do not attempt to write everything down during the interview but prepare detailed notes immediately following the interview to avoid losing important facts.

Analyzing Information Collected

Well-developed analytical skills are a key attribute for effective internal auditors. Reding and colleagues (2009) caution internal auditors that they "must always remember to apply a healthy level of professional skepticism when evaluating audit evidence. Professional skepticism means that internal auditors take nothing for granted; they continuously question what they hear and see and critically assess audit evidence."

A key component to effective analysis is the application of critical thinking processes.

Critical Thinking

Internal auditors need to display high-level critical thinking skills in order to provide value-adding recommendations. Greenawalt (1997) observes, "The skill and the propensity for critical thinking are attributes that are vital to effective functioning as an internal auditor." She argues that there is a knowledge component to critical thinking, followed by reflective skepticism.

Internal auditors should have a good understanding of the area or activity being reviewed in order to apply reflective skepticism. Without a depth of knowledge they will be unable to challenge the effectiveness or appropriateness of controls. Internal auditors need to be problem solvers with an ability to apply inductive and deductive reasoning.

Root Cause Analysis

Root cause analysis focuses on the primary causes of adverse events that need to be addressed by solutions. For internal auditors, focusing on root causes adds significant value to the audit engagement, as it moves the engagement beyond articulating known issues, to a process of working with management to identify systemic solutions.

Keith (2005) said:

One of the best ways internal auditing can add value is by providing recommendations that not only correct problems, but also address the cause of those problems. This is the difference between "cleaning up the spider webs" (simply fixing the current problem) and "killing the spider" (addressing the root cause to mitigate future occurrences). If auditors only clean up the spider web, at some point the web will be back.

ISHIKAWA (FISHBONE) DIAGRAMS   Ishikawa, or fishbone, diagrams were developed by Kaoru Ishikawa as a model for identifying the causes of particular problems (or effects). These were introduced in Chapter 2 and are shown in Figure 14.1.

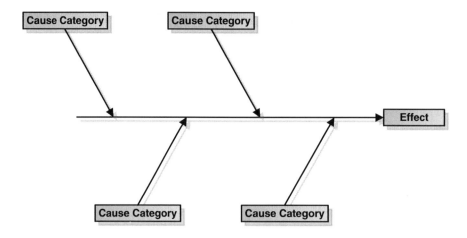

FIGURE 14.1 Ishikawa Diagram

5 WHYS   The 5 Whys process is used as part of the Six Sigma methodology (introduced in Chapter 2) to determine root causes. It is related to the Ishikawa diagram and relies on asking a series of *why* questions in an attempt to drill down to a causal factor. It involves identifying a specific problem, and asking, "Why did this problem happen?" If the answer does not indicate a root cause, the question is repeated at the next level.

Example 14.3 Using the 5 Whys to Identify Causal Issues

Through fieldwork, an internal auditor may identify that a manager did not authorize particular purchases. The 5 Whys process could be used as follows:

- Why did management not authorize the purchases?
  - Because the employee did not provide the purchase order to management for approval.

- Why did the employee not provide the purchase order to management for approval?
  - Because the employee did not know the purchase order was required for approval.
- Why did the employee not know the purchase order was required for approval?
  - Because the employee was not aware the organization had documented financial delegations that included this requirement.
- Why was the employee not aware of the financial delegations?
  - Because the financial delegations were normally discussed during induction training, but the employee was not provided with induction when they first commenced.
- Why was the employee not provided with an induction?
  - Because the organization had cancelled its induction program as a cost-saving exercise.

QAIP Hint

Maturity Model

Internal audit functions could incorporate *engagement fieldwork—analyzing evidence* into an internal audit maturity model, as a key process area in its maturity model. For example, level 4 of a five-stage maturity model could identify that the internal audit function utilizes root-cause analysis as part of its audit fieldwork.

Engagement Findings

According to Hubbard (2001), "the term 'finding' is actually a misnomer. If a problem exists, auditors are not usually the ones who discover or identify it. Instead, it's more likely that the workers or management in the area already knew of the problem but just haven't addressed it yet."

After applying the audit methodology, internal auditors determine how well the process under review is operating relative to the agreed criteria, which were discussed in Chapter 13. Any gaps between the expected and observed levels of performance should be noted for further investigation, or, if consider significant, discussed with the engagement client.

The internal auditor should record their findings or observations as part of their working papers. IIA Practice Advisory 2410–1 recommends that observations are recorded based on these attributes: *criteria, condition, cause,* and *effect.*

Criteria

- The criteria provide the standard that should be expected and answer the question *What ought to be?*

- The criteria may be internal or external to the organization:
  - Internal criteria are formalized in policy and procedure manuals, employee handbooks, guidelines, and other similar documents.
  - External criteria are formalized in government regulations and laws, as well as external standards. Criteria may also represent general principles, such as accounting principles or good business practices.

Condition

- The condition refers to a problem or opportunity noted during fieldwork and answers the question "What are the facts?"
- The condition states the problems factually. It identifies what actually exists by telling what is happening now or what has occurred in the past and should provide enough information for an external party to understand.
- An example of a condition statement is "The manager did not authorize the expenditure by the employee."

Cause

- The cause explains the discrepancy between the condition and the criteria and answers the question "Why?"
- Causes should identify the underlying reason behind a problem—that is, the root cause.

Effect

- The effect identifies the type or degree of risk the organization is exposed to, or could be exposed to, if the cause is not addressed, and answers the question "So what?"

Audit Moderation Workshops

Some internal audit functions hold audit moderation workshops among internal auditors working on an engagement to discuss, challenge, and agree on audit findings and the significance of these findings. They may also invite additional stakeholders to these workshops such as the chief audit executive and senior manager(s) from other parts of the internal audit function.

QAIP Hint

Internal audit functions could incorporate *engagement fieldwork—audit findings* into an internal audit maturity model or a balanced scorecard.

Maturity Model

Internal audit functions could include *engagement fieldwork—audit findings* as a key process area in its maturity model. For example:

- Level 4 of a five-stage maturity model could identify that the engagement working papers identify the criteria, condition, cause, and effect for all engagement findings and observations.
- Level 5 could identify that the internal audit function holds audit moderation workshops for all engagements.

Balanced Scorecard/KPI

Internal audit functions could include a performance indicator such as "The cause and effect of all findings and observations documented within working papers."

Closing Interviews

The closing interview is a critical element of the engagement and helps to embed transparency in the audit process. It provides an opportunity to:

- Identify areas of good practice in the area under review.
- Identify, and clarify, any significant findings and their likely impact on the achievement of objectives.
- Resolve any issues of fact.
- Seek the audit sponsor's response to any agreed management actions or recommendations and agree on a timeframe when these will be provided.
- Clarify the process for finalization of the engagement report.

Issues Papers

Internal audit functions sometimes develop issues papers or presentations in preparation for the closing interview. These document tentative findings and associated evidence and allow the internal auditors to seek feedback on them from the engagement client. They may or may not be provided to the engagement client.

Using issues papers or presentations provides assurance that:

- Facts are correct.
- The program or activity, including any significant controls, is well understood by the engagement team.
- Causes of control breakdowns have been accurately determined.
- The significance of findings is mutually understood.
- Management has agreed to appropriate actions to address findings.

Chief audit executives should attend closing interviews wherever possible, as a means of fully understanding the client's response to the audit findings and recommendations, as well as a way to retain good client relationships.

QAIP Hint

Internal audit functions could incorporate *closing interviews* into an internal audit balanced scorecard with performance indicators such as:

- Closing interviews held for all audit engagements
- The chief audit executive attending all closing interviews.

Efficient Fieldwork

Internal auditors should strive to commence and complete fieldwork within the time frames agreed with the engagement client. This demonstrates a level of professionalism to the organization and helps ensure that internal audit operates in an efficient manner.

QAIP Hint

Internal audit functions could incorporate *efficient fieldwork* into an internal audit balanced scorecard with performance indicators such as:

- Timeliness of fieldwork
- Percentage audit plan completed (include target)
- Number of audits completed (include target)
- Proportion of audits completed within prescribed time frames or days from planned to actual completion of fieldwork (include target)
- Proportion of audits completed within prescribed budget (include target)
- Proportion of billable/recoverable hours versus nonbillable/nonrecoverable hours (include target)
- Level of engagement client satisfaction (include target)
- Actual time spent versus budget (include target)

Management and Supervision

Effectively managing the internal audit function promotes the internal auditing objectivity and is a requirement under the IIA *Standards*.

Supervision will generally encompass:

- Approval of the engagement plan
- Oversight of opening and closing meetings
- Direction, supervision, and review of engagement fieldwork
- Review of working papers to ensure conformance with agreed processes and professional standards
- Assurance that significant issues are properly documented, appropriately pursued, and reported adequately
- Resolving differences of professional judgment among staff involved in engagement

- On-the-job training of internal auditors to assist their development of appropriate skills and competence
- Overall review of engagements to ensure that the quality of each audit meets professional standards

---

Mid-Conduct Reviews

For large engagements, it can be useful to undertake a semi-formal, mid-conduct review between the engagement team and the chief audit executive to alert him or her to emerging issues. Allan Gaukroger, General Manager, Audit and the Chief Audit Executive at the Australian Government Department of Human Services, values these mid-conduct reviews for a number of reasons.

First, such reviews provide an opportunity for the chief audit executive to ensure that the engagement objective and scope remain relevant. Drawing on ongoing interactions with senior managers, the chief executive, and the audit committee, as well as emerging findings from other audits, the chief audit executive can quickly assess the extent to which an engagement remains aligned with the organization's rapidly evolving priorities and risks, and approve prompt changes to the plan if required. This minimizes the risk of a mismatch between the engagement's objective and changing organizational arrangements, which could limit the value of the assurance provided by the chief audit executive and reduce stakeholder confidence. It also provides an opportunity for the chief audit executive to learn about and communicate emerging issues to senior counterparts in the business, supporting a no surprises approach.

Second, mid-conduct reviews provide a more formal opportunity to escalate emerging and persistent issues that may be troubling the engagement team and that may require more senior expertise to resolve. Discussing these issues with the internal auditors allows the chief audit executive to provide a sense of perspective about their relative importance in a broader organizational context, to suggest approaches for resolution drawing on lessons learned from other engagements, and to reach out to senior colleagues in the business, as required, to broker solutions. Examples of such issues include a reluctance to acknowledge key shortcomings in governance, risk, and control arrangements; to communicate emerging audit conclusions that cross organizational boundaries; and to tackle challenges to the authority and independence of the internal audit function. This steering by the chief audit executive can keep an engagement from drifting off track to pursue less important issues, maintain the quality of relationships between the engagement team and the engagement client, and overcome resistance and inertia that can delay audit delivery.

Finally, these reviews provide an opportunity for the chief audit executive to shape the key messages delivered throughout the fieldwork and in the engagement report. Effective communication of engagement outcomes relies heavily on the tone, nuance, and emphasis given to each finding, and the manner in which

(continued)

(continued)

these are drawn together to form persuasive, credible conclusions and recommendations. If the first opportunity afforded to chief audit executives to shape the engagement communications is at the draft or even final report stage, it may be too late to weave their independent, more strategic perspective into the narrative of the report. This can result in a more technical, detail-focused report, less likely to influence senior decision makers. Conversely, even brief suggestions or questions during a review meeting can be enough for the engagement team to recognize the sensitivity or importance of a particular issue, and to tailor its communications accordingly.

Taken together, these opportunities for the chief audit executive to receive and give advice about the conduct of an audit mitigate a range of risks to audit quality and timeliness, while at the same time harnessing opportunities to take advantage of timely advice about evolving strategic priorities.

Working Papers

Internal auditors should retain appropriate working papers for their audit engagements. Quality working papers do the following:

- Support internal auditors to plan and perform the engagement.
- Demonstrate alignment between engagement planning and fieldwork.
- Assist internal auditors to find information they need quickly and easily.
- Demonstrate the extent to which engagement objectives were achieved.
- Support the preparation of a complete, accurate, and timely engagement report.
- Support any further action or investigation emerging from the engagement.
- Provide assurance that engagement is conducted in an orderly, efficient, and accountable manner.
- Support knowledge transfer to other internal audit staff.
- Support the review of engagements.
- Provide transparency to audit clients regarding engagement findings and conclusions.
- Provide a basis for assuring the quality of audits.
- Provide a historical record of the engagement.
- Demonstrate conformance with professional standards.

The IIA *Standards* recognize the value of adequate working papers—specifically, IIA Standards 2310 and 2330.

Standard 2310—Identifying Information

Internal auditors must identify sufficient, reliable, relevant, and useful information to achieve the engagement's objectives.

Standard 2330—Documenting Information

Internal auditors must document relevant information to support the conclusions and engagement results.

Wueste (2008) identifies the five essential characteristics of high-quality working papers as completeness, accuracy, organization, relevance, and conciseness. Working papers should be arranged in a logical manner to expedite both their review and knowledge sharing. At a minimum, working papers should include:

- The engagement plan and program
- Planning material, including relevant policies, procedures, and process maps
- Records from the opening and closing interviews
- Sufficient evidence to justify the conclusions drawn, including notes from interviews undertaken
- Copy of the draft report shared with management, any subsequent changes, and the rationale for these
- Copy of the final report
- Evidence of supervisory review

Quality working papers will be well structured and easy to follow. They will contain sufficient information to draw conclusions against engagement objectives but not contain excessive information that would make the relevant material difficult to find.

Automated Working Papers

For internal audit functions of a sufficient size, automated working papers can maximize efficiency and expedite knowledge management. However, significant effort is required to embed an automated working paper process, and the chief audit executive should provide appropriate resources to ensure its effective implementation. If these resources are not available, the chief audit executive should consider whether the organization is better off, at least in the short term, retaining a manual process.

PRIVACY CONSTRAINTS Some countries have legislation preventing information from being transferred across borders, which has implications for global audit functions retaining working papers on centralized servers. In these cases, it may be necessary for working papers to be retained locally, rather than centrally.

Common Quality Issue

Common quality issues related to *working papers* include:

- There is inadequate documentation of work performed, such as entry and exit interviews.

(continued)

(*continued*)

- Documents are missing from working papers.
- Audit supervision is not documented.
- Files do not have clear cross-referencing to demonstrate that each of the audit objectives had been completed, and that adequate work was performed to support the conclusions in the report.
- Review of working papers is not undertaken or documented.
- There is an inconsistent approach to documenting engagements across the internal audit function.
- Service providers do not retain adequate engagement documentation.
- Excessive and/or irrelevant material is retained on file.

QAIP Hint

Internal audit functions could incorporate *engagement working papers* into an internal audit maturity model or a balanced scorecard.

Maturity Model

The internal audit function could include *engagement working papers* as a key process area in its maturity model. For example:

- Level 2 of a five-stage maturity model could identify that working papers are completed in an ad hoc manner.
- Level 3 could identify that working papers are completed and appropriately reviewed for all engagements.
- Level 4 could identify that the internal audit function uses a template or automated process for capturing engagement working papers as well as checklists to document their independent review.
- Level 5 could identify that automated working papers are used and that engagement working papers:
  - Link to professional standards for each internal audit element
  - Link to policies and procedures for each internal audit element
  - Include quality checklists and quality control sign-off points

Balanced Scorecard/KPI

The internal audit function could include a performance indicator such as "Working papers are completed and appropriately reviewed for all engagements."

Questions about Performing the Engagement

Table 14.1 provides a range of questions about performing the engagement. These can be formally incorporated into a quality assurance and improvement program, or, less formally, into ongoing assessment activities. Questions may be variously posed to the chief audit executive, internal auditors, or audit stakeholders.

TABLE 14.1 Quality Questions

Questions	Evidence of Quality
Are opening and closing interviews held?	Working papers Internal audit staff interviews
Is there evidence that the engagement plan and work program were followed for each engagement?	Working papers
Does the internal audit function retain adequate working papers for each engagement?	Working papers
Are working papers clear, complete, and referenced back to the audit scope?	Working papers
Do working papers contain sufficient, reliable, relevant, and useful information to adequately support engagement findings?	Working papers
Are working papers for all audit engagements reviewed by the audit manager and chief audit executive (or designee)?	Working papers
Do working papers contain appropriate and adequate information to support the findings and conclusions?	Working papers
Does the internal audit function use automated working papers to maximize efficiency and expedite knowledge management?	Working papers
Does the internal audit function utilize continuous auditing techniques, such as repeatable CAATs?	Working papers Chief audit executive and internal audit staff interviews
Does the internal audit function appropriately challenge the control environment, including questioning the existence and relevance of some controls?	Working papers Chief audit executive and internal audit staff interviews Senior management and audit committee interviews
Do audit engagements identify causal risks and systemic issues?	Working papers Senior management and audit committee interviews
Have internal audit staff members demonstrated consideration of the relative significance and materiality of findings?	Working papers
Does the internal audit function work collaboratively with clients to identify mutually agreeable outcomes?	Senior management and audit committee interviews Chief audit executive and staff interviews Post-audit surveys
Does the internal audit function have documented processes for assuring adequate engagement supervision?	Policies and procedures

Conclusion

A high-quality internal audit function should operate as a critical friend to management—with sufficient independence to provide an impartial assessment of operations, but with the ultimate goal of supporting organizational success. By collaborating with management to achieve quality organizational outcomes, internal audit has the potential to add significant value.

Internal audit functions should adopt a systematic and transparent approach to its audit fieldwork. It should draw on established policies and procedures to maximize the potential that fieldwork is undertaken in a professional manner.

References

Craig, T. (1991). Effective interviewing skills for auditors. *Journal of Accountancy* 172(1): 121.

Dogas, C. (2011). Effective audit supervision. *Internal Auditor*. http://www.theiia.org/intauditor.

Gleim, I. N. (2004). *CIA Review: Part 2 Conducting the Internal Audit Engagement*. Gainesville, FL: Gleim Publications.

Greenawalt, M. B. (1997). The internal auditor and the critical thinking process: A closer look. *Managerial Auditing Journal* 12(2): 80–86.

Hubbard, L. D. (2001). What's a good audit finding? *Internal Auditor* 58(1): 104, 2001.

The Institute of Internal Auditors. (2013). *International Professional Practices Framework*. Altamonte Springs, FL: The Institute of Internal Auditors.

Keith, J. T. (2005). Killing the spider. *Internal Auditor* 62(2): 25–27, 2005.

Ratliff, R. L. and R. I. Johnson. (1998). Evidence. *Internal Auditor* 55(4): 56–61.

Reding, K. F., et al. (2009). *Internal Auditing: Assurance and Consulting Services*. Altamonte Springs, FL: The Institute of Internal Auditors Research Foundation.

Sawyer, L. B., M. A. Dittenhofer, and J. H. Scheiner. (2005). *Sawyers Internal Auditing*, 5th ed. Altamonte Springs, FL: The Institute of Internal Auditors Research Foundation.

Seipp, E., and D. Lindberg. (2012). A guide to effective audit interviews. *CPA Journal* 82(4): 26–31.

Wueste, B. (2008). Producing quality workpapers. *Internal Auditor*. http://www.theiia.org/intauditor.

CHAPTER 15

Communication and Influence

Begin with the end in mind.

—Stephen Covey

An internal auditor cannot be truly great without being an excellent communicator. Analytical skills and technical expertise will allow internal auditors to identify key improvement opportunities within an organization. However, without an ability to communicate well, both verbally and in writing, internal auditors are unlikely to influence management to make requisite changes.

Excellent communication is required at every stage of the internal audit process. During strategic planning, the chief audit executive needs to communicate with the audit committee and senior managers to ensure their expectations are realistic and appropriately reflected in the internal audit strategy and charter.

Communication with a broad range of stakeholders during annual audit planning maximizes the potential for the plan to accurately reflect the strategic priorities and risks of the organization. Likewise, effective communication throughout engagement planning and fieldwork provides assurance that engagement objectives will be met in a fair, accurate, and impartial manner.

Chief audit executives should develop clear communication pathways with internal and external stakeholders. These should help position the internal audit function as a professional, strategic partner, and enhance the overall influence that internal audit wields.

Understanding Stakeholder Needs

Baker (2011) notes, "Every great communicator tailors his or her message to the needs of the audience." Chief audit executives should have a clear understanding of the intended audience for each message. Audit committee needs may not be the same as those of middle management. Chief audit executives should understand what each of their stakeholders value and ensure that they develop their communications appropriately.

Stakeholder Mapping

As noted in Chapter 6, Rezaee (1996) described the evolution of stakeholders from management to the organization as a whole. Chief audit executives should have a clear picture of their key stakeholders from their strategic planning processes. They should also have identified the areas of greatest importance for each of these stakeholders in endeavoring to meet stakeholder expectation.

Chief audit executives may identify stakeholders and their needs in a formal or informal capacity. Visual processes, such as stakeholder mapping (Figure 15.1) can sometimes assist in identifying each of the stakeholders.

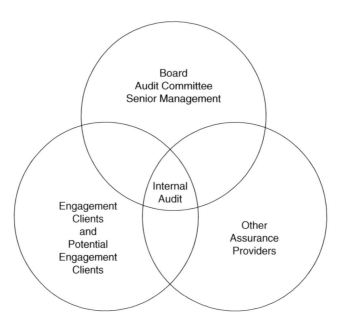

FIGURE 15.1 Stakeholder Mapping

Internal Stakeholders

Internal audit functions have a range of internal stakeholders that can be generally grouped as governance and oversight stakeholders, engagement clients, and other assurance providers. Governance and oversight stakeholders include the board and audit committee, the chief executive officer, and other senior management.

IIA Standards 2060, 2440.C2, and 2600 impose specific reporting requirements for some of these stakeholders.

Standard 2060—Reporting to Senior Management and the Board

The chief audit executive must report periodically to senior management and the board on the internal audit activity's purpose, authority, responsibility, and performance relative to its plan. Reporting must also include significant risk exposures and control issues, including fraud risks, governance issues, and other matters needed or requested by senior management and the board.

Standard 2440.C2—Disseminating Results

During consulting engagements, governance, risk management, and control issues may be identified. Whenever these issues are significant to the organization, they must be communicated to senior management and the board.

Standard 2600—Communicating the Acceptance of Risks

When the chief audit executive concludes that management has accepted a level of risk that may be unacceptable to the organization, the chief audit executive must discuss the matter with senior management. If the chief audit executive determines that the matter has not been resolved, the chief audit executive must communicate the matter to the board.

Chief audit executives should be clear regarding the primary recipient of their engagement reports. This will allow the report to be structured in a manner that best meets stakeholder needs.

Who Are We Providing Assurance To?

Greg Hollyman, Chief Internal Auditor at the Australian Taxation Office, believes there are times that internal auditors can lose sight of who they are providing assurance for. He sees internal audit assurance as being fundamentally directed to the audit committee and the chief executive. Therefore, Hollyman believes, it is important that reports are written in a manner that meet the needs of these primary stakeholders, while still providing clarity to operational management about identified control weaknesses and agreed management actions to resolve these issues.

AUDIT COMMITTEE REPORTS   Internal audit functions typically prepare audit committee reports for each meeting that commonly include the following elements:

- An update or overview from the chief audit executive
- Report on the quality assurance and improvement program, including performance against key performance indicators (KPIs)
- Progress against the approved plan and any proposed changes
- Results of internal audit engagement and a summary of reports issued since the last meeting
- Resolution status for audit recommendations

The report could also include other elements such as systemic issues, emerging risks, and updates on assurance coverage across the organization.

Common Quality Issue

Some chief audit executives do not report against internal audit performance or the quality assurance and improvement program. This reduces the visibility of senior management and the audit committee to internal audit's performance—both good and bad.

External Stakeholders

The internal audit function should embed processes to ensure effective communication with external stakeholders, including external audit and regulatory compliance functions. This should include conversations regarding the nature and scope of proposed engagements on the annual internal audit plan and the extent to which each party will rely on the other's work. The IIA's 2012–2013 chairman of the board, Phil Tarling (2012), advises internal auditors of the need to communicate effectively with other assurance providers in order to maximize risk and control benefits.

QAIP Hint

Internal audit functions could incorporate *stakeholder engagement* into an internal audit maturity model or a balanced scorecard.

Maturity Model

Internal audit functions could include *stakeholder engagement* as a key process area in its maturity model. For example:

- Level 2 of a five-stage maturity model could identify that the chief audit executive relies on ad hoc interaction with stakeholders.
- Level 3 could identify that the chief audit executive routinely engages key stakeholders, although these stakeholders may not be formally identified.
- Level 4 could identify that the chief audit executive has formally mapped stakeholders, and has a structured and documented process for engaging with each stakeholder.
- Level 5 could identify that regular (e.g., monthly) meetings are held between the chief audit executive and senior management and the chief audit executive and the audit committee chair. It could also identify that findings are aggregated into themes and across locations, and reported to senior management and the audit committee.

Balanced Scorecard/KPI

Internal audit functions could include performance indicators such as:

- The number of times the chief audit executive meets privately with the chief executive officer and other senior management (include target)
- The number of times the chief audit executive meets privately with the audit committee (include target)
- The completion and update of a stakeholder engagement map on an annual basis

Communication versus Influence

Communication and influence are interrelated but separate, as it is possible to communicate without influence but impossible to influence without communication. Although different, communication and influence are both integral elements of the internal audit quality and value equation. In terms of the internal audit logic model introduced in Chapter 3, effective communication and engagement reports are key outputs of the internal audit function; influence is a key outcome.

Communication encompasses a broader spectrum of activity than just engagement reports. Communication includes how the internal audit function interrelates with the audit committee, senior management, and engagement clients as well as other assurance providers.

According to Smith (2005):

Internal auditors need to possess excellent communication skills in order to succeed and advance in the changing, complex international global marketplace. Auditors utilize communication skills in almost every situation they encounter. Auditors must create an image of adding value to the organization and not just being investigators. Auditors must possess strong listening and interpersonal skills. Auditors have to be careful in using certain voice reflections when working with different types of individuals at various levels within an organization. Auditors must be aware of how their mannerisms impact auditees.

Tarling (2012) noted that *how* we communicate is as important as *what* we communicate. He was so committed to this message that he selected the phrase "say it right" as his primary theme for his term as chairman of the Institute of Internal Auditors.

The Institute of Internal Auditors–Australia (2013) identifies the following communication skills that are prevalent among good leaders:

- Being open and approachable
- Being prepared/thinking before speaking
- Being direct and clear
- Using superior listening skills
- Speaking with confidence
- Tailoring the communication to the audience
- Having integrity
- Having good body language and delivery style
- Removing barriers to communication

Influence

The Macquarie Dictionary (1991) defines influence as (1) invisible or insensible action exerted by one thing or person on another; or (2) power of producing effect by invisible or insensible means.

Essentially, influence is the ability to get things done with and through other people without necessarily having the formal power to mandate the action. Often the aim of influence is to impact others and have them support your agenda.

Influence is based on interpersonal relationships rather than power—power can create a result by force; influence creates a result voluntarily. This allows influence to be used in situations where individuals have no direct authority, which is important for internal auditors, as the best internal audit functions can create significant positive change in organizations without delegated authority or responsibility.

Creating the positive relationships necessary to support influence takes time and effort. By investing in time to build relationships across the organization, internal auditors can maximize their potential influence.

Influence is also dependent on creating and maintaining good reputations and respect across the organization. Internal auditors need to be seen as being knowledgeable, fair, ethical, respectful, and empathic before they are likely to be able to wield influence.

Influence: The Internal Audit Product

Mike Lynn, IT Audit Director at a major global financial services company and Vice Chairman of the IIA's Professional Issues Committee, believes the final product of a great audit is influence, not the report. "The report is just words on paper, and there are times there may not need to be a formal report but you can still influence an outcome," says Lynn.

INTERNAL AUDITORS AND INFLUENCE Internal auditors regularly use influence to achieve their goals, meet the requirements of their engagements, and implement their plans and strategies. Effective chief audit executives can influence the audit committee, senior management, engagement clients, other assurance providers, and internal audit staff.

Internal auditors may need to influence the ideas and actions of management and engagement clients to have them recognize control breakdowns, agree to audit findings, or adopt better practice.

Influencing Consciousness

Teis Stokka, Chief Internal Auditor at Tax Norway and leader of the Chief Audit Executive Network in Norway, advises that the mere fact that you are auditing an area will influence consciousness as well as behavior. Stokka emphasizes, "We own the process; the auditee and the organization have the knowledge and the responsibility."

Influence is not necessarily an innate skill for internal auditors. However, by recognizing it as a requisite competency in an internal audit capability plan, appropriate training and development can be provided to ensure the necessary skills are learned and are able to be applied.

Conflict Resolution

The nature of internal auditing means that conflict is always a possibility. Well-managed conflict can actually be advantageous to an organization. It can increase understanding among a team, enhance team cohesion and productivity and improve self-awareness. However, poorly managed conflict can be a destabilizing and destructive effect that impacts morale, reduces productivity, and increases staff turnover. Conflict can severely damage relationships across an organization, and reduce the potential for influence.

UNDERSTANDING THE CONFLICT   Johnson and colleagues (1998) suggest a number of key questions for understanding a potential conflict situation:

- Is the conflict real or is it actually just a case of poor communication?
- What is the conflict—what is the actual cause or source of the conflict?
- Is the conflict task-oriented or emotional—is the basis of the conflict logical and tangible, or is it values-based?

Internal auditors may experience conflict both internal and external to the internal audit function. Internal conflicts can relate to issues such as the way the function is structured, personnel processes, the nature of work undertaken, auditing tools and techniques, or management styles. External conflicts can arise when internal auditors critique organizational management—internal auditors are responsible for assessing the adequacy and effectiveness of governance, risk management, and control processes, and there will be times that management is sensitive to this critical review.

THE STAGES OF CONFLICT   Conflicts generally pass through a number of recognizable stages. Pastor (2007) suggests that there are three main stages of conflict:

1. Stage 1: Warning signs
2. Stage 2: Erupting differences in expectations
3. Stage 3: Open conflict

Other researchers have defined the conflict stages in a number of different ways, and the number of stages generally ranges from three to six. Using a combination of approaches, typical stages can be defined as follows.

Stage 1: Discomfort/Warning Signs   Although the actual problem may not yet be apparent, this stage is typified by a sense of uneasiness or discomfort, often characterized by a feeling that something is not quite right. Warning signs may include sudden changes in behavior or attitude.

Stage 2: Differences in Expectations   Although the problem may become apparent, parties to the conflict may have difficulty understanding the facts of a situation or the motives of others. The relationship a person has with the other party in the conflict may be more difficult, due to negative opinions and attitudes. The perceptions of, and feelings about, the colleague or client may be different from what they were before. There is constant worrying about the relationship with the colleague or client.

Stage 3: Open Conflict   This is the extreme manifestation of a conflict. Parties to the conflict may now behave in a manner that is not normal for them and their reactions to situations are uncharacteristic. They may be very emotive and the relationship with the colleague or client may now be ruptured and in a state that is unable to be repaired.

MANAGING CONFLICT   Managing conflicts requires an understanding of the individual characteristics of the conflict. There is no single approach to conflict management that will work, or that is even necessarily appropriate, in all situations. Conflicts arise for varying reasons, in a variety of settings, and with different potential consequences. The approach for dealing with a conflict will depend on the unique combination of these elements.

One of the most frequently cited models for conflict resolution was developed by Thomas and Kilmann in the 1970s. It proposes five basic conflict management styles, each defined by the combination of how much effort is put into satisfying individual concerns and how much effort is put into satisfying the other party's concerns. The five styles are *accommodate*, *avoid*, *collaborate*, *compete*, and *compromise*. They are characterized as follows.

Accommodate   These individuals are unassertive and cooperative. They effectively give in to the other person's desires or position, generally at the expense of their own. This approach is a *lose-win* strategy, often taken by people considering themselves a self-sacrificing *martyr*.

Avoid   These individuals are assertive and uncooperative—essentially refusing to deal with the conflict at all. The conflict may be ignored under the pretense that it doesn't exist or delegated to someone else. This is a *lose-lose* strategy.

The dangers in avoiding conflict are that if left unaddressed, it will worsen and escalate into a more serious issue, breed resentment, and create the perception of the individual involved as being weak and ineffective.

Collaborate   These individuals are assertive and cooperative. There is an attempt to meet the needs of all people involved. Collaborating is a traditional *win-win* strategy and will often involve galvanizing a group to work on and solve an issue together.

Compete   These individuals are assertive and uncooperative and are the opposite of the accommodating person. They generally operate from a position of power to impose a solution. This is a *win-lose* approach, with individuals often pursuing their own concerns at the expense of others.

The danger in using this style of conflict management is that it can lead to resentment and anger, particularly if this approach is used regularly, as the default approach, or in less urgent situations.

Compromise   These individuals lie somewhere between assertive and cooperative. They generally seek a solution that will at least partially satisfy the needs of all parties. This is a "middle ground" approach characterized by everybody giving up something in order to reach a mutually satisfactory outcome for all.

Compromise may be an appropriate strategy when:

- There are time pressures and deadlines approaching.
- Collaboration has not worked.
- Parties of similar strength are deadlocked.

The problem with a compromise approach is that issues and possible solutions are not explored in as much depth as they may be using a collaborative strategy, thus the optimal solution may not be reached.

CHOOSING A CONFLICT MANAGEMENT STYLE Although internal auditors may have a personal preference for one of the five conflict management styles, to work effectively they should be able to use any of the styles (or combinations of them) depending on the issue at hand. Generally, the style used should be driven by the situation, not by the personal predisposition of the internal auditor.

Culture and Conflict

Sadri (2013) has researched the impact of culture on conflict and conflict resolution and found this influence to be significant. She established that different cultures approach conflicts differently and that employees from the United States, Australia, Great Britain, Canada, and the Netherlands are typically individualistic, whereas Asian, Latin, and Middle Eastern cultures are typically collectivistic.

Individualistic cultures tend to look for speedy closure of conflicts, use more direct forms of communication, and pursue a higher incidence of social interactions (which tend to be shorter and less intimate). Collectivistic cultures value face-saving, often by using indirect communication, and have fewer (longer and more intimate) social interactions.

STEPS IN CONFLICT RESOLUTION Clarke and Lipp (1998) developed a seven-step conflict resolution model that they believe works effectively across cultures. It involves:

1. Problem identification
2. Problem clarification
3. Cultural exploration
4. Organizational exploration
5. Conflict resolution
6. Impact assessment
7. Organizational integration

Pastor (2007) proposes a seven-step process for collaborative negotiations in an audit setting.

Step 1: Prepare for the Process   Assemble all the information regarding the conflict and consider the information objectively. Decide on the specific outcome that is desired, the second-best outcome, and the minimum acceptable outcome (the bottom line). Chose an approach to the discussion and plan how to facilitate the process.

Step 2: Set the Scene and the Tone   Open the discussion with a framing statement and emphasize the desire for a collaborative (win-win) approach. Use positive language and nonverbal communication.

Step 3: Listen and Get the Issues out onto the Table   Make sure that people bring out all the relevant issues through excellent questioning skills, well-developed active listening skills, and positive body language.

Step 4: Look for Common Ground   Look for areas where there is broad agreement, while still leaving room for discussion of points of difference.

Step 5: Try for Collaboration   Use problem-solving techniques such as brainstorming to identify solutions that may be mutually acceptable to all parties.

Step 6: Make Decisions and Document Them   Evaluate all possible solutions that arise through the brainstorming session and decide together on the solution that is most acceptable to all parties (keeping in mind the bottom-line position derived in Step 1 of the process).

Step 7: Close and Summarize   Conclude conflict resolution discussions with a clear summary of what has taken place, what has been resolved, and what the process will be from this point on. Circulate summary documentation, including the decisions made and expectations on parties to all participants for acknowledgement.

Engagement Communications

The engagement communication, often a report, is the output of the engagement. In many cases it is the only visible artifact that the organization sees from the internal audit engagement. It is therefore extremely important that the communication reflects the professionalism of the internal audit function and provides stakeholders with a sense of confidence regarding the work undertaken and the conclusions drawn. HM Treasury (2010) states, "A good audit report communicates the auditor's conclusions effectively and makes recommendations persuasively so that management understands the issues, accepts the conclusions and acts appropriately. An inadequate report may negate the best audit work and finest conclusions. It may also damage the reputation and status of internal audit."

Effective communication outputs can lead to the achievement of the internal audit outcome of influence. IIA Standards 2400, 2410, and 2440 include specific criteria regarding the communication of engagement findings.

Standard 2400—Communicating Results

Internal auditors must communicate the results of engagements.

Standard 2410—Criteria for Communicating

Communications must include the engagement's objectives and scope as well as applicable conclusions, recommendations, and action plans.

Standard 2440—Disseminating Results

The chief audit executive must communicate results to the appropriate parties.

A typical internal audit engagement report includes the following elements:

- Date of report and timeframe of the engagement
- Executive summary
- Introduction, including engagement objectives and scope
- Findings or observations
- Recommendations or agreed management actions
- Overall conclusion and opinion on the engagement objectives
- Appendices with details of methodology, criteria, and interviews

Reporting Better Practices

Reporting is critical in producing a quality audit outcome. Better practices for engagement reporting include:

- Using a one-page executive summary for reports that identifies individual issues, why the engagement has added value, and thanks the engagement client
- Producing individual assurance reports for major programs, activities, or organizational areas
- Developing a reporting quality dashboard and producing quarterly reports against the dashboard for the audit committee
- Documenting the reporting flow from the annual audit plan to annual internal audit reports to the audit committee
- Staff training in report writing

Executive Summary

The executive summary is a brief, stand-alone synopsis of the entire engagement report. It provides the audit committee and senior management with an opinion against the objectives of the review, either as an overall opinion or an opinion against each of the key engagement questions.

The executive summary should include a précis of key findings, both positive and negative, and agreed recommendations or management actions. Readers should gain a sense of the overall significance of matters raised in the body of the report, without having to read the full detail. In other words, the executive summary should answer the "So what?" question in relation to the internal auditor's conclusions.

The executive summary should be consistent with the body of the report and should not include additional information from the remainder of the report.

Findings or Observations

The findings (or observations) section of the report describes the results of the engagement. Quality reports will include both positive and negative observations, but will generally be limited to issues that directly lead to the conclusion or ratings included in the report. Less significant findings can be communicated verbally or in a memorandum to management—the internal audit function should still retain records of this informal communication.

The findings should flow logically, taking the reader through a structured process that allows them to build an image of the program or activity reviewed and the significance of the observations made by the internal audit function.

In accordance with IIA Practice Advisory 2410–1, findings should generally reflect the following attributes:

- **Criteria**—the standards, expectations, or values used to determine the finding (what should exist)
- **Condition**—the evidence that was found
- **Cause**—the reason for the difference between the expected and actual condition
- **Effect**—the risk or impact of the condition

These were discussed in greater detail in Chapter 14. The internal audit function may choose to describe each of these attributes as separate headings within each finding, or, more typically, use these attributes to guide an overall narrative for each finding.

Focus on Key Findings

Rune Johannessen, Senior Audit Manager and Head of Competence and Development at Nordea Bank AB in Norway, warns internal auditors to avoid the temptation of including all audit findings in their report. He recommends that internal auditors focus on the most important findings, as this will increase the potential for the audit report to influence change.

Recommendations and Management Actions

Schleifer and Greenawalt (1996) recognize, "In order to function as a value-adding component of their organizations, internal auditors must go beyond the tasks of evaluation and passing judgment to make recommendations for improvement."

Recommendations, or agreed management actions, answer the question "What is to be done?" Some internal audit functions prefer to use agreed management actions, rather than recommendations, as they see these as a more collaborative outcome of the audit engagement. In contrast, recommendations are suggestions for corrective actions, still requiring management's acceptance. This acceptance will most likely occur if the recommendations have been developed in consultation with management.

Recommendations or agreed management actions should focus on what must be done to address the causal issue, and so correct the condition that was observed. In this way, the condition can be prevented from recurring.

Schwarz (1999) wrote, "A good recommendation maintains the proper balance between the risk presented and the cost to control it." He suggests that, before making a recommendation, the auditor consider the following questions:

- Does the recommendation solve the problem and eliminate or reduce the risk?
- Can the recommendation be implemented within the current environment?
- Is the recommendation cost-effective?
- Will the recommendation act as a temporary bandage or a permanent solution?

Additional questions that could be asked are:

- Does the recommendation stimulate action?
- Is the recommendation precise, clearly describing the procedures that will affect the required change?
- Does the recommendation address the root cause?
- Is the recommendation directed to an appropriate person with authority to implement the recommendation?
- Is the recommendation problem-specific, and is the corrective action measurable?

Recommendations and agreed management actions should be clear, specific, and concise and address the causal issue of the finding. A general rule of thumb is that if a recommendation asks management to continue an action already commenced, indicating that management is already addressing the condition found, the finding and recommendation should not be included in the report.

Conclusions, Opinions, and Ratings

There are many approaches to expressing opinions against the audit objectives and rating the significance of findings. This variation is reflected in IIA Standard 2410.A1.

POSITIVE FINDINGS AND OBSERVATIONS Some internal auditors are reluctant to identify positive findings while at the same time are prepared to identify negative findings. A common justification is that there is a risk that their positive finding may be incorrect. However, the same argument could be made against identifying negative findings.

Quality internal auditing recognizes that there is a level of evidence necessary for identifying both positive and negative performance. Internal auditors are not meant to be infallible, and provided that evidence gathered resulting in positive findings addresses the *reasonable person* test described in Chapter 14, internal auditors should feel comfortable in identifying positive as well as negative findings. This approach is reinforced in IIA Standard 2410.A2.

Standard 2410.A1

Final communication of engagement results must, where appropriate, contain the internal auditor's opinion and/or conclusions. When issued, an opinion or conclusion must take account of the expectations of senior management, the board, and other stakeholders and must be supported by sufficient, reliable, relevant, and useful information.

Interpretation:

Opinions at the engagement level may be ratings, conclusions, or other descriptions of the results. Such an engagement may be in relation to controls around a specific process, risk, or business unit. The formulation of such opinions requires consideration of the engagement results and their significance.

Standard 2410.A2

Internal auditors are encouraged to acknowledge satisfactory performance in engagement communications.

OPINIONS   Better practice internal audit reports include an opinion for every engagement against the objectives of the engagement. Spencer Pickett (2012) said, "The primary role of internal audit is to provide independent assurances that the organization is, or is not, managing risk well. Internal audit can provide assurance on the extent to which controls are able to address risks but cannot give any absolutes." The form of the opinion can vary between internal audit functions.

IIA Standard 2450 includes specific requirements regarding audit opinions.

Standard 2450—Overall Opinions

When an overall opinion is issued, it must take into account the expectations of senior management, the board, and other stakeholders and must be supported by sufficient, reliable, relevant, and useful information.

RATINGS   Quality engagement reports often include formalized ratings. These ratings can be against the overall objective, subobjectives, individual findings, or recommendations. The internal audit function should determine a suitable scale to be used for categorizing the control environment within the organization. Examples 15.1, 15.2, and 15.3 illustrate different approaches.

Example 15.1 Sample Overall Audit Ratings

Satisfactory—Internal controls, governance, and risk management processes were adequately established and functioning well. No issues were identified that would significantly affect the achievement of the objectives of the audited entity.

Partially Satisfactory—Internal controls, governance, and risk management processes were generally established and functioning, but needed improvement. One or several issues were identified that may negatively affect the achievement of the objectives of the audited entity.

Unsatisfactory—Internal controls, governance, and risk management processes were either not established or not functioning well. The issues were such that the achievement of the overall objectives of the audited entity could be seriously compromised.

Example 15.2 Sample Ratings for Engagement Findings

Satisfactory—Adequate controls exists that are operating as intended.

Improvement Opportunity—Some additional controls might be required and/or control effectiveness could be enhanced.

Unsatisfactory—Controls are missing or obsolete, or controls exist but are not operating effectively.

Example 15.3 Sample Rating for Engagement Recommendations

Critical—High likelihood of an event that will significantly impact the organization or activity if the recommendation is not effectively implemented within the proposed time frame.

Major—Likelihood of an event that will significantly impact the organization or activity if the recommendation is not effectively implemented within the proposed time frame.

Minor—Possibility of an event that will moderately impact the organization or activity if the recommendation is not effectively implemented within the proposed time frame.

Improvement Opportunity—Opportunity to enhance control effectiveness.

Quality Engagement Communications

Internal audit functions are often judged by the quality of their engagement reports. Gray (1996) supports the importance, and highlights the challenge of quality reporting: "One of the most difficult and most important aspects of the auditing profession is presenting the audit results in a clear, convincing manner. If the reader of the report is not convinced of the need to implement the recommended corrective actions, all of the audit work has been for naught."

In accordance with IIA Standard 2420, quality engagement communications will be accurate, objective, clear, concise, constructive, complete, and timely.

Standard 2420—Quality of Communications

Communications must be accurate, objective, clear, concise, constructive, complete, and timely.

ACCURATE COMMUNICATIONS   Accurate communications are dependent on sufficient, reliable evidence and appropriate analysis of the evidence to support conclusions. The accuracy of findings and conclusions should be determined prior to the preparation of the engagement report by maintaining an ongoing dialogue with the engagement client throughout the fieldwork.

OBJECTIVE COMMUNICATIONS   Internal audit is by nature a critical activity. The internal auditor's role is to objectively evaluate organizational activities and recommend opportunities for improvement where appropriate. Human nature being what it is, engagement clients are more likely to accept this criticism when it is delivered in an objective and nonemotive manner.

Using an established rating scale can support engagement objectivity, as it allows the significance of the findings and/or recommendations to be compared across engagements.

Assisting Organizations to Manage their Reputation

Goh Boon Hwa, Head of Corporate Audit at the Singapore Economic Development Board, believes the primary role of the internal auditor is to help the organization manage its reputation by identifying issues and reporting them in a neutral manner.

CLEAR COMMUNICATIONS   A quality engagement report should answer the question "So what?" regarding the audit findings. It should provide clarity on what was expected and what the engagement actually found, and should leave the reader with a clear understanding of the importance of any issues and their significance for the organization.

Each finding or observation should describe the condition, criterion, cause, and effect. Recommendations or agreed management actions should be specific and cost-effective, and flow logically from key findings and observations.

Using active (rather than passive) language in the reports also supports their readability. Didis (1997) suggests that clear writing first of all requires proper organization of ideas and information to be communicated. He said, "The auditor's judgment normally should prevail in determining how topics should be sequenced, although thought should be given to whether issues should be placed in order of importance or matched to the sequence of events in the process audited."

Report clarity can be assisted by utilizing style guidelines. Some larger organizations develop their own style manual, while others use publicly available guides. For example, many Australian government departments use the *Style Manual: For Authors, Editors and Printers*.

Using graphics and photographs (as appropriate) in reports can also aid interpretation and add visual interest. Chief audit executives should determine the style of the report that best suits their organization, and develop standardized reporting that supports these preferences.

The Challenge of Finding Great Communicators

Vanessa Johnson, Group Manager of Corporate Risk and Assurance at New Zealand Inland Revenue, believes it is a challenge to find people who can communicate well and ask the right questions.

Internal auditors are no different from other groups in an organization—they must be seen to deliver value for money. In their case, that doesn't necessarily translate directly into monetary terms. How and what they communicate significantly impacts their effectiveness and their ability to influence change in their organization. They need to have conversations with their customers. This requires good listening skills, the ability to pick up nuances, and a good understanding of their customers' strategic objectives and challenges so that there is useful dialogue. They need to communicate more formally in a way that is clear and to the point. They can no longer rely on organizational mandate to be effective. Whether communication is verbal or in writing they need to engage with their customers, constantly *selling* why it makes sense to invest to reduce a risk or implement a more efficient process.

CONCISE COMMUNICATIONS Internal auditors should communicate concisely, balancing the need for completeness and clarity in reports with respect for the time pressures facing the report's audience.

Conciseness can be enhanced by producing succinct executive summaries for senior management and the audit committee. The complete report can then be made available as required. Brief executive summaries can also be included verbatim in periodic internal audit reporting to the audit committee.

Rating, and listing in order of importance, the findings and recommendations in the executive summary allows senior management and the audit committee to focus on important areas. Using ratings also allows for comparison of the effectiveness of the control environment relative to other programs or activities.

For very large organizations (producing a large number of internal audit reports) the internal audit function may produce both full and abbreviated report formats. The full reports can be provided to engagement clients, and the abbreviated reports to senior management and the audit committee.

Common Quality Issue

A common quality issue internal auditors face is determining which findings and observations to include in the report. Internal auditors should avoid including every finding from fieldwork, and instead focus on the key areas likely to impact the achievement of objectives.

An alternative to going into excessive detail in the main report is to use appendices for information such as the audit methodology, criteria, and people interviewed as part of the engagement.

CONSTRUCTIVE COMMUNICATIONS   Engagement reports need to be useful. They should assist management to make beneficial change to governance, risk management, and control processes, and ultimately support organizational effectiveness. Internal auditors should be constantly mindful as to whether the reports are providing constructive criticism, or are unnecessarily destructive.

Constructiveness can be enhanced by offering insight through the report. Internal auditors should start by identifying the root causes for issues, and work with management to develop long-term, systemic solutions.

Reports should provide senior management and the audit committee with clarity regarding the extent to which the organization is effectively managing its key risks.

Identifying Root Causes

Goh Thong, Chief Internal Auditor at SPRING Singapore, believes that one of the greatest quality issues for internal auditors is their ability to identify and communicate the root cause of issues. He considers that reports are not often written in a way that enables management to appreciate the value of an issue. Ideally, he believes that a report needs to be able to capture people's attention in the first paragraph.

COMPLETE COMMUNICATIONS   Internal auditors need to constantly balance conciseness and completeness. They should incorporate each of the significant issues found while also using opportunities such as verbal reports and management letters to communicate additional issues.

Including the engagement client's response to the findings and recommendations in the report enhances the transparency of the reports and supports the follow-up process.

TIMELY COMMUNICATIONS Audit reports should be issued in a timely manner to engagement clients. The chief audit executive should ensure that internal auditors have sufficient time to draft the report after the completion of fieldwork, and internal audit managers should make themselves available to review the report as early as possible.

Embedding preset time limits between completion of fieldwork and issue of the report helps ensure quality, and reduces the risk that delays in communications may lead to organizational changes reducing the impact of findings.

Chief audit executives may develop formal agreements with management (possibly through a service level agreement) specifying the maximum time period between completion of fieldwork, issue of draft report, and issue of final reports. This should also include a maximum time period for review of reports by the engagement client and completion of management comments.

Common Quality Issue

Organizational managers commonly complain about the lateness of engagement reports. Often there is a significant lag between the completion of fieldwork and the issue of the draft report, especially for larger performance and operational audits.

Insight and Influence

The IIA (2013) recognizes that the provision of insight by internal auditors is one of their greatest value offerings. The IIA defines the key elements of insight as catalyst, analyses, and assessments and believes internal auditing is a "catalyst for improving an organization's effectiveness and efficiency by providing insight and recommendations based on analyses and assessments of data and business processes."

Making Issues Relevant for Stakeholders

Tan Peck Leng, Head of Internal Audit at Defence, Science and Technology Agency in Singapore, believes that senior management and the audit committee highly value the independent perspective that internal audit can bring. She sees this being reinforced through the internal audit function identifying both issues and the impact of these issues on the organization. By making the issues relevant for stakeholders, they are then more likely to respond positively to the finding.

Insight and influence are interrelated, and a quality internal audit function requires both attributes. Providing insight will increase internal audit's influence; although a level of influence is necessary for the insight to be accepted.

Verbal Reporting

While written reports are most commonly provided after internal audit engagements, there may be times when a verbal report would suffice (particularly for smaller compliance or follow-up engagements where no adverse issues were noted). However, regardless of what is provided to management or the engagement client, there will still need to be a notation of these findings in reporting to the audit committee.

Rather than replacing written communication, verbal reporting most often complements the written communication. Verbal reporting can be used effectively during presentations, particularly in situations where:

- The internal auditor needs to update the chief audit executive and other members of the internal audit function regarding preliminary findings and recommendation.
- Management's feedback to preliminary findings is being sought, particularly at the exit interview.
- Internal auditors want to workshop potential recommendations with the engagement client.
- Complex issues are being communicated that would be simplified through appropriate visuals.

The UK's HM Treasury (2010) cautions that the challenge for chief audit executives with verbal reporting (particularly presentations) is that these verbal reports are not usually subject to the same degree of quality control as written communications. If communicated poorly, a verbal report may lead to misunderstanding regarding facts or emphasis. HM Treasury notes that the key to successful presentations are training, preparation, and practice.

Example 15.4   Using Presentations to Influence People

Effective presentations have the ability to dramatically influence people. They can be used to impart a new idea or concept or to challenge the prevailing wisdom. There are a number of key elements to an effective presentation.

Preparation

Effective presentations begin with preparation. Kaye (2009) wrote, "There is only one good reason to give a presentation and that is to cause change. Your first step in planning a presentation is to determine why you are speaking. What decision do you want the audience to make? What outcome/conclusion do you want them to reach? What action do you want them to take? Your presentation is a success when you deliver the result that was expected."

Preparation provides an opportunity to collect ideas, identify the three to five main points of the presentation, and determine the evidence needed to support these ideas. Visual aids can be used to support the presentation, although these should not become the default presentation—they should simply reinforce the main ideas. For example, a closing interview presentation may incorporate graphs or photos to clearly illustrate the nature of the findings.

Effective presentations are rehearsed. Presenters should have a good idea of the time the presentation requires and ensure that this aligns with the time available. Rehearsing the presentation helps to add energy and commitment, and can reduce nerves associated with public speaking.

Delivery

Effective presentations starts with a powerful impact statement that may only last one to two minutes, but that clearly defines the purpose of the presentation up front. These statements introduce the presenter, very simply articulate the purpose of the presentation, and structure the presentation into key sections. Using an engagement closing presentation as an example:

Hello. I'm Mary Smith, and I am the lead auditor for this engagement. Over the next hour I plan to take you through our key findings from the engagement, provide an opportunity for you to comment on our conclusions, and work with you to develop some actions to address these findings.

Weissman (2003) believes an effective presentation leads the audience to a clear objective. "The journey gives the audience a psychological comfort level that makes them ready to respond positively to the presenter's call to action—as well as to the presenter," says Weissman.

It is not unusual for people to be nervous about public speaking. Presenters should channel their adrenaline into enthusiasm, manage their nerves through positive self-talk, and control their breathing.

To increase their connection with the audience, presenters should make eye contact and understand how the audience is responding to the presentation— they should be observant of the audience's body language. Brody (2000) suggests that "hitting the emotional buttons will create more impact and action than pure data. Include stories, analogies, and metaphors to reinforce the key points."

Closing

The closing section provides an opportunity to create a mutual dialogue with the audience—to offer the floor to the audience to ask questions and to provide clarification as required. Rather than introducing new material during the closing, it should reinforce the call to action and main points of the presentation.

QAIP Hint

Internal audit functions could incorporate *engagement reporting* into an internal audit maturity model or a balanced scorecard.

Maturity Model

Internal audit functions could include *engagement reporting* as a key process area in its maturity model. For example:

- Level 2 of a five-stage maturity model could identify that the findings and recommendations from engagements are reported in an inconsistent or ad hoc manner.
- Level 3 could identify that the internal audit function uses a structure approach to engagement reporting and that reports are accurate, objective, clear, concise, constructive, complete, and timely.
- Level 4 could identify that engagement reports include positive opinions and findings, and/or recommendations are rated.
- Level 5 could identify that engagement reports provide insight and the internal audit function delivers formal presentations for each closing meeting.

Balanced Scorecard/KPI

Internal audit functions could include performance indicators such as:

- Elapsed time for issue of reports—completion of engagement fieldwork to issue of draft report (include target)
- Elapsed time for finalization of report—issue of draft report to issue of final report (include target)

Follow-Up

Follow-up, or monitoring, is the important final step in the engagement process. Without this, recommendations or agreed management actions may not be implemented in a complete or timely manner due to management complacency or competing demands.

IIA Standard 2500 includes specific requirements for monitoring.

Standard 2500—Monitoring Progress

The chief audit executive must establish and maintain a system to monitor the disposition of results communicated to management.

Internal audit functions can adopt various processes for engagement monitoring, and the appropriateness of each will depend on the size and sourcing of the internal audit function, as well as the needs and maturity of the broader organization. Regardless of the follow-up approach used by the internal audit function, the process should include the following key elements:

- Management advice regarding status of recommendations or agreed management actions
- Management provision of supporting evidence
- Review of supporting evidence by the internal audit function
- Update of database or system for monitoring actions
- Reporting of follow-up results

Keating (1995) suggests the following criteria to determine the quality of corrective actions implemented by management:

- Was the action responsive to the defect?
- Was the action complete in correcting all material aspects of the defect?
- Is the corrective action continuing?
- Is the corrective action monitored to ensure effectiveness and to prevent recurrence?

The chief audit executive should provide regular advice to the audit committee of the status of recommendations or agreed management actions. This should incorporate the age of open issues, the rating of issues, business area responsible, and nature of the issue.

Common Quality Issue

Inadequate follow-up is relatively common across internal audit functions. This may be due to a lack of motivation by the chief audit executive, inadequate understanding of the importance of follow-up, or a failure to allocate specific time for this activity in the internal audit plan.

QAIP Hint

Internal audit functions could incorporate *follow-up* into an internal audit maturity model or a balanced scorecard.

Maturity Model

Internal audit functions could include *follow-up* as a key process area in its maturity model. For example:

- Level 2 of a five-stage maturity model could identify that the internal audit function does not routinely follow up on the results of internal audit engagements.
- Level 3 could identify that the internal audit function has in place a formal follow-up process.

- Level 4 could identify that the internal audit function has in place an automated follow-up process that allows for direct updates by management. In addition, the internal audit function provides a status report to the audit committee each meeting identifying outstanding recommendations, the name of the responsible officer, the nature of the action to be taken, and the expected completion date.
- Level 5 could identify that the internal audit function uses analytics to identify trends for specific business processes, categorize audit issues, and identify root causes. Responsible officers for long-overdue items (say, 6 to 12 months) report in person to the audit committee.

Balanced Scorecard/KPI

Internal audit functions could include performance indicators such as:

- Percentage of recommendations accepted (include target)
- Perceived importance of audit findings and recommendations (include target)
- Percent of audit recommendations implemented (include target)

Communicating the Acceptance of Risk

Management is ultimately responsible for mitigating risks associated with its own area activities. While the internal audit function can provide advice to management regarding the effectiveness and adequacy of controls, it relies on management to accept this advice. However, if management chooses to accept a risk that the internal audit function considers inappropriate the chief audit executive should discuss this with senior management.

IIA Standard 2600 addresses this issue.

Standard 2600—Communicating the Acceptance of Risks

When the chief audit executive concludes that management has accepted a level of risk that may be unacceptable to the organization, the chief audit executive must discuss the matter with senior management. If the chief audit executive determines that the matter has not been resolved, the chief audit executive must communicate the matter to the board.

Questions about Communication and Influence

Table 15.1 provides a range of questions about communication and influence. These can be formally incorporated into a quality assurance and improvement program, or, less formally, into ongoing assessment activities. Questions may be variously posed to the chief audit executive, internal auditors, or audit stakeholders.

TABLE 15.1 Quality Questions

Questions	Evidence of Quality
Does the internal audit function have a process or criteria that supports the production of high quality reports?	Evidence of process or criteria
Are engagement reports approved by the chief audit executive or their delegate prior to distribution?	Evidence of approval
Have engagement results been communicated to appropriate parties?	Engagement communication Evidence of dissemination of engagement communication
Is the internal audit function honest, fair, and consistent in its identification of issues?	Senior management and audit committee interviews Post-audit surveys
Do engagement reports include the engagement's objectives and scope, as well as applicable conclusions, recommendations, and action plans?	Engagement communication
Do engagement reports include management comments and agreed actions with timing and responsibility?	Engagement communication
Do reports released to external parties include limitations on the distribution of results?	Evidence of limitation wording in engagement communication
Is the statement "conforms with the International Standards for the Professional Practice of Internal auditing" used in any engagement reports or communications?	Engagement communication
If so, has an external assessment supported this statement?	Quality assurance and improvement program reports
Does the chief audit executive report periodically to the audit committee on performance against the internal audit plan?	Record of communications Chief audit executive interview Senior management and audit committee interviews
Are significant risk exposures and control issues reported to the audit committee?	Record of communications Chief audit executive interview Senior management and audit committee interviews
Do the chief audit executive and internal audit staff members have well-developed communication skills?	Senior management and audit committee interviews
Does the internal audit function disseminate lessons learned from its work, and from external audit, to relevant areas of the entity to contribute to organizational learning?	Chief audit executive interview Senior management and audit committee interviews
Does the chief audit executive regularly inform the audit committee of progress on the implementation of agreed internal and external audit and other relevant report recommendations?	Chief audit executive interview Audit committee interviews Audit committee minutes
Does the chief audit executive facilitate communication between external audit and entity management, where appropriate?	Chief audit executive interview Senior management and audit committee interviews External audit interviews Audit committee minutes Chief audit executive interview

(continued)

TABLE 15.1 (*continued*)

Questions	Evidence of Quality
Have there been any instances where the chief audit executive believed that management had accepted a level of risk that may be unacceptable to the organization?	
If so, did the chief audit executive discuss the matter with senior management?	Chief audit executive interview Senior management interviews
If so, and the chief audit executive did not believe the matter was resolved, did the chief audit executive communicate the matter to the audit committee?	Chief audit executive interview Audit committee interviews Audit committee minutes Any tangible evidence (e-mail records, internal memos, reports on meetings, etc.) demonstrating that the board had been informed
Are periodic meetings held with external audit and other assurance providers?	Records of meetings Chief audit executive interview Senior management and audit committee interviews External audit interviews
Are engagement results shared between assurance providers where appropriate and beneficial?	Records of meetings Chief audit executive interview Senior management interviews
Does the internal audit function provide overall assurance on governance, risk management, and control?	Assurance statements
Is the internal audit function recognized as an agent of change?	Senior management and audit committee interviews
Does internal audit provide foresight (i.e., commentary on emerging or potential issues/risks) in addition to hindsight?	Engagement communication Senior management and audit committee interviews Post-engagement surveys
Do engagement reports include internal audit's opinion or conclusion?	Engagement communication
Do engagement reports note satisfactory performance, where applicable?	Engagement communication Senior management and audit committee interviews Post-engagement surveys
Are any overall opinions supported by sufficient, reliable, relevant, and useful information?	Engagement communication Senior management and audit committee interviews Post-engagement surveys
Are reasons given for any unfavorable overall opinion?	Engagement communication
Has the internal audit function established a follow-up process?	Policy and procedure
Is the status of reported recommendations periodically determined and reported to the audit committee?	Audit committee reports Audit committee interviews
Does the chief audit executive or the audit supervisor have discussions with internal audit staff regarding the audit findings and report?	Evidence of engagement supervision Internal audit staff interviews
Does the chief audit executive undertake surveys (or other processes) to gauge client satisfaction at the end of engagements?	Client satisfaction surveys (or similar)

Conclusion

Communication is one of the most important elements of the internal audit function. When done effectively, it allows the chief audit executive and internal auditors to wield positive influence over an organization. It positions the internal audit function as a strategic and professional partner, and maximizes the value that internal audit can offer an organization.

References

Baker, N. (2011). A stronger partnership. *Internal Auditor*. http://www.theiia.org/intauditor.

Brody, M. (2000). Marketing: 10 little-known, rarely discussed, highly effective presentation techniques. *Commercial Law Bulletin* 15(6): 2.

Clarke, C. C., and G. D. Lipp. (1998). Conflict resolution for contrasting cultures. *Training & Development* 52(2): 20–33.

Cutler, S. (2009). *Audit Committee Reporting: A Guide for Internal Audit*. Altamonte Springs, FL: The Institute of Internal Auditors Research Foundation.

Cutler, S. (2001). *Designing and Writing Message-Based Audit Reports*. Altamonte Springs, FL: The Institute of Internal Auditors.

Didis, S. K. (1997). Communicating audit results. *Internal Auditor* 54(5): 36–38.

Gray, R. E. (1996). The everyday guide to effective report writing. *Government Accountants Journal* 45(2): 20–22.

HM Treasury. (2010). *Good Practice Guide: Reporting*. http://www.hm-treasury.gov.uk.

Hubbard, L. D. (2001). What's a good audit finding? *Internal Auditor* 58(1): 104.

The Institute of Internal Auditors. (2013). *International Professional Practices Framework*. Altamonte Springs, FL: The Institute of Internal Auditors.

The Institute of Internal Auditors. The Value of Internal Auditing for Stakeholders. https://na.theiia.org/about-ia/PublicDocuments/10405_GOV-Global_Value_Proposition_Flyer_Update-FNL-Hi.pdf.

The Institute of Internal Auditors–Australia. (2013). *Graduate Certificate in Internal Audit Module 1 Unit 1*. Unpublished.

Johnson, G. H., T. Means, and J. Pullis. (1998). Managing conflict. *Internal Auditor* 55(6): 54–59.

Kaye, S. (2009). It's showtime! How to give effective presentations. *SuperVision* 70(9): 13–15.

Keating, G. (1995). The art of the follow-up. *Internal Auditor* 52(2): 59.

Macquarie University. (1991). Macquarie Dictionary. New South Wales: Macquarie Library, Macquarie University.

Pastor, J. (2007). *Conflict Management & Negotiation Skills for Internal Auditors*. Altamonte Springs, FL: The Institute of Internal Auditors Research Foundation.

Reding, K. F., P. J. Sobel, U. L. Anderson, M. J. Head, S. Ramamoorti, M. Salamasick, and C. Riddle et al. (2009). *Internal Auditing: Assurance and Consulting Services*. Altamonte Springs, FL: The Institute of Internal Auditors Research Foundation.

Rezaee, Z. (1996). Improving the quality of internal audit functions through total quality management. *Managerial Auditing Journal* 11(1): 30–34.

Rezaee, Z. (2010). The importance of audit opinions. *Internal Auditor*. http://www
    .theiia.org/intauditor.
Sadri, G. (2013). Choosing conflict resolution by culture. *Industrial Management*
    55(5): 10–15.
Sawyer, L. B., M. A. Dittenhofer, and J. H. Scheiner. (2005). *Sawyers Internal Auditing*,
    5th ed. Altamonte Springs, FL: The Institute of Internal Auditors Research
    Foundation.
Schleifer, L. L. F., and M. B. Greenawalt. (2013). The internal auditor and the critical
    thinking process. *Managerial Auditing Journal* 11(5): 5–13.
Schwartz, Brian M. (1999). Documenting audit findings. *Internal Auditor* 56(2): 48–49.
Seipp, E., and D. Lindberg. (2012). A guide to effective audit interviews. *CPA Journal*
    82(4): 26–31.
Smith, G. (2005). Communication skills are critical for internal auditors. *Managerial
    Auditing Journal* 20(5): 513–519.
Spencer Pickett, K. H. (2012). *The Essential Guide to Internal Auditing*, 2nd ed. West
    Sussex, England: John Wiley & Sons.
Style Manual for Authors, Editors and Printers, 6th ed. (2011). Hoboken, NJ: John
    Wiley & Sons.
Tarling, P. (2012). Say it right. *Internal Auditor*. http://www.theiia.org/intauditor.
United Nations Office for Project Services. (2013). (sample) *Internal Audit Report*.
    http://www.unops.org/SiteCollectionDocuments/Accountability%20documents/
    Internal_audits/2013–11–25%20IAIG3211-Project%2077260-GFATM%20-%20PR%
    20-%20Internal%20Audit%20Report.pdf.
Weissman, J. (2003). Inspiring presentations. *Executive Excellence* 20(7): 14–15.

CHAPTER 16

Knowledge Management and Marketing

The aim of marketing is to know and understand the customer so well the product or service fits him and sells itself.

—Peter Drucker

Internal auditing is a knowledge-based activity. It relies on internal auditors being proficient in identifying and analyzing data to gain a depth of knowledge about processes and activities. The quality of internal auditing increases directly with the degree to which this knowledge can be shared and reused. Knowledge only has value when it is managed appropriately.

There is a direct link between knowledge management and marketing. Marketing requires knowledge of the needs and expectations of key stakeholders, and an ability to promote potential solutions for meeting these expectations. Marketing an internal audit function helps the organization to enhance its knowledge of internal auditing and the services that internal audit can provide.

Knowledge Management

Knowledge has become the most important factor in economic life. It is the chief ingredient of what we buy and sell. It is the raw ingredient with which we work. Intellectual capital—not natural resources, machinery, or even financial capital—has become the one indispensable asset of corporations.

Tom Stewart, Editor of Fortune

Effectively managing knowledge in a knowledge-focused environment such as internal audit can add significant value to an organization. Internal audit functions are privy to a vast amount of organizational information and are required to be abreast of a range of emerging technical and operational areas. Mukherjee (2011) identifies knowledge sharing as essential to keeping internal auditors up to date with frequent changes in a fast-moving business world, and considers the establishment of a knowledge-sharing culture as critical for internal audit success.

Internal auditors should utilize knowledge management techniques to create efficiencies within internal audit functions. In addition, they should position themselves to effectively capture and disseminate corporate knowledge to the broader organization, to leverage better practices across the organization, and to help promote organization-wide risk mitigations.

Example 16.1 Key Knowledge Questions

When developing a **knowledge management** approach, key questions for internal auditors to consider are:

- **Who** knows? Who in the organization possesses particular expertise and skills?
- **What** do we need to know? Factual knowledge that helps achieve objectives and tasks.
- **Where** is the knowledge located? Location of material in electronic and hard copy formats.
- **When** do we need to know it by? Timetables and deadlines.
- **Why** do we need to know? Knowledge about corporate vision, objectives, and values.
- **How** do we know? Procedural and process knowledge.

Knowledge Management Opportunities

Chief audit executives can incorporate knowledge management strategies as an explicit element within their strategy and planning processes. However, Anderson and Leandri (2006) believe that ideally:

> *Knowledge management activities are integrated into internal audit operations, helping to increase awareness among auditors and their stakeholders about the benefits of effective knowledge sharing. Staff training of auditors on knowledge management as a core audit process should start when new auditors are hired or rotated into the department.*

Anderson and Leandri recommend that internal audit functions adopt a systematic approach to knowledge management that incorporates the following actions:

1. Define a knowledge management strategy.
2. Embed knowledge management into the audit process.
3. Acquire enabling technology.
4. Look for risk-profile changes and trends.
5. Centralize storage of risk and control data.
6. Create a best practices database.
7. Become the education hub.
8. Monitor, measure, and reward results.

HANDOVER OF ENGAGEMENT AND CLIENT INFORMATION BETWEEN INTERNAL AUDIT STAFF AND OUTSOURCED PROVIDERS The internal audit function should formalize processes for handing over engagement client information between staff, and to and from outsourced providers, taking into account confidentiality requirements. This could include the sharing of electronic and physical files as well as debriefing meetings.

Using the knowledge gained through previous internal audit engagements or discussions with management enhances the quality of internal audit's work and increases the opportunity for internal audit to provide insight. For internal audit functions using a co-sourced or outsourced model, it is particularly important that this information is shared and not lost.

IDENTIFY AND INCORPORATE INTERNAL AUDIT PROCESS IMPROVEMENTS A quality internal audit function should continually assess its own performance and look for ongoing process improvements. Sharing lessons learned about the internal audit process following an engagement will help support continuous improvement. This can occur informally, through conversations between internal auditors, or formally, such as through the completion of checklists identifying improvement opportunities.

IDENTIFY AND DISSEMINATE SYSTEMIC ISSUES, EMERGING RISKS, AND BETTER PRACTICES TO THE ORGANIZATION Internal auditors have access to a vast amount of corporate information. Taking into account the need for confidentiality, internal auditors can categorize and share (de-identified) systemic issues and emerging risks, allowing the knowledge to be leveraged across the organization.

Internal auditors can also utilize the knowledge gained through audit engagements to help populate an organization-wide assurance map and refine the organization's risk management processes.

SHARE TECHNICAL KNOWLEDGE Internal auditors can formally and informally share technical knowledge within the organization and with their peers in other organizations. Professional associations such as the IIA provide an excellent opportunity for professional networking and for sharing knowledge about new and emerging practices.

Example 16.2 Communities of Practice

Communities of practice are a form of professional networking that involves groups of people voluntarily meeting to share experiences and discuss job-related issues. Usually, the community of practice operates within an organization and it often shares some features of Ishikawa's quality circles, discussed in Chapter 2. Retna and Ng (2011) have found that communities of practice "can facilitate the creation, sharing and utilization of knowledge in an organization, positively affecting its strategy, operations and bottom line."

Internal auditors could form part of a community of practice with other internal assurance providers. This would provide an opportunity to discuss systemic issues, emerging risks, and better practices across the organization. It would also allow for the development of collaborative approaches to the provision of assurance.

QAIP Hint

Internal audit functions could incorporate *knowledge management* into an internal audit maturity model or a balanced scorecard.

Maturity Model

The internal audit function could include *knowledge management* as a key process area in its maturity model. For example:

- Level 2 of a five-stage maturity model could identify that information is shared throughout the internal audit function in an informal manner.
- Level 3 could identify that the internal audit function has regular meetings to share information; and the chief audit executive prepares reports for each audit committee meeting.
- Level 4 could indicate that the internal audit function reflects knowledge management processes to share knowledge within the internal audit function and across the organization.
- Level 5 could identify that the internal audit function has a formal knowledge management strategy and utilizes a range of processes, including:
  - Communities of practice to discuss emerging issues and share ideas
  - Social networking and blogs to share contemporary internal audit practices
  - Teleconferencing, videoconferencing, and social networking to connect with remotely based staff

Balanced Scorecard/KPI

Internal audit functions could include performance indicators such as:

- Knowledge management strategies implemented (include target)
- Professional networking events attended by staff (include target)
- Systemic audit issues identified and shared with organization (include target)
- Communities of practice established and meetings held (include target)

Marketing

In an age of increasing transparency, marketing the internal audit function can provide clarity to stakeholders about internal audit's role, as well as transparency over the processes used by internal audit. Marketing also provides an opportunity for the internal audit function to promote the value it provides to the organization, and for this reason, Rickard (1994) cautions internal auditors that it would be unwise to think that their services do not need to be marketed.

Marketing Strategy and Plan

Developing a strategic approach to marketing can assist the internal audit function in maximizing its potential to deliver a clear, consistent, and positive message. A

Protecting Your Reputation

Cesar Martinez, member of the IIA Professional Issues Committee, recommends that new chief audit executives spend time looking at the way professional services firms build and protect their reputation. He believes that some internal auditors become complacent, and take the attitude that they will be able to continue delivering engagements regardless of how well they are performing.

Martinez recommends that internal auditors change their mindset—to view the organization as a discretionary client, and to approach each engagement from the perspective that the client could chose to work with another provider. He warns, "Even an organization with a fully in-house function can chose to change its delivery model."

---

marketing strategy can define the nature of the internal audit function, which should be closely aligned to the internal audit strategy.

In developing a marketing strategy, Rickard (1994) recommends that chief audit executives consider the following questions:

- What services is the internal audit function currently offering to management?
- In what way can these services be improved or expanded?
- What are the emerging trends in the organization (both operational and strategic) that need to be considered by the internal audit function?
- What are the emerging trends in the industry that need to be considered by the internal audit function?
- What are the emerging trends in the profession that can assist the internal audit function to improve its value-added activities?

The marketing strategy might be combined with the internal audit strategic plan, or it might be a stand-alone document.

Cheskis (2012) believes that a strong, winning internal audit brand helps to drive the effectiveness and influence of an internal audit function. He identifies a number of benefits to specific branding, shown in Table 16.1.

Cheskis (2012) warns that an internal audit function's role and brand need to fit in with the organization and its needs. Internal audit functions may feel more comfortable portraying a conservative, dependable image in a traditional, risk-averse organization or where the organization has a conservative audit committee. Other, more entrepreneurial and risk-tolerant organizations may be looking for a contemporary, best practice internal audit function. The image of internal audit will also vary across cultures.

Internal Audit Website

The Internet provides a valuable tool for internal auditors, and its marketing potential can be leveraged through the development of an internal audit website. Potential users of the website could include internal audit staff, management and employees, other assurance providers, and the audit committee.

TABLE 16.1 Branding and Department Effectiveness

Branding Element (i.e., Perception of Internal Audit)	Resulting Actions with the Organization	Increased Audit Department Effectiveness
Fair/balanced, open, transparent	Management is more open with the internal audit function; management brings more concerns to the internal audit function.	The internal audit function prevents more problems before they happen.
Knowledgeable about business; talented team	Stakeholder support brings access to key projects and committees; support for more expansive internal audit.	The internal audit function is more influential.
Unpretentious, practical, fair/balanced	Management is more receptive to internal audit self-assessment tools and controls education; diminished fear of raising problems.	The internal audit function is more effective at promoting a risk-aware culture within the organization.
High impact; helps business to achieve objectives, knowledgeable	Internal audit is viewed as a training ground for future leaders in the organization.	Internal audit attracts a more talented team.

Elements of an internal audit website could include:

- Composition and structure of the internal audit function
- Internal audit charter
- Audit plan
- Completed audits (names and dates)
- Internal audit annual report
- Systemic issues and better practices observed
- Assurance map
- Links to a follow-up database
- Internal audit policies and procedures
- General information about governance, risk management, and control
- Audit committee composition and role
- Audit committee charter
- Contact details and email links
- FAQs

Workshops and Seminars

Cameron and Reeb (2008) view workshops and seminars as a potentially valuable marketing tool for professional areas such as internal audit. They caution, however, that the purpose of the workshop or seminar should be clear (such as educating and interacting with engagement clients) and the presenter should be able to present an in-depth knowledge of a specialized area.

Workshops and seminars also provide an opportunity for the internal audit team to network informally, and for new internal audit staff to be introduced to stakeholders.

Example 16.3 Frequently Asked Questions

The internal audit website can provide an opportunity to answer common questions that people have about internal audits. Spencer Pickett (2011) identifies a number of frequently asked questions:

- What is internal audit, and why do we need it?
- What is the audit objective?
- Who are the internal auditors?
- What is the difference between the audit and management role?
- What is the difference between external and internal audit?
- How is internal audit independent?
- Where does the audit committee come in?
- How are areas selected for audit?
- How does internal audit fit in with risk management?
- Where do the reports go?
- Does internal audit accept requests from management?
- Does internal audit conduct surprise audits?
- What does an internal audit not do?
- Who audits the auditor?

Marketing Collateral

Internal audit functions can use a variety of marketing collateral—from newsletters and flyers to online blogs and videos. The chief audit executive should develop marketing collateral consistent with the culture and tone of the organization—flyers may be more suited to small, conservative organizations whereas online videos may be appropriate for a larger, tech-savvy organization.

Social Media

Social media is both the angel and the devil as a marketing tool. It can be used to build the image and reputation of internal auditors through their intelligent participation in online discussions and the posting of well-considered thought pieces. However, it can also be the downfall of internal auditors when they inadvertently or deliberately share confidential information, present themselves in an unprofessional or unflattering light, or are the subject of online criticism. Nonetheless, social media is increasingly emerging as a major marketing tool, and chief audit executives should consider ways to use it effectively.

Internal Audit Annual Reporting

The annual report provides a summary of internal audit activity for the year and affords transparency regarding the internal audit function's performance against its strategy and annual audit plan. It should include commentary regarding the internal audit function's quality assurance and improvement program and any significant procedural or staffing changes within the internal audit function.

The report should provide an assessment, based on the work performed during the previous year, of any systemic control issues or inefficiencies within the organization, and any significant or recurrent findings from engagements.

The report may also include an overall opinion regarding the status of internal control for the organization, and the adequacy and effectiveness of governance and risk management processes for the organization. In instances where the chief audit executive relies on the work of others to form this opinion, this reliance should be explicitly stated.

QAIP Hint

Internal audit functions could incorporate *marketing* into an internal audit maturity model or a balanced scorecard.

Maturity Model

The internal audit function could include *marketing* as a key process area in its maturity model. For example:

- Level 4 of a five-stage maturity model could identify that the internal audit function:
  - Has and maintains a website
  - Uses a range of marketing collateral
  - Produces an annual report
- Level 5 could identify that the internal audit:
  - Has a formal marketing strategy
  - Produces a semiannual analysis and report of trends in audit activities to provide insight to senior management and the audit committee
  - Conducts regular information sessions for the organization

Balanced Scorecard/KPI

Internal audit functions could include performance indicators such as:

- The level of awareness of internal audit across the organization (include target)
- The proportion of internal audit time devoted to marketing activities (include target)
- The number of general information sessions provided by the internal audit function to the organization (include target)
- The development and maintenance of an internal audit website
- The amount of marketing collateral produced by the internal audit function (include target)

Questions about Knowledge Management and Marketing

Table 16.2 provides a range of questions about knowledge management and marketing. These can be formally incorporated into a quality assurance and improvement program, or, less formally, into ongoing assessment activities. Questions may be variously posed to the chief audit executive, internal auditors, or audit stakeholders.

TABLE 16.2 Quality Questions

Questions	Evidence of Quality
Has the chief audit executive developed a formalized approach to knowledge management?	Knowledge management strategy
Does the internal audit function utilize knowledge management processes as part of its operations?	Examples of knowledge management processes
Does the internal audit function have processes in place to promote professional networking?	Chief audit executive interview Internal audit staff interviews
Does the internal audit function share lessons learned from audits and work collaboratively to achieve continuous improvement?	Documented lessons learned Internal audit annual report Senior management and audit committee interviews
Does the internal audit function have a process for capturing systemic issues identified across engagements?	Evidence of process
Does the internal audit function have a process for communicating systemic issues with operational managers, senior managers, and the audit committee?	Evidence of process
Does the internal audit function have a process for incorporating knowledge of risks gained from consulting engagements back into organizational processes?	Evidence of process
Does the internal audit function have a process for informing the organization of any emerging risks?	Evidence of process
Does the internal audit function have a process for disseminating better practices to the organization?	Evidence of process
Does the internal audit function make appropriate use of social media audit to share knowledge and/or for professional development?	Chief audit executive interview Internal audit staff interviews
Has the chief audit executive developed a formalized marketing strategy?	Marketing strategy
Does the chief audit executive use marketing techniques to promote the role of internal audit?	Examples of marketing techniques
Does the internal audit function maintain an intranet site to share relevant information with its organization?	Intranet
Does the internal audit function have any marketing collateral to promote the role and structure of internal audit to the organization?	Marketing collateral
Do the chief audit executive and other internal audit staff attend and present periodically at management meetings to promote the role of internal audit?	Evidence of meetings attended Chief audit executive interview Internal audit staff interviews

(continued)

TABLE 16.2 (*continued*)

Questions	Evidence of Quality
Does the chief audit executive prepare an annual report for senior management and the board?	Internal audit annual report
Has the chief audit executive agreed to a reporting format with senior management and the audit committee?	Chief audit executive interview Senior management and audit committee interviews Audit committee minutes
Does the chief audit executive advise the audit committee and senior management of patterns, trends, or systemic issues arising from internal audit work?	Chief audit executive interview Senior management and audit committee interviews Audit committee minutes
Does the internal audit annual report, or another report, include insight into the organization's operations (i.e., are the chief audit executive's comments forward looking and proactive, rather than just being reactive)?	Engagement communication and other communications Internal audit annual report
Does the internal audit annual report, or another report, include an annual assessment of performance of the quality assurance and improvement program?	Internal audit annual report

Conclusion

Knowledge management and marketing will both support the internal audit function to increase the value it offers to the organization. Chief audit executives could consider developing formalized knowledge management and marketing strategies, or could incorporate these practices into daily activities.

References

Anderson, R. J., and S. Leandri. (2006). Unearth the power of knowledge. *Internal Auditor* 63(5): 58–68.

Cameron, M., and W. Reeb. (2008). The fortress and the empire: A marketing strategy for the professional services firm. *Southern Business Review* 33(2): 1–12.

Cheskis, A. L. (2012). What's your brand? *Internal Auditor*. http://www.theiia.org/intauditor.

Greenawalt, M. B. (1997). The internal auditor and the critical thinking process: A closer look. *Managerial Auditing Journal* 12(2): 80–86.

Mukherjee, U. (2011). Knowledge sharing. *Internal Auditor*. http://www.theiia.org/intauditor.

Retna, K. S., and P. T. Ng. (2011). Communities of practice: Dynamics and success factors. *Leadership & Organization Development Journal* 32(1): 41–59.

Rickard, P. (1994). Marketing internal audit. *Australian Accountant* 64(8): 21.

Scott, P. R., and J. M. Jacka. (2012). *The Marketing Strategy—a Risk and Governance Guide to Building a Brand*, Altamonte Springs, FL: The Institute of Internal Auditors Research Foundation.

CHAPTER 17

Quality and the Small Audit Shop

A small body of determined spirits fired by an unquenchable faith in their mission can alter the course of history.

—Mahatma Gandhi

S mall internal audit shops face a number of unique challenges, because of their size and the common requirement for their internal auditors to wear *multiple hats*. Often small audit shops exist in organizations with limited staff and resources.

Nonetheless, small audit shops present a range of opportunities for internal auditors, and many people working in these environments prefer these challenges to larger or better-resourced internal audit functions. The key to success in a small audit shop is effective planning, flexibility, and great communication.

What Is a Small Audit Shop?

The IIA, in its *Practice Guide: Assisting Small Internal Audit Activities in implementing the Standards* (2011), defines a small internal audit function, commonly referred to as a small audit shop, as having one or more of the following characteristics:

- One to five auditors
- Productive internal audit hours below 7,500 a year
- Limited level of co-sourcing or outsourcing

The characteristics of a small audit shop will vary between countries and sectors, with some places considering 5 internal auditors to be a medium-sized activity, and others seeing 10 to be small. Contrary to the IIA's definition, some fully outsourced internal audit functions still consider themselves to be small. Regardless, most chief audit executives will have their own understanding as to whether they are small, medium, or large.

Delivering Value in a Small Audit Shop

Despite their size, there is still potential to deliver value from within a small audit shop. Often, these functions exist in smaller organizations, and there is real potential for the chief audit executive to have significant influence over the broader organization.

Small audit shops offer a number of advantages over larger internal audit functions. Cuzzetto (1994) cites a number of these, including the potential for the chief audit executive to stay close to organizational activities, broad exposure to the entire organization, and reduced staff management activities.

Ridley and Chambers (2012) encourage chief audit executives in small audit shops to undertake the following 12 actions to increase their value offering:

1. Be expert in governance.
2. Teach management how to control.
3. Promote use of self-assessment techniques.
4. Use your organization's objectives when planning audits.
5. Relate objectives for each audit test to your organization's objectives.
6. Establish management commitment to all the elements of governance.
7. Learn to recognize the influence and effect of change.
8. Focus auditing into the future.
9. Consider revolutions as well as evolution in your internal auditing practices.
10. Use teamwork in all your audit work.
11. Measure, measure, and measure again.
12. Embed characteristics such as talented people and capable leadership into the internal audit team.

Quality Assurance and Improvement Program

Chief audit executives should develop a quality assurance and improvement program, regardless of the size of the internal audit function. As described in Chapter 3, the program should comprise ongoing internal assessments, periodic internal assessments, and external assessments.

Some very small audit shops have only a sole internal auditor. For them, the idea of expending resources on developing a quality assurance and improvement program may seem frivolous. They might not see the immediate benefit of formalizing processes to check their own work.

However, even a very small audit shop can gain substantial value from a quality assurance and improvement program. Often, the smaller the audit shop, the greater the pressure and demands that are placed on it. Under these circumstances, there is an increased risk that chief audit executives may not meet their independence requirements. There is also the potential for the internal audit function to fail in its provision of effective assurance over governance, risk management, and control processes.

One way a small audit shop can embed an effective periodic internal assessment program is to undertake reviews of its conformance with a small number of standards at one time. For example, it could review conformance with one standard every week or two. This would allow it to have assessed conformance with all of the IIA *Standards* on an annual basis.

Small audit shops with limited budgets can undertake external quality assessments using the peer review process described in Chapter 5. This avoids the direct cost attached to the external assessment, as it instead requires an investment of staff time. Nonetheless, there are limitations to this approach, as it reduces the time available to undertake assurance and consulting activities. It might also be a lost opportunity to gain input from an expert external assessor, which can be particularly valuable for small audit shops with limited opportunities to share better practices and emerging internal audit techniques.

Delivering Value in a Small Audit Shop

Chin Ooi, Head of Internal Audit at Toyota Financial Services, knows firsthand the challenges of delivering value in a small audit shop. "There are ongoing pressures on companies from external factors such as economic conditions, competition and regulatory changes," says Ooi. "Everyone is trying to do more with less, or at least the same. It is important for internal audit to ensure its focus will continue to be on areas important to the company and senior management." Ooi suggests the following strategies for small audit shops to add value and meet stakeholder expectations:

- Avoid continually focusing on, or raising, issues that are not material or perceived as not material to senior management.
- Look for areas that senior management values the most, articulate your value proposition, and implement ways to deliver against this.
- Invest in activities for internal auditors to keep abreast of company priorities; try to understand management's needs and their real areas of concern.
- Be aware that these concern and priorities could change from time to time due to external factors and changes (such as regulation and competition), and internal changes (such as cost pressure, reorganization, maturity of processes, and capabilities).
- It is important for internal auditors to understand key drivers for the business, the organization's focus, and its limitations. Ooi says, "Thinking like a CEO is what I believe internal auditors should do more of."

Quality Challenges for Small Audit Shops Related to Governance Structures

Chief audit executives of small audit shops will understand the specific challenges they face. Nonetheless, they might not fully appreciate that they are not alone in facing these challenges, and that there are a range of potential strategies for meeting many of these challenges.

Internal Audit Strategy

Some chief audit executives of small audit shops see time devoted to strategic planning as a luxury rather than a priority. While it's true that small audit shops can get caught up in the day-to-day challenges of delivering audit engagements, a failure to strategically plan may lead to the chief audit executive focusing on low-priority areas. It can also create a disconnect between the expectations of the chief audit executive and stakeholders.

An efficient way for small audit shops to undertake strategic planning is to do this in collaboration with the audit committee and the person to whom the chief audit executive reports. Engaging the audit committee at the earliest stages of the strategic planning process allows for immediate buy-in of these important stakeholders, and helps the chief audit executive to address these stakeholder expectations in the internal audit strategy.

Independence

IIA Standard 1110 requires that chief audit executives report to a level within the organization that allows them to fulfill their responsibilities.

Standard 1110—Organizational Independence

The chief audit executive must report to a level within the organization that allows the internal audit activity to fulfill its responsibilities. The chief audit executive must confirm to the board, at least annually, the organizational independence of the internal audit activity.

Standard 1110.A1

The internal audit activity must be free from interference in determining the scope of internal auditing, performing work, and communicating results.

Standard 1130.A2

Assurance engagements for functions over which the chief audit executive has responsibility must be overseen by a party outside the internal audit activity.

The standard is intended to prevent management from unduly influencing the engagements selected for the annual plan or the outcomes of individual engagement. This can sometimes be challenging for organizations without the resources to recruit a senior internal auditor with the experience to report directly to the chief executive officer.

It can be problematic when an internal auditor is expected to perform internal auditing tasks alongside other management responsibilities. Where this occurs, the internal auditor should actively engage the audit committee to reduce the risk that internal audit's independence is impaired. The audit committee can assist in maintaining internal audit's independence and can support the internal auditor to procure external resources to periodically review areas the internal auditor is operationally responsible for.

Assurance and Consulting Activities

Small audit shops need to balance the competing value of assurance and consulting engagements in their annual audit plan. While the limited resources available to most small audit shops mean that they may need to focus on a discrete number of assurance activities, having an experienced chief audit executive within a smaller organization can provide access to consulting services it could not otherwise afford.

The key to determining the right mix of assurance and consulting services will lie in effective engagement with key stakeholders such as the chief executive officer and the audit committee.

Nature of Engagements

Internal auditing helps an organization to improve its governance, risk management, and control processes. The extent to which the internal audit function will focus on any of these areas will be determined through its annual audit planning processes.

GOVERNANCE AUDITS   Bahrmam (2011) recommends that chief audit executives adopt the following strategies when considering undertaking audits of governance in a small audit shop:

- Select staff with the right capabilities to undertake governance audits
- Complement staff with governance subject matter experts, either from within the organization (as guest auditors) or externally (through co-sourcing)
- Create/expand and maintain networks with management responsible for governance
- Nurture governing board relationships
- Expand external networks (to share advice)
- Get involved with the IIA at a local or international level
- Develop peer networks

Internal Audit Charter

The internal audit charter is a critical document for small audit shops, but it is often overlooked. Although its development will require the application of scarce internal audit resources, small audit activities often experience multiple, competing demands, and a well-developed charter can help determine how these demands are best met. An internal audit charter can also clarify the independence requirements of internal audit functions.

Quality Challenges for Small Audit Shops Related to Staffing

Internal auditing is a knowledge-based activity. Small audit shops will maximize their value by ensuring that they have appropriately skilled and experienced staff.

Staffing the Small Audit Shop

With a limited number of staff, chief audit executives of small audit shops place greater reliance on each staff member. Performance issues are magnified in small audit shops—with high performance being more readily identified and low performance having a major impact on the total effectiveness of the internal audit function.

ATTRACTING EXPERIENCED STAFF   Often, small audit shops exist in organizations with below-average numbers of senior management and operating budget. This can affect the organization's ability to recruit a senior and experienced chief audit executive who reports to the chief executive officer. These organizations may need to utilize creative ways to attract good staff.

Example 17.1 Attracting Good Staff through Flexible Arrangements

Experienced staff can be attracted to small audit shops through the promise of working in a smaller, more intimate environment and the associated autonomy this presents. Other people may be attracted through flexible work arrangements. Experienced professionals nearing retirement and parents returning to work may welcome the opportunity for part-time employment or flexible working conditions.

Internal Auditor Proficiency

Regardless of the size of the internal audit function, it must collectively have the knowledge, skills, and competencies to undertake the work required. It may not be possible for a small audit shop to always have the level of proficiency it requires in-house to meet the requirements of its annual audit plan. At times, the small audit shop may need to outsource internal audit skills and capability. Small audit shops could adopt a co-source arrangement to maximize the collective pool of skills and experience.

Knowing When to Listen and Ask Questions

When employing staff in small audit shops, it is important to look for people who are well rounded and mature, and most important, who will listen and ask questions. New staff should not be expected to have all the answers, but instead, should recognize what they don't know, and ask questions to fill in any knowledge gaps.

Individual Professional Development

Organizations with small audit shops may see professional development as a luxury rather than a professional requirement. However, these internal audit functions often have the highest professional development needs—not because staff members are less competent than their counterparts in other organizations but because staff are expected to undertake a broader range of internal audit and consulting activities.

Example 17.2 Creative Approaches to Professional Development

Limited resources may require small audit shops to be more creative about the way in which they gain professional development. Examples could include:

- Developing communities of practice, or peer networks, to meet with other internal auditors from similar organizations on a regular basis
- Participating in in-house training provided by the broader organization
- Participating in freely available webinars
- Offering to deliver presentations or training in exchange for complimentary registration at conferences

---

Professional Networks

Professional networks provide a valuable opportunity for chief audit executives in small audit shops to receive professional support, share ideas, and seek feedback on new initiatives. These networks may be from within the organization, between compatible organizations, or from within professional associations such as the Institute of Internal Auditors.

Quality Challenges for Small Audit Shops Related to Professional Practices

Chief audit executives from small audit shops will undertake many of the same activities as would be expected from a larger internal audit function. The only difference may be the size and scope of the task being undertaken. For example, an annual audit plan from a small audit shop may only identify 6 to 10 engagements for a year, compared with a large internal audit function that may undertake between 50 and 100 engagements. There will be times, however, that a chief audit executive from a small audit shop needs to look for different ways of conforming to professional standards.

Policies and Procedures

Internal audit functions should develop standardized processes to ensure that they operate in a consistent and transparent manner. This is reflected in IIA Standard 2040.

Standard 2040—Policies and Procedures

The chief audit executive must establish policies and procedures to guide the internal audit activity.

Small audit shops, and particularly those with three or fewer staff, often fail to adequately document their internal audit processes, in the incorrect assumption that a formalized, detailed manual is required. However, the IIA *Standards* require that policies and procedures be appropriate to the size of the internal audit function. The chief audit executive should maximize the potential benefit from standardization while balancing the associated costs.

Example 17.3 Using Templates to Document Processes

Very small audit shops can document their processes through a series of standardized templates, which can be readily updated as processes change within the internal audit function.

Annual Audit Planning

Some small audit shops may be concerned about their ability to provide effective audit coverage. Ultimately, however, it is the decision of the audit committee and the chief executive officer as to the level of resources that will be provided to the internal audit function. Rather, the chief audit executive is responsible for developing a risk-based audit plan in accordance with IIA Standard 2010.

Standard 2010—Planning

The chief audit executive must establish a risk-based plan to determine the priorities of the internal audit activity, consistent with the organization's goals.

Salierno (2003) recommends that small audit shops focus on defining the risks to the organization: "When resources are scarce, prioritizing becomes essential for ensuring efficiency, if not survival. Many with experience in small audit shops find that risk assessment plays a key role in their prioritizing efforts as well as their ability to ensure adequate coverage of the audit universe."

In consultation with the audit committee and the chief executive officer, the chief audit executive can identify the "cut-off" point for the annual audits from the rolling audit plan based on the internal audit resources. The chief audit executive should clarify to the audit committee and senior management that only some of the audits can be completed, and allow these stakeholders to determine whether more resources are required to achieve more of the plan. Further information about rolling audit plans is provided in Chapter 12.

Achieving the Annual Audit Plan

Chief audit executives in small organizations are often asked to provide support and assistance to management. Although this demonstrates respect for the chief audit executive, it can potentially distract the small audit shop from achieving its annual audit plan.

To reduce the risk of this occurring, chief audit executives should allocate a proportion of time for ad hoc work and management requests but be firm when this has been exceeded. At this point, the chief audit executive needs to determine the value of the request against the value of the planned audit engagements. If the requested work is deemed to be of a significantly high priority, the chief audit executive should seek input from the audit committee and senior management regarding proposed changes to the annual audit plan.

Example 17.4 Allocating Time to Management Requests

Chief audit executives may choose to allocate up to 10 percent of their available engagement time to management requests. In doing so, however, chief audit executives should ensure they do not adversely impact their independence.

Supervising Engagements

Achieving conformance with the supervision requirements under IIA Standard 2340 can present a challenge for very small audit shops.

Standard 2340—Engagement Supervision

Engagements must be properly supervised to ensure objectives are achieved, quality is assured, and staff is developed.

Chief audit executives need to make informed decisions regarding the level of supervision required by their staff. Recruiting senior internal auditors will naturally reduce the level of supervision necessary. However, there may be insufficient internal audit budget to recruit experienced staff, and under these circumstances, chief audit executives should put in place practices for ensuring that less experienced staff are supported in their activities.

Example 17.5 Ongoing Self-Assessments

Chief audit executives could develop checklists and self-assessment processes for staff use during engagements. The chief audit executive could then review these on a regular basis during the engagement to confirm that accepted practices have been followed. The chief audit executive could also use the checklists as part of the small audit shop's health check or periodic internal assessment.

Assessing quality on an ongoing basis will ultimately reduce the cost of any type of external assessment activity.

Managing Scarce Resources (Including Time)

Small audit shops and scarce resources go hand-in-hand. When faced with limited resources, chief audit executives need to be creative about the way that they utilize staff and budgets.

DOCUMENTATION   Chief audit executives in small audit shops need to constantly balance priorities. Although working papers are important for audit engagements, excessive documentation can be wasted effort. Durmisevic and Fazlik-Frjak (2012) advise chief audit executives of small audit shops to not overdocument. Although they recognize that well-documented findings are valuable, they challenge auditors to judge what constitutes a reasonable amount of supporting evidence.

Example 17.6 Simplifying Working Papers

Internal auditors can reduce the time spent on documentation by:

- Using tablet computers or mobile devices to capture key issues during interviews rather than retyping handwritten notes
- Using bulleted lists to document issues rather than long narratives
- Using photos and videos to illustrate conditions rather than written narratives
- Using handheld devices to scan or photograph evidence on-site
- Avoiding the inclusion of material that does not directly support an observation or finding

---

COMMUNICATING RESULTS AND CLIENT MEETINGS   Durmisevic and Fazlik-Frjak (2012) recommend that chief audit executives in small audit shops identify opportunities for holding exit meetings with multiple managers at once. They recommend that invitees be limited to those that are necessary to discuss each particular type of issue—operational managers for operational issues and executive management for strategic issues.

CONCISE REPORTING   Chief audit executives from small audit shops should work with their key stakeholders to develop a brief but concise reporting format. Wherever possible, the format should avoid duplication of information and make use of formatting techniques such as bulleted lists.

TEAM MEETINGS   There is a definite balance to be found by small audit shops between having excessive meetings and working in isolation.

The value of regular team meetings, even for a very small internal audit function of two or three people, is the promotion of continuous improvement. Meetings provide an opportunity for sharing information that may impact multiple engagements. They also allow for specific audit-related issues to be discussed as they arise, potentially expediting the reporting process.

The downside to team meetings is the time that these take away from client-facing work. To avoid this, chief audit executives need to be well-prepared for each meeting.

Conclusion

Small audit shops present a range of challenges. By their nature, they often have limited staff and budget, requiring the chief audit executive, or broader organization, to give real consideration to the resourcing model that will be used.

Small audit shops need to be staffed by people with appropriate skills, experience, and attitude. One nonperforming staff member in a team of three can have a major negative impact on morale and productivity, unlike in large, internal audit functions where nonperformers can remain relatively inconspicuous.

Despite the added complexity associated with small audit shops, many internal auditors view them as a dynamic and stimulating place to work presenting the internal auditor with vast, constant opportunities to demonstrate creativity and innovation.

References

Bahrmam, P. D. (2011). *Advancing Organizational Governance: Internal audit's Role.* Altamonte Springs, FL: The Institute of Internal Auditors Research Foundation.

Cuzzetto, C. E. (1994). Lean, mean, auditing machines. *Internal Auditor* 51(6): 26.

Durmisevic, A., and Fazlic-Frjak, B. (2012). The dos and don'ts of small audit shops. *Internal Auditor.* http://www.theiia.org/intauditor.

Hubbard, L. D. (2001). What's a good audit finding? *Internal Auditor* 58(1): 104.

The Institute of Internal Auditors. (2011). *Practice Guide: Assisting Small Internal Audit Activities in Implementing the International Standards for the Professional Practice of Internal Auditing.* Altamonte Springs, FL: The Institute of Internal Auditors.

The Institute of Internal Auditors. (2013). *International Professional Practices Framework.* Altamonte Springs, FL: The Institute of Internal Auditors.

Reding, K. F., et al. (2009). *Internal Auditing: Assurance and Consulting Services.* Altamonte Springs, FL: The Institute of Internal Auditors Research Foundation.

Ridley, J., and A. Chambers. (1998). *Leading Edge Internal Auditing.* Hertfordshire, England: ICSA Publishing.

Salierno, D. (2003). Savvy solutions for small audit shops. *Internal Auditor* 60(5): 33–39.

Sawyer, L. B., M. A. Dittenhofer, and J. H. Scheiner. (2005). *Sawyers Internal Auditing*, 5th ed. Altamonte Springs, FL: The Institute of Internal Auditors Research Foundation.

Seipp, E., and D. Lindberg. (2012). A guide to effective audit interviews. *CPA Journal* 82(4): 26–31.

Zeigenfuss, D. E. (1994). *Challenges and Opportunities of Small Internal Audit Organizations.* Altamonte Springs, FL: The Institute of Internal Auditors Research Foundation.

International Standards for the Professional Practice of Internal Auditing

Attribute Standards

1000 – PURPOSE, AUTHORITY, AND RESPONSIBILITY

The purpose, authority, and responsibility of the internal audit activity must be formally defined in an internal audit charter, consistent with the Definition of Internal Auditing, the Code of Ethics, and the Standards. The chief audit executive must periodically review the internal audit charter and present it to senior management and the board for approval.

1010 – Recognition of the Definition of Internal Auditing, the Code of Ethics, and the Standards in the Internal Audit Charter   The mandatory nature of the Definition of Internal Auditing, the Code of Ethics, and the Standards must be recognized in the internal audit charter. The chief audit executive should discuss the Definition of Internal Auditing, the Code of Ethics, and the Standards with senior management and the board.

1100 – INDEPENDENCE AND OBJECTIVITY

The internal audit activity must be independent, and internal auditors must be objective in performing their work.

1110 – Organizational Independence   The chief audit executive must report to a level within the organization that allows the internal audit activity to fulfill its responsibilities. The chief audit executive must confirm to the board, at least annually, the organizational independence of the internal audit activity.

1111 – Direct Interaction with the Board   The chief audit executive must communicate and interact directly with the board.

1120 – Individual Objectivity   Internal auditors must have an impartial, unbiased attitude and avoid any conflict of interest.

1130 – Impairment to Independence or Objectivity   If independence or objectivity is impaired in fact or appearance, the details of the impairment must be disclosed to appropriate parties. The nature of the disclosure will depend upon the impairment.

1200 – PROFICIENCY AND DUE PROFESSIONAL CARE

Engagements must be performed with proficiency and due professional care.

1210 – Proficiency   Internal auditors must possess the knowledge, skills, and other competencies needed to perform their individual responsibilities. The internal audit activity collectively must possess or obtain the knowledge, skills, and other competencies needed to perform its responsibilities.

1220 – Due Professional Care   Internal auditors must apply the care and skill expected of a reasonably prudent and competent internal auditor. Due professional care does not imply infallibility.

1230 – Continuing Professional Development   Internal auditors must enhance their knowledge, skills, and other competencies through continuing professional development.

1300 – QUALITY ASSURANCE AND IMPROVEMENT PROGRAM

The chief audit executive must develop and maintain a quality assurance and improvement program that covers all aspects of the internal audit activity.

1310 – Requirements of the Quality Assurance and Improvement Program   The quality assurance and improvement program must include both internal and external assessments.

1311 – Internal Assessments   Internal assessments must include:

- Ongoing monitoring of the performance of the internal audit activity; and
- Periodic self-assessments or assessments by other persons within the organization with sufficient knowledge of internal audit practices.

1312 – External Assessments   External assessments must be conducted at least once every five years by a qualified, independent assessor or assessment team from outside the organization. The chief audit executive must discuss with the board:

- The form and frequency of external assessment; and
- The qualifications and independence of the external assessor or assessment team, including any potential conflicts of interest.

1320 – Reporting on the Quality Assurance and Improvement Program The chief audit executive must communicate the results of the quality assurance and improvement program to senior management and the board.

1321 – Use of "Conforms with the International Standards for the Professional Practice of Internal Auditing" The chief audit executive may state that the internal audit activity conforms with the *International Standards for the Professional Practice of Internal Auditing* only if the results of the quality assurance and improvement program support this statement.

1322 – Disclosure of Nonconformance When nonconformance with the Definition of Internal Auditing, the Code of Ethics, or the Standards impacts the overall scope or operation of the internal audit activity, the chief audit executive must disclose the nonconformance and the impact to senior management and the board.

Performance Standards

2000 – MANAGING THE INTERNAL AUDIT FUNCTION

The chief audit executive must effectively manage the internal audit activity to ensure it adds value to the organization.

2010 – Planning The chief audit executive must establish a risk-based plan to determine the priorities of the internal audit activity, consistent with the organization's goals.

2020 – Communication and Approval The chief audit executive must communicate the internal audit activity's plans and resource requirements, including significant interim changes, to senior management and the board for review and approval. The chief audit executive must also communicate the impact of resource limitations.

2030 – Resource Management The chief audit executive must ensure that internal audit resources are appropriate, sufficient, and effectively deployed to achieve the approved plan.

2040 – Policies and Procedures The chief audit executive must establish policies and procedures to guide the internal audit activity.

2050 – Coordination The chief audit executive should share information and coordinate activities with other internal and external providers of assurance and consulting services to ensure proper coverage and minimize duplication of efforts.

2060 – Reporting to Senior Management and the Board The chief audit executive must report periodically to senior management and the board on the internal audit activity's purpose, authority, responsibility, and performance relative to its plan. Reporting must also include significant risk exposures and control issues, including fraud risks, governance issues, and other matters needed or requested by senior management and the board.

2070 – External Service Provider and Organizational Responsibility for Internal Auditing
When an external service provider serves as the internal audit activity, the provider must make the organization aware that the organization has the responsibility for maintaining an effective internal audit activity.

2100 – NATURE OF WORK

The internal audit activity must evaluate and contribute to the improvement of governance, risk management, and control processes using a systematic and disciplined approach.

2110 – Governance   The internal audit activity must assess and make appropriate recommendations for improving the governance process in its accomplishment of the following objectives:

- Promoting appropriate ethics and values within the organization;
- Ensuring effective organizational performance management and accountability;
- Communicating risk and control information to appropriate areas of the organization; and
- Coordinating the activities of and communicating information among the board, external and internal auditors, and management.

2120 – Risk Management   The internal audit activity must evaluate the effectiveness and contribute to the improvement of risk management processes.

2130 – Control   The internal audit activity must assist the organization in maintaining effective controls by evaluating their effectiveness and efficiency and by promoting continuous improvement.

2200 – ENGAGEMENT PLANNING

Internal auditors must develop and document a plan for each engagement, including the engagement's objectives, scope, timing, and resource allocations.

2201 – Planning Considerations   In planning the engagement, internal auditors must consider:

- The objectives of the activity being reviewed and the means by which the activity controls its performance;
- The significant risks to the activity, its objectives, resources, and operations and the means by which the potential impact of risk is kept to an acceptable level;
- The adequacy and effectiveness of the activity's governance, risk management, and control processes compared to a relevant framework or model; and
- The opportunities for making significant improvements to the activity's governance, risk management, and control processes.

2210 – Engagement Objectives   Objectives must be established for each engagement.

2220 – Engagement Scope   The established scope must be sufficient to achieve the objectives of the engagement.

2230 – Engagement Resource Allocation   Internal auditors must determine appropriate and sufficient resources to achieve engagement objectives based on an evaluation of the nature and complexity of each engagement, time constraints, and available resources.

2240 – Engagement Work Program   Internal auditors must develop and document work programs that achieve the engagement objectives.

2300 – PERFORMING THE ENGAGEMENT

Internal auditors must identify, analyze, evaluate, and document sufficient information to achieve the engagement's objectives.

2310 – Identifying Information   Internal auditors must identify sufficient, reliable, relevant, and useful information to achieve the engagement's objectives.

2320 – Analysis and Evaluation   Internal auditors must base conclusions and engagement results on appropriate analyses and evaluations.

2330 – Documenting Information   Internal auditors must document relevant information to support the conclusions and engagement results.

2340 – Engagement Supervision   Engagements must be properly supervised to ensure objectives are achieved, quality is assured, and staff is developed.

2400 – COMMUNICATING RESULTS

Internal auditors must communicate the results of engagements.

2410 – Criteria for Communicating   Communications must include the engagement's objectives and scope as well as applicable conclusions, recommendations, and action plans.

2420 – Quality of Communications   Communications must be accurate, objective, clear, concise, constructive, complete, and timely.

2421 – Errors and Omissions   If a final communication contains a significant error or omission, the chief audit executive must communicate corrected information to all parties who received the original communication.

2430 – Use of "Conducted in Conformance with the International Standards for the Professional Practice of Internal Auditing"   Internal auditors may report that their engagements are "conducted in conformance with the *International Standards for the Professional*

Practice of Internal Auditing," only if the results of the quality assurance and improvement program support the statement.

2431 – Engagement Disclosure of Nonconformance When nonconformance with the Definition of Internal Auditing, the Code of Ethics or the *Standards* impacts a specific engagement, communication of the results must disclose the:

- Principle or rule of conduct of the Code of Ethics or Standard(s) with which full conformance was not achieved;
- Reason(s) for nonconformance; and
- Impact of nonconformance on the engagement and the communicated engagement results.

2440 – Disseminating Results The chief audit executive must communicate results to the appropriate parties.

2450 – Overall Opinions When an overall opinion is issued, it must take into account the expectations of senior management, the board, and other stakeholders and must be supported by sufficient, reliable, relevant, and useful information.

2500 – MONITORING PROGRESS

The chief audit executive must establish and maintain a system to monitor the disposition of results communicated to management.

2600 – COMMUNICATING THE ACCEPTANCE OF RISKS

When the chief audit executive concludes that management has accepted a level of risk that may be unacceptable to the organization, the chief audit executive must discuss the matter with senior management. If the chief audit executive determines that the matter has not been resolved, the chief audit executive must communicate the matter to the board.

List of Quality Questions

Quality Framework

Questions	Evidence of Quality
Do stakeholders clearly understand their roles and responsibilities with regard to internal audit quality?	Position descriptions Outsourced provider contracts Stakeholder interviews
Do internal audit staff members understand their responsibilities for internal audit quality?	Internal audit staff interviews
Are quality considerations part of the ongoing dialogue between the chief audit executive, senior management, and the audit committee?	Senior management and audit committee interviews
Are there regular discussions regarding internal audit quality between the chief audit executive and the outsourced providers?	Outsourced provider interviews Records of meetings
Does the internal audit function have a documented approach to monitoring quality and performance?	Documented quality assurance and improvement program
Has a quality assurance and improvement program been developed and documented?	Documented quality assurance and improvement program
Does the quality assurance and improvement program include both internal and external assessments?	Documented quality assurance and improvement program
Does the chief audit executive consider the drivers of quality in its quality program?	Documented quality assurance and improvement program
Does the chief audit executive consider inputs, outputs, and outcomes in the consideration of quality?	Documented quality assurance and improvement program
How does the chief audit executive determine whether the internal audit function has been successful?	Assessment processes and measures Documented quality assurance and improvement program
Can the chief audit executive articulate what success looks like?	Success statement
How do senior managers and the audit committee define success for the internal audit function?	Senior management and audit committee interviews

Does the internal audit function's approach to monitoring quality and performance include health checks, self-assessments, or assessments by another person within the organization with sufficient knowledge of internal audit practices?

Reports and documentation of internal assessments including any relevant action plans

Internal Assessment

Questions	Evidence of Quality
Has the internal audit function built quality checkpoints into policies and procedures?	Policies and procedures
Are supervision processes formalized?	Policies and procedures
Has the internal audit function formalized its processes for internal assessments and health checks?	Policies and procedures
Does the internal audit function undertake periodic assessments and health checks?	Results of periodic assessments and health checks
Do internal assessments include the level of adherence to professional standards?	Scope or terms of reference of assessments
Do internal assessments include the adequacy and appropriateness of the internal audit charter, vision, and mission?	Scope or terms of reference of assessments
Do internal assessments include the adequacy, appropriateness, and level of adherence to internal audit policies and procedures?	Scope or terms of reference of assessments
Do internal assessments consider stakeholder's perspectives regarding the value of the internal audit function?	Scope or terms of reference of assessments
Do the internal auditors have a clear understanding of the internal audit function's level of conformance with professional standards?	Internal audit staff interviews
Do the internal auditors have a clear understanding of the internal audit function's level of efficiency and effectiveness?	Internal audit staff interviews
Is client, management, and audit committee satisfaction considered as part of internal assessments and health checks?	Satisfaction surveys
Is the maturity of the internal audit function formally assessed?	Results of maturity assessment
Has the internal audit function been formally benchmarked against industry data?	Benchmarking results
Does the chief audit executive provide the audit committee with periodic benchmarking on audit capability including experience, average years, qualifications and professional certifications?	Minutes of audit committee meetings
Are the results of quality activities such as periodic assessments and health checks reported to the audit committee?	Minutes of audit committee meetings

External Assessment

Questions	Evidence of Quality
Have external assessments been performed (either a full external assessment or a self-assessment with independent validation)?	External quality assessment report Board minutes
Was the last external assessment performed within the last five years?	External quality assessment report Board minutes
Did a qualified and independent assessor perform the external assessment?	List of competencies for the assessor leader and assessment team
Does the external assessment include an opinion on the level of conformance with the standards and the effectiveness of the internal audit function?	Results of external assessment
Is the audit committee actively involved in the external assessment of the internal audit function, including the frequency and scope of review as well as the selection of the reviewer?	Chief audit executive interview Audit committee interviews
Have the results of the external assessment been reported to senior management and the audit committee?	Audit committee minutes Senior management and audit committee interviews

Strategy and Planning

Questions	Evidence of Quality
Has the internal audit function developed a formal strategy or strategic plan?	Internal audit strategy Strategic plan
Is the internal audit strategy aligned to the strategic risks and priorities of the organization?	Linkages between audit plan and strategic risks
Does the strategy effectively support key organizational initiatives?	Linkages between audit plan and key organizational initiatives Senior management and audit committee interviews
Is there a documented vision for the internal audit function?	Documented vision statement
Is this vision shared and understood by all internal audit staff members?	Staff interviews
Have senior management and the audit committee been consulted about, and do they support, the vision statement?	Senior management and audit committee interviews
Does the vision meet the strategic objectives of the organization?	Linkages between vision and strategies objectives Senior management and audit committee interviews

Has consideration been given to how the internal audit function can be a proactive driver of value and innovation rather than a reactive reviewer?	Senior management and audit committee interviews Inclusion of value-adding engagements in the audit plan
Can the chief audit executive articulate what the organization sees as value from the internal audit function?	Chief audit executive interview Senior management and audit committee interviews
Does the chief audit executive understand the value requirements of different stakeholders?	Chief audit executive interview Senior management and audit committee interviews
Can the chief audit executive articulate what the organization needs the internal audit function to focus on to maximize organizational success and to deliver on the organization's quality expectations?	Chief audit executive interview Senior management and audit committee interviews
Does the chief audit executive actively engage senior management in discussion regarding what stakeholders see as the internal audit function's value?	Chief audit executive interview Records of interviews and conversations
Does the internal audit function add value to the organization?	Senior management and audit committee interviews Audit coverage and alignment with strategic objectives and priorities
What capacity does the internal audit function have to adapt to changing business priorities?	Assessment of staff capabilities and resourcing
Do stakeholders demonstrate trust of, and respect for, the internal audit function?	Management-initiated engagements
Does the internal audit function display courage in its review and analysis of difficult or sensitive areas and its dealings with challenging clients?	Senior management and audit committee interviews Post-audit surveys
Is constructive criticism of the internal audit function welcome?	Senior management and audit committee interviews Post-audit surveys
Does the internal audit function deal with sensitive issues discretely?	Senior management and audit committee interviews Post-audit surveys
Does the internal audit function have the confidence of the audit committee and senior management?	Senior management and audit committee interviews
Does the internal audit function undertake risk assessments (at least annually) of the internal audit function?	Internal audit risk assessment and/or risk management plan (prepared or updated in previous 12 months)
Has the internal audit function undertaken capability and resource planning?	Capability and resource plans (prepared or updated in previous 12 months)
Has the chief audit executive discussed resourcing models with senior management and the audit committee?	Records of interviews/conversations
Has the internal audit function undertaken business continuity planning for its own activities?	Business continuity plans (prepared or updated in previous 12 months)

Areas of Responsibility

Questions	Evidence of Quality
Does the internal audit charter define the nature of assurance services provided to the organization?	Internal audit charter
Does the internal audit charter specifically define consulting activities?	Internal audit charter
Are compliance audits based on identified, prioritized risks?	Internal audit plan Details of engagements completed
Are any compliance audits undertaken because they always have been (without considering risk)?	Internal audit plan Details of engagements completed Senior management and audit committee interviews
Are operational or performance audits undertaken?	Internal audit plan Details of engagements completed
Does the internal audit function undertake integrated auditing?	Internal audit plan
Does the internal audit function undertake consulting activities?	Internal audit plan Details of engagements completed
Is there any evidence that the internal audit function has undertaken consulting engagements in areas beyond its expertise?	Internal audit plan Details of engagements completed Post-engagement surveys
Is there evidence that the internal audit function has considered the potential value of a consulting engagement to the organization before accepting the engagement?	Evidence of discussions with management requesting consulting engagements
Do planned consulting engagements appear in the annual audit plan?	Internal audit plan
Does the internal audit function respond appropriately to management requests for consulting or assurance engagements?	Senior management interviews Post-engagement surveys
Do internal auditors consider risks as part of consulting engagements?	Evidence of risk assessment Post-engagement surveys
Is knowledge of controls gained through consulting engagements incorporated back into an evaluation of control processes?	Internal audit staff interviews Senior management and audit committee interviews
Is there evidence that internal auditors plan consulting engagements with engagement clients?	Planning documentation Evidence of discussions with stakeholders Post-engagement surveys Senior management interviews
Have internal auditors documented their mutual understanding (with clients) for significant consulting engagements?	Planning documentation Post-engagement surveys
Does the internal audit function undertake engagements that evaluate and contribute to the improvement of governance?	Internal audit plan Details of engagements completed Senior management and audit committee interviews

Does the internal audit function undertake engagements that evaluate and contribute to the improvement of risk management?	Internal audit plan Details of engagements completed Post-engagement surveys
Does the internal audit function undertake engagements that evaluate and contribute to the improvement of control processes?	Internal audit plan Details of engagements completed
Does the internal audit function assess and make appropriate recommendations for improving governance processes?	Internal audit working papers and reports Post-engagement surveys Senior management and audit committee interviews
Does the internal audit function evaluate the design, implementation, and effectiveness of the organization's ethics-related objectives, programs, and activities?	Internal audit plan Details of engagements completed
Does the internal audit function assess whether IT governance supports the organization's strategies and objectives?	Annual audit plan Details of engagements completed Engagement working papers
Does the internal audit function assess the adequacy and effectiveness of governance controls?	Annual audit plan Details of engagements completed Engagement working papers
Do internal audit engagements include an assessment of risk management practices within the engagement subject area?	Engagement working papers Post-engagement surveys
Does the internal audit function periodically review the organization's risk management framework?	Details of engagements completed
Is there a mechanism for the internal audit function to input risks from individual engagements back into the risk management framework?	Internal audit staff interviews
Does the internal audit function evaluate operational risks such as: ■ Reliability and integrity of financial and operational information ■ Effectiveness and efficiency of operations and programs ■ Safeguarding of assets ■ Compliance with laws, regulations, policies, procedures, and contracts	Annual audit plan Details of engagements completed Engagement working papers Senior management and audit committee interviews
Does the internal audit function evaluate strategic risks that can impact the achievement of strategic objectives?	Annual audit plan Details of engagements completed Engagement working papers Senior management and audit committee interviews
Does the internal audit function have any operational responsibility for managing risks beyond those specifically connected to internal audit activities?	Internal audit charter
Does the internal audit function evaluate the potential for the occurrence of fraud and how the organization manages fraud risk?	Annual audit plan Details of engagements completed Engagement working papers
Does the internal audit function evaluate the adequacy and effectiveness of controls?	Annual audit plan Details of engagements completed Engagement working papers

Does the internal audit function offer recommendations to support the continuous improvement of controls?	Internal audit reports Senior management and audit committee interviews Post-engagement surveys
Does the internal audit function feed knowledge gained of controls through consulting engagements back into a broader evaluation of controls?	Internal audit staff interviews Senior management and audit committee interviews

Internal Audit Charter

Questions	Evidence of Quality
Is there an internal audit charter defining the purpose of the internal audit function?	Internal audit charter
Has the internal audit charter been approved by senior management and the audit committee?	Evidence of consultation and/or approval
Has the internal audit charter been reviewed and endorsed by the audit committee in the last 12 months?	Evidence of review and/or endorsement
Does the internal audit charter define the internal audit function's purpose?	Internal audit charter
Does the internal audit charter define the internal audit function's authority?	Internal audit charter
Does the internal audit charter define the internal audit function's responsibilities?	Internal audit charter
Does the internal audit charter recognize the mandatory nature of the IIA's Code of Ethics (if the IIA Standards are used)?	Internal audit charter
Does the internal audit charter recognize the mandatory nature of the definition of "internal audit" in the IIA's Standards (if the IIA Standards are used)?	Internal audit charter
Has the internal audit function documented any legislation, regulation, or policy that it is required to conform with?	Formal internal audit documentation
Does the internal audit charter establish the position of internal audit within the organization?	Internal audit charter
Does the internal audit charter or other formal document specify the nature of the chief audit executive's reporting relationship to the audit committee?	Internal audit charter Organization charts demonstrating the internal audit function's reporting lines
Does the chief audit executive report functionally to the audit committee?	Internal audit charter Organization charts demonstrating the internal audit function's reporting lines
Does the audit committee approve the appointment, removal, and remuneration of the chief audit executive?	Internal audit charter Audit committee interviews

Is the audit committee actively involved in the performance management of the chief audit executive?	Chief audit executive interview Audit committee interviews
Does the audit committee approve the internal audit budget, scope, and resource plan?	Internal audit charter Audit committee interviews
Does the chief audit executive attend audit committee meetings in person, and interact directly with audit committee members?	Internal audit charter Audit committee minutes Audit committee interviews
Does the chief audit executive have direct and unrestricted access to senior management and the audit committee?	Internal audit charter Organization charts demonstrating the internal audit function's reporting lines Chief audit executive interview Senior management and audit committee interviews
Does the audit committee contribute to setting the tone at the top by having its chair meet one-on-one at least quarterly with the chief audit executive?	Chief audit executive interview Senior management and audit committee interviews
Is the internal audit function structured to maintain independence and objectivity, while also allowing a close enough relationship with the business to build understanding and networks?	Chief audit executive interview Senior management and audit committee interviews
Does the organization perceive the internal audit function as being independent?	Senior management interviews
Does the audit committee perceive the internal audit function as being independent?	Audit committee interviews
Is the internal audit function considered to be a critical friend or an impartial observer?	Senior management and audit committee interviews
Is there any evidence that the internal audit function has been restricted in audit planning?	Senior management and audit committee interviews Unsupported changes to audit planning
Is there any evidence that the internal audit function has provided assurance over activities for which the chief audit executive is responsible?	Record of engagements undertaken
Does the chief audit executive have a process for obtaining external assurance over activities for which he or she is responsible?	Documented process (possibly in the internal audit charter) Chief audit executive interview
Does the internal audit charter authorize access to records, physical property, and personnel relevant to the performance of engagements?	Internal audit charter
Is the internal audit function involved in key organizational committees, either as an active participant or as an observer?	Committee participant lists Committee minutes Senior management and audit committee interviews
Do senior managers actively encourage internal audit involvement in key organizational committees?	Senior management interviews Chief audit executive interview

Are the internal auditors' opinions heard and valued?	Senior management and audit committee interviews
	Chief audit executive and internal audit staff interviews
Do senior management and the audit committee regularly seek the chief audit executive's perspective on trends in risk and control issues?	Senior management and audit committee interviews
	Chief audit executive interview

Resourcing

Budget

Questions	Evidence of Quality
Does the internal audit function have a detailed, documented budget?	Budget
Is the internal audit plan used to drive the resource requirements for the internal audit function?	Budget
	Staffing analysis and annual operating plans
	Internal audit plan
Does the budget reflect the sourcing model and include capacity for purchasing additional resources or specialist resources as required?	Staffing plans make provisions for the knowledge, skills and other competencies required to perform the internal audit responsibilities
Do the current internal audit resourcing levels allow sufficient audit coverage of higher-risk areas?	Budget
	Risk management plan
	Senior management and audit committee interviews

Staffing

Questions	Evidence of Quality
Do internal audit staff members have the skills and experience to deal with challenging or contentious issues?	Assessment of staff capabilities and resourcing
Do job descriptions exist, and do they clearly articulate the roles and responsibilities of the chief audit executive and internal audit staff members?	Job descriptions/position descriptions
	Internal audit staff interviews
Are internal audit staff accountabilities clearly defined?	Job descriptions/position descriptions
	Accountability framework
	Internal audit staff interviews
Can internal audit staff members clearly articulate their respective accountabilities?	Internal audit staff interviews
Do job descriptions reflect the qualifications and experience necessary for undertaking the position's requirements?	Job descriptions

Do internal audit staff members have appropriate qualifications and experience for the position they occupy?	Details of staff qualifications and experience Internal audit staff interviews
Do internal audit staff members collectively possess the knowledge, skills, and competencies necessary for the internal audit function to operate effectively?	Details of staff qualifications and experience
Are the skills, knowledge, and competencies of internal audit staff members aligned to the resource requirements of the internal audit plan?	Details of staff qualifications and experience Internal audit plan
Do internal audit staff members possess the attributes necessary to operate effectively?	Performance reviews Staff interviews Post-engagement surveys
Does the chief audit executive provide the audit committee with periodic benchmarking of audit capability, including experience, average years, qualifications, and professional certifications?	Minutes of audit committee meetings
Does the chief audit executive have structured and documented retention strategies in order to maintain an appropriate level of staff turnover?	Human resources policies or documentation
Has the chief audit executive undertaken succession planning to retain important corporate knowledge?	Succession plan Capability plan
Does the chief audit executive have structured and documented secondment and rotation strategies in order to develop staff members and import organizational knowledge into the team?	Succession plan Capability plan
Are internal audit staff members offered flexible work practices?	Internal audit staff interviews Documentation formalizing flexible work practices
Are internal audit staff members provided with an appropriate balance of travel in order to attract and retain high-performing staff?	Internal audit staff interviews
Has the chief audit executive considered staff location in terms of the potential to attract and retain high-performing staff?	Internal audit staff interviews Capability plan

Outsourcing

Questions	Evidence of Quality
Has the chief audit executive considered the cost/benefit of alternative sourcing models?	Chief audit executive interview Senior management interviews
Has the chief audit executive discussed resourcing models with senior management and the audit committee?	Senior management and audit committee interviews
Has the internal audit function followed organizational procurement processes for sourcing capacity?	Contract documentation

Does the chief audit executive have processes in place for assessing the quality of external service providers and feeding this assessment into the quality assurance and improvement program?

Quality assurance and improvement program
Key performance indicators
Policies and procedures
Feedback from outsourced providers demonstrating an understanding of the policies and procedures

Does the quality assurance and improvement program specify quality assessment activities specific to external service providers?

Quality assurance and improvement program

Do contracts for external service providers specify performance standards and performance indicators?

Service provider contracts

Are performance requirements for external service providers cost effective for both parties?

Service provider performance measures
Service provider interviews

Do performance requirements for external service providers encourage performance over the life of their contract?

Service provider performance measures
Service provider interviews

Are there specific policies and procedures for external service providers to ensure the quality of their work?

Policies and procedures
Service provider interviews

Are outsourced providers given a written understanding for engagements about objectives, scope, respective responsibilities, and other expectations, including restrictions on distribution of the results of the engagement and access to engagement records?

Engagement memorandum
Service provider interviews

Performance Management

Questions	Evidence of Quality
Do staff management practices provide assurance that engagements are conducted with proficiency and due professional care?	Engagement supervision Post-engagement surveys
Do internal audit staff members demonstrate proficiency through their internal audit work?	Engagement supervision Working paper review Post-engagement surveys
Do internal audit staff members demonstrate due professional care through their internal audit work (including both consulting and assurance engagements) by considering the following: ■ Needs and expectations of clients, including the nature, timing, and communication of engagement results; ■ Relative complexity and extent of work needed to achieve the engagement's objectives; and ■ Cost of the consulting engagement in relation to potential benefits?	Working paper review Engagement supervision Post-engagement surveys

Do internal audit staff members undertake their work professionally and cause minimal disruption to organizational activities?	Senior management and audit committee interviews Post-engagement surveys Working paper review Engagement plan
Have internal audit staff members considered the extent of work needed to achieve the engagement's objectives?	
Have internal audit staff members demonstrated consideration of the relative significance and materiality of findings?	Working paper review Post-engagement surveys
Is senior management confident that the internal audit function can identify the root causes of control breakdowns?	Senior management interviews
Have internal audit staff members demonstrated consideration of the cost of assurance versus the potential benefits?	Working paper review
Do the chief audit executive and audit managers have a strategic mindset?	Chief audit executive interview Internal audit staff interviews Senior management and audit committee interviews Post-engagement surveys
Do internal audit staff members sign a code of conduct or code of ethics?	Internal audit staff code of conduct/code of ethics
Does the code of conduct or code of ethics make reference to the IIA's Code of Ethics?	Internal audit staff code of conduct/code of ethics
Do internal audit staff members maintain an objective, unbiased mindset when undertaking engagements?	Working paper review Senior management interviews Post-engagement surveys
Do internal audit staff members avoid any conflicts of interest in undertaking engagement?	Chief audit executive interview
Is there evidence that any impairment to objectivity is appropriately documented for assurance engagements?	Working paper review
Do internal audit staff members avoid providing assurance over areas they have been involved in in the previous 12 months?	Chief audit executive interview
Is there evidence that consulting engagement clients are advised of any impairment to independence or objectivity prior to the engagement being accepted?	Engagement client feedback
Are internal audit staff members provided with regular, formal performance evaluations?	Chief audit executive interview Internal audit staff interviews
Does the internal audit function utilize 360-degree feedback as part of its internal performance processes?	Chief audit executive interview Staff interviews
Does the internal audit function adopt peer review processes particularly with regard to completed engagements?	Chief audit executive interview Internal audit staff interviews Report from peer reviews
Does the internal audit function utilize staff satisfaction surveys as part of its human resources management and internal quality processes?	Internal audit staff satisfaction surveys

Professional Development

Questions	Evidence of Quality
Have internal audit staff members demonstrated proficiency through the attainment of professional certifications?	Internal audit staff training register Lists of staff certification
Has the chief audit executive developed a strategic capability plan to allow for strategic human resources management	Capability plan
Has the chief audit executive considered the availability of external service providers as part of its capability planning?	Chief audit executive interview Internal audit staff interviews
Is professional development offered to internal audit staff members?	Training register Chief audit executive interview Internal audit staff interviews
Is there a clear career continuum for internal audit staff members, outlining expected skills, knowledge, and attributes across the different levels within the internal audit function?	Internal audit staff interviews Capability plan
Is professional development targeted appropriately to provide internal audit staff members with the proficiency necessary to undertake engagements?	Internal audit staff training plans and records
Do processes exist to feed back development needs identified through internal audit engagements into individual training plans?	Chief audit executive interview
Does the chief audit executive maintain a training register for individual staff members?	Training register
Are internal audit staff members offered the opportunity to attend external courses as required and in accordance with a structured professional development plan?	Internal audit staff training plans and records Internal audit staff interviews
Are external courses assessed to ensure that they meet professional development requirements and offer value for money?	Chief audit executive interview
Do internal audit staff members participate in professional or industry conferences?	Internal audit staff training plans and records Internal audit staff interviews
Do internal audit staff members attend in-house training?	Internal audit staff training plans and records Internal audit staff interviews
Do internal audit staff members utilize online training?	Internal audit staff training plans and records Internal audit staff interviews
Does team-wide competency planning include consideration of fraud awareness?	Internal audit staff training plans and records
Does team-wide competency planning include consideration of technology-based audit techniques?	Internal audit staff training plans and records

Are regular team meetings held to allow for professional development and knowledge sharing?	Chief audit executive interview
	Internal audit staff interviews
	Meeting minutes
Has the chief audit executive developed a formal communication strategy for sharing information among internal audit staff members?	Internal audit communication strategy
Are internal audit staff members provided opportunities to attend training that supports team building?	Internal audit staff training plans and records
	Internal audit staff interviews
Has the chief audit executive adopted formal or informal mentoring strategies for staff members?	Chief audit executive interview
	Internal audit staff interviews
Are internal audit staff members supported to obtain or retain professional membership?	Records of professional membership
	Internal audit staff interviews
Do internal audit staff members attend professional meetings?	Internal audit staff interviews
Does the chief audit executive actively support the IIA or other relevant professional associations?	Chief audit executive interview
Are the chief audit executive and/or senior internal audit staff office bearers within the IIA or other relevant professional associations?	Chief audit executive interview
	Internal audit staff interviews
Does the internal audit budget make allowance for professional development?	Internal audit budget
Are internal audit staff members committed to continuous learning?	Internal audit staff interviews
	Records of professional development

Policy and Procedures

Questions	Evidence of Quality
Are there internal audit policies and procedures in place that are appropriate to the size of the internal audit function?	Policies and procedures
Are internal audit staff members aware of the policies and procedures?	Internal audit staff interviews
Do policies and procedures include key audit stages (engagement planning, fieldwork, etc.)?	Policies and procedures
Does the internal audit function have adequate policies and procedures for annual audit planning?	Policies and procedures
Do policies and procedures reflect contemporary audit practice?	Policies and procedures
Does the internal audit function have communication protocols (including report distribution, timing, etc.) that have been approved by management and the board?	Communication protocols
Do standardized processes/templates exist for engagement reports/communications?	Standardized processes and templates

Does the internal audit function use contemporary, or leading-edge, audit processes and tools?	Assessment of internal audit processes including the use of CAATs
Do policies and procedures cover the use of technology-based audit and data analysis techniques?	Policies and procedures
Are there specific policies regarding potential conflicts or impairments to objectivity?	Policies and procedures
Do policies and procedures cover access to engagement records?	Policies and procedures
Do policies and procedures include retention requirements for engagement records consistent with organizational guidelines and any regulatory requirements?	Policies and procedures
Do policy requirements provide for internal audit personnel to ensure security of engagement documents and information?	Policies and procedures
Do policies and procedures exist for dissemination of results with external parties?	Policies and procedures
Are policies and procedures updated on a regular (at least annual) basis?	Evidence of review
Does the chief audit executive discuss the need for changes to policies and procedures with staff members?	Internal audit staff interviews

Annual Planning

Questions	Evidence of Quality
Do the chief audit executive and internal auditors spend time in the business to develop an understanding of key issues?	Senior management and audit committee interviews
Does the scope of work in the annual audit plan meet the role of internal audit under the internal audit charter?	Annual audit plan
Does the annual audit plan consider an environmental scan of the wider external context of the organization such as legislative compliance requirements, industry risks, and economic factors?	Annual audit plan
Does the annual audit plan align with the strategic and operational risks of the organization?	Annual audit plan
Is the annual audit plan based on a documented risk assessment of the organization's risks?	Annual audit plan Documented risk assessment
Is this risk assessment performed at least annually?	Annual audit plan Documented risk assessment
Does the annual audit plan consider the organization's risk management framework, including any risk appetite set by management?	Annual audit plan Senior management interviews

Does the annual audit plan adequately account for new and emerging risk areas?	Annual audit plan Senior management interviews
Is the annual audit plan dynamic and flexible, adapting as the risk profile of the organization changes (e.g., changes occur to the annual audit plan during the year if the risk profile changes)?	Annual audit plan Senior management interviews
Has the internal audit function identified the auditable areas across the organization?	Audit universe
Does the internal audit function have a process for ensuring optimal budget allocation and adherence for annual planning such as prioritizing projects?	Annual audit plan Chief audit executive interview
Is input to the annual audit plan obtained from senior management and the audit committee?	Documented evidence of input Senior management and audit committee interviews
Has the internal audit function applied a consistent approach to assessing risks and potential auditable areas?	Audit planning methodology Senior management interviews
Does the annual audit plan include an appropriate mix of engagements covering the scope of organizational function?	Annual audit plan
Are senior management and the audit committee satisfied with the assurance coverage provided through the annual audit plan?	Senior management and audit committee interviews
Are the annual audit plan and any significant changes communicated to senior management and the audit committee for approval?	Documented evidence of input Senior management and audit committee interviews
Is there alignment between the internal audit function and other assurance providers?	Chief audit executive interview Senior management and audit committee interviews
Are there any instances where the internal audit function has unnecessarily duplicated the work of other assurance providers?	Senior management and audit committee interviews
Are other assurance providers consulted during the development of the annual audit plan?	Senior management and audit committee interviews
Does the internal audit function have a formal process for engaging with external audit regarding the audit plan?	Chief audit executive interview
Is the annual audit plan shared with other assurance providers?	Documented evidence of input Assurance providers interviews

Engagement Planning

Questions	Evidence of Quality
Do plans exist for each internal audit engagement?	Engagement plans
Are work programs developed to support the engagement plan for each internal audit engagement?	Work programs

Are all work programs (and subsequent adjustments) approved in writing by the chief audit executive or designee prior to the engagement commencing?	Electronic/hard copy work program papers reviewed before commencing review
Does the engagement sponsor approve the engagement scope/terms of reference prior to the engagement commencing?	Documented evidence of sponsor approval
Has the internal audit function considered external factors or contemporary best practice when planning each engagement (i.e., are there lessons to be learned from other organizations and are there implications to risks/controls based on external factors)?	Chief audit executive interview Internal audit staff interviews Engagement plans
Do engagement plans and work programs consider significant risks to the function, its objectives, resources, and operations and the means by which the potential impact of risk is kept to an acceptable level?	Engagement plans Work programs
Do engagement plans include an objective?	Engagement plans
Is there evidence that the internal audit function has considered the probability of significant errors, fraud, noncompliance, and other exposures when developing the engagement objectives?	Engagement plans
Does the internal audit function use relevant criteria for evaluating governance, risk management, and control?	Engagement plans
Do consulting engagements address governance, risk management and control to the extent agreed upon with the engagement client?	Engagement plans
Are consulting engagement objectives consistent with the organization's values, strategies, and objectives?	Engagement plans
Do engagement plans include scopes sufficient to achieve engagement objectives?	Engagement plans
Do engagement plans and/or engagement work programs document the required resources and procedures for identifying, analyzing, evaluating, and documenting information during the engagement?	Engagement plans Work programs
Is there evidence the internal audit function has considered the use of technology-based audit and other data analysis techniques?	Engagement plans Work programs
Are resources for individual engagements assigned based on an analysis of the scope, complexity, time constraints, and available resources?	Engagement plans Work programs
Are special resources sourced where required?	Engagement plans Work programs
Do engagement plans include milestones?	Engagement plans

Engagement Performance

Questions	Evidence of Quality
Are opening and closing interviews held?	Working papers Internal audit staff interviews
Is there evidence that the engagement plan and work program were followed for each engagement?	Working papers
Does the internal audit function retain adequate working papers for each engagement?	Working papers
Are working papers clear, complete, and referenced back to the audit scope?	Working papers
Do working papers contain sufficient, reliable, relevant, and useful information to adequately support engagement findings?	Working papers
Are working papers for all audit engagements reviewed by the audit manager and chief audit executive (or designee)?	Working papers
Do working papers contain appropriate and adequate information to support the findings and conclusions?	Working papers
Does the internal audit function use automated working papers to maximize efficiency and expedite knowledge management?	Working papers
Does the internal audit function utilize continuous auditing techniques, such as repeatable CAATs?	Working papers Chief audit executive and internal audit staff interviews
Does the internal audit function appropriately challenge the control environment, including questioning the existence and relevance of some controls?	Working papers Chief audit executive and internal audit staff interviews Senior management and audit committee interviews
Do audit engagements identify causal risks and systemic issues?	Working papers Senior management and audit committee interviews
Have internal audit staff members demonstrated consideration of the relative significance and materiality of findings?	Working papers
Does the internal audit function work collaboratively with clients to identify mutually agreeable outcomes?	Senior management and audit committee interviews Chief audit executive and staff interviews Post-audit surveys
Does the internal audit function have documented processes for assuring adequate engagement supervision?	Policies and procedures

Communication and Influence

Questions	Evidence of Quality
Does the internal audit function have a process or criteria that supports the production of high quality reports?	Evidence of process or criteria
Are engagements reports approved by the chief audit executive or their delegate prior to distribution?	Evidence of approval
Have engagement results been communicated to appropriate parties?	Engagement communication Evidence of disseminations of engagement communication
Is the internal audit function honest, fair, and consistent in its identification of issues?	Senior management and audit committee interviews Post-audit surveys
Do engagement reports include the engagement's objectives and scope, as well as applicable conclusions, recommendations, and action plans?	Engagement communication
Do engagement reports include management comments and agreed actions with timing and responsibility?	Engagement communication
Do reports released to external parties include limitations on the distribution of results?	Evidence of limitation wording in engagement communication
Is the statement "conforms with the International Standards for the Professional Practice of Internal auditing" used in any engagement reports or communications?	Engagement communication
If so, has an external assessment supported this statement?	Quality assurance and improvement program reports
Does the chief audit executive report periodically to the audit committee on performance against the internal audit plan?	Record of communications Chief audit executive interview Senior management and audit committee interviews
Are significant risk exposures and control issues reported to the audit committee?	Record of communications Chief audit executive interview Senior management and audit committee interviews
Do the chief audit executive and internal audit staff members have well-developed communication skills?	Senior management and audit committee interviews
Does the internal audit function disseminate lessons learnted from its work, and from external audit, to relevant areas of the entity to contribute to organizational learning?	Chief audit executive interview Senior management and audit committee interviews
Does the chief audit executive regularly inform the audit committee of progress on the implemcntation of agreed internal and external audit and other relevant report recommendations?	Chief audit executive interview Audit committee interviews Audit committee minutes

Does the chief audit executive facilitate communication between external audit and entity management, where appropriate?	Chief audit executive interview Senior management and audit committee interviews External audit interviews Audit committee minutes
Have there been any instances where the chief audit executive believed that management had accepted a level of risk that may be unacceptable to the organization?	Chief audit executive interview
If so, did the chief audit executive discuss the matter with senior management?	Chief audit executive interview Senior management interviews
If so, and the chief audit executive did not believe the matter was resolved, did the chief audit executive communicate the matter to the audit committee?	Chief audit executive interview Audit committee interviews Audit committee minutes Any tangible evidence (e-mail records, internal memos, reports on meetings, etc.) demonstrating that the board had been informed
Are periodic meetings held with external audit and other assurance providers?	Records of meetings Chief audit executive interview Senior management and audit committee interviews External audit interviews
Are engagement results shared between assurance providers where appropriate and beneficial?	Records of meetings Chief audit executive interview Senior management interviews
Does the internal audit function provide overall assurance on governance, risk management, and control?	Assurance statements
Is the internal audit function recognized as an agent of change?	Senior management and audit committee interviews
Does internal audit provide foresight (i.e., commentary on emerging or potential issues/risks) in addition to hindsight?	Engagement communication Senior management and audit committee interviews Post-engagement surveys
Do engagement reports include internal audit's opinion or conclusion?	Engagement communication
Do engagement reports note satisfactory performance, where applicable?	Engagement communication Senior management and audit committee interviews Post-engagement surveys
Are any overall opinions supported by sufficient, reliable, relevant, and useful information?	Engagement communication Senior management and audit committee interviews Post-engagement surveys
Are reasons given for any unfavorable overall opinion?	Engagement communication
Has the internal audit function established a follow-up process?	Policy and procedure

Is the status of reported recommendations periodically determined and reported to the audit committee?	Audit committee reports Audit committee interviews
Does the chief audit executive or the audit supervisor have discussions with internal audit staff members regarding the audit findings and report?	Evidence of engagement supervision Internal audit staff interviews
Does the chief audit executive undertake surveys (or other processes) to gauge client satisfaction at the end of engagements?	Client satisfaction surveys (or similar)

Knowledge Management

Questions	Evidence of Quality
Has the chief audit executive developed a formalized approach to knowledge management?	Knowledge management strategy
Does the internal audit function utilize knowledge management processes as part of its operations?	Examples of knowledge management processes
Does the internal audit function have processes in place to promote professional networking?	Chief audit executive interview Internal audit staff interviews
Does the internal audit actively share lessons learned from audits and work collaboratively to achieve continuous improvement?	Documented lessons learned Internal audit annual report Senior management and audit committee interviews
Does the internal audit function have a process for capturing systemic issues identified across engagements?	Evidence of process
Does the internal audit function have a process for communicating systemic issues with operational managers, senior managers, and the audit committee?	Evidence of process
Does the internal audit function have a process for incorporating knowledge of risks gained from consulting engagements back into organizational processes?	Evidence of process
Does the internal audit function have a process for informing the organization of any emerging risks?	Evidence of process
Does the internal audit function have a process for disseminating better practices to the organization?	Evidence of process
Does the internal audit function make appropriate use of social media audit to share knowledge and/or for professional development?	Chief audit executive interview Internal audit staff interviews

Marketing

Questions	Evidence of Quality
Has the chief audit executive developed a formalized marketing strategy?	Marketing strategy
Does the chief audit executive use marketing techniques to promote the role of internal audit?	Examples of marketing techniques
Does the internal audit function maintain an intranet site to share relevant information with its organization?	Intranet
Does the internal audit function have any marketing collateral to promote the role and structure of internal audit to the organization?	Marketing collateral
Do the chief audit executive and other internal audit staff members attend and present periodically at management meetings to promote the role of internal audit?	Evidence of meetings attended Chief audit executive interview Internal audit staff interviews
Does the chief audit executive prepare an annual report for senior management and the board?	Internal audit annual report
Has the chief audit executive agreed to a reporting format with senior management and the audit committee?	Chief audit executive interview Senior management and audit committee interviews Audit committee minutes
Does the chief audit executive advise the audit committee and senior management of patterns, trends, or systemic issues arising from internal audit work?	Chief audit executive interview Senior management and audit committee interviews Audit committee minutes
Does the internal audit annual report, or another report, include insight into the organization's operations (i.e., are the chief audit executive's comments forward looking and proactive, rather than just being reactive)?	Engagement communication and other communications Internal audit annual report
Does the internal audit annual report, or another report, include an annual assessment of performance of the quality assurance and improvement program?	Internal audit annual report

List of Key Performance Indicators

Quality Indicators

Quality Assurance and Improvement Program

- Quality assurance and improvement program implemented

Internal Assessment

- Periodic assessments and/or health checks performed on a biannual basis
- All policies and procedures covered through health checks
- Conformance with policies and procedures
- Professional standards covered through health checks
- Conformance with professional standards
- Numbers of improvements embedded (include target)
- Proportion of engagement working papers reviewed through health checks (include target)
- Level of management satisfaction (include target)
- Level of audit committee satisfaction (include target)

External Assessment

- External assessment undertaken at least once every five years

Strategy and Planning Indicators

- Annual review of the internal audit strategy
- Endorsement of the strategy by the audit committee
- Endorsement of the internal audit values by the audit committee
- Level of management satisfaction with strategy (include target)
- Level of audit committee satisfaction with strategy (include target)
- Internal audit risk assessments conducted annually
- Capability and resource planning undertaken annually
- Business continuity planning undertaken annually

Areas of Responsibility Indicators

- Total number of engagements completed by the internal audit function (include target)
- Time spent on functional engagements, program-based engagements, and integrated auditing (include target)
- Number of assurance engagements completed by the internal audit function (include target)
- Number of assurance engagements performed by the internal audit function as a proportion of overall plan (include target)
- Number of compliance audits, operational/performance audits, IT audits, management initiated reviews, and consulting engagements completed (include target)
- Number of compliance audits, operational/performance audits, IT audits, management initiated reviews, and consulting engagements as a proportion of overall plan (include target)
- Time spent on compliance audits, operational/performance audits, IT audits, and consulting engagements as a proportion of overall plan (include target)
- Time spent on fraud investigations as a proportion of the overall plan (include target)
- Time spent on management-initiated reviews as a proportion of the overall plan (include target)
- Time spent on follow-up audits (include target)
- Time spent on audit support activities (include target)
- Relative proportion of time spent on consulting versus assurance engagements (include target)
- Relative proportions of time spent on governance, risk management, and control assurance (include target)
- Number of engagements incorporating governance, risk management, and control elements (include target)
- Number of engagements focused exclusively on governance, risk management, or control assurance (include target)

Internal Audit Charter Indicators

- The number of times the chief audit executive meets privately with the chief executive officer and other senior management (include target)
- The number of times the chief audit executive meets privately with the audit committee (include target)
- The number of strategic committees that internal auditors are involved in (include target)
- Annual review of the internal audit charter
- Compliance with internal audit charter

Resourcing Indicators

Budget

- Delivery of operations in accordance with approved budget
- Resources allocated to the internal audit function relative to international benchmarks
- Levels of expenditure (budget versus actual, costs per auditor day, ratio of payroll to other costs, comparison between audit sections, comparison with previous periods)
- Cost of audit as a proportion of total corporate operating costs (include target)
- Comparison of audit budget to actual costs
- Ratio of audit payroll costs to other audit costs (include target)
- Ratio of productive to unproductive audit time (include target)
- Costs per implemented audit recommendation (include target)
- Ratio of outputs (products, programs, or services) to inputs (resources utilized) meets or exceeds established standards, targets, or benchmarks

Staffing

- Capability plan reviewed on an annual basis
- Number of auditors per 1,000 staff average compared to sector average (include target)
- Number of auditors as a percentage of total corporate staff (include target)
- Average years of staff experience (include target)
- Number of years of audit experience (include target)
- Number of years in area of current audit (include target)
- Proportion of internal auditors with degree and postgraduate qualifications (include target)
- Number of professional certifications/percentage of staff certified (include target)
- Absenteeism rates (include target)
- Level of internal audit staff turnover (include target)
- Number of new hires versus total number of staff on audit team (include target)
- Levels of internal audit staff satisfaction (include target)
- Levels of internal audit staff grievances (include target)
- Existence and annual update of a flexible work policy
- Flexible work practices offered to all staff
- Proportion of staff utilizing flexible work practices (include target)
- Candidate satisfaction with recruitment and/or induction processes (include target)
- Time taken to successfully recruit to vacant position (include target)
- Cost of recruitment/cost per hire (include target)
- Completion of induction by all new recruits
- Number of times guest auditors utilized on engagements (include target)
- Number of internal audit staff seconded to other parts of the organization (include target)
- Number of staff rotated into internal audit (include target)

Outsourcing

- Relative proportions of the internal audit plan insourced and outsourced (include target)
- Turnover of staff within the service provider allocated to engagements for the organization (include target)
- Years of relevant experience among service provider staff allocated to engagements for the organization (include target)
- Time allocated by external providers to share learning with in-house staff (include target)
- Number of better practices recommended by the service provider (include target)
- Number of systemic issues identified by the service provider (include target)
- Proportion of time spent by the service provider in meeting with management (include target)

Professional Development Indicators

- Proportion of internal audit staff performance evaluations completed on an annual basis (include target)
- Development and review of a capability plan on an annual basis
- Proportion of budget allocated to professional development (include target)
- Regularity of staff meetings (include target)
- Proportion of individual training/development plans implemented (include target)
- Average training hours per internal auditor (include target)
- Attendance at professional meetings
- Number of internal audit staff involved as volunteers in professional associations (include target)
- Number of internal audit staff involved in mentoring activities (include target)

Policy and Procedures Indicators

- Existence of policies and procedures
- Annual review of policies and procedures
- Extent to which policies and procedures are being applied by internal audit staff

Annual Planning Indicators

- Proportion of senior managers consulted as part of the planning process (include target)
- Level of senior management satisfaction with the audit plan (include target)
- Proportion of the organization's strategic priorities addressed in the audit plan (include target)
- Conduct of a periodic, at least annual, comprehensive risk assessment
- Percentage of key risks audited per annum (include target)

- Proportion of audit universe addressed in the audit plan (include target)
- Extent of coverage of strategic priorities (include target)
- Extent of coverage of key business activities (include target)
- Proportion of geographic and functional areas addressed in the audit plan (include target)
- Percentage of major projects audited per annum (include target)
- Percentage of major systems audited per annum (include target)
- Percentage of systems under development audited per annum (include target)
- Existence of audit committee concerns regarding unaddressed risks
- Completion of audit plan
- Numbers of management initiated requests (include target)

Engagement Planning Indicators

- Engagement client consulted prior to the engagement commencing
- Risk assessments conducted of the auditable areas as part of engagement planning
- Analytical procedures and CAATs are used in a minimum number of engagements (include target)
- Engagement risk assessments conducted for 100 percent of operational/performance audits
- Total hours used in planning versus scheduled hours used (include target)
- Total hours planning versus total engagement hours (include target)

Engagement Performance Indicators

- The cause and effect of all findings and observations documented within working papers
- Closing interviews held for all audit engagements
- The chief audit executive attending all closing interviews
- Working papers completed and appropriately reviewed for all engagements
- Timeliness of fieldwork
- Percentage audit plan completed (include target)
- Number of audits completed (include target)
- Proportion of audits completed within prescribed time frames (include target)
- Proportion of audits completed within prescribed budget (include target)
- Proportion of billable/recoverable hours versus nonbillable/nonrecoverable hours (include target)
- Level of engagement client satisfaction (include target)
- Actual time spent versus budget (include target)

Communication Indicators

- The number of times the chief audit executive meets privately with the chief executive officer and other senior management (include target)

- The number of times the chief audit executive meets privately with the audit committee (include target)
- The completion and update of a stakeholder engagement map on an annual basis.
- Elapsed time for issue of reports—completion of engagement fieldwork to issue of draft report (include target)
- Elapsed time for finalization of report—issue of draft report to issue of final report (include target)
- Percentage of recommendations accepted (include target)
- Perceived importance of audit findings and recommendations
- Percent of audit recommendations implemented (include target)

Knowledge Management Indicators

- Knowledge management strategies implemented (include target)
- Professional networking events attended by staff (include target)
- Systemic audit issues identified and shared with organization (include target)
- Communities of practice established and meetings held (include target)

Marketing Indicators

- The level of awareness of internal audit across the organization (include target)
- The proportion of internal audit time devoted to marketing activities (include target)
- The number of general information sessions provided by the internal audit function to the organization (include target)
- The development and maintenance of an internal audit website
- The amount of marketing collateral produced by the internal audit function (include target)

Glossary

Accountability The obligation to answer for a responsibility that has been conferred. It presumes the existence of at least two parties: one who allocates responsibility and one who accepts it with the undertaking to report upon the manner in which it has been discharged.

Active listening A technique where the listener feeds information back to the speaker, confirming an understanding of both the content of the message and the emotions and feelings underlying the message, thus ensuring that understanding is accurate. There is a high degree of correlation between the speaker's intended message and what the listener understands.

Add value Maximize the potential to positively contribute to an organization or activity.

Adequate evidence Enough relevant and reliable evidence to support findings and conclusions. Adequacy does not, however, indicate that all possible evidence has been obtained.

Analytical auditing procedures Used to obtain an understanding of an entity and its environment by studying and comparing the relationships of information. They highlight unexpected information and unusual or nonrecurrent transactions or events.

Annual audit planning Planning that determines the priorities of the internal audit function over a period of time (often over a one- to three-year period).

Appropriate evidence Relevant and reliable evidence to support findings and conclusions.

Assurance An objective examination of evidence for the purpose of providing an independent assessment on governance, risk management, and control processes for the organization. Examples may include performance, compliance, system security, and due diligence engagements.

Assurance mapping Mapping both internal and external assurance coverage across the key risks in an organization. This allows an organization to identify and address any gaps in the assurance process, and gives stakeholders comfort that risks are being managed and reported on, and that regulatory and legal obligations are being met.

Assurance services Involve the internal auditor's objective examination of evidence for the purpose of providing an independent assessment on governance, risk management, and control processes of the organization. Examples may include financial, performance, compliance, system security, and due diligence engagements.

Audit committee A committee of the board, often with specific responsibility for assurance over the organization's governance and financial management frameworks.

Audit committee chair A member of the audit committee with oversight responsibilities for the effective operation of the committee.

Audit committee report Internal audit functions typically prepare audit committee reports for each meeting, which commonly include the following elements:

- An update or overview from the chief audit executive
- Report on the quality assurance and improvement program including performance against KPIs
- Progress against the approved plan and any proposed changes
- Results of internal audit engagement and a summary of reports issued since the last meeting
- Resolution status for audit recommendation

Auditee The manager or supervisor with responsibility for the area or activity being audited. May also be referred to as the engagement client.

Audit evidence Information collected through an audit that determines the extent to which criteria are met and any deviations from expected conditions.

Audit manual A collection of policies and procedures that set the operating standards for the internal audit function.

Audit observations Description of what the auditor observed (often referred to as the *audit finding*). Often this involves comparison against agreed performance criteria.

Audit sampling The process that the internal auditor follows to select items (sample items) from a larger whole (population). The internal auditor performs audit tests on those sample items, and uses the results of the tests to extrapolate them to the larger population.

Audit universe The list of all the possible audits that could be performed in an organization, taking into account the organizational structure and activities.

Authority The explicit or implicit delegation of power or responsibility for a particular activity.

Balanced scorecard First proposed by Kaplan and Norton in 1992, the balanced scorecard focused on translating strategy into actions, and promoted a move away from traditional financial measures. Instead, organizations were encouraged to develop a broad range of financial and nonfinancial lead and lag measures that provided insight into overall operating performance.

Benchmarking A standard or point of reference used in measuring or judging quality or value—it is the process of comparing and measuring an organization against other like organizations to gain information that will help improve performance.

Board The highest level of governing body charged with the responsibility to direct and/or oversee the activities and management of the organization. Typically, this includes an independent group of directors.

Business continuity plan (BCP) This refers to the documented procedures and information that enable the organization and or business unit/third party agent to respond to a disruption, recover, and resume critical business functions.

Capability plan A structured approach to identifying the skills and experience needed across a program or activity to address current and emerging needs.

Cause Explains the discrepancy between the condition and the criteria (the expected and actual conditions).

Chief audit executive As per the IIA definition, this describes a person in a senior position responsible for effectively managing the internal audit function in accordance with the internal audit charter and the definition of internal auditing, the Code of Ethics, and the *Standards*. The chief audit executive or others reporting to the chief audit executive will have appropriate professional certifications or qualifications. The specific job title of the chief audit executive may vary across organizations and historically was more commonly known as the *chief internal auditor*.

Closing interview In relation to internal audit, an interview held with an engagement client, and sometimes senior management, at the conclusion of fieldwork to share key observations and preliminary findings.

Code of Ethics Expression of fundamental ethical principles that provides guidance on decision making and behavior in cases where no specific rule is in place or where matters are genuinely unclear.

Combined assurance The coordination of assurance between different assurance providers. Often, this assurance crosses the three lines of defense, incorporating management, second-line providers such as compliance and quality assurance areas, internal external, and external audit.

Community of practice A form of professional networking that involves groups of people voluntarily meeting to share experiences and discuss job-related issues.

Compliance audit Assess financial and operating controls to determine conformance with mandatory requirements such as laws, legislation, regulations, internal and external policies, operating plans, documented procedures, and contract provisions. Elements of compliance audits can merge with financial auditing and IT auditing.

Computer-assisted audit techniques (CAATs) This includes automated audit techniques such as generalized audit software, test data generators, computerized audit programs, and specialized audit systems.

Conclusions The internal auditor's evaluations of the effects of the observations and recommendations on the activities reviewed.

Condition States the facts related to the activity and tells what actually exists at present or what has occurred in the past.

Conflict of interest A situation in which an individual or organization is involved in multiple interests, one of which could possibly corrupt the motivation for an act in the other. This also encompasses an interest or relationship that would have, or would be perceived as having, a negative impact on the objectivity of a person's decision-making ability.

Conformance In relation to internal audit, a statement indicating that an audit engagement meets all the requirements of professional standards such as those of the IIA.

Consulting services As per the IIA definition, advisory and related client service activities, the nature and scope of which are agreed with the client, and are intended to add value and improve an organization's governance, risk management, and control processes without the internal auditor assuming management responsibility. Examples include counsel, advice, facilitation, and training.

Continuous improvement   Management concept introduced by Deming that seeks to create ongoing positive change in an organization.

Control   As per the IIA definition, any action taken by the management, the board, and other parties to manage risk and increase the likelihood that established objectives and goals will be achieved. Management plans, organizes, and directs the performance of sufficient actions to provide reasonable assurance that objectives and goals will be achieved.

Co-sourcing   In relation to internal audit, resourcing an internal audit function with both in-house staff and outsourced providers.

Criteria   Standards or expectation specifying what should exist (what success looks like).

Data analysis   Process of applying statistical techniques to evaluate data.

Deductive reasoning   Reasoning that relies on the absolute certainty of a particular outcome, rather than probability of an outcome (inductive reasoning).

Deming, J. Edward   (1900–1993) A pioneer of the quality management movement and architect of the Deming cycle.

Deming cycle   A model for continuous improvement, also known as the plan, do, check, and act (PDCA) cycle.

Disaster recovery   The coordinated activity to enable the recovery of IT (and other) systems due to a disruption.

Due professional care   In accordance with IIA *Standards*, the application of the care and skills expected of a reasonably prudent and competent internal auditor.

Economy   In relation to performance/operational auditing, the acquisition of the appropriate quality and quantity of financial, human, physical, and information resources at the appropriate times and at the lowest cost.

Effect   Answers the question *So what?* and details the potential impact and/or degree of risk the organization is exposed to or could be exposed to if the cause is not addressed.

Effectiveness   In relation to performance/operational auditing, the achievement of the objectives or other intended effects of activities (such as the delivery of a product or service to specification).

Efficiency   In relation to performance/operational auditing, the use of financial, human, physical, and information resources such that output is maximized for any given set of resource inputs, or input is minimized for any given quantity and quality of output.

Embedded maturity level   The fourth level within a five-stage maturity model. Typically service provision meets stakeholder expectations and is focused on strategic priorities; staff are provided with structured and systematic development; services include a range of consulting and assurance engagements.

Emerging maturity level   The second level within a five-stage maturity model. Typically standards are recognized but not routinely adhered to; professional practices are ad hoc or individualized; service provision is ad hoc; staff have some qualifications and/or experience but knowledge is not systematically shared.

Engagement   In relation to internal audit, a specific internal audit assignment, task, or review activity. Includes both assurance engagements and consulting engagements.

Engagement client The manager or supervisor with responsibility for the area or activity being audited. May also be referred to as the *auditee*.

Engagement leader Internal auditor with responsibility to lead an individual engagement.

Engagement objectives The key questions that will be answered through the engagement or the purpose of the engagement.

Engagement opinion The rating, conclusion, and/or other description of results of an individual internal audit engagement relating specifically to the engagement objective.

Engagement plan A document that specifies an engagement's objectives, scope, timing, and resource allocation, and the standards to which the work will be performed. The engagement plan is required under the IIA Standards.

Engagement planning The planning specific to an individual internal audit engagement that typically includes:

- Background
- Risk assessment/key risks
- Audit objectives (and subobjectives if used)
- Criteria
- Audit scope
- Methodology

Engagement report The report on an individual audit or consulting engagement that typically includes:

- Date of report and time frame of the engagement
- Executive summary
- Introduction, including engagement objectives and scope
- Findings or observations
- Recommendations or agreed management actions
- Overall conclusion and opinion on the engagement objectives
- Appendices with details of methodology, criteria, and interviews

Engagement risk assessment An assessment of the risks associated with conducting a specific internal audit engagement.

Engagement scope A statement that defines the exact boundaries of the engagement, covering what aspects are included in the review and what are not.

Engagement test plan A plan designed to gather sufficient appropriate evidence to support an evaluation of how well the key controls function. This may be developed as part of an engagement work program or may replace the engagement work program.

Engagement work program A document that lists the procedures to be followed during an engagement, designed to achieve the engagement plan.

Enterprise risk management (ERM) The application of risk management approaches across an organization in a structured and disciplined manner.

Environmental audit A specialized field of auditing focused on issues affecting the natural or built environment.

Environmental scanning A process of reviewing the internal and external environments of the organization to identify potential threats and opportunities.

Established maturity level The third or middle level within a five-stage maturity model. Typically professional practices are standardized, conform with standards and are routinely applied; staff collectively have the skills and experience required to perform services.

Ethical climate Refers to an organization's culture, environment, motives, and pressures, and the way in which an organization handles issues with an ethical element to them.

Ethics The moral principles that govern a person's or organization's behavior or the conducting of an activity.

Evidence In relation to internal audit, information collected through an engagement that determines the extent to which criteria are met and any deviations from expected conditions.

Executive management/senior management A group of managers at the highest level of an organization.

External assessment In relation to internal audit, a quality assessment undertaken by a reviewer independent of the organization in which internal audit operates.

External assessor/reviewer The qualified and independent person charged with responsibility for undertaking an external quality assessment.

External service provider A person or firm outside of an organization engaged by the organization for specialized knowledge or skills.

Financial audit Assesses the financial aspects of an organization, including the integrity of financial and operating information and the accuracy of what is reported. This can include examination of controls providing assurance over the integrity of financial information, compliance with legislative and regulatory requirements, and the prevention of fraudulent public financial reporting.

Finding The determination of the extent to which a process or activity under review is operating relative to agreed criteria.

Fishbone diagram (cause and effect) A pictorial diagram in the shape of a fishbone showing all possible variables that could affect a given process output measure. The model is used for identifying cause and effect. Also known as an Ishikawa diagram after its creator, Kaoru Ishikawa.

Flexible work practices Management practices that facilitate flexibility in employment arrangements to accommodate lifestyle and family responsibilities.

Follow-up Designed to determine whether corrective actions have been appropriately implemented.

Follow-up audit A secondary engagement to determine the extent to which findings and recommendations from a primary engagement have been addressed.

Forensic audit A specialized field of auditing, often used as part of or following a fraud investigation, to collect evidence suitable for a court of law.

Foundation maturity level The first (or lowest) level within a five-stage maturity model. Typically standards have not been established; routine professional practices are absent; services are not routinely provided; staff are unqualified or inexperienced.

Fraud Dishonest activity characterized by deceit or concealment that causes loss or financial loss to a person or party, or results in personal or business advantage (includes misappropriation or theft of funds or property by employees or people outside of the organization and misuse of information or position for improper benefit).

Fraud investigation A specific engagement (often ad hoc) to assist management to detect or confirm the presence of fraudulent activities.

Functional engagements Engagements associated with a specific activity or process and that usually assess the entire life cycle of the activity or process. For example, staff recruitment processes could form the basis of a functional engagement.

Governance The combination of processes and structures implemented by the board to inform, direct, manage, and monitor the activities of the organization toward the achievement of its objectives.

Guest auditor An employee from outside the internal audit function invited to participate in a specific engagement.

Health check In relation to internal audit, a periodic internal quality assessment.

Human resources (HR) processes Processes that support the management of staff such as recruitment, induction, and performance management.

Independence As per the IIA definition, the freedom from conditions that threaten the ability of the internal audit activity to carry out internal audit responsibilities in an unbiased manner.

Individual objectivity In relation to internal audit, an unbiased mental attitude that avoids internal auditors subordinating their views or opinions to others.

Inductive reasoning Reasoning that relies on the probability of a particular outcome, rather than absolute certainty of an outcome (deductive reasoning).

Influence Invisible or insensible action exerted by one thing or person on another, or the power of producing effect by invisible or insensible means.

Information technology (IT) audit Assesses the controls within an organization's IT systems and processes. This could include the efficiency and effectiveness of new or ongoing IT and related systems, and the adequacy of controls supporting systems under development.

In-house The resourcing of an activity, or a specific project, with employees (as opposed to outsourced providers).

Inputs Often used in relation to logic models, the resources required by an activity or program to achieve a specific result.

Insight In relation to internal audit, the added value provided by internal audit acting as catalyst for improving an organization's effectiveness and efficiency. This occurs through providing understanding and recommendations based on analyses and assessments of data and business processes

Insourced Permanent in-house functions that may be fully staffed by permanent, full-time employees or may include part-time, casual, or contract staff.

The Institute of Internal Auditors (IIA) The professional body representing internal auditors established in the United States in 1941.

Integrated auditing Engagements that incorporate a range of auditing types and techniques to provide assurance over a program or activity.

Internal assessment Undertaken by the internal audit function to determine the efficiency and effectiveness of the function, as well as conformance with professional standards. Internal assessments can be undertaken on an ongoing basis or as a period assessment (otherwise known as a *health check*).

Internal audit activity A department, division, team of consultants, or other practitioners that provides independent, objective assurance and consulting services designed to add value and improve an organization's operations.

Internal auditing An independent, objective assurance and consulting activity designed to add value and improve an organization's operations. It helps an organization accomplish its objectives by bringing a systematic, disciplined approach to evaluate and improve the effectiveness of risk management, control, and governance processes.

Internal audit charter A formal document that defines the internal audit function's purpose, authority, and responsibility. The internal audit charter establishes the internal audit function's position within the organization; authorizes access to records, personnel, and physical properties relevant to the performance of engagements; and defines the scope of internal audit activities.

Internal audit engagement A specific internal audit assignment or activity designed to accomplish an established objective.

Internal audit risk assessment An assessment of the risks associated with the operation of an internal audit function.

Internal audit strategy A means of establishing the internal audit function's purpose and determining the nature of the contribution it intends to make while predefining choices that will shape decisions and actions. Strategy for the internal audit function enables the allocation of financial and human resources to help achieve these objectives as defined in the activity's vision and mission statements (which contribute to the achievement of the organization's objectives). This benefits the internal audit function through its unique configuration of resources aimed at meeting stakeholder expectations.

Internal control A process, affected by an entity's board of directors, management, and other personnel, designed to provide reasonable assurance regarding the achievement of objectives in the following three categories:

1. Effectiveness and efficiency of operations.
2. Reliability of financial reporting.
3. Compliance with applicable laws and regulations.

International Professional Practices Framework **(IPPF)** The conceptual framework that organizes the authoritative guidance issued by the Institute of Internal Auditors (IIA).

ISACA A global professional body focused on IT governance and support of IT auditing professionals. It was originally known as the Information Systems and Control Association but now goes by its acronym alone.

Ishikawa diagram A model used for identifying cause and effect. Also known as a fishbone diagram and named after its creator, Kaoru Ishikawa.

ISO 9000 The International Organization for Standardization (ISO) first published its ISO 9000 series of quality standards in 1987 as a model for quality assurance standards in design, development, production, installation, and service. The system provides a universal framework for quality assurance and quality management.

Job design Work arrangements designed to maximize employee performance and job satisfaction.

Juran, Joseph (1904–2008) A contemporary of Deming who introduced the *quality trilogy*, incorporating quality planning, quality control, and quality improvement.

Kaizen A Japanese management theory of continuous improvement, literally translated as "change for good" or "improvement."

Kansayaku Japanese statutory auditors appointed by the chief executive officer and endorsed by the board.

Key drivers or enablers Critical links that ensure business objectives are achieved. These may include capital, facilities, technology, resources, processes, and activities.

Key performance indicator (KPI) A measure that indicates the achievement of a specific objective.

Key process area Often used within maturity models to describe the key processes or activities required to achieve a particular level of maturity.

Knowledge management The process of capturing, using, leveraging, and sharing organizational knowledge.

Leadership A process of influencing others to accomplish a goal and build commitment and cohesion within an organization or team.

Leading maturity level The fifth (or highest) level within a five-stage maturity model. Typically service provision represents better/leading practice; staff collectively are highly skilled and experienced; professional practices utilize leading technologies and processes.

Logic model A graphical representation of the interrelationship between the resources available for a project or program, the activities proposed, and the results intended (also known as *program logic*).

Management information Information available to management and staff that allows them to make informed decisions about performance.

Management-initiated review Engagements commissioned, and sometimes funded, by operational or senior management to assess a specific issue, operation, or process.

Mandate The purpose for the entity or activity existing.

Marketing The activities associated with making people aware of an organization's products and services and motivating them to procure these products or services.

Marketing collateral The collection of media used to undertake and support marketing activities.

Materiality The external impact and significance of an activity or area to the overall program or organization.

Maturity In relation to organizations or activities, the level of sophistication or development of a specific program or activity.

Maturity ladder The pictorial hierarchy of maturity levels.

Maturity models First introduced by the Carnegie Mellon Software Engineering Institute in 1991 to improve the process of software development. However, their broader applicability was recognized, and the model was expanded in 2000 to apply to enterprise-wide process improvement.

Mentoring An opportunity for a more experienced person to impart knowledge and expertise to a less experienced person.

Milestone A key event within a project (including an audit engagement), selected for its importance in the project. For an audit engagement these could include completion of planning, completion of fieldwork, and completion of final report.

Nonstatistical sampling A sampling approach that allows more latitude regarding sample selection and evaluation than statistical sampling—it follows a nonrandom selection technique to select a sample that is expected to be representative of the population.

Objectivity   As per the IIA definition, an unbiased mental attitude that allows internal auditors to perform engagements in such a manner that they believe in their work product and that no quality compromises are made.

Observation   In relation to internal audit, a finding or judgment derived from the engagement conduct.

Ongoing internal monitoring   An element of an internal audit quality assurance and improvement program that involves assessing quality on a continuous basis.

Opening interview   An interview held with an engagement client, and sometimes senior management, at the commencement of fieldwork or engagement planning to share audit objectives and the proposed methodology.

Opinion   In relation to internal audit, a conclusive statement regarding the effectiveness of controls and/or the extent to which an objective has been achieved.

Organizational context   The environment in which an organization operates. For example, the regulatory and policy environment, political environment, major competitors, and customer demographics.

Organizational ethics   How an organization ethically responds to an internal or external stimulus. It expresses the values of an organization to its employees and/or other entities irrespective of governmental and/or regulatory laws.

Organizational independence   The specific line of reporting—often to the chief audit executive—that allows the internal audit function to operate free from interference.

Outcomes   The effects of the products or services produced by an organization or activity on the organization and its customers or stakeholders—the longer-term benefits or changes that result from the outputs.

Outputs   The products or services that an organization or activity produces.

Outsourcing   The procurement of external resources to undertake specific tasks or activities.

Overall opinion   The rating, conclusion, and/or other description of results provided by the chief audit executive addressing, at a broad level, governance, risk management, and/or control processes of the organization. An overall opinion is the professional judgment of the chief audit executive based on the results of a number of individual engagements and other activities for a specific interval.

Peer review   In relation to internal audit, a form of external assessment that involves a minimum of three organizations assessing each other's internal audit functions using a round-robin approach (A reviews B who reviews C who reviews A).

Performance   The manner in which organizations achieve results (i.e., the way they behave and operate to effect actions), as well as the outputs and outcomes of these actions (i.e., the results they achieve).

Performance management   An ongoing process where a manager and a team member work together to create a work environment that enables people to work to their full potential. It includes feedback and development components and mechanisms for dealing with underperformance.

Performance measures   A specific target for achievement (what success looks like). For example, 90 percent of draft reports are written within two weeks of completing fieldwork.

Performance metrics Indicators of an organization, program, or activity's level of performance. For example, draft reports written within two weeks of completing fieldwork.

Performance monitoring A systematic process of assessing performance against defined targets.

Performance/operational audit Sometimes referred to as value for money audits or 3 Es audits, these audits assess the extent to which business objectives are achieved, or goods and services are delivered, in an efficient, effective, and/or economical manner.

Performance reporting A systematic process of reporting on performance against defined targets.

Periodic self-assessment An element of an internal audit quality assurance and improvement program that involves a discrete internal assessment.

Persuasive evidence Evidence or information that can be relied on in full without additional corroboration.

Post-implementation review (PIR) A formal review that details what aspects of the project worked well and what areas need improvement.

Professional networking Processes or opportunities for establishing professional contacts.

Professional practices The methodologies, systems, and processes used to deliver results. In relation to internal audit, they define the entity as a professional internal audit function distinct from external audit, evaluation, or quality assurance activities.

Professional skepticism The state of mind that prevents a professional from taking things for granted, and requires him or her to critically assess information and evidence.

Proficiency Possessing the knowledge, skills, and other competencies required to perform individual responsibilities.

Program-based engagement An engagement that focuses on a range of activities that collectively lead to a particular outcome. For example, they could include the activities associated with an organizational program such as human resources management.

Program logic A graphical representation of the interrelationship between the resources available for a project or program, the activities proposed, and the results intended (also known as *logic models*).

Quality A relative and unique concept that in effect refers to the standard of something as measured against other things of a similar kind; the degree of excellence of something.

Quality assurance and improvement program (QAIP) A formal program established by a chief audit executive to measure the quality of an internal audit function and to identify opportunities for improvements. Under the IIA Standards, the QAIP must include both internal and external assessment of quality.

Quality checkpoints Process points designed specifically to embed quality.

Quality circles A group of volunteers from within an organizational area who work together to introduce and implement quality improvements.

Quality control Review of all elements of development and production, often reliant on inspection.

Quality drivers The inputs (such as budget, staffing, and professional practices) required to achieve particular outputs and outcomes.

Quality gates Process points embedded to ensure that previous elements have been satisfactorily completed before allowing the process to continue (e.g., chief audit executive sign-off of an audit plan may be a quality gate preventing the audit from continuing until this is completed).

Quality improvement According to Juran, the creation of beneficial change to achieve unprecedented levels of performance.

Quality management system The organizational structure, systems, and processes designed to promote quality.

Quality planning According to Juran, identification of customers and their needs.

Quality team In relation to internal audit, a group from within the internal audit function tasked with ongoing and/or periodic assessment of internal audit quality.

Relevant evidence Evidence that specifically addresses the engagement objective.

Reliable evidence Evidence determined by the internal audit function as being credible, reasonable, and accurate. It accurately represents the observed phenomena and can be independently verified.

Resource planning Identification and analysis of the various resources required to undertake an activity. Can also refer to human resources planning, which specifically relates to the human resources required.

Resourcing Providing the inputs such as staffing and budgets to undertake a particular activity.

Risk The possibility of an event occurring that will have an impact on the achievement of objectives. Risk is measured in terms of impact and likelihood.

Risk appetite The level of risk than an organization is willing to accept.

Risk consequence The effect that the occurrence of a risk will have.

Risk likelihood The probability that a risk will occur.

Risk management A process to identify, assess, manage, and control potential events or situations to provide reasonable assurance regarding the achievement of the organization's objectives.

Risk register A documented collection of the risks impacting an activity or organization.

Rolling audit plan A complete list of potential audit engagements prioritized according to the risk and materiality of the auditable area. Normally it would identify the time since the last audit and the proposed duration between audits.

Root cause analysis Focuses on the primary causes of adverse events that need to be addressed by solutions.

Sampling A process used in statistics to select a predetermined number of objects from a larger population, with the intention that the smaller collection is representative of the whole.

Secondment A temporary transfer to another job position, usually in the same organization.

Self-assessment with independent validation (SAIV) A form of internal audit external quality assessment that involves the external validation of a self-assessment undertaken by the internal audit function.

Six Sigma A business management strategy originally developed by Motorola in the 1980s. It is essentially a business problem-solving methodology that supports process improvements through an understanding of customer needs, identification of causes of quality variations, and disciplined use of data and statistical analysis.

Small audit shop An internal audit function that generally has one of more of the following characteristics:

- One to five auditors
- Productive internal audit hours below 7,500 a year
- Limited level of co-sourcing or outsourcing

SMART performance measures Performance measures that are **s**pecific, **m**easurable, **a**ction-oriented, **r**elevant, and **t**imely.

Sourcing model The model used to resource an activity—generally based on insourcing, co-sourcing, or outsourcing.

Stakeholder Any party who affects, or is affected by, a project or activity (within and external to an organization). For an internal audit function, stakeholders include the board and audit committee, chief executive office, senior management, audit clients, and the external auditors.

Standard As per the IIA definition, a professional pronouncement promulgated by the Internal Audit Standards Board that delineates the requirements for performing a broad range of internal audit functions and for evaluating internal audit performance.

Statistical sampling A sampling approach that uses mathematics to determine the sample size and methodology for selection of a subset of individuals from within a population to yield some knowledge about the whole population.

Strategic context Aspects that need to be considered when formulating an organization's mission and vision statement, and can include the motivation behind the organization's existence, the environment in which it operates, key challenges that it faces, and what value it adds to its stakeholders.

Strategic human resources (HR) planning/staffing strategy/workforce planning Procedures used within an organization to maximize the efficiency and effectiveness of employment practices, and to mitigate workforce risks to meeting organizational objectives.

Strategy A means of establishing the organization's purpose and determining the nature of the contribution it intends to make while predefining choices that will shape decisions and actions.

Succession planning Process for identifying and developing successors to key positions in an organization.

Sufficient evidence Typically, a reasonable person test is used to determine sufficiency—there is enough evidence if a reasonable person can be persuaded that the audit findings are valid.

Teamwork Group of people with a shared vision working optimally toward a common goal.

Three lines of defense The different roles and responsibilities across an organization for effective coordination of risk management and control oversight. Within the first line of defense, management has a responsibility for providing assurance over its controls. The second line of defense incorporates other internal assurance providers, such as compliance and quality functions, and internal audit is positioned as the third line of defense.

Time recording Recording of time spent by individuals on specific activities.

Total quality management (TQM)   A management philosophy from the 1940s and 1950s, consisting of various strategies to ensure quality products and services.

Transparency   Processes or behaviors that are well documented or defined, authorized, communicated, and understood by relevant parties.

Trend analysis   A form of statistical analysis used to analyze activities over a period of time.

***U.S. Sarbanes-Oxley Act* (2002) (SOX)**   This act has had a significant influence on internal audit in the United States. Section 404 of the act requires management's development and monitoring of the procedures and controls for making its required assertion about the adequacy of internal controls over financial reporting, as well as the required attestation confirmation by an external auditor of management's assertion. Section 302 requires management's quarterly certification of not only financial reporting controls but also disclosure controls and procedures.

Value   According to Benjamin Graham, "Price is what you pay—value is what you get."

Value proposition   A commitment, promise, or expectation of value that will be delivered by an organization or individual.

Values/guiding values   Relate to an organization's or individual's morals and ideals.

Vision   A statement that defines where an organization wants to be in the future.

Working papers   Records of an audit engagement.

360-degree process   Appraisal system where feedback is provided to individuals from their subordinates, peers, managers, and sometimes clients. A questionnaire is usually used, and feedback is provided anonymously.

About the Author

Sally-Anne Pitt, CMIIA (Australia), CIA, CGAP, is the Managing Partner of Pitt Group Pty Ltd., an Australian-based consulting firm specializing in assurance and evaluation services.

Pitt Group commenced operations in 2003, working primarily with public sector agencies. Key audit clients include the Australian Government Department of Human Services, the Australian National Audit Office, the Commonwealth Department of Finance, and the Victorian Auditor-General's Office.

Between 2008 and 2012, Sally-Anne was engaged by the Institute of Internal Auditors-Australia to oversee its external quality assessment program, and through this role she commenced her involvement with the international committees of the Institute of Internal Auditors, joining the Committee for Quality. Sally-Anne led the team responsible for authoring the Institute of Internal Auditors' 2012 *Practice Guide: Quality Assurance and Improvement Program.*

She has undertaken in excess of 60 external quality assessments for major Australian and international organizations. She is recognized as an expert in internal audit quality assurance and has delivered training courses and presentations in Australia, South Africa, Malaysia, Fiji, Singapore, Thailand, and the United States.

She has continued to volunteer at an international level and is currently the vice chair of the Institute of Internal Auditors Professional Issues Committee.

Sally-Anne's qualifications include a bachelor's degree in applied science and a master's in public policy, and she has undertaken postgraduate management studies at the Darden School of Business at the University of Virginia.

Index

Page numbers with *f* or *t* indicate figure or table.

Printed and bound by CPI Group (UK) Ltd, Croydon, CR0 4YY

24/04/2025

14661394-0001